FOURTH EDITION

A GUIDE TO SERVICE DESK CONCEPTS

DONNA KNAPP

COURSE TECHNOLOGY
CENGAGE Learning™

Australia • Brazil • Japan • Korea • Mexico • Singapore • Spain • United Kingdom • United States

COURSE TECHNOLOGY
CENGAGE Learning™

A Guide to Service Desk Concepts, Fourth Edition
Donna Knapp

Executive Editor: Kathleen McMahon

Senior Product Manager: Alyssa Pratt

Development Editor: Deb Kaufmann

Editorial Assistant: Sarah Ryan

Brand Manager: Kay Stefanski

Content Project Manager:
    Jennifer Feltri-George

Art Director: Cheryl Pearl, GEX

Cover Designer: GEX

Cover Photo: ©iStockphoto/sambarfotos

Print Buyer: Julio Esperas

Copyeditor: Mary Kemper

Proofreader: Lisa Weidenfeld

Indexer: Sharon Hilgenberg

Compositor: Integra

Library of Congress Control Number: 2013930322

ISBN-13: 978-1-285-06345-4

ISBN-10: 1-285-06345-7

Course Technology
20 Channel Center Street
Boston, MA 02210
USA

Some of the product names and company names used in this book have been used for identification purposes only and may be trademarks or registered trademarks of their respective manufacturers and sellers.

Any fictional data related to people, companies, or URLs used throughout this book is intended for instructional purposes only. At the time this book was printed, any such data was fictional and not belonging to any real people or companies.

Course Technology, a part of Cengage Learning, reserves the right to revise this publication and make changes from time to time in its content without notice.

The programs in this book are for instructional purposes only. They have been tested with care, but are not guaranteed for any particular intent beyond educational purposes. The author and the publisher do not offer any warranties or representations, nor do they accept any liabilities with respect to the programs.

Cengage Learning is a leading provider of customized learning solutions with office locations around the globe, including Singapore, the United Kingdom, Australia, Mexico, Brazil, and Japan. Locate your local office at **www.cengage.com/global**

Cengage Learning products are represented in Canada by Nelson Education, Ltd.

To learn more about Course Technology, visit **www.cengage.com/coursetechnology**

Purchase any of our products at your local bookstore or at our preferred online store **www.cengagebrain.com**

Printed in the United States of America
2 3 4 5 6   22 21 20 19 18

Brief Contents

Contents

CHAPTER 3

The People Component: Service Desk Roles and Responsibilities **75**

CHAPTER 4

The Process Component: Service Desk Processes and Procedures 113

CHAPTER 5   The Technology Component: Service Desk Tools and Technologies **183**

Preface

It has been close to 15 years since the first edition of this text was published as *A Guide to Help Desk Concepts*. In some respects, little has changed since that first edition. The function we now call the service desk is still first and foremost a customer service organization. What has changed, and what continues to change, are the customers themselves. Today's technology users are increasingly technically savvy and self-sufficient. They expect technology to work, and when it doesn't, they expect easy access to a wide range of support services. They expect options! Businesses expect the service desk to offer these options and also to pave the way for the business and technological changes to come. They expect the service desk to proactively anticipate customer needs, and they expect the people working in the service desk to meet those needs in the most innovative, cost-effective ways possible.

This edition, *A Guide to Service Desk Concepts, Fourth Edition*, describes the strategically important role service desks now hold in organizations. In reality, every aspect of the service desk has changed since the first edition of this text was published—its people, processes, technology, and information, even its physical setting. We are not, however, "done." This edition describes why and how organizations are making the transition from a traditional, reactive help desk (or service desk) to a more strategic, proactive service desk.

For the past 20 years, I have provided help desk and service desk–related consulting and training services. Looking back, it amazes me how much the role of the service desk has changed, but I'm even more amazed at the prospect of changes to come. It's a dynamic time for this industry. It's interesting to examine the strategies companies are using to address trends influencing the service desk such as social support, self-help, bring your own device (BYOD), desktop virtualization, and cloud computing. As an educator in the field, it's gratifying to see how organizations are successfully using best practice frameworks and standards such as IT Infrastructure Library® (ITIL®) and ISO/IEC 20000 to improve their services and processes, while at the same time adapting those practices to their organization's unique business needs and unique customer preferences.

This text provides both a historical perspective and a "crystal ball" look into the future, along with current best practices relative to this exciting and dynamic industry. It looks at the real-world challenges service desks are facing in their efforts to support a global, mobile, multigenerational workforce whenever they need assistance (anytime), wherever they are (anywhere), regardless of the device they are using (any device).

In the real world, the heroes of this industry are the front-line service providers who day in and day out maintain a *can do* attitude and do the best they can to help their customers. This book was written with these heroes in mind. It was also written for all of the people who are bringing about the positive and lasting change that is enabling this diverse industry to thrive and for the people who are reaping the benefits of their efforts. Through this book, I hope to shed light on this exciting and challenging field and provide the information people need to pursue not only a job, but a career in customer support. This book explores all aspects of the service desk and the service desk industry. It is designed to provide a solid foundation upon which individuals entering the service desk industry, or striving to advance in the industry, can build their skills and knowledge.

Intended Audience

This book is primarily intended for three kinds of readers:

- Readers who are considering career opportunities in a service desk, and who want an introduction to the field. They can use this book to explore the different types of service desks, the available service desk career paths, and the kinds of knowledge, skills, and abilities they need to be successful.

- Readers who are working in a service desk and want a better understanding of how people, processes, technology, and information affect the typical service desk. They can use this book to obtain additional knowledge and depth about how these components and best practices enable the service desk to operate efficiently and effectively. They can also use this book to obtain clear definitions and explanations of key concepts.

- Readers who are taking a course in help desks, service desks, customer support, or a related degree program. They can use this book to obtain a high-level overview of the service desk. These readers will especially benefit from the end-of-chapter activities that provide practical experience with the concepts and skills they will use on the job.

Service Desk Curriculum

This book is designed for a first course in any Service Desk (or Help Desk) curriculum. It is also a relevant addition to an IT Service Management (ITSM) curriculum. It is intended for use in community and technical college courses, such as Introduction to Service Desks, Service Desk Concepts, Customer Service and the Service Desk, and Problem Solving for the Service Desk. These courses are part of rapidly emerging programs that aim to prepare students for the following degrees or certificates: IT Support Professional, Computer Service Desk Specialist, Computer Technical Support, Service Desk Support Specialist, Computer User Support, and Computer Support Technician. As the need for and the quantity of service desks grows, companies are turning to community colleges, technical colleges, training centers, and other learning institutions to prepare their students to fill new and existing entry- and higher-level positions in the service desk industry.

Technical skills are no longer the only requirement for the field of technical support. Companies now also want to attract individuals who have the appropriate balance of business, technical, soft, and self-management skills that contribute to making their service desks successful. Increasingly, organizations that are committed to providing quality customer support view their service desks as a strategic asset. These companies are seeking individuals who have the desire and skills needed to achieve the service desk's mission. Whether a service desk provides support to the customers who use its company's products or the service desk provides technical support to the company's employees, the need for service desk professionals is great.

Approach

This book is designed to provide an overview of each of the topics relevant to working at a service desk. My goal is to provide an in-depth understanding of the concepts that the reader needs to understand to succeed in the service desk industry and to bring these concepts to life by providing real-world examples of these concepts in action. To this end, separate chapters are dedicated to subjects such as people, processes, technology, and information. Collectively, these chapters offer one of the most current and inclusive compilations of service desk-related information available today. These chapters also show how the people, processes, technology, and information components when well designed and managed come together seamlessly in the workplace. Like a puzzle, each piece is required, and when all of the pieces are assembled, the picture comes into view. If one piece is missing, the picture is incomplete.

To derive the maximum benefit from this book, the reader must be an active participant in the learning process. The end-of-chapter activities are designed specifically to develop the reader's knowledge and help the reader assimilate the chapter concepts. They encourage the reader to expand his or her knowledge through self-study as well as prepare the reader for the team-oriented service desk environment by having the reader work with other students in project groups, teams, or via a forum or class message board. Many of the end-of-chapter activities encourage the reader to search the web, retrieve and use information resources, and solve problems: skills that are essential in the dynamic service desk industry.

Assumed Knowledge

This book assumes that readers have experience in the following areas, either through course work, work experience, or life experience:

- Basic customer service concepts
- Basic information technology (IT) concepts or computer literacy
- Internet and web concepts

Overview

The outline of this book takes a holistic view of the service desk. Each chapter explores a particular component of the service desk in detail and builds on the information presented in previous chapters.

CHAPTER 1, INTRODUCTION TO SERVICE DESK CONCEPTS. Explains the evolution of technical support in the IT industry, the evolution from help desk to service desk within a technical support department, the components of a successful service desk, and why customer service is the bottom line for service desks.

CHAPTER 2, SERVICE DESK OPERATIONS. Describes the different types of customer service and support organizations, the roles and operations of internal and external service desks, and how size influences service desk operations. It also explores the benefits and challenges of centralized and decentralized service desks as well as of managing service desks as cost centers and profit centers, along with the role of outsourcing in the support industry.

CHAPTER 3, THE PEOPLE COMPONENT: SERVICE DESK ROLES AND RESPONSIBILITIES. Describes the business, technical, soft, and self-management skills and job and professional responsibilities required for the front-line service provider, management and supporting job categories at a service desk. It also explains the necessity of working as a team.

CHAPTER 4, THE PROCESS COMPONENT: SERVICE DESK PROCESSES AND PROCEDURES. Describes the anatomy and evolution of processes and the role of process frameworks and standards, along with leading quality management and IT service management frameworks and standards such as TQM, ISO 9000, ITIL, and ISO/IEC 20000, to name just a few. The chapter also discusses the most common processes used in service desks, how they are integrated, their importance, and their benefits to the service desk.

CHAPTER 5, THE TECHNOLOGY COMPONENT: SERVICE DESK TOOLS AND TECHNOLOGY. Covers the wide array of tools and technology used in service desks. It introduces the common service desk technologies, the technologies used by service desk managers, and the relationship between processes and technology. It also provides a seven-step method for evaluating, selecting, and implementing service desk technology.

CHAPTER 6, THE INFORMATION COMPONENT: SERVICE DESK PERFORMANCE MEASURES. Explains how information is used in the service desk as a resource, describes the most common data categories captured by service desks, and discusses the most common team and individual performance metrics.

CHAPTER 7, THE SERVICE DESK SETTING. Briefly examines the factors that influence the location and layout of service desks and describes how analysts can improve the ergonomics of their personal workspace. It also explores how to design and maintain work habits that enable analysts to stay organized and achieve personal success.

CHAPTER 8, CUSTOMER SUPPORT AS A PROFESSION. Explores service desk industry trends and directions, explains the role of certification in the service desk, and provides ways to prepare for a future as a service desk professional. It also provides transition tips for individuals who choose to pursue a service desk management position.

New to this Edition!

Key concepts and features new to this edition include:

- **Up-to-date Concepts.** Up-to-date research, trends, case studies, and resources such as web sites are referenced throughout the text.

- **Technology Trends.** The impact of technology trends on the service desk is discussed throughout the text including virtualization, cloud computing, consumerization (bring your own device), mobile technologies, and social support.

- **ITIL 2011.** References to ITIL best practices have been updated to reflect ITIL 2011.

- **Updated Hands-On and Case Projects.** Hands-on projects and case projects have been added to reflect current trends and updated to support a blended learning strategy.

- **Chapter 2 – Bring your own Device.** Updates have been made to the section on Service Level Agreements to discuss customer responsibilities in a company that allows employees to bring their own devices.

- **Chapter 4 – Knowledge Sharing.** Updates have been made to the Knowledge Management Process section to discuss ways to address both formal knowledge sharing and informal knowledge sharing and collaboration through the use of communities of practice, mentoring programs, webinars, wikis, blogs, and social media.

- **Chapter 5 – Service Desk Tools and Technologies.** Updates have been made to describe the benefits of the software as a service (SaaS) delivery model and the many different roles a service desk plays in a SaaS model. This chapter also describes the use of social media in a service desk setting.

- **Chapter 8 – Service Desk Industry Trends and Directions.** Updates have been made to describe the service desk's transition to a more strategic, proactive role within organizations. This chapter also describes current challenges facing the industry such as the need to deliver multigenerational, multichannel, and anytime, anywhere, any device support, in addition to enabling social support channels.

Features

To aid you in fully understanding service desk concepts, the following features in this book are designed to improve its pedagogical value:

CHAPTER OBJECTIVES. Each chapter in this book begins with a list of the important concepts to be mastered within the chapter. This list provides you with a quick reference to the contents of the chapter as well as a useful study aid.

ILLUSTRATIONS, PHOTOGRAPHS, AND TABLES. Illustrations and photographs help you visualize common components and relationships. Tables list conceptual items and examples in a visual and readable format.

NOTES. Notes expand on the section topic and include resource references, additional examples, and ancillary information.

TIPS. Tips provide practical advice and proven strategies related to the concept being discussed.

WANT MORE INFO? POINTERS. Want More Info? pointers direct you to other chapters in the text or the Internet for more information about a topic, an example related to the chapter content, and other points of interest.

BULLETED FIGURES. Selected figures contain bullets that summarize important points to give you an overview of upcoming discussion points and to later help you review material.

INTERVIEWS. Interviews detail real-life examples of the chapter topic. Using a case study approach, interviews describe actual experiences and confirm the importance of the topic. Also, interviews with industry experts expand upon and give additional insight into real-world applications of the topic.

CHAPTER SUMMARIES. Each chapter's text is followed by a summary of chapter concepts. These concise summaries provide a helpful way to recap and revisit the ideas covered in each chapter.

KEY TERMS. Each chapter contains a listing of the boldfaced terms introduced in the chapter and a concise definition of each. This listing provides a convenient way to review the vocabulary you have learned.

REVIEW QUESTIONS. End-of-chapter assessment activities begin with a set of 25 or more review questions that reinforce the main ideas introduced in each chapter. These questions ensure that you have mastered the concepts and have understood the information you have learned.

HANDS-ON PROJECTS. Although it is important to understand the concepts behind service desk topics, no amount of theory can improve on real-world experience. To this end, along with conceptual explanations, each chapter provides eight to ten Hands-On Projects aimed at providing practical experience in service desk topics. Some of these include applying service desk concepts to your personal life and researching information from printed resources, the Internet, and people who work in or have experience with the support industry. Because the Hands-On Projects ask you to go beyond the boundaries of the text itself, they provide you with practice implementing service desk concepts in real-world situations.

CASE PROJECTS. The Case Projects at the end of each chapter are designed to help you apply what you have learned to business situations much like those you can expect to encounter in a service desk position. They give you the opportunity to independently synthesize and evaluate information, examine potential solutions, and make recommendations, much as you would in an actual business situation.

Instructor Resources

The following teaching tools are available for download at our Instructor Companion Site. Simply search for this text at *login.cengage.com*. An instructor login is required.

- **Electronic Instructor's Manual:** The Instructor's Manual that accompanies this textbook includes additional instructional material to assist in class preparation, including items such as Overviews, Chapter Objectives, Teaching Tips, Quick Quizzes, Class Discussion Topics, Additional Projects, Additional Resources, and Key Terms. A sample syllabus is also available.

- **ExamView®:** This textbook is accompanied by ExamView, a powerful testing software package that allows instructors to create and administer printed, computer (LAN-based), and Internet-based exams. ExamView includes hundreds of questions that correspond to the topics covered in this text, enabling students to generate detailed study guides that include page references for further review. The computer-based and Internet testing components allow students to take exams at their computers, and they save the instructor time by grading each exam automatically. These test banks are also available in Blackboard-compatible formats.

- **PowerPoint Presentations:** This text provides PowerPoint slides to accompany each chapter. Slides may be used to guide classroom presentations, to make available to students for chapter review, or to print as classroom handouts. Files are provided for every figure in the text. Instructors may use the files to customize PowerPoint slides, illustrate quizzes, or create handouts.

- **Solutions:** Solutions to all Review Questions are available.

Acknowledgments

Publishing a book is a team effort and each and every person's contribution is valued and appreciated. I wish to thank the staff at Course Technology who contributed their talents to the creation of this book, including Alyssa Pratt, Senior Product Manager, Deb Kaufmann, developmental editor, Abby Reip, permissions and photo research, along with all of the individuals who have worked "behind the scenes" to bring this book to life.

I want to express my great appreciation to the industry professionals and educators who reviewed the draft manuscript and made suggestions that significantly enhanced the quality and completeness of the book and its usefulness as a learning tool. The reviewers are Cay Robertson, TECO Energy; and Hillary Rosenfeld, Boston University. Special thanks to my good friend Joyce Parker, independent ITSM consultant and trainer, who has reviewed all the editions of this text and also contributes to the project by writing exam questions.

I am also very grateful to the following people for their valuable contributions to the "Interview with . . . " sections that offer a real-world view of the subject matter presented in each chapter: Meg Franz, CompuCom Systems, Inc.; Malcolm Fry, Fry-Consultants; Rick Joslin, HDI; Pete McGarahan, McGarahan & Associates; John Rakowski, Forrester Research, Ltd.; and Carole Wacey, MOUSE.

As always, love and thanks to my family who tolerate the clutter, neglect, and forgetfulness that a book project inevitably brings. I greatly appreciate your support and encouragement.

Finally, I want to dedicate this book to the thousands of professionals who are currently working in the service desk industry. Your efforts have enabled this industry to become what it is—an exciting and growing professional career choice. I hope this book will further elevate the service desk as a profession and encourage the knowledgeable and enthusiastic students who complete this course to enter the field and help it continue to grow.

Donna Knapp
Tampa, Florida

CHAPTER 1

Introduction to Service Desk Concepts

In this chapter you will learn:[1]

- ◎ The evolution of technical support
- ◎ The evolution of the service desk within a technical support department
- ◎ The components of a successful service desk
- ◎ Why customer service is the bottom line for service desks

---

[1]All ITIL definitions © Crown copyright 2014. All rights reserved. Material is reproduced with the permission of the Cabinet Office under delegated authority from the Controller of HMSO.

In today's fast-paced and fiercely competitive business environment, people and the companies they work for depend on complex technology. This results in an enormous challenge: supporting the growing number of technology users when they need help. The **service desk**—a single point of contact within a company for managing customer incidents and service requests—provides this support.

And the need for support is great. Equipment manufacturers and software publishers receive millions of help requests annually from frustrated users of personal computers (PCs), laptop computers, tablets, mobile telephones, and smartphones. The number of requests made to service desks within companies is estimated to be larger still. Why? Some of the factors that contribute to this increasing demand for support include:

 The widespread use of smartphones is obsoleting older technologies such as personal digital assistants (PDAs) and pagers.

- The rising number of mobile devices and Internet-based applications that people use on a daily basis and the need to integrate and synchronize those various technologies.

- Questions and problems stemming from infrastructure changes as companies adopt virtual, cloud-based technologies and more environmentally sustainable computing practices such as smaller data centers.

- The seemingly constant installation and updating of security and compliance-related systems such as antivirus, firewall, and data protection systems.

- Regular and frequent upgrades to existing systems, such as office systems (database management, spreadsheet, and word processing), operating systems, collaboration systems, and messaging systems.

- Problems with outdated equipment and legacy systems, such as mainframe-based accounting and human resources systems.

- Home and school use of systems once used only in offices, including presentation tools, photo-editing tools, tax software, money-management systems, and travel planning systems.

Of the service desks surveyed by HDI (an international membership association that focuses on the needs of internal and external support organizations), 66 percent report that the monthly number of tickets they receive is increasing and only 12 percent reported a decrease (*2012 Support Center Practices and Salary Report*, HDI).

The term *ticket* is a throwback to the days when service desks used paper forms. Today, customer contacts are logged electronically, but the term *ticket* is still widely used. Tickets may also be called records, cases, incidents, requests, and work orders.

This huge demand for support, coupled with a shortage of information technology (IT) professionals, has created a tremendous career opportunity in the field of customer service and technical support. According to the United States Department of Labor, computer support is projected to increase by 18 percent from 2010 to 2020 (*Occupational Outlook Handbook, 2012– 13 Edition*, U.S. Department of Labor Bureau of Labor Statistics).

To work at a service desk, you must understand what is involved in delivering technical support services and what role the service desk plays within a technical support department. You must have excellent communication and problem-solving skills as well as applicable technical skills. Above all, you must understand that the service desk is first and foremost a customer service organization that contributes to a company's bottom line by delivering services that meet the needs of its users.

The Evolution of Technical Support

As people and companies worldwide struggle to manage costs and justify the benefits of their technology investments, they are finding that technical support is one of the most significant costs. **Technical support** refers to the wide range of services that enable people and companies to effectively use the information technology they have acquired or developed. Technical support is a considerable part of the **total cost of ownership (TCO)** of information technology, which is the total amount that a company or person spends on information technology over its lifetime.

Historically, the term *problem* was used to describe an event that disrupts service or access to products. The evolution of this term is described later in this chapter.

In the early 1970s, companies did little to support technology users. The same highly skilled developers of the software or hardware also handled technical support questions and problems. As the computer industry grew, people used a wider variety of systems, often on different computer platforms. Some people used mainframe-based systems developed internally by their company's IT department. Others used PC-based **off-the-shelf** products— personal computer software products developed and distributed commercially. Increasingly, people used systems on both platforms. This growing complexity made technical support even more challenging and time consuming.

Users often had no idea whom to call for help. Sometimes, companies gave users a list of numbers to call—one for hardware problems, another for telephone- or network-related problems, and others for help using mainframe-based systems or PC-based software packages. As shown in Figure 1-1, users were bewildered. When in doubt, users would contact anyone or everyone they thought could help resolve their problems.

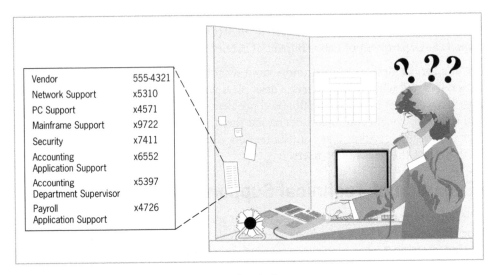

Vendor	555-4321
Network Support	x5310
PC Support	x4571
Mainframe Support	x9722
Security	x7411
Accounting Application Support	x6552
Accounting Department Supervisor	x5397
Payroll Application Support	x4726

Figure 1-1 Obtaining support without a service desk
© Cengage Learning 2014

The costly, negative effects of companies' prolonged failure to recognize the need for technical support accumulated. Developers missed deadlines because they were diverted to technical support calls, leaving little time for their primary job of programming. Information was not being collected, so developers had to discover the same solution repeatedly. Recurring problems were neither identified nor resolved. Technology users who expected quick and accurate solutions to their problems and requests were extremely dissatisfied when their expectations were not met on a timely basis.

Companies began realizing that they had to distinguish between **development**—the construction of new systems—and **support**—services that enable the effective use of a system. In addition, companies learned that they had to support not only technology, but also the *users* of that technology. They recognized that each user should be treated and referred to as a **customer**, a person who buys products or services. Today, the service industry makes the distinction that a customer *buys* products or services and a **user** *consumes* products or services. This distinction clarifies that customers are individuals with budgeting responsibilities and so are responsible for making purchasing decisions and for negotiating agreements or contracts. For example, the managers (customers) within an organization typically make purchasing decisions based on both their employees' (users) requirements and the organization's financial constraints. However, it is important to note that in practice, many organizations – and this text – informally use the term customer in lieu of user in recognition of the service desk's role as a customer service organization.

In the 1970s, companies realized that their highly skilled developers often lacked the interpersonal skills and communication skills required to interact directly with customers. Developers' skills were better suited for projects and activities such as product planning, system design, and programming.

At about the same time, some vendors (most notably, IBM) began to offer discounts to customers who "screened" problem calls internally before calling the vendor. Calls were screened to determine the nature of the problem. If the problem required the services of a field engineer, the company would contact the vendor, who would then **dispatch**, or send, a field engineer to the customer's site. Otherwise, the company would handle the problem internally. Although the vendor's goal was to minimize the number of times a field engineer was dispatched unnecessarily to a customer site, it introduced technology users to the idea of calling a central point of contact for help. This trend paved the way for a concept that IBM called the "help desk," a forerunner of the service desk. A **help desk** is a single point of contact within a company for technology-related questions and incidents.

 The evolution from help desk to service desk is discussed in the next section.

In the early 1980s, a number of factors caused even more companies to focus on supporting the users of technology, not merely the technology itself, and viewing those technology users as customers. These factors included:

- The explosion of PC tools and the accompanying increase in the number of companies competing in the computer industry.

- The growing number of knowledgeable but frustrated technology users who were willing and able to take their business elsewhere.

- A business realization that a broader set of support services, delivered efficiently and effectively, could reduce the total cost of owning technology, enhance customer productivity, improve customer satisfaction, and, ultimately, increase revenue by helping to sell more products.

- The quality movement, a business trend that began in the late 1970s and challenged companies to measure and monitor quality and to take corrective action when products or services failed to satisfy customers' requirements.

The quality movement introduced the concept that a customer can be either external or internal to the company. Today, the service industry recognizes an **external customer** as a person or company that buys another company's products and services. An **internal customer** is a person who works at a company and at times relies on other employees at that company to perform his or her job.

This increase in customer focus in the early 1980s prompted companies to expand their definition of technical support to include a set of activities known as customer support. **Customer support** includes services that help a customer understand and benefit from a product's capabilities by answering questions, solving problems, and providing training. The term *technical support* has taken on new meaning and now includes services that span the complete lifecycle of information technology. Technical support begins with selecting and installing the hardware, software, network, and application components that enable technology users to do their work. Ongoing support includes keeping the system in good repair, upgrading hardware and software when needed, and providing customer support. Ongoing support also includes proactive activities such as having a regular maintenance schedule with steps such as backing up data and using system utilities such as Disk Defragmenter. Technical support for a particular piece of hardware or software ends when the technology becomes unusable.

In the early 1990s, the World Wide Web was developed, resulting in the rampant expansion and commercialization of the Internet. The **World Wide Web (WWW or web)** is a collection of documents on the Internet with point-and-click access to information that is posted by government agencies, businesses, educational institutions, nonprofit organizations, and individuals around the world. The **Internet** is a global collection of computer networks that are linked to provide worldwide access to information.

 Today, more than 2 billion users have access to the Internet (World Internet Users, *www.internetworldstats.com*, December 2011).

The rapid commercialization of the Internet, coupled with more affordable and portable technology, led to an explosion in the number of people using computers on a daily basis—and, therefore, in the number of people needing technical support. The exploding number of computer users and the constant influx of new technologies solidified the concept of technical support and its importance. Companies that once had little need for technical support realized the need to give serious thought to how and by whom technical support services are delivered.

During the mid-1990s, IT organizations worldwide began adopting the **Information Technology Infrastructure Library® (ITIL®)**, a set of best practices for IT service management. ITIL was developed in the 1980s in the United Kingdom by the government's Central Computer and Telecommunications Agency (CCTA). It consists of a series of books that gives best practice guidance on IT service management-related topics. A **best practice** is a proven way of completing a task to produce a near optimum result. Best practices are proven over time through experience and research to work for a large number and variety of people and organizations. **IT service management (ITSM)** is a discipline for managing IT services that focuses on the quality of those services and the relationship that the IT service provider has with its customers. ITIL defines a **service** as a means of delivering value to customers by facilitating outcomes customers want to achieve without the ownership of specific costs and risks. An **IT service** is based on the use of information technology and supports business processes of the IT service provider's customers.

 ITIL has evolved and expanded since it was first introduced. The newest edition was released in 2011 by the Cabinet Office, a part of the government of the United Kingdom.

ITIL considers technical and customer support vitally important and introduced organizations to the concept of the service desk. Simply put, the service desk is a help desk with a broader scope of responsibility and the goal of providing faster service and improving customer satisfaction. In addition to managing customer incidents and service requests, the service desk also handles communication with customers.

ITIL defines an **incident** as an unplanned interruption to an IT service or a reduction in the quality of an IT service. Historically, such unplanned events were referred to as "problems." ITIL, however, defines a **problem** as the cause of one or more incidents. A **service request** is a request from a user for information, advice, or a standard change.

 Incidents, problems, and service requests are further discussed in Chapter 4.

Figure 1-2 illustrates the evolution of technical support.

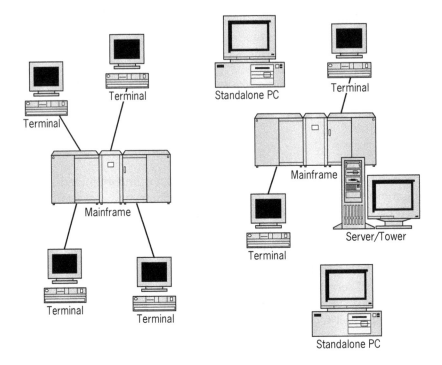

Figure 1-2   Evolution of technical support

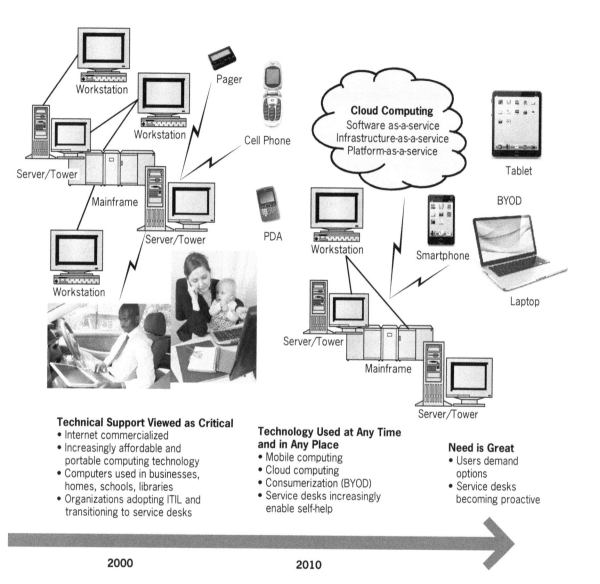

Technical Support Viewed as Critical
- Internet commercialized
- Increasingly affordable and portable computing technology
- Computers used in businesses, homes, schools, libraries
- Organizations adopting ITIL and transitioning to service desks

Technology Used at Any Time and in Any Place
- Mobile computing
- Cloud computing
- Consumerization (BYOD)
- Service desks increasingly enable self-help

Need is Great
- Users demand options
- Service desks becoming proactive

2000   2010

During the 2000s, rapid acceptance of innovations such as mobile and wireless computing, cloud computing, and Web 2.0 radically changed when, where, and how people interact with information technology. This in turn impacted when, where, and how people obtain support for that technology. Technically savvy customers increasingly began looking for self-help services such as online knowledge bases and frequently asked questions (FAQs). They also turned to social networking sites such as Facebook and Twitter, as well as online support communities and forums. Although the telephone and email continued to be the most widely used support channels, service desks also saw a significant increase in the use of web forms and online chat services.

Cloud computing involves delivering hosted services over the Internet. **Web 2.0** is a concept that emphasizes enabling web users to interact, collaborate, and generate content via, for example, blogs, wikis, and social networking sites, rather than passively view content created by others.

The use of social media by the service desk is discussed in greater detail in Chapter 5.

A trend that emerged in the mid-2000s and that is gaining wider acceptance in the 2010s is the **consumerization** of IT, where consumer preferences drive the adoption of technology in the workplace. This trend is prompting many companies to adopt "bring your own device" policies in an effort to reduce costs and increase employee satisfaction. **Bring your own device (BYOD)** involves using personally-owned mobile devices to access business applications. Gartner, Inc., an information technology research company, predicts that by 2014, 90 percent of organizations will support corporate applications on personal devices (*Bring Your Own Device: Dealing With Trust and Liability Issues*, Forbes, August 2011). The service desk is on the leading edge of this trend as organizations work out how to address the security, liability, and technical support challenges associated with this trend.

Another trend that is gaining acceptance in the 2010s and that is affecting the service desk is the move to desktop virtualization. **Desktop virtualization** separates a PC desktop environment from a physical machine using the client–server model of computing. With desktop virtualization, each user's desktop, which includes the operating system and applications, is delivered over the network in real time to the user's PC. The user's PC may be a thin client or a smart mobile device. This approach is being driven by factors such as the move to more mobile and cloud-based computing practices, the need to optimize costs, and the need to reduce the time required to resolve incidents and handle service requests. The approach means that many of the incidents and service requests that were traditionally handled at the desktop by the field services group can now be handled remotely by the service desk.

A field service group is composed of technicians who work 'in the field' handling incidents and service requests related to equipment such as desktop computers, laptops, printers, scanners, and mobile devices. This group may also be called desktop support, technical support, or deskside support.

The technical support services that a company delivers, as well as how and by whom those services are delivered, vary according to company size, company goals, and customer expectations. Some companies, particularly smaller ones, deliver technical support informally by people who are knowledgeable about computers but who have little or no specialized training. Coworkers direct their computer-related questions or incidents to these resident experts. Technical support in such companies is often highly personalized. For example, a computer expert may go to the desk of a user and provide one-on-one support. Or, a user may walk up to an expert in an effort to obtain immediate assistance. According to HDI's *2012 Support Center Practices and Salary Report*, 53 percent of survey respondents offer walk-up support services. Such services are most common in smaller companies and in the education industry. Although users tend to greatly appreciate such "high touch" service, the computer expert may quickly become overburdened, particularly if technical support is not his or her primary job function. As a result, most companies take a more formal approach to technical support. They often have an official help desk or service desk that users can contact. This practice enables the company to maximize its technical resources and ensures that the people providing support services have the required skills.

The informal support delivered by companies that don't have a help desk or service desk can also occur within companies that have an established help desk or service desk. For example, users occasionally may turn to **peer-to-peer support**, a practice in which users bypass the formal support structure and seek assistance from their coworkers or someone in another department. Peer-to-peer support is effective when a coworker can help a person in the same department understand how to use a product or system for department-specific work. Peer-to-peer support has its drawbacks, however. For example, when a person asks a coworker for help solving a complex incident that neither one has the skill to resolve, they not only waste time trying to solve the incident, they could also make the incident worse. Or, they may "fix" the incident incorrectly so that it is likely to recur. Also, because incidents solved via peer-to-peer support are typically not logged, the help desk or service desk does not know about the incidents and so it cannot help others who experience similar incidents.

As the computer industry has evolved, so has the concept of technical support, which has moved from a narrow focus on fixing technical problems to a much more comprehensive focus on supporting customers and helping them use technology to achieve business goals. Many companies still deliver that support via a traditional help desk. However, organizations are increasingly delivering a broader set of services via a service desk.

The Evolution from Help Desk to Service Desk

The role of the service desk has evolved considerably since IBM coined the term *help desk* in the late 1970s. The help desk was originally established simply to screen calls, but now the service desk is the first and sometimes only point of contact that customers have with a company or a company's IT department. Many companies consider the service desk a strategic corporate resource because of its constant interaction with the company's customers or employees.

 According to HDI's *2012 Support Center Practices and Salary Report*, more than 35 percent of the organizations that are experiencing an increase in ticket volume cite a broader scope of services as a reason.

This section describes the dramatic changes that prompted the evolution from help desk to service desk.

In the early 1980s, developers and computer operators working in data centers—not help desks—handled questions from customers who did not know how to operate their computers. As in the early days of technical support, this misuse of highly skilled resources was costly, to say the least. Slowly at first, companies implemented, and then expanded, the role of the help desk.

The help desk began to answer simple questions and *resolve* problems instead of just passing them on. Support organizations and customers both realized the benefits of a well-implemented help desk, prompting companies to expand the help desk's role further. During the mid-1980s, many companies redesigned their help desk support processes. Some help desks began to acquire and use sophisticated telephone systems, problem management systems, a forerunner of incident management systems (discussed below), and remote control and diagnostic systems. **Remote control and diagnostic systems** allow the service desk to take remote control of the keyboard, screen, or mouse of connected devices and then troubleshoot problems, transfer files, and even provide informal training by viewing or operating the customer's screen. Some help desks took on new activities, such as:

- Conducting and scheduling training sessions

- Coordinating hardware and software installations

- Distributing software electronically

- Creating reports for customers and managers that detailed opportunities to improve the company's products and services, problem areas, training needs, and trends

- Maintaining system and network status and availability information

- Managing programs designed to attract and keep customers

- Marketing help desk services as well as the services offered by other departments, such as training

- Monitoring the efficiency and effectiveness of delivered services to ensure customers' needs are met

- Participating in the development of hardware and software standards

- Performing customer satisfaction surveys

- Processing service requests, such as orders for new products or services, enhancement requests, and requests to move, add, or change equipment

- Resolving complex problems

All these activities meant that the help desk role was more *proactive*—that is, better able to anticipate problems and prevent them—than *reactive*—that is, merely responding to problems. A proactive help desk meant better training, relevant information, timely system status information, fully resolved problems, and feedback. As a result, customers were less likely to have problems, and when they did, the help desk had a much better chance of resolving those problems quickly. This trend toward proactivity led to more effective help desks than ever before.

In the 1980s, some organizations began to **outsource** their help desks—that is, to have services provided by an outside supplier instead of providing them in-house. Some help desks outsourced all of their services, whereas others outsourced only a portion of their services. For example, some help desks outsourced only their support for off-the-shelf products such as Microsoft Office products or only their after-hours support. This outsourcing trend had a profound effect on the support industry because it forced companies to recognize and determine the real costs associated with delivering the support services needed by their customers. As labor is typically one of a service desk's greatest costs, companies often found that the use of onshore, near-shore, or offshore outsourcing services enabled them to reduce their labor costs or to obtain a tax savings. **Onshore outsourcing** involves obtaining services from another company in the same country. **Near-shore outsourcing** involves obtaining services from another company in a neighboring country. **Offshore outsourcing** is the exporting of work from one country to another part of the world.

 Companies often outsource services to a **call center**, a place where telephone calls are made or received in high volume. Some large companies that provide global services also use call centers to serve their internal customers. Call centers are discussed in Chapter 2.

By the early 1990s, it became clear that help desks could positively affect the bottom line of their companies by delivering efficient and effective support services. In an effort to demonstrate their contribution, help desks began to assess their efficiency and effectiveness by creating performance measures, or **metrics**, and evaluating customer satisfaction levels. They ranked their performance in relation to their own past performance and in relation to other help desks. Having a "world class" help desk became a goal for the most ambitious and progressive companies. **World class** describes a company that has achieved and sustains high levels of customer satisfaction. For example, a world class manufacturing company is considered excellent by its customers when compared to other companies, regardless of what industry they are in. World class is different than **best-in-class**, which describes a company that is the finest in its industry peer group. For example, a best-in-class manufacturing company is considered excellent by its customers when compared only to other manufacturing companies.

World class help desks resolve a high percentage of problems and try to avoid dispatching or sending problems to other support groups. Also, their practices are proactive, rather than reactive, in nature. Figure 1-3 illustrates the characteristics of a world class help desk.

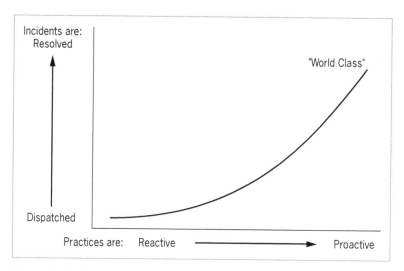

Figure 1-3   Characteristics of a world class help desk
© Cengage Learning 2014

During the mid-1990s, companies began adopting ITIL and the service desk concept versus the traditional help desk concept. Rather than handling only computer failures—a practice often referred to as "break/fix"—the service desk took on a much broader set of responsibilities that included serving as the single point of contact for managing customer incidents and service requests and communicating with customers.

By the late 1990s, service desks began to fully realize the benefits of technologies introduced earlier, such as incident management systems (discussed below) and remote control and diagnostic systems. Service desks also began using technology to perform tasks that various other support groups performed historically. For example, network management tools made it possible for the service desk to perform proactive network monitoring. Also, in an effort to reduce the time required to satisfy a customer's request, some service desks began performing system and network administration tasks.

Around this time, service desks also began to capitalize on the power of the web. They worked hard to streamline and automate their key processes and to empower technology users to help themselves. Many organizations found that moving some support activities such as "how to" requests, FAQs, and password resets to a self-service delivery method enabled them to reduce costs. Providing self-help tools also enabled organizations to free up the their analysts to develop the skills needed to support the technology innovations that were taking hold during the 2000s and 2010s, such as mobile computing, cloud computing, BYOD, and desktop virtualization.

During the 2010s, these technology innovations continue to prompt changes to the service desk and to the skills required by service desk analysts. For example, as companies adopt cloud-based services, the service desk continues to play an invaluable role as a single point of contact for users and must also develop the skills needed to support this more complex environment. Service desk analysts must also become skilled at working with vendors to isolate and determine the root cause of incidents and problems. As companies move to desktop virtualization, many organizations are more closely aligning and in some cases merging their service desk and field services functions. This means that many of the responsibilities traditionally handled by the field services group are being shifted to the service desk and handled remotely. As service desks expand the scope of their services to include mobile, Internet-enabled devices such as tablets and smartphones, clear policies must dictate the levels of service to be provided. This expanded scope also requires that service desk analysts become more highly-skilled at not only supporting mobile devices themselves, but also at handling security- and connectivity-related issues.

According to HDI, 40 percent of support organizations indicate that they are keeping up with emerging technologies, while 52 percent indicate that they are struggling. Only three percent of survey respondents indicate that they are staying ahead of emerging technologies. (*Supporting Mobile Devices in 2011*, HDI Research Corner, January 2012)

These technology innovations make it possible for people to access information at any time and in any place. This environment, where people have access to their information from multiple computing devices and systems and even from public shared access points, is called **ubiquitous computing**.

Customers who adopt this anywhere, anytime approach to computing can be quite demanding and can expect to be offered a variety of ways to obtain support. As a result, today's service desks typically offer customers several ways to contact the service desk, such as the telephone, voice mail, and email, along with web-based options such as self-help and online chat. These various routes of communication to and from the service desk are called **channels**. Service desks also continue to provide self-help tools to their customers and to enable self-services. By 2012, 84 percent of organizations that contributed to HDI's *2012 Support Center Practices and Salary Report* were providing their customers access to self-help tools such as obtaining the status of outstanding tickets (48 percent), reading FAQs (52 percent), searching knowledge bases and documentation libraries (50 and 35 percent respectively), resetting passwords (48 percent), and downloading documents, software, and patches (34 percent).

 According to HDI's *2011 Support Center Practices and Salary Report*, 31 percent of organizations experiencing a decrease in ticket volume cite self-help as a reason.

Table 1-1 summarizes how the role of the help desk has evolved to that of service desk.

Decade	Role
1970s	IBM coined the term *help desk*
	Help desks simply screened calls
1980s	Help desks dispatched even simple questions
	Help desks began to answer simple questions and resolve problems
	Companies redesigned help desk processes
	Help desks began to use sophisticated telephone, problem management, and remote control and diagnostic systems
	Help desk role became more proactive than reactive
	Some companies outsourced their help desk services
1990s	Companies realized help desks could positively impact the bottom line
	Help desks began measuring performance and customer satisfaction levels
	Help desks ranked their performance with other help desks
	Becoming a world class help desk became a goal
	Companies began adopting ITIL and the service desk concept
	Service desks began to exploit the capabilities of the web
	Service desks began empowering technology users to help themselves
	Service desks began using technology to perform tasks such as network monitoring and system and network administration
2000s	Help desks evolved into service desks
	Service desks began offering a variety of support channels
	Service desks began positioning themselves to support technology innovations such as mobile computing, cloud computing, BYOD, and desktop virtualization
2010s	Service desks are supporting ubiquitous computing
	Service desks are transitioning from reactive to proactive

Table 1-1 Evolution of the service desk role

As customers increasingly expect service in real time, traditional reactive service desks are becoming less effective and so service desks must put in place policies and processes aimed at proactively meeting the business' strategic needs. Companies are in varying stages of this transition from reactive help desk to proactive service desk. Some companies have invested heavily in the service desk. Other companies provide only basic or minimal help desk assistance—either because they have yet to fully recognize the service desk opportunity or because other priorities take precedence. Other companies still are taking the service desk even one step further, which is to focus on enhancing customer self-sufficiency and incident prevention rather than just incident resolution. These companies are responding to trends that are determining the direction in which the service desk industry is heading and are affecting the opportunities available to people pursuing a service desk career. As with technical support services, the role of the service desk varies based on the company's size, goals, and customers' expectations.

Chapter 8 explores service desk industry trends and directions.

INTERVIEW WITH. . .

Courtesy of Rick Joslin, Executive
Director of Certification and
Training, HDI
(www.thinkhdi.com)

RICK JOSLIN
EXECUTIVE DIRECTOR OF CERTIFICATION & TRAINING HDI
COLORADO SPRINGS, COLORADO
www.thinkhdi.com

Rick Joslin, interviewed by Donna Knapp, May 2012

The support industry has evolved and the service desk is maturing into a business function that is critical to the success of corporations, governments, and institutions that leverage technology to enable business processes. Help desks were once characterized as reactive and were only responsible for minimizing the impact of service disruptions on IT resources—a very IT-centric focus. Now this function has a service focus and is responsible for minimizing the impact of disruptions on the business. This means that support professionals, regardless of their role in the organization, need to understand how the business uses technology and how it is affected by service disruptions.

As our industry has matured, best practices have emerged, such as the Information Technology Infrastructure Library (ITIL), Knowledge-Centered Support (KCS), and HDI Standards. These frameworks and standards provide a common language and guidance based on the experiences of others that technical support professionals can use to optimize their services. They have also enabled the reactive help desk to mature into a proactive service desk that provides a single point of contact for IT services. Organizations now recognize the value of the service desk and continue to expand its role. The next step in the evolution of the service desk is to a customer- and business-centric support center that makes it easy for customers to obtain support for business processes, telecommunications, and facilities management, as well as IT. Options such as multiple contact methods, self-service, community support, and social networks also make it easy for customers and provide the choices customers demand in the environment they prefer to work.

As our industry continues to evolve, support professionals must evolve as well. Technical support professionals must be dedicated to learning. They must continually grow their knowledge of technology and the business, enhance their customer service and business skills, leverage best practices and the experiences of others, and take steps to continually learn and improve. IT certifications enable professionals to demonstrate their mastery of specific knowledge and skills and to promote their credentials to various stakeholders. Certifications are raising the performance expectations and are improving the quality of services delivered by these individuals. Support professionals do not just take IT certifications and use them to improve their personal knowledge and skills. They must give back to the community by sharing their knowledge and experiences to help others. They must also understand that in the support industry, what we do has a positive, bottom-line impact on our customers and our business. That's why we do it.

Components of a Successful Service Desk

Companies that attain high levels of customer satisfaction have learned that many factors influence how customers perceive their experiences with the service desk. These companies have also learned that they must constantly monitor and manage their level of service because customer expectations are constantly changing and being raised. Most importantly, companies have learned that there is no quick fix or "magic pill." They must pay attention to the four critical components—people, processes, technology, and information—that determine a service desk's success. See Figure 1-4.

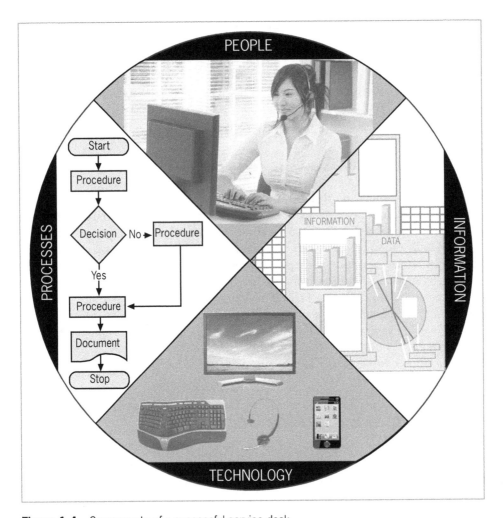

Figure 1-4 Components of a successful service desk

PEOPLE SOURCE: © Norman Pogson / Shutterstock.com
MONITOR SOURCE: © Denis Tabler / Shutterstock.com
KEYBOARD SOURCE: © Creativa / Shutterstock.com
HEADSET SOURCE: © KariDesign / Shutterstock.com
SMARTPHONE SOURCE: © tele52 / Shutterstock.com

People

The first and most important component of the service desk is people. The **people**
component consists of the staff and structure put in place within a company or department to
support its customers by performing processes. The support services delivered by a company
or department are often represented as a multi-level structure through which customer
contacts might pass prior to being resolved.

The different types of customer transactions—questions, incidents, and service requests—are often called **contacts**.

The service desk, often referred to as level one or tier one, is the initial point of contact for customers when they have an incident or service request. People at this level attempt to handle as many customer contacts as possible. If they cannot solve an incident or complete a service request, they pass it up the structure to the level two or level three group that has the experience, authority, or physical proximity needed to resolve the incident or service request. Having level one people handle as many contacts as possible ensures economical use of a company's resources. This approach also promotes customer satisfaction because customers receive solutions more quickly and are not just passed from one support person to another.

Although once an entry level position, the service desk is increasingly considered a skilled profession that requires analysts to hold applicable certifications. Chapter 8 explores the role of certifications.

As a primary point of contact, members of the service desk team must also promote and enforce their company's or department's policies on privacy, security, and computer usage. Figure 1-5 shows a sample computer usage policy. These policies may cover topics such as abiding by software licensing agreements, protecting the company's data assets by using only authorized IDs and passwords, and using email, web-based systems, and social media appropriately and only for business reasons. As overseers of these policies, members of the service desk team must conduct themselves at all times in a professional and ethical manner.

Financial scandals in the business world and dilemmas such as the ease with which Internet sources can be misused have prompted increased awareness of the need for ethics. **Ethics** are the rules and standards that govern the conduct of a person or group of people. Such rules and standards dictate, or provide guidance, about what is considered right and wrong behavior. **Ethical behavior** is conduct that conforms to generally accepted or stated principles of right and wrong. The policies of a department or company dictate what is right and wrong behavior; these policies may vary from one department or company to the next. For example, some companies permit limited personal use of the company's email system, whereas others restrict company email to work-related correspondences. **Governance** is how an organization controls its actions. Governance ensures that the policies and processes that drive right and wrong behavior are put in place and are correctly followed.

IT governance is a subset of corporate or enterprise governance that focuses on IT systems and their performance. Gartner, Inc. defines **IT governance** as "the processes that ensure the effective and efficient use of IT in enabling an organization to achieve its goals." (IT Glossary, Gartner, Inc., *www.gartner.com/it-glossary/it-governance*) The service desk plays an important role in IT governance by maintaining efficient and effective processes and by providing timely responses to user incidents and service requests.

ABC COMPANY
COMPUTER USAGE POLICY

I understand and agree to the following conditions governing the use and care of computer hardware and software assigned to me.

1. I agree to abide by the license agreement between the software publisher and the ABC Company and I understand that the improper reproduction of proprietary software by any means is prohibited.

2. I will not use proprietary software that is NOT the property of the ABC Company on any computing devices of the ABC Company unless I have specific authorization to do so.

3. I understand that safeguarding the software is my responsibility.

4. I have read the policies and procedures in the computer usage policies memorandum and agree to abide by them.

5. I will access the ABC Company's local area network only with my user ID and password. I will not use unauthorized passwords to gain access to other employees' files.

6. I understand that Internet and World Wide Web access should be used only for work-related purposes.

7. I understand that the email system is designed to facilitate business communication among employees and other business contacts. In addition, I understand the following about the email system:
   • Email communications may be considered ABC Company documents and may be subject to review.
   • The email system is not to be used for personal gain or to solicit outside business ventures or political or religious causes.
   • The ABC Company reserves the right to review the contents of employees' email when necessary for business purposes.
   • Foul, inappropriate, or offensive messages are prohibited.
   • Email messages are capable of being forwarded without the express permission of the original author. Accordingly, due caution should be exercised when sending email messages.

I understand that ABC Company personnel who violate any of these guidelines are subject to disciplinary actions or dismissal.

Signed:_____   Dated:_____

Figure 1-5 Sample computer usage policy
© Cengage Learning 2014

The support industry must continuously change in an effort to align itself with business goals and policies aimed at gaining and keeping customer loyalty. In this dynamic environment, companies have difficulty finding and keeping people who possess the mix of skills needed to take on the expanding responsibilities of the service desk. The principal skills required to work successfully at a service desk include:

- **Business skills**—The skills people need to work successfully in the business world, such as the ability to understand and speak the language of business and the ability to analyze and solve business problems. Business skills also include the skills people need that are unique to the profession their service desk supports, such as accounting skills or banking skills, and the skills that are unique to the service industry, such as understanding the importance of meeting customers' needs and managing their expectations.

- **Technical skills**—The skills people need to use and support the specific products and technologies the service desk supports. Technical skills also include basic computer and software literacy.

- **Soft skills**—The skills people need to deliver great service, such as listening skills, verbal communication skills, customer service skills, problem-solving skills, writing skills, and teamwork skills.

- **Self-management skills**—The skills, such as stress and time management, people need to complete their work effectively, feel job satisfaction, and avoid frustration or burnout. Self-management skills also include the ability to get and stay organized and to learn new skills continuously and quickly.

 Chapter 3 explores the people component of a successful service desk.

Although clearly defined processes and technology enable people to be more efficient and effective at the service desk, often satisfying customers requires human qualities such as empathy, patience, and persistence. Successful service desks hire and train people who have good soft skills, who sincerely enjoy working with customers, and who like helping others solve problems. The most service-oriented companies try to ensure employee satisfaction as well as customer satisfaction.

Processes

The processes that people perform are the next important component of a successful service desk. Processes determine the procedures people follow relative to their specific area of the business. People often confuse the terms *process* and *procedure*. A **process** is a collection of interrelated work activities that take a set of specific *inputs* and produce a set of specific *outputs* that are of value to a customer. For example, incident management is the process of tracking and resolving incidents. Incident management takes evidence that an incident has occurred (input) and produces a resolution (output). A **procedure** is a step-by-step, detailed set of instructions that describes how to perform the tasks in a process. The directions that show how to record information about an incident or how to determine a resolution are examples of procedures. In other words, processes define the tasks to be performed and procedures describe how to perform the tasks.

Some processes found in a service desk environment include:

- **Incident management**—The process of tracking and resolving incidents—for example, a jammed printer or an illegal operation error message when using software. The goal is to minimize the impact of incidents that affect a company's systems, networks, and products to ensure the best possible levels of service quality and availability are maintained.

- **Request fulfillment**—The process of collecting and maintaining information about customer requests for new products or services and enhancements to existing products or services—for example, a request for new software or a laptop computer. The goal is to identify and document the tasks required to satisfy requests and ensure that appropriate resources are assigned.

- **Access management**—The process responsible for granting authorized users the right to use a service in accordance with the company's security policies, while preventing access to nonauthorized users. The goal is to control access to services, thus ensuring that the organization effectively maintains the confidentiality of its information and that employees have the right level of access to effectively execute their jobs.

- **Service level management**—The process of negotiating and managing customer expectations, with regard to, for example, how and when customers contact the service desk, the service desk's hours of operation, target response and resolution times, and so on. The goal is to promote a common (two-way) level of expectation about the services to be delivered and provide measurable performance objectives.

The rigorous, consistent use of processes leads to customer confidence, employee satisfaction, and, ultimately, process improvement. Companies find that in today's competitive business climate, it is not enough to do things right; rather, they must do the *right* things right. In other words, companies must perform the correct processes and they must perform them well. Processes must be continuously fine-tuned and occasionally redesigned to ensure that customers' ever-rising expectations are met.

Chapter 4 explores the processes component of a successful service desk.

Technology

The third integrated component of a successful service desk is technology. **Technology** is the tools and systems people use to do their work. Service desk technology includes the data collection and management systems, monitoring systems, and reporting mechanisms that employees and managers use to perform processes. Successful service desks use technology to capture, store, and deliver the information needed to satisfy the needs of both its customers and the company.

Some tools found in a typical service desk include:

- **Incident management systems**—The technology used to log and track customer incidents and service requests.

- **Knowledge management systems**—The technology used to capture and distribute known solutions to incidents and answers to FAQs.

- **Self-service systems**—The technologies such as self-help and self-healing systems that enable customers to, for example, reset their own passwords or restore the configuration of their desktops in the event of a crash.

- **Telephone systems**—The technology used to manage incoming and outgoing telephone calls.

- **Web-based systems**—The technology used to enable customers to submit incidents and service requests or solve incidents through the web without calling the service desk.

According to The Association of Support Professionals (ASP), an international membership organization for customer support managers and professionals, the Ten Best Web Support Sites of 2012 were Cisco Systems, Infor, Informatica, Quest Software, Red Hat, SAS Institute, Yahoo!, Blackbaud, TiVo, and Tricentis.

Because service desk technology is sophisticated, many companies require that service desk candidates meet predefined computer literacy standards. Then their on-the-job training can focus on the specific tools the company uses, not on the basics of telephone systems and computers. The most successful people in a service desk combine those all-important business skills and soft skills with proficiency at using the company's tools.

Chapter 5 explores the technology component of a successful service desk.

Information

The final component of a successful service desk is **information**, data that is organized in a meaningful way. People need information to do their work. Similarly, management needs information to control, measure, and continually improve processes.

It is difficult to find a book or an article about service desks that does not describe the tools and technologies that enable service desk analysts and managers to do their work. Such tools and technologies are useless, however, if they do not provide and produce meaningful information. For example, it is a waste of time for service desk analysts to log every incident in an incident management system if they cannot later search the system and retrieve information about the incidents they logged. Similarly, managers must be able to use the incident management system to run reports and produce charts that show trends.

People working in a service desk must understand that the data they collect on a daily basis becomes information. This information is not used just to track outstanding incidents and service requests. It is also used to measure their individual performance, the overall performance of the service desk, and, more importantly, customer satisfaction with the department and the company. Failing to record events and activities accurately and completely can have negative results for the department or company, the service desk, and the service desk employee. Figure 1-6 shows a sampling of the types of data and information collected and used by service desks.

24

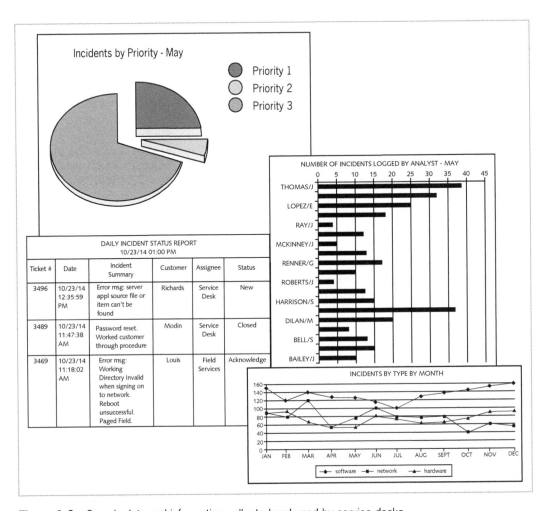

Figure 1-6   Sample data and information collected and used by service desks
© Cengage Learning 2014

Forward-thinking companies use the data they capture at the service desk to spot trends and discover the causes of incidents. By doing so, companies can increase customer satisfaction, enhance productivity, improve the quality of products and services, increase the efficiency and effectiveness with which services are delivered, and create new products and services. People working in a service desk enjoy a unique opportunity to capture an enormous amount of information about customers' wants and needs. Successful service desks design and implement processes and technologies that enable them to capture and use customer information efficiently. Because of this, people interested in a service-industry career must learn how to interpret data and how to share and add value to information.

Chapter 6 explores the information component of a successful service desk.

Of the four service desk components, people are by far the most important and expensive component. This is because when customers—living, breathing human beings with feelings and expectations—contact the service desk for support, they expect to be assisted by competent, friendly, and efficient people. Finding qualified people to deliver excellent customer service is one of the greatest challenges the support industry faces.

Customer Service—The Bottom Line

High-quality customer service is the goal of every customer-oriented company or department. **Customer service** involves ensuring that customers receive maximum value for the products or services they purchase. **Value** is the perceived worth, usefulness, or importance of a product or service to the customer. Customers' definitions of value are influenced by every service encounter they experience, which is why every contact a customer has with a service desk is an opportunity for the company to enhance its customer service image.

The most recognized membership organizations and associations that provide information, guidance, and networking opportunities to support industry professionals are Association of Support Professionals (*www.asponline.com*), HDI (*www.thinkhdi.com*), IT Service Management Forum (*www.itsmfi.org*), and Technology Services Industry Association (*www.tsia.com*).

At one time, young, leading-edge companies could get by with mediocre service if they were delivering a phenomenal new product. However, as these companies grew and competition increased, they needed to quickly rethink their customer service strategy. Some internal IT departments have historically taken a "We'll give you what we think is best" attitude, but they, too, have had to adopt a more customer-driven approach. Otherwise, their companies may replace them with a supplier that focuses on customer needs.

26

Customer service does not mean giving customers everything they ask for, whenever they ask for it. This misinterpretation of customer service can cripple the most well-meaning company or cause it to fail completely. For example, sending a technician to a customer site without attempting to resolve the incident over the telephone is very costly and quickly overworks the company's pool of technicians. Likewise, failing to define what products the service desk supports causes them to receive calls about products for which they are not trained and have difficulty supporting. Instead, a service desk must manage customer expectations, which, in turn, leads to customer satisfaction. **Customer satisfaction** reflects the difference between how a customer expects to be treated and how the customer perceives he or she was treated. Managing expectations involves clearly communicating to customers what the service desk can and cannot do to meet their needs, given available resources.

Managing expectations is a challenge because expectations can vary from one person to another, one situation to another, and even one day to another. Left unmanaged, customer expectations quickly exceed the resources and capabilities of even the most successful service desk. Failing to recognize the importance of managing customer expectations can cause a service desk to fall into one of four traps:

- Promising more than it can deliver
- Delivering more than it promises, which raises the bar on customer expectations
- Promising one thing and delivering something else
- Not promising anything specific, leaving the customer to set expectations

Any of these scenarios, in the end, leads to customer dissatisfaction. Companies that provide world class customer service work diligently to determine what services are important to their customers and how customers expect services to be delivered. These companies are gaining market share and increasing the size of their client base by delivering superior customer service and support before and after the customer purchases or uses a product. Customers increasingly use customer service to differentiate companies and products, leading to an ever-increasing demand for quality service. Establishing a responsive, competent service desk is no longer an option; it is a critical factor for success.

Chapter Summary

- A vastly increased dependence on technology has created a tremendous demand for technical support. Technical support services enable individuals and corporations to effectively use the information technology they have acquired or developed.

- A well-thought-out and properly implemented service desk provides a company with a primary mechanism for measuring and managing the delivery of technical and customer support services to the customer community. The role of the help desk has evolved from that of a reactive dispatch function to that of a proactive service desk that is focused on meeting strategic business needs.

- People, processes, technology, and information are the tightly integrated components that contribute to the success of a service desk. By far, people are the most important and expensive component. Tremendous opportunity exists for people who have the mix of business, technical, soft, and self-management skills needed to work in the support industry and who sincerely enjoy working with customers and helping others.

- High-quality customer service is the goal of every customer-oriented company or department. To deliver high-quality customer service, a service desk must manage customer expectations. Managing expectations involves clearly communicating to customers what the service desk can and cannot do, given the available resources. Because savvy customers use customer service to evaluate companies and products, establishing a responsive, competent service desk is no longer an option for companies; it is a critical success factor.

Key Terms

best-in-class—Refers to a company that is the finest in its industry peer group. For example, a best-in-class manufacturing company is considered excellent by its customers when compared to other manufacturing companies.

best practice—A proven way of completing a task to produce a near optimum result.

bring your own device (BYOD)—A practice that involves using personally-owned mobile devices to access business applications.

call center—A place where telephone calls are made or received in high volume.

channel—A route of communication to and from the service desk, such as the telephone, voice mail, email, and the web.

contact—A generic term used to describe different types of customer transactions such as questions, incidents, and service requests.

customer—A person who buys products or services.

customer satisfaction—The difference between how a customer expects to be treated and how the customer perceives he or she was treated.

customer service—Services that ensure customers receive maximum value for the products or services they purchase.

customer support—Services that help a customer understand and benefit from a product's capabilities by answering questions, solving problems, and providing training.

development—The construction of new systems.

dispatch—To send.

ethical behavior—Conduct that conforms to generally accepted or stated principles of right and wrong.

ethics—The rules and standards that govern the conduct of a person or group of people.

external customer—A person or company that buys another company's products and services.

governance—How an organization controls its actions.

help desk—A single point of contact within a company for technology-related questions and incidents.

incident—An unplanned interruption to an IT service or a reduction in the quality of an IT service. (ITIL definition)

information—Data that is organized in a meaningful way.

Information Technology Infrastructure Library (ITIL)—A set of best practices for IT service management.

internal customer—A person who works at a company and at times relies on other employees at that company to perform his or her job.

Internet—A global collection of computer networks that are linked to provide worldwide access to information.

IT governance—The processes that ensure the effective and efficient use of IT in enabling an organization to achieve its goals. (Gartner, Inc. definition)

IT service—A service that is based on the use of information technology and supports business processes.

IT service management (ITSM)—A discipline for managing IT services that focuses on the quality of those services and the relationship that the IT organization has with its customers.

metrics—Performance measures.

near-shore outsourcing—Obtaining services from another company in a neighboring country.

off-the-shelf—Personal computer software products that are developed and distributed commercially.

offshore outsourcing—The exporting of work from one country to another part of the world.

onshore outsourcing—Obtaining services from another company in the same country.

outsource—To have services provided by an outside supplier instead of providing them in-house.

peer-to-peer support—A practice in which users bypass the formal support structure and seek assistance from their coworkers or someone in another department.

people—The service desk component that consists of the staff and structure put in place within a company or department to support its customers by performing processes.

problem—The cause of one or more incidents. (ITIL definition)

procedure—A step-by-step, detailed set of instructions that describes how to perform the tasks in a process.

process—A collection of interrelated work activities that take a set of specific inputs and produce a set of specific outputs that are of value to a customer.

remote control and diagnostic systems—Systems that allow the service desk to take remote control of the keyboard, screen, or mouse of connected devices and then troubleshoot problems, transfer files, and even provide informal training by viewing or operating the customer's screen.

service—A means of delivering value to customers by facilitating outcomes customers want to achieve without the ownership of specific costs and risks. (ITIL definition)

service desk—A single point of contact within a company for managing customer incidents and service requests.

service request—A request from a user for information, advice, or a standard change.

support—Services that enable the effective use of a system.

technical support—A wide range of services that enable people and companies to effectively use the information technology they have acquired or developed.

technology—The tools and systems people use to do their work.

total cost of ownership (TCO)—The total amount that a company or person spends on information technology over its lifetime. A considerable portion of the TCO is technical support.

ubiquitous computing—An environment where people have access to their information from multiple computing devices and systems and even from public shared access points.

user—A person who consumes products or services.

value—The perceived worth, usefulness, or importance of a product or service to the customer.

Web 2.0—A concept that emphasizes enabling web users to interact, collaborate, and generate content via, for example, blogs, wikis, and social networking sites, rather than passively view content created by others.

world class—Refers to a company that has achieved and sustains high levels of customer satisfaction. For example, a world class manufacturing company is considered excellent by its customers when compared to other service companies, regardless of what industry they are in.

World Wide Web (WWW or web)—A collection of documents on the Internet with point-and-click access to information that is posted by government agencies, businesses, educational institutions, nonprofit organizations, and individuals around the world.

Review Questions

1. What two factors create the need to provide help to a growing number of technology users?

2. What is a service desk?

3. What is the purpose of technical support?

4. What are four negative consequences for companies that fail to distinguish between development and support?

5. What action on the part of vendors began the move toward help desks?

6. What concept about customers did the quality movement introduce?

7. How is the focus of customer support different from that of technical support?

8. In the 1990s, what two factors led to an explosion in the number of people using computers on a daily basis?

9. What trend affecting the service desk is being driven by the consumerization of IT?

10. What are the three factors that influence the technical support services a company delivers?

11. Why do some companies take a more formal approach to technical support?

12. What is it called when a person bypasses the formal support structure and seeks computer-related assistance from a coworker?

13. Why do many companies consider the service desk a strategic corporate resource?

14. Describe the difference between a world class company and a best-in-class company.

15. Describe the characteristics of a world class help desk.

16. How is a service desk different than a help desk?

17. What are the benefits of having the service desk perform tasks such as network monitoring that various other support groups performed historically?

18. List the four components of a successful service desk, and briefly describe each one.

19. What is IT governance?

20. In addition to technical skills, list and briefly describe the three other types of skills people need to work successfully at a service desk.

21. What are three characteristics that successful service desks look for in people they hire and train?

22. A(n) _____ is a collection of interrelated work activities that take inputs and produce outputs that are of value to the customer.

23. What must service desks do to ensure that processes meet their customers' ever-rising expectations?

24. How do successful service desks use technology?

25. List four ways that information is used at a service desk.

26. What must people interested in a career in the service industry learn to do with data and information?

27. _____ involves ensuring customers receive maximum value for the products and services they purchase.

28. What influences a customer's definition of value?

29. Customer service means giving customers everything they ask for, whenever they ask for it. True or False? Briefly explain your answer.

30. What are the consequences of leaving customer expectations unmanaged?

31. What are four traps companies can fall into if they do not manage customer expectations?

32. Why is establishing a service desk a critical success factor in business today?

Hands-On Projects

1. **Evaluate technical support experiences.** The quality of technical support varies greatly from company to company. Talk to at least three people about their experiences with technical support. Ask each person the following questions:

   - What kind of technical support did you need recently?

   - When and how did you contact the company?

   - Did the company you contacted have a service desk?

   - What expectations did you have before you contacted the company for support?

   - What led you to have those expectations?

   - Did the company meet your expectations?

   - Could the company have done anything better? If so, what?

   Write a report that summarizes each experience and presents your conclusions about each experience.

2. **Determine how to obtain technical support.** Be prepared by knowing what company or department to contact when you need technical support. Perform an inventory of the hardware and software you use on a regular basis. Determine how you obtain help when you have a problem or a question with each piece of hardware and software. Make a list for future reference that includes the names of the products and the telephone numbers or web addresses you would use to obtain support.

3. **Perform proactive technical support services.** Technical support includes reactive activities such as resolving incidents; however, it also includes proactive activities such as having a regular PC maintenance schedule. Complete the following steps:

    1. Search the web for articles about PC maintenance.

    2. Prepare a list of the 10 most frequently suggested PC maintenance tips.

    3. If you have a PC, perform each of the suggested maintenance activities on your PC. If you do not have a PC, offer to perform each of the suggested maintenance activities on the PC of a classmate, friend, or family member. Provide him or her with a copy of your maintenance tips for future reference.

    4. Share your tips with your classmates and add to your list any new tips that your classmates identified.

    5. As a class, prepare a list of three to five benefits that are derived from having a regular PC maintenance schedule.

4. **Explore perceptions about customer support.** Customer support services include answering questions and providing training, in addition to resolving incidents. Mobile Internet-enabled devices, such as tablets and smartphones, are extremely popular. These devices are perceived to be fairly easy to use. Do they need to be supported? Talk to three people who regularly use one of these devices. If you use one of these devices regularly, you can count yourself as an interviewee. Ask each person the following questions:

    - How did you learn to use this device?

    - If you had questions, how did you get answers?

    - Are you using all of the features and functionality this device provides? If not, why?

    - Have you had any trouble using this device? If so, how were the incidents resolved?

    Determine each person's *expectations* about how they would obtain user information and support for the device. Compare their expectations to their *perceptions* about any support services they actually received from a service desk (such as the service desk where they work) or from the product's manufacturer. Conclude whether the support services each person received failed to meet, met, or exceeded his or her expectations. Summarize your interviewees' responses by briefly describing how their expectations influenced their perceptions and ultimately their satisfaction with customer support services.

5. **Compare reactive and proactive employees and companies.** The term *fire fighting* is often used to describe the reactive way in which employees and companies approach their work. For example, it is not uncommon to hear an executive exclaim that he or she spent most of the day "fighting fires." Assemble a team of at least three of your classmates or use your school's online message or discussion board. Discuss the challenges and drawbacks of fire fighting at work. Brainstorm and prepare a list of ways that real fire fighters are proactive. For example, fire fighters promote fire safety in an effort to prevent fires. See how many analogies you can draw between the way

fire fighters work and the way a service desk works. When you are done, share your list with the rest of the class.

6. **Uncover processes and procedures.** Many activities you are involved in follow specific processes and procedures. Think about a hobby or sport that you enjoy. Determine the "process" your hobby or sport requires and the "procedures" that make up that process. For example, if your hobby is flying model airplanes, flying the plane to its target destination is a process. Procedures include selecting a destination, preparing the plane for flight, taking off, avoiding obstacles, landing, and so on. Briefly describe the process your hobby or sport involves and list its associated procedures.

7. **Evaluate a company's technical support services.** Visit the web site for a hardware or software company that you do business with now or are considering doing business with in the future. For example, you could contact the company that manufactured your computer or that published a frequently used software package. Or visit one of the web sites selected for The Association of Support Professionals' Ten Best Web Support Sites award. From the web site you choose, do the following:

- Determine all the ways the company delivers technical support. Does it have a service desk?

- Find out what commitments, if any, the company makes about how it delivers customer support. For example, does it promise to respond to all inquiries within a certain time? Does it make any promises about how it handles telephone calls, emails, or online chat sessions? Does it promise to provide access to knowledgeable analysts?

Critique the company's technical support services based on the information you found. Was it easy to locate this information about the company's support services? Do its technical support services encourage or discourage you from using the company's products? Write a report that summarizes your findings.

8. **Understand the implications of bring your own device (BYOD).** Many companies and schools are implementing bring your own device policies for their employees and students. Such polices must address the associated risks and liabilities. Use the Internet to research this trend and then answer the following questions:

- What are the benefits of BYOD to (1) the organization and (2) the technology users?

- What technologies are typically involved?

- What risks and liabilities must be considered?

- Provide at least three examples of BYOD policies.

- Provide a checklist of at least three steps that organizations must take when implementing BYOD policies.

9. **Compare your positive and negative customer experiences.** Think about situations within the past week or two in which you were a customer. For example, you may have been a customer while dining out or shopping. Select one positive experience and one negative experience. For each experience, do the following:

- Briefly describe the situation.

- Explain what made the customer service experience positive or negative.

- Suggest how the service encounter could have been handled better.

- Determine if your recommendation is feasible. For example, would you be willing to pay more or wait longer for service if that was a byproduct of implementing your suggestion?

- Summarize what you learned from these experiences in a report.

10. **Determine the value of a product.** Recall that value is the perceived worth, usefulness, or importance of a product or service to a customer. Assemble a team of at least three of your classmates or use your school's online message or discussion board. Select a product that everyone is familiar with and has purchased at some point. It does not have to be a hardware or software product (for example, you could select a clothing item or a common over-the-counter medicine). Brainstorm and document the value of the selected item to you and your classmates.

Case Projects

1. **Bulldog Boards Manufacturing Company.** The Bulldog Boards Manufacturing Company, a producer of high-quality wakeboards, bindings, and boots, recently won an international contract that will significantly increase its sales. You have been hired to set up a service desk for the company's employees who will be using a newly introduced sales ordering and product manufacturing system. The company's Chief Information Officer (CIO) has expressed interest in using a best practice framework such as ITIL. Search the web for information about ITIL and prepare a brief presentation that includes an overview of ITIL, its history, and its benefits.

2. **Creating an Information Security Policy.** You manage the service desk and have been asked to participate on a team of representatives from IT and the business to create an Information Security Policy (ISP). The service desk plays an important role in enforcing these policies and you will play an active role on the team. Search the web for information about how to create an ISP. Prepare a set of notes in preparation for the first meeting that includes the following:

- Information about how to create and implement an ISP

- Typical responsibilities, policies, and procedures included in an ISP

- The role a service desk plays in enforcing information security policies and promoting security awareness

CHAPTER 2

Service Desk Operations

In this chapter you will learn:

◎ The different types of customer service and support organizations

◎ The components of a service desk mission

◎ The role and operation of internal service desks

◎ The role and operation of external service desks

◎ How size influences a service desk's operation

◎ The benefits and challenges of centralized and decentralized service desks

◎ The benefits and challenges of managing a service desk as a cost center or a profit center

◎ The role of outsourcing in the support industry

◎ How the service desk model is evolving

Service desks, like any customer service and support organization, are the first point of contact for customers and exist to ensure customer satisfaction. Although this underlying purpose is the same from one organization to the next, the specific services offered and the operating characteristics such as type, size, and structure vary, depending on the needs of the customers. Customer needs determine the mission of both the larger corporation and the service desk. For example, if a company is highly committed to ensuring a positive customer experience, then the service desk's mission reflects this. If a company is committed to improving the lives of its customers, or if a company is committed to improving the quality of its products through innovation, then the service desk's mission reflects this. The amount of resources such as staffing and equipment that the company gives the service desk reflects the company's mission and the priority it places on customer satisfaction.

To work in a service desk, you must understand the different types and sizes of service desks that exist, how they are structured, and the daily activities that employees perform. Understanding these characteristics will enable you to seek out opportunities that align with your career goals and broaden your resume. So that you can be successful, it is also important to know that your individual performance as a service desk employee will be measured against how well you contribute to the service desk's mission and to the company's mission.

Types of Customer Service and Support Organizations

Customer service and support organizations come in all shapes and sizes and deliver a wide range of services. These organizations can be either a company or a department within a company.

One type of customer service and support organization is a call center, which is a place where telephone calls are made or received in high volume. An **inbound call center** receives telephone calls from customers and may answer questions, take orders, respond to billing inquiries, and provide customer support. An **outbound call center** makes telephone calls to customers, primarily for telemarketing. **Telemarketing** is the selling of products and services over the telephone. Some call centers are **blended call centers**, which means that they receive incoming calls and make outgoing calls. The term **contact center** refers to a call center that uses technologies such as e-mail and the web in addition to the telephone to communicate with its customers.

Major businesses use call or contact centers because they need to handle a high volume of customer contacts. A cost-efficient solution is to handle these contacts from one or more centralized locations. The actual services delivered by each call center vary.

Examples of call centers and contact centers include airline reservation centers, catalog ordering centers, and home shopping centers. Software publishers and equipment manufacturers such as Apple, Dell, Hewlett-Packard (HP), and Microsoft use call or contact centers to provide technical and customer support. Large corporations may use call or contact centers to provide technical and customer support to internal employees. They may also outsource their support services to a supplier that runs a call center that serves the employees or customers of many corporations.

Customers directed to contact a help desk or service desk for support may in fact reach an analyst who physically resides in a call or contact center.

Two other common types of customer service and support organizations are help desks and service desks. Although help desks and service desks both are a single point of contact within a company for managing customer contacts, help desks typically have a narrower scope of responsibility than service desks and handle only incidents. Service desks handle service requests and communications with customers as well as incidents.

The service desk plays a critical role as it may be the only contact that a technology user has with an IT organization. Given a clear mission and adequate resources, a service desk can compensate for deficiencies elsewhere in the organization by, for example, improving customer service and therefore customers' perception of the organization. The service desk can also deliver bottom line benefits by ensuring effective use of IT resources and increasing customer productivity.

Conversely, a poorly run service desk can make even the most effective IT organization look bad. Poorly trained or insufficient service desk staff and incorrect or inadequate procedures can leave customers with a bad impression of the entire organization.

Although the service desk plays a critical role, it cannot function independently and must build positive working relationships with other parts of the organization to succeed. As a result, service desks are often structured in a series of levels or lines, an approach commonly known as a **multi-level support model**. In a multi-level support model, customers contact the service desk when they are unable to solve incidents on their own. The service desk refers incidents it cannot resolve to the appropriate internal group, external vendor, or subject matter expert. A **subject matter expert (SME)** is a person who has a high level of experience or knowledge about a particular subject.

In the context of a multi-level support model, customers solving incidents on their own is known as **level zero** or tier zero and may also be referred to as **self-help**. Self-help services such as a service desk web site that contains answers to FAQs and a knowledge base of solutions empower customers to support themselves.

Chapter 5 explores how service desks use the Internet to provide self-services.

Level one is the first point of contact for customers and is typically the service desk. If the level one service desk cannot resolve an incident, it hands off the incident to the next highest level, a practice known as escalation. **Escalation** (or **escalate**) means to raise an incident from one level to another, such as from level one to level two, to dedicate new or additional resources to the incident. **Level two** is the person or group that resolves incidents that are beyond the scope or authority (such as system access rights or permissions) of level one. Level two might consist of a support group for a particular software application, a network support group, or an expert in a particular service. Level two might be a specialist group within the service desk team that has greater technical skills or authority than the front-line service desk analysts who initially handle incidents. If level two cannot resolve the incident, then it hands off the incident to level three, which is usually a developer or system engineer, a vendor, or a subject matter expert. **Level three** is the person or group that resolves complex incidents that are beyond the scope of level two. The service desk's ultimate goal is to resolve a high percentage of incidents at level one and to escalate a very low percentage of incidents to level three. Figure 2-1 shows a multi-level support model. The goal of the multi-level support model is to resolve incidents in the most efficient and cost-effective manner possible.

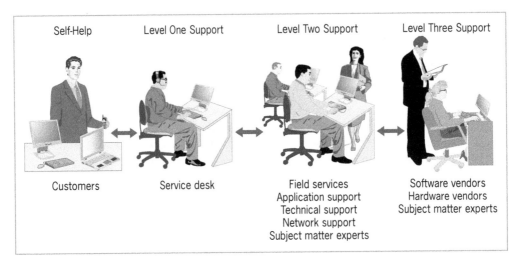

Figure 2-1   Multi-level support model
© Cengage Learning 2014

Not all service desks require three levels of support. For example, it is not uncommon for small service desks to have only two levels of support. This is particularly true in organizations that support primarily off-the-shelf software products. In those organizations, if a level one analyst cannot resolve an incident, he or she contacts the appropriate software vendor.

 Chapter 4 explores the responsibilities of groups within a multi-level support model.

Technology such as knowledge management systems, network monitoring systems, and remote control and diagnostic systems make it possible for the service desk to absorb many of the activities that relate directly to the customer from other support groups, such as network support, field service, and system administration. These other groups then can focus on tasks such as projects, operations activities, and maintenance activities. Thus, a service desk handles incidents and service requests with greater efficiency than a traditional help desk because it hands off fewer incidents and service requests to other groups. This increases the value of its services to customers and the company. Customers receive faster service, the other support groups can focus on their primary missions, and the company achieves a maximum return on its investment in the service desk. This book focuses on the service desk, a successor to the help desk. Unlike call centers, customers can typically contact the service desk using a number of methods, or channels. These include the telephone, fax, email, and services on the web such as web forms and online chat. In some companies, customers can even walk in to the service desk for support. Also, service desks typically handle technology-oriented incidents and questions, whereas call centers handle a wide range of transactions that may or may not be technology oriented.

Service Desk Mission

Without a clearly defined mission that is determined by its customers' needs, a service desk can fall prey to the "all things to all people" syndrome. A service desk's **mission** describes the customers the service desk serves, the types of services the service desk provides, and how the service desk delivers those services. In other words, a mission defines who the service desk supports, what it supports, and how it provides that support. These things determine the type, size, and structure of the service desk. The mission is like a roadmap the service desk can use to determine how it operates. A service desk's mission reflects the values expressed in the company's mission. A clearly defined mission also provides service desk management, staff, and customers with an overall objective against which they can measure performance. The essence of the mission is often captured in a mission statement. Figure 2-2 shows an example of a mission statement for a service desk.

The service desk mission is to provide our customers with a centralized point of contact for responsive support. We are committed to quality help through teamwork and a proactive approach to identifying and solving incidents. We will strive to exceed our customers' expectations in our ongoing pursuit of service excellence.

Figure 2-2 Sample service desk mission statement
© Cengage Learning 2014

It is important that every service desk employee understand the service desk's mission—and how it fits into the company's mission—and his or her role in that mission. Companies whose employees understand both the company mission and their department mission attain considerably higher customer satisfaction rates than companies whose employees do not. These companies also tend to experience high employee satisfaction because employees understand their purpose and know how to contribute to the department's mission and the company's mission.

When a department's mission reflects the company's mission, employees perform activities that support the mission and customers are satisfied. For example, if a company's mission is to be a low-cost provider of quality products, the service desk's mission may be to enhance product quality by delivering efficient, effective, and low-cost services. The mission of a service desk determines the type of service desk and how it operates.

There are two principal types of service desks: internal service desks and external service desks. An internal service desk supports internal customers, or the employees who work at its company. An external service desk supports external customers, the people who buy a company's products and services. A blended service desk supports both internal customers and external customers. Whether the service desk has internal or external customers, it is still a customer service organization, and as such, must strive to meet its customers' needs.

Just under 53 percent of the companies that responded to HDI's *2012 Support Center Practices and Salary Report* provide blended support.

Internal Service Desks

An **internal service desk** responds to questions, distributes information, and handles incidents and service requests for its company's employees. A company can have several types of internal help desks or service desks that employees contact for support, each with a clearly defined scope of responsibility. For example, employees usually go to the human resources (HR) department for questions about medical insurance or to receive directories of health-care providers. They contact the facilities department to have office fixtures installed or repaired. Similarly, they contact the company's IT department about the hardware and software they use to accomplish their work. These departments all function as internal service desks because they serve internal customers and are responsible for satisfying those customers. This section focuses on the IT service desk, which may also be known as an IT support desk, technical support desk, customer support center, or support services.

Internal Service Desk's Role

Historically, IT departments focused solely on the technology for which they were responsible, such as hardware, software, applications, and networks, and concentrated on ensuring that the systems were "up and running." They did not always focus on the technology users, nor did they always emphasize doing things as efficiently and cost-effectively as possible. Although IT departments provided a necessary function in the company, their role was limited.

IT departments must now function as internal service providers. An **internal service provider** is a department or a person within a company that supplies information, products, or services to another department or person within the same company. Like an external service provider, an internal service provider must supply a high-quality product on an agreed-upon schedule at an agreed-upon price. As an internal service provider, the IT department must supply competitively priced services that help the company's employees use technology to improve productivity and increase corporate profitability. To do this, the IT department must acknowledge that it is a customer service organization and provide a high level of service to its customers. It is no longer enough for the IT department to simply keep the company's information technology in good working order. As a customer service organization, it must also ensure that customers receive maximum value for that technology. In other words, the IT department must ensure that customers perceive that the information technology is useful. To do this, many IT departments are establishing service desks or enhancing their existing help desks and adopting the service desk concept. The IT service desk provides company employees a single point of contact within the IT department. The service desk acts as a customer advocate and ensures that quality services are provided.

An internal service desk may provide some support directly to the company's external customers, such as technical support for the company's web site or proprietary software customers use to interface with the company. In this capacity, the internal service desk is acting as a blended service desk.

In an effort to satisfy their customers, most IT service desks strive to resolve a high percentage of reported incidents at the first point of contact. According to HDI's *2012 Support Center Practices and Salary Report*, 69 percent of incidents are resolved by the person who initially received the call. They also take ownership of all incidents, whether or not they can resolve them. Taking **ownership** of an incident means tracking the incident to ensure that the customer is kept informed about the status of the incident, that the incident is resolved within the expected time frame, and that the customer is satisfied with the final resolution.

Chapter 4 further explores the concept of ownership.

An internal service desk often participates in other activities besides assisting internal customers with incidents. Especially in smaller organizations, the service desk can serve as a jack-of-all-trades and be actively involved in performing other functions, such as those listed in Figure 2-3. In larger organizations, separate groups and possibly even external vendors may perform some or all of these functions.

- Training
- Network and system administration
- Request fulfillment

Figure 2-3 Additional service desk functions
© Cengage Learning 2014

Training

Training involves preparing and delivering programs that provide people the knowledge and skills they need to use technology effectively. The service desk may also provide ad-hoc, or informal, and one-on-one training in the course of responding to users' questions and incidents. Training is often a significant expense. Companies must spend a lot of time and money to develop and deliver the training, and users must leave their regular duties to attend the training. Not giving formal training to users and service desk staff can, however, be just as costly. The cost comes in the form of lost productivity as employees and service desk staff waste time trying to informally learn how to use systems, fix incidents, and correct mistakes made because of lack of training.

Training might take place in a physical classroom setting with an instructor, in an online or virtual classroom with an instructor, or one-on-one in a user's office. Training might also take place through media such as audio, video, computer-based training, Internet-based training, podcasts, and webinars. These various forms of technology-supported learning and training are commonly referred to as **electronic learning**, or **eLearning**. **Computer-based training (CBT)** uses computer software packages to train and test people on a wide range of subjects. **Internet-based training (IBT)** uses training systems that people access from any device that has an Internet connection and a browser. **Podcasts** distribute digital media files over the Internet to personal computers and portable media players. Podcasts are used both by teachers to provide training and by students to deliver assignments or to share their expertise. **Webinars**, short for web-based seminars, are used to deliver presentations, lectures, workshops, or seminars over the web. CBT, IBT, and podcasts tend to be fairly passive forms of learning where students are completing assignments or listening to content independently. Webinars typically enable attendees to interact with the instructor and other attendees by, for example, responding to polling questions, submitting questions, or communicating with others via online chat, over the telephone, or via Voice over Internet Protocol (VoIP).

A strong trend in the training industry is **social learning,** which involves people learning by interacting with other people. This learning may occur by observing others or by others sharing their expertise and experience through, for example, social networking sites, discussion forums, wikis, and blogs. A **wiki** is a web site whose users add, modify, or delete its content using a Web browser. Wikis are often used by subject matter experts to share their expertise and draw upon the expertise of others in their community. A **blog**, short for web log, is a journal kept on the Internet. Blogs are typically updated frequently and display journal entries in reverse chronological order.

Some service desks use social media sites such as YouTube to post videos created by service desk analysts or by users providing "how to" type information. Some service desks facilitate users interacting with other users via, for example, discussion forums, particularly for noncritical services. Service desk analysts often monitor these ad hoc forms of training to ensure customers are getting the information and answers that they need in a timely fashion.

People benefit most when training programs deliver the appropriate content at the appropriate level. A training program should include basic or introductory classes for new users and advanced classes for those who have already mastered the basics. An effective training program reduces support costs and increases employee productivity and satisfaction. In other words, proper training means fewer calls to the service desk.

Network and System Administration

Network and system administration activities include day-to-day tasks such as setting up and maintaining user accounts, ensuring that the data the company collects is secure, and performing email and database management. Administrators protect the company's data by performing regular backup and restore procedures and by ensuring that backup and restore processes are in place and working. Other activities include file management, printer and server management, monitoring server and network performance, and performance tuning.

Request Fulfillment

Request fulfillment activities involve handling service requests from IT users. Common service requests include answering questions such as "how to" questions, resetting a password, or providing equipment to a new employee. Service requests may also include standard changes. A **standard change** is a preapproved change that is low risk and follows a procedure. Examples of standard changes may include moving equipment, installing and configuring new systems, and upgrading existing systems. These activities are often referred to as **moves, adds, and changes (MACs)** or **installations, moves, adds, and changes (IMACs)**. Although some organizations use the same process to handle incidents and service requests, an increasing number handle these activities through separate processes.

 Service requests and the request fulfillment process are defined in greater detail in Chapter 4.

As the internal service desk's role has expanded, so has the variety of skills needed to keep it functioning smoothly. These skills vary considerably from one service desk to the next because the service desk must support the specific services, hardware, software, network, and application components a particular company uses. For example, supporting Microsoft Windows is very similar from one company to the next, whereas internally developed, or "home-grown," applications change from company to company. Analysts who support these home-grown applications usually receive specialized training.

In the past, the internal service desk was viewed as an entry-level position for new IT hires, regardless of their skills. The problem with such an approach is that new hires often do not understand the company's business and technical infrastructure well enough to function as efficiently and effectively as today's customers demand. As a result, organizations are increasingly taking care to ensure that service desk staff, including new hires, have appropriate skills and are provided adequate training.

Internal service desks expose analysts to a variety of technologies, technology-related problems, and customers. They offer career advancement opportunities and can also expose analysts to and prepare them for opportunities that exist in other parts of the company. What better way to learn about the company than to interact regularly with people who work in different areas of the business? Some internal service desks operate very informally. Others have very formal processes and require users to follow clearly defined procedures to obtain services. For example, some organizations have established Service Level Agreements with their internal customers. A **Service Level Agreement (SLA)** is a written document that spells out the services the service desk will provide to the customer, the customer's responsibilities, and how service performance is measured. Examples of customer responsibilities include:

- Calling the service desk (not someone else in the company) when there is an incident or service request

- Complying with technology usage and information security policies

- Attending training

In a company that allows employees to bring their own devices, the customer responsibilities specified in an SLA may include:

- Purchasing devices that are eligible for the bring your own device (BYOD) program

- Maintaining vendor maintenance or support contracts for their devices (when required by the program)

- Contacting the vendor to obtain support for their devices (when required by the program)

- Complying with information security policies and protecting corporate data

- Maintaining their systems by, for example, backing up their data, using antivirus software, and maintaining software licenses (when these tasks aren't performed by the company itself)

- Removing corporate data and company-licensed software if a personal device is no longer being used in a professional capacity

 Some internal service desks offer "best effort" support or time-specified support (such as 30 to 60 minutes of support) for employee devices, but provide full support for incidents relating to corporate applications or connectivity to the corporate network.

An SLA helps to set customer expectations so customers don't have an unrealistic view of what support they should be getting. It also enables the service desk to know its limits for supporting internal customers and what it must do to satisfy them. It is important to note that, because SLAs are between internal parties, SLAs are agreements, not legally binding contracts. The goal when establishing SLAs is to build and manage the relationship between an internal IT service provider and its customers. SLAs are necessary as organizations struggle to balance the need to satisfy ever-increasing internal customer demands with the costs associated with meeting those demands.

 Chapter 6 explores how SLAs are used to manage customer expectations and measure service desk performance.

Internal Service Desk's Position in the Organization

Establishing and maintaining a service desk can be costly. One ongoing challenge that internal service desks face is proving their worth to the company. Although people, processes, and technology are expensive, they are investments that help the company avoid lost productivity and lost opportunity, which are also costly but harder to quantify. Because productivity and opportunity cannot be purchased, there are no invoices for them. Yet the loss of them has a very real cost, even if it does not seem that "real" dollars are being spent. An efficient, effective service desk can help lower those costs by increasing the effectiveness with which customers can use technology. The service desk can also lower those costs by reducing the time customers cannot use technology because of incidents or lack of information.

The technologies that internal service desks use to do their work usually reflect the company's willingness to invest in the service desk. Some companies have rudimentary systems, such as simple databases the service desk has developed in-house, whereas other companies have commercially developed, state-of-the-art incident management systems that were customized to meet the company's needs. Because people are the most expensive component of a service desk, companies are often willing to invest in technology in an effort to maximize their human resources.

Few companies have the human resources required to provide unlimited customer service; this is particularly true for an internal service desk. IT departments are notoriously understaffed, and because internal service desks have not historically charged for their services, they also tend to be underfunded. This situation is compounded by the fact that some internal service desks try to be all things to all people. In these cases, the service desk may ineffectively use its resources by stretching them too thin.

The best service desks strive to provide high-quality service within the limits of their funding. For example, an internal service desk may limit the products it supports or its hours of operation. This approach enables service desks to provide quality service for fewer products or hours rather than mediocre service for all products at all times. Or, instead of rejecting service requests that are beyond their capabilities (sometimes called **out-of-scope service requests**), underfunded service desks can provide the best possible alternative by directing the customer to another source that can help. These service desks are aware of their limitations and work diligently to balance customer needs with available resources.

External Service Desks

External service desks support customers who buy their company's products and services. In other words, the customers they support are not employees of the company. Most hardware and software companies have external service desks to support their customers, as do most telecommunications companies and internet service providers. Major companies may use a call or contact center to deliver support services because they need to handle a high volume of contacts.

The services that external service desks provide vary by industry and by the role a service desk plays within its organization. For example, the external service desk of an equipment manufacturer may be responsible primarily for ensuring that field service representatives are dispatched to a customer site when an incident occurs. That incident may have already been diagnosed by the internal service desk at the customer site. That same equipment manufacturer may offer another service that diagnoses incidents to determine if the problem is with the actual equipment or with the software being used to run the equipment. The external service desk of a software publisher may handle questions about or incidents related to all of the company's products. Another software publisher may have multiple service desks that specialize in a particular product or set of products.

External Service Desk's Role

External service desks can provide a variety of services to customers. Some external service desks provide **pre-sales support**, meaning that they answer questions for people who have not yet purchased the company's products or services. They may also take orders and respond to billing inquiries. Most external service desks provide traditional **post-sales support**, which involves helping people who have purchased a company's product or service. Post-sales support activities include answering questions, helping the customer learn to use the product, explaining the advanced features that the product offers, and resolving incidents.

The role of the external service desk is evolving as companies start to fully appreciate the fact that positive customer experiences help sell products and services. These companies recognize the enormous contribution the service desk makes by capturing and sharing customer feedback with the appropriate groups in the company. The company can then use this information to develop new and more desirable products and services. External service desks are continuously being challenged to build customer relationships and contribute to corporate growth and profitability. Many companies use customer relationship management programs in an effort to serve their customers better. **Customer relationship management (CRM)** involves using customer contact and relationship information to generate additional sales and to increase levels of customer service and retention. A CRM initiative involves implementing software products and processes that enable the service desk to collect, maintain, and share information about the company's customers with other authorized company employees.

External Service Desk's Position in the Organization

In much the same way that an internal service desk shares information with other IT groups, such as development and network support, an external service desk exchanges information with its company's sales, marketing, field services, development, and research and development (R&D) departments. By collecting and disseminating information about the company's customers, how those customers use the company's products, and how customers would like those products enhanced, the external service desk provides an invaluable service to the company. Figure 2-4 illustrates how the external service desk collects information about the company's customers and shares that information with other departments.

Figure 2-4   External service desk sharing information
© Cengage Learning 2014

External service desks have become a major focal point for customer interactions. They are responsible for capturing information about customers, including the products and services they are using and their preferences. They are also responsible for recording all transactions relevant to a given customer. This information can then be used by others in the organization. For example, a sales representative who is planning to call a customer and suggest a new product can refer to this information to find out if that customer has had problems with any existing products. A service desk analyst who is working with a customer to resolve an incident can use this information to suggest that the customer upgrade to the next release of a product or note the benefits the customer might receive from training provided by the company.

External service desks do not always face the same budget and staffing constraints as do internal service desks. Some external service desks cover their own costs by either (1) charging for their services or (2) including the support costs with the cost of the product.

 The services an external service desk provides are typically determined by a warranty or legally binding contract. These contracts may be referred to as SLAs, but they contain legal conditions and ramifications that true SLAs do not.

However, other external service desks experience the same underinvestment and understaffing problems as internal service desks. This occurs because some companies place a higher priority on selling and shipping products than on supporting products they have sold. External service desks may also experience an excessive and perhaps underfunded workload when the engineering department, in response to an extremely competitive situation, distributes a product before it has been fully tested.

As with internal service desks, the resources available to an external service desk reflect the company's commitment to customer satisfaction and willingness to invest in the service desk. For example, some external service desks invest heavily in technologies that enable them to deliver exceptional services, such as highly sophisticated telephone systems and web-based systems. These companies may, however, become so highly automated that customers feel alienated and view the service desk as an impenetrable point of entry to the company. Other companies invest heavily in training their service desk analysts and providing opportunities for them to specialize and attain a high level of knowledge and experience. Companies that become too highly automated and do not invest in their staff fail to understand that the service desk is the "front door" into the company.

The best companies realize they must deliver high-quality products *and* superior customer support to retain today's savvy customers, who have high expectations. These companies value the service desk as a nucleus for customer service and as a primary means to capture and disseminate customer information. Also, they appreciate and reward people who understand the company's goals and actively contribute to them.

CASE STUDY: Service Industry Awards

HDI annually presents Team Excellence Awards to the internal and external teams that most enhance the image of the service desk profession by setting and achieving the highest standards of excellence in customer support. HDI also presents the HDI Analyst of the Year Award to the industry's best first-level support analysts. To learn more, go to www.thinkhdi.com/ membership *and click* Member Awards*. The Technology Services Industry Association (TSIA) presents an annual STAR Award to recognize technology companies that display exceptional leadership, innovation, and commitment in both service excellence and in developing and implementing best practices. To learn more, go to* www.tsia.com *and click* Awards & Certification*.*

Sizes of Service Desks

Whether internal, external, or blended, service desks range in size. Although it may seem logical for small companies to have small service desks and large companies to have large service desks, this is not always the case. The size of a service desk is determined by its mission and the scope of its responsibilities. For example, the more customers and products a service desk supports, the larger it tends to be in terms of staffing, budget, and so on. The number of additional activities the service desk performs, such as training, network and system administration, and so forth, also influences its size.

Small Service Desks

Small service desks have anywhere from one to 10 people on staff. Companies may have small service desks for a number of reasons. For example, the service desk may be new and just getting started; or it may be small if the company has limited its initial scope of responsibility to give it a chance to get off to a good start. Some service desks remain small simply because they do not receive a high volume of contacts, they support products that are fairly stable and easy to use, or customers have other ways to obtain support such as from a web site. Figure 2-5 illustrates a small service desk setting.

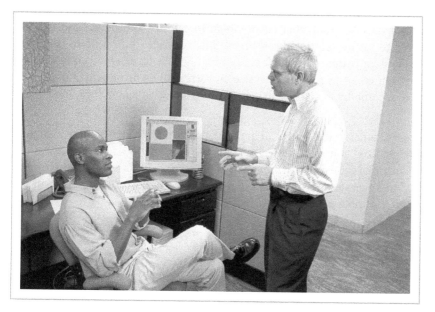

Figure 2-5 Small service desk setting
Comstock / Photos.com

Some companies have a single-person service desk, although most will grow to have more people in time, if only to provide backup for the primary analyst. Efficient and effective one-person service desks are rare. It takes a very organized, easygoing person to manage the stress that comes from being the only person available to handle contacts.

Some large companies prefer to have a number of small service desks rather than one large service desk. For example, a company might place a small service desk in each district office. Specialized departments, such as engineering or product testing, also might have separate service desks if they use highly specialized and sophisticated equipment.

Some smaller companies set up their service desks as a **one-stop shop**, which means that the service desk is fully responsible for resolving all incidents and service requests, even if the solution requires extensive research or even programming changes. They don't hand off incidents to other groups, such as development or engineering groups, as in the multi-level support model. Although this may sound like a good way to provide support, it works well only if customers have simple incidents or are willing to occasionally wait for a solution. This is because complex or high-priority incidents that require an immediate resolution can quickly consume the service desk's limited resources. As a result, customers with simpler incidents can end up waiting for service.

Small service desks can be world class, but they also face challenges. For example, small service desks tend to be people-dependent, which means that individual analysts specialize in a particular area, such as a customer community, vendor, product, or suite of products. As a result, the service desk can be severely affected when a key person leaves the company or is out because of illness or vacation. Small service desks may find it difficult to provide adequate training for their staff because every available person is needed to serve customers, and small service desks may not have the tools that enable them to capture knowledge and the information required to justify additional resources. Small service desks tend to be more informal, which is good for people who don't enjoy a highly structured environment or doing paperwork, but this can result in a highly reactive and stressful environment. All these challenges can be overcome by effectively using people, processes, technology, and information.

Working in small service desks can be gratifying to people who are highly motivated and capable of staying organized and managing stress. People working in small service desks can get to know their customers, tend to relate well to them, and fully understand their customers' needs. Small service desks usually offer people the opportunity to perform a diversity of tasks and assemble a broad base of skills.

 Medium service desks have between 10 and 25 people on staff and can take on the characteristics of both small and large service desks.

Large Service Desks

Large service desks vary in size, depending on whether they are internal or external. Internal service desks are considered large when they have more than 25 people on staff, whereas external service desks can have as many as several hundred people.

Large service desks evolved in several ways. Many grew from small service desks over the years as the company produced or took on support for more products. Some large service desks were consolidated from several smaller service desks, an initiative that many companies undertook in the 1980s to reduce redundant support efforts and maximize their return on investment in people, processes, technology, and information. A large service desk can also occur as a result of a corporate merger or acquisition. Figure 2-6 shows a large service desk setting.

Figure 2-6 Large service desk setting
Courtesy of CompuCom

It is common for large service desks to be subdivided into specialty teams. Specialty teams can be product oriented—one team supports a particular product or category of products—or customer oriented—that is, one team supports a particular segment of the customer community or a specific customer account.

The challenges that large service desks face are different than those for small service desks. For example, large service desks, particularly those that have evolved over time, may lack the discipline required for a large work force. They sometimes retain the informal ways of a smaller service desk far longer than they should. As a result, in such organizations, many people make independent decisions about how to handle incidents, which can cause inconsistent service. On the other hand, some large service desks are extremely performance oriented. For example, they place an excessive emphasis on efficiency (such as answering the phone quickly) and forsake effectiveness and quality. Either of these characteristics can lead to high stress levels that companies must work hard to manage.

Large service desks enable people to work in a team setting and usually offer many opportunities for training and advancement. People working in a large service desk can either choose to specialize in a particular product or customer set, or they can be a generalist and support a wide range of technologies and customers.

Working in a large service desk also exposes people to the many tools and best practices needed to run a successful service desk and satisfy its customers. Because achieving efficiencies through the use of technology and best practices is a priority in many IT organizations, this is invaluable experience for individuals interested in advancing their careers and pursuing IT management positions.

Service desk size is a critical issue for companies, because it determines how much they invest in the service desk, which, in turn, determines the quality of service the service desk can deliver. Another factor that influences service desk size is its structure.

Service Desk Structures

There are many ways of structuring service desks. Some companies have a single **centralized service desk** that supports all of the technologies used by its customers. Others have multiple **decentralized service desks** that support specific products or customer communities. More often, companies use a combination of centralized and decentralized service desk structures to meet the needs of their customers.

Centralized Service Desks

A centralized service desk provides customers with a single point of contact for support services. Customers appreciate this approach because they do not have to determine whom to call within the company. This approach can also be more efficient and cost effective for the company. For example, a centralized service desk exposes service desk analysts to a wider variety of contacts. This exposure typically leads to higher skill levels and a greater ability to resolve incidents. Centralizing and formalizing the processes and tools used by the service desk reduces the inefficiencies and costs that can occur with a decentralized approach. Having all incidents logged in a centralized manner also makes it possible to identify trends more quickly and easily so that proactive steps can be taken to prevent incidents and questions.

Service desks can be centralized in several ways. For example, some companies locate all of their service desk analysts in a single location. For larger organizations with high contact volumes, this single location may be a call or contact center. Other companies use technology to establish a virtual service desk. A **virtual service desk** gives the impression of a centralized service desk by using sophisticated telephone systems and the Internet. In reality, the service desk analysts may be located in any number of locations, including their homes.

 Chapter 5 explores the concept of a virtual service desk in greater detail.

Let's look at the centralized service desk approach in action. A common practice is for companies to have a centralized level one service desk and establish level two resources at remote offices. This practice uses the multi-level support model. Customers contact the level one service desk, which contacts the level two resources at the remote site *only* when the level one service desk cannot resolve an incident.

A challenge with this approach is that some customers at remote offices search out these on-site resources by going directly to level two staff or stopping the level two staff in the hall, rather than first calling the level one service desk. Customers often perceive that they are receiving a very high level of service when they can call or visit an on-site resource. In reality, customers who directly contact level two resources quickly become dissatisfied if these limited local resources are not available because they are already working on an incident, attending training, or taking vacation. Also, because on-site resources are constantly pulled in different directions, they may not log customer incidents, which might then be lost or forgotten.

Another downside of incidents not being logged is that their solutions typically are not logged either. As a result, the level one service desk and the on-site resources at all of the company's sites may solve the same incident multiple times because a solution identified at one site is not available to the others. A trend is to provide on-site analysts with smart mobile devices that can be used to capture information about customer incidents and service requests when they cannot readily access the company's incident management system.

A centralized service desk receives a wide diversity of calls on any given day. Because of this, effective tools and adequate training are key. Without them, analysts can find the centralized service desk a frustrating place to work. However, a clear management vision, an effective training program, and the need to continuously learn new skills make the centralized service desk an exciting and dynamic place to work.

Decentralized Service Desks

Some companies establish multiple decentralized service desks in an effort to provide a high level of service to customers with specific needs. When service desk services are decentralized, procedures or technology must direct customers to the appropriate service desk, based on their incidents or service requests. A decentralized service desk can provide fast resolutions for incidents because customers receive expert assistance immediately from someone familiar with their needs. However, if customers contact the wrong service desk for an incident or service request, resolution can take longer.

Service desks can be decentralized in several ways. Some companies establish local service desks at each of their corporate offices. A **local service desk** is located close to its customers. This approach provides customers with on-site assistance, but it can duplicate the same services from office to office. Other companies have specialized service desks that customers contact based on their needs. For example, users call one set of numbers for support with particular business applications, and customers experiencing network-related problems or problems using a mobile device call another set of numbers. Although the goal is to match customers with the service desk best able to assist them, customers can find it difficult to determine which service desk to call. Users accessing applications through a local area network (LAN) or from a mobile device, for instance, might call either the network service desk *or* the application service desk *or* the mobile service desk.

Some companies establish regional service desks to make their customers feel more comfortable. For example, global companies commonly establish one service desk in the Americas to support customers there and, possibly, customers in Canada, another in Europe to support customers there, and still another in Asia to support customers in the Pacific Rim. These companies have found that factors such as language, culture, legal issues, and time zone considerations warrant a decentralized approach. Some companies integrate these service desks using the virtual service desk concept discussed above to achieve an approach known as "follow the sun." A **follow the sun** service desk approach enables an organization to provide 24-hour coverage by scheduling regional service desks to work only during the usual business hours for their location.

Decentralized service desks face challenges in providing quality support and service. For example, they sometimes have difficulty justifying the resources that a centralized service desk can justify. As a result, resource limitations can cause the service desk to become overwhelmed. Another challenge that decentralized service desks must overcome is communicating to customers what they should do—what service desk they should contact—when incident symptoms are unclear. Also, they must define procedures for handling those times when the customer has contacted the "wrong" service desk. Without clearly defined procedures for handling these situations, customers may be referred continually from one part of the company to another without getting their questions answered. Ultimately, the customer will become dissatisfied.

INTERVIEW WITH...

Courtesy of MOUSE

CAROLE WACEY
EXECUTIVE DIRECTOR
MOUSE
NEW YORK, NEW YORK
WWW.MOUSE.ORG

MOUSE empowers underserved youth to learn, lead, and create with technology, preparing them with skills essential for their academic and career success.

The MOUSE Squad program trains students to become digital media and technology experts in their schools, improving the use of technology to enhance learning, while also building confidence and developing skills for 21st century innovation. MOUSE connects students around shared interests as a national network of youth technology leaders.

Founded in 1997, MOUSE programs are having a positive and lasting impact on over 4,000 students each year in 345 sites, including in New York, California, Illinois, and Texas. In partnership with Microsoft, the MOUSE Help Desk curriculum is accessible in more than 50 countries worldwide.

High school students across New York City can advance their MOUSE Squad experience by participating in MOUSE Corps, a youth-centered design and technology program in which students explore career pathways through professional mentors and internships and develop technology projects that address a social need.

Since 2000, more than 23,000 students have participated in MOUSE programs, providing valued technical support and leadership for more than 1.5 million students, teachers and administrators in their schools and communities.

Organization. MOUSE Squads are specialized teams of students who support and improve their school and after school learning communities and are a critical part of MOUSE's broader youth development programming. These youth-led level one technology help desks provide educators, administrators, and students with a trained support staff to troubleshoot and solve technical problems. On average, Squads provide their sites with more than 20 hours of level one technical support each week, equivalent to up to 1,000 hours throughout the school year. Each squad has an average of 10 students.

Developed using help desk industry best practices, the MOUSE Squad program includes operating processes and procedures, training for Squad Coordinators and student participants, and certification activities for students that provide hands-on, team-based ways to build work and technology skills. The program also includes a collaborative online workspace (web site) that includes a web-based CaseTracker tool for ticket tracking and tools for project communication. Cases may be submitted to individual Squads through the web site or documented and submitted by Technicians responding to help requests in person. Squads can use the web site to offer self-services such as answers to frequently asked technical questions and solutions to known issues. They can also use the site to collaborate with members of their team or with their peers at other schools to troubleshoot problems, brainstorm, and conduct demonstrations.

Courtesy of MOUSE

Each MOUSE Squad has a Squad Coordinator who has direct responsibility for his or her school's squad. The Coordinator also functions as a point person for communication between MOUSE's national network and the site. At the start of each school year, MOUSE orients prospective Coordinators through hands-on Information Sessions that help educators and administrators to reframe their ideas about effectively involving young people in the support and deployment of new technologies in the greater learning community. Squads in regional learning communities come together and engage in a series of hands-on workshops designed to get them started not only in the process of setting up technical help desks, but also in thinking about how to apply these new skills to their careers and lives beyond school.

In their schools, Squads establish a base of operations where students and Coordinators meet, store technical equipment, and carry out their roles and responsibilities. Each Squad conducts an inventory of their school's technology and ensures that the MOUSE Squad is aligned with the school's technology plan. Squads orient educators and administrators on using the ticket tracking system to report technology problems, design projects and activities to improve technology integration, and regularly report progress and promote their services to fellow students and school leaders.

Tasks. Students participating in the MOUSE Squad program can assume one or more of three roles: Technician, Team Leader, or Information Manager. All members of the Squad serve as Technicians, providing an average of at least five hours of weekly service on the help desk. Technicians respond to ticket requests to the best of their ability, complete scheduled maintenance projects, log ticket requests on a daily basis, and participate in weekly team meetings and required training sessions.

The Team Leader is the student manager of the MOUSE Squad Help Desk. In addition to his or her duties as a Technician, it is the Team Leader's responsibility to coordinate the weekly schedule to ensure maximum help desk coverage, oversee responses to ticket requests, ensure maintenance activities are being completed, ensure that help desk data is being properly logged, and facilitate communication among Squad members. The Team Leader also provides the Coordinator with periodic updates and oversees the help desk's base of operations.

The Information Manager (IM) manages data and information related to the help desk's activities, in addition to his or her duties as a Technician. In keeping with the program's commitment to work documentation and reporting, the IM catalogs completed ticket requests on his or her Squad's online CaseTracker and compiles regular reports for Squad members. The IM also organizes efforts to use help desk data to support and modify services and to identify the Squad's training needs.

MOUSE Squads handle basic activities such as fixing computers that are frozen and troubleshooting hardware failures; installing, upgrading, and configuring operating systems; configuring web browsers; loading and configuring software applications; and troubleshooting software problems. Most Squads also handle more advanced activities, such as working on high-level design and integration projects. MOUSE Squads develop work portfolios that include web site and multimedia production, open-source consulting for school labs, digital music production, and technology integration coaching. MOUSE also offers specialist certifications in Robotics and Serious Games.

In keeping with their commitment to provide polite, prompt, and skilled technical support, many Squads develop and hand out Customer Satisfaction Surveys once per semester that measure not only how quickly and how well squads handle requests, but also how well they serve their school community in general.

Philosophy. MOUSE maintains three specific goals for the successful implementation of MOUSE Squads in schools and community based sites:

- To broaden the learning and "life opportunities" of youth by providing authentic hands-on experiences that build skills and the motivation to succeed in school and life
- To support effective practices in learning with technology for educators and inspire innovation in the classroom
- To provide a student-centered solution to the technical support crisis facing public schools

This program is more than just establishing help desks in schools. More importantly, MOUSE Squad creates an opportunity for young people to serve as conduits between schools and communities and the increasingly ubiquitous world of information technologies. While learning technical, teamwork, problem solving, and other career readiness skills, MOUSE Squad members are given the chance to build knowledge, understand how technology impacts the world around them, and envision themselves applying their skills and passion to the contexts of work and life.

Centrally Decentralized Service Desks

Some companies, particularly large companies, take a "centrally decentralized" approach to delivering services. This approach combines a single, central service desk with multiple, specialized service desks. Customers contact the central service desk first. If it is unable to assist them, the central service desk uses common tools and processes to seamlessly transfer the customer to the appropriate specialized service desk within the company. This approach eliminates the need for customers to determine what service desk to call and yet enables the individual service desks to focus on their specific scope of responsibility. The process of determining a customer's need and routing the customer to the appropriate support group is known as **triage**. If it is determined that the customer has an immediate need, his or her incident may be escalated more quickly or given a higher priority.

Service Desks as Cost Centers or Profit Centers

Service desks can cost companies a considerable amount of money. Whether internal or external, small or large, centralized or decentralized, service desks need many resources—tangible and intangible—to run. Figure 2-7 shows some common service desk expenses. To pay for these expenses, service desks are run either as cost centers or as profit centers.

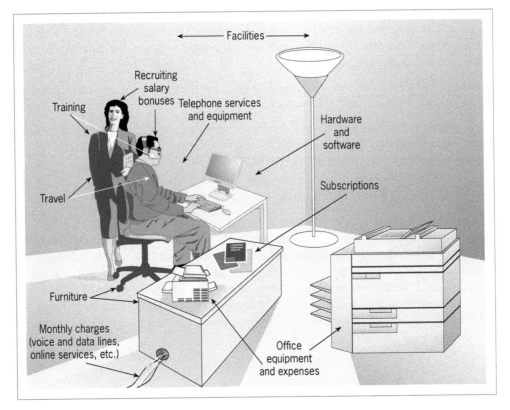

Figure 2-7 Service desk expenses
© Cengage Learning 2014

Service Desks as Cost Centers

Historically, service desks, particularly internal service desks, have been **cost centers**, in which the budget items required to run the service desk are considered a cost (or expense) to the company. When a service desk is run as a cost center, management's main objective is to minimize and eliminate expenses so that profits are as high as possible. In the past, some service desks tried to recover some of their expenses by charging customers for each contact. This approach was not always successful because customers were instructed by their managers, who also wanted to contain costs, not to contact the service desk. They would then waste precious time trying to resolve incidents themselves or with coworkers. Managers couldn't always see that this approach incurred "hidden" costs in the form of lost productivity and peer-to-peer support. The cost of peer-to-peer support often equals or even exceeds the cost of formal service desk support. For example, imagine the cost to a company if a lawyer or an engineer spends a portion of his or her day assisting coworkers with their technology-related questions and incidents. If managers understood these hidden costs, perhaps they would be more willing to pay "real" dollars to the service desk for support.

Running a service desk as a cost center can reduce the need to track expenses and effort in the detailed manner the service desk would have to if it were a profit center. Also, service desks run as cost centers can focus on existing customers because they do not have to market their services and generate new customers the way a profit center does. On the other hand, service desks run as a cost center may not be given the resources and management support they need, despite the fact that they often support millions of dollars' worth of technology investments and customer relationships.

To remedy this, many service desks define standards that limit service desk services in some way. For example, service desks may support only certain products or they may limit the hours that the service desk is open. By defining standard services, the service desk can ensure that it is staffed properly and has the resources it needs (such as hardware, software, training, and so on) to deliver high-quality support.

Service Desks as Profit Centers

Some service desks are run as **profit centers**, in which the service desk must cover its expenses and perhaps make a profit by charging a fee for support services. Rather than charge for each contact, as in the past, many service desks base the fee for their services on the company's actual cost to provide the services, plus a reasonable profit margin.

Some organizations, particularly internal service desks, establish the service desk as an overhead expense; each department in the company is assessed a fee based on how great its need is for service desk services. For example, a department might be assessed a fee based on the number of devices it has. This fee might cover standard service desk services during normal business hours. Departments can then opt to obtain premium services—such as after-hours support or holiday support—at an additional fee.

Other organizations, particularly external service desks, establish detailed pricing structures that allow customers to choose free services (such as web-based, self-help services), fee-based standard services, or premium services. In charging for service desk services, organizations recognize the increased cost of delivering nonstandard services.

Service desks run as profit centers can often justify expenses and acquire needed resources by demonstrating their benefit in the form of increased revenue. This is a positive benefit of profit centers because lack of resources, such as tools, training, and procedures, contributes to the stress and frustration of analysts. One drawback to the service desk as a profit center is that the staff must account for every activity they perform throughout the day.

Whether run as a cost center or profit center, service desks are under increasing pressure to analyze and control their costs, market the value of their services, and—without alienating customers—charge a premium for "customized" services. This approach requires that each and every person appreciate the fact that his or her actions contribute to the company's bottom line.

Service Desk Outsourcing

In the 1980s, organizations began to outsource their service desk services—that is, to have services provided by an outside supplier instead of providing them in-house. Outsourcing is a business sourcing strategy that can reduce costs, make more efficient use of resources, or enable existing resources to focus on the primary purpose (or core competency) of the business. Contracts are typically used to determine the services that a supplier will provide.

In the early days of this trend, managers thought outsourcing would be more cost effective. In many cases, however, this strategy didn't save the companies any money. The reason was that few companies understood what it cost to deliver services internally, so they could not make an accurate cost comparison. For example, companies whose internal staff were not logging all the contacts they were handling did not know their actual contact volume and were shocked when the supplier began billing them for a higher number of contacts than expected.

Some companies naively hired an outsourcer in the mistaken notion that they could wash their hands of service-related problems. They found, however, that outsourcing support did not make service-related problems go away. Instead, it added another layer of complexity to the situation. For example, the issue of who retains ownership of outstanding incidents and service requests when the supplier is unable to deliver a solution is a hotly debated topic when contracts are being negotiated. Companies "assume" the supplier will retain ownership, while suppliers try to make it clear that companies must be willing to pay for that service. When such a policy is unclear, it is often the customer who suffers, thus causing customer complaints and dissatisfaction to increase. As a result, many early outsourcing engagements failed, and companies reestablished their internal service desks.

Despite these early misconceptions and failings, service desk outsourcing continues to be a consideration, although the practice is declining. Of the organizations surveyed by HDI in their *2012 Support Center Practices and Salary Report*, 29 percent of organizations outsource some or all services, down from 46 percent in 2010. A 2011 survey conducted by Computer Economics, an IT industry research firm, presents a similar finding and shows how organization size influences the decision to outsource. Figure 2-8 illustrates that, according to the Computer Economics study, 14 percent of small and midsized organizations, and 32 percent of large organizations outsource at least part of their service desk activities.

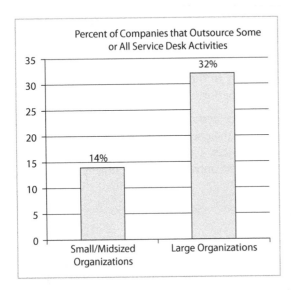

Figure 2-8   Percent of companies that outsource service desk activities
Source: *IT Help Desk Management Series,* Computer Economics, 2011

An important aspect of this statistic is that outsourcing is not an "all or nothing" business strategy, nor is it a permanent strategy. According to the 2011 Computer Economics survey, the small and midsized organizations that outsource service desk activities have less than one-third of their workload being handled by external suppliers, while large organizations outsource 71 percent of their work. Figure 2-9 illustrates the top five services being outsourced according to HDI.

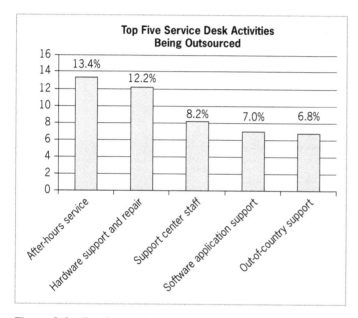

Figure 2-9 Top five services outsourced
Source: *2012 Support Center Practices and Salary Report*, HDI

The reasons companies outsource and the approaches they take are many. Some companies have internal service desks that support their employees and outsource support for their external customers, or vice versa. Some companies handle support internally during regular business hours and conditions but may outsource support after-hours or for peak call loads. Some companies outsource support for a legacy application they are preparing to retire to free their employees to learn a new technology. When the new technology is deployed, the company may terminate the relationship with its supplier and resume providing support internally.

Some companies—48 percent according to HDI—do not outsource services at all and have no plans to outsource (*2012 Support Center Practices and Salary Report*, HDI). Some companies believe that internal resources are better suited to understand and meet the needs of customers. These companies choose to maintain internal control over services in an effort to ensure service quality and customer acceptance. Some companies do not have a sufficiently high volume of services to warrant the cost of outsourcing. Some companies have such high security concerns that they are unwilling to give a third party access to their company's customer data and records. Figure 2-10 shows the most common reasons companies do not outsource more, according to HDI.

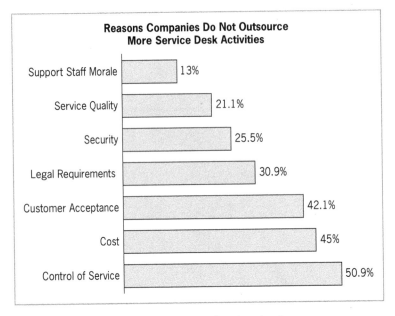

Reasons Companies Do Not Outsource More Service Desk Activities

- Support Staff Morale — 13%
- Service Quality — 21.1%
- Security — 25.5%
- Legal Requirements — 30.9%
- Customer Acceptance — 42.1%
- Cost — 45%
- Control of Service — 50.9%

Figure 2-10 Common reasons companies do not outsource
Source: *2012 Support Center Practices and Salary Report,* HDI

There are an equal number of reasons that companies do outsource some or all services. First, many companies realize that although the service desk is a critical service for their customers, they lack either the ability or the desire to build and manage this function internally. These companies may not consider the service desk their company's core competency and choose to hire a company that does. Second, some companies are unwilling to make the capital investments required to deliver competitive service desk services. Third, some companies want to deliver after-hours or multilingual services or accommodate peak volumes that arise as a result of seasonal or project-driven business fluctuations (such as a new release of software) without increasing staffing levels.

A better understanding of how to negotiate contracts and monitor those legally binding agreements has led to more successful outsourcing engagements. For example, many suppliers now monitor contact volumes and proactively notify companies if the contact volume is higher than usual or approaching a predefined threshold. Also, many suppliers are moving beyond traditional reactive service desk services and offering incident prevention services. For example, a supplier may produce and analyze trend reports and recommend ways the company can reduce or prevent certain types of incidents.

The Service Desk Supplier Role

Service desk suppliers offer a variety of technical support services. Outsourcers can act as an external service desk, such as when they provide support for original equipment manufacturers (OEMs); or they can act as an internal service desk, such as when they provide support for the employees of a company. As discussed above, a supplier can take over all or part of a company's support services.

Leading service desk suppliers include CompuCom Systems, Inc., Computer Sciences Corporation (CSC), Dell Inc., HCL Technologies Limited, Hewlett-Packard Company (HP), and International Business Machines Corporation (IBM).

Suppliers' charges to customers vary. For example, some suppliers pay their employees an hourly rate and then charge customers that rate plus a reasonable profit. Some suppliers charge customers a fee for each call; this fee may increase during certain times, such as after-hours or on weekends. Still other suppliers offer a "menu" of standard and optional services, such as the one shown in Table 2-1, that enable customers to determine the level of service they want. Frequently, suppliers are paid for performance, based on measurable indicators spelled out in their service contracts. Measurable indicators include how quickly suppliers respond to customers, the percentage of incidents they resolve, how well they keep customers informed, and overall customer satisfaction.

Supplier employees must keep careful records of their time and effort. The suppliers use these records to create customer invoices and to measure employee performance. Because the success and profitability of the supplier is based on the quality of the services their staff delivers, many suppliers carefully screen applicants, offer extensive training for new hires, and provide ongoing training. These companies expect to see a return on their training investment in the form of satisfied customers.

Companies now realize that when they outsource, they are establishing a complex partnership in an effort to focus on their mission, expand their services, or contain costs. These companies recognize that when they outsource certain services, they do not outsource their customers. Therefore, companies that outsource services must show that they remain deeply committed to their customers' satisfaction by rigorously measuring and managing their supplier's performance.

Fee	Service	Cost per Call
Standard	Standard support hours (HH:MM – HH:MM, x days per week)	$
Optional	Extended support hours (24 hours per day, 7 days per week)	$
Optional	Holiday support (standard support hours)	$
Optional	Holiday support (extended support hours)	$
Standard	Toll-free service	$
Standard	Web-based service	$
Optional	Email service	$
Optional	Customized interfaces (for example, to a customer's incident management system)	$
Standard	Entitlement verification • To service desk services • To level two/level three services (such as on-site support)	$
Optional	Incident ownership	$
Standard	Incident logging and tracking	$
Standard	Incident diagnosis	$
Optional	Remote diagnosis (using remote control software)	$
Standard	Incident resolution	$
Standard	Dispatching or escalating to level two or level three support	$
Optional	Multivendor management	$
Optional	Weekly performance reporting	$
Standard	Monthly performance reporting	$
Optional	Customized reports	$
Optional	Trend and root cause analysis	$
Standard	Customer satisfaction verification and follow-up prior to incident closure	$
Optional	Independent survey services (such as to measure customer satisfaction)	$
Total Cost per Contact		$

Table 2-1   Sample pricing "menu" for service desk services

© Cengage Learning 2014

The Service Desk Model

As the support industry has evolved, there has been an important shift toward consolidating support services. First, many companies consolidated multiple decentralized help desks into fewer help desks or a single, centralized help desk. Now, companies are further consolidating their support services and evolving their help desks into service desks. In 2011, the term "service desk" topped the term "help desk" as the name that respondents use for their support organizations for the first time in the history of HDI's *Support Center Practices and Salary Report*.

The number of companies adopting ITIL worldwide is fueling adoption of the service desk model. ITIL views the service desk as a vitally important part of an IT organization and provides guidance on how to ensure that the service desk delivers value to both its customers and IT. ITIL also describes how to make the service desk an attractive place to work in an effort to attract and retain people with the needed experience and skills.

The needed experience and skills are changing because the service desk model challenges managers throughout the organization to move customer-related transactions into the service desk. This approach provides customers a single point of contact for services and also enables the service desk to deliver a broader set of services directly to customers.

Companies adopt the service desk model because of customer demand for faster service, the desire to streamline processes by reducing handoffs, and a need to reduce costs. By expanding their services beyond those traditionally offered by the help desk, the service desk can avoid engaging groups unnecessarily, thus delivering services more efficiently and cost-effectively to customers. Figure 2-11 shows the expanded services offered by service desks.

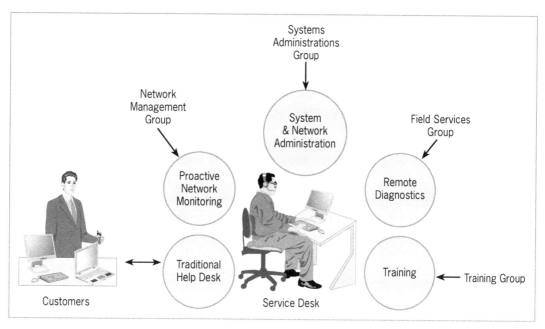

Figure 2-11 Expanded services offered by service desks
© Cengage Learning 2014

Technology is enabling this further consolidation of support services. For example, monitoring tools make it possible for the service desk to perform proactive monitoring of the network and applications rather than waiting to hear about an incident from the network management or application management groups. Because the service desk now can do proactive monitoring, it can detect incidents more quickly, contact the appropriate group, and then inform customers that the company is aware of a network- or application-related incident and that it is being resolved.

Another area in which technology is consolidating support services is remote support. In the past, the help desk or service desk dispatched a field service technician to investigate incidents it could not properly diagnose, or it required customers to ship their equipment to the service desk. Both resulted in a delay of hours or even days. With remote support technologies, the service desk can take control of networked devices to resolve incidents, distribute software, and deliver informal training on the spot. This leaves field service technicians free to work on complex incidents, determine the cause of incidents, or make progress on projects such as installing new systems.

A third example of consolidation is in the area of system administration. Rather than hand off a service request to the system administration group, many service desks set up and maintain user accounts and perform some security-related activities, such as granting access to services. Taking over these activities has reduced the time required to satisfy these requests.

Chapter 5 explores the technologies used by service desks.

Under the service desk model, companies can deliver services more efficiently and effectively, increasing customer satisfaction. Some organizations further enhance this model by rotating subject matter experts (such as application developers and customer representatives) through the service desk so they can share their knowledge with the permanent staff and enhance communications between coworkers. Many companies that have adopted the service desk model see an increase in employee satisfaction because service desk analysts have expanded responsibilities and are given the tools and skills needed to resolve incidents quickly and correctly.

The service desk industry is growing and changing, and clearly, one size does *not* fit all. Because there are so many different types and sizes of service desks, people who want to enter the service desk industry can choose from a range of opportunities. The dramatic rise in the number of service desk classes in colleges and technical schools is evidence that the service desk industry is becoming increasingly important and that the available opportunities are growing. Companies are actively recruiting candidates for the thousands of new service desk positions opening up around the world.

Chapter Summary

- Although the underlying purpose of the service desk is the same from one organization to the next, the services it offers and its operating characteristics such as type, size, and structure vary, depending on the needs of the company and its customers. A company's commitment to satisfying its customers determines its service desk's mission as well as its investment in the service desk.

- Call centers, contact centers, help desks, and service desks are all examples of customer service and support organizations. Call centers make or receive telephone calls in high volume and handle a wide range of transactions. Contact centers are call centers that use technologies such as email and the web in addition to the telephone. Help desks and service desks tend to handle technology-oriented questions and incidents. Service desks have a broader scope of responsibility and also handle service requests and communications with customers. Customers contact service desks using a variety of channels, including the telephone, email, and the web.

- The two principal service desk types are internal service desks and external service desks. An internal service desk supports the employees of its company, whereas an external service desk supports the people who buy its company's products or services. Within these two categories, some organizations are small and others are large, some are centralized and others are decentralized, and some are run as cost centers and others as profit centers. All have strengths and all have challenges.

- The skills required to work in these different organizations vary. People who consider the strengths and challenges of the different service desk types can determine the type of service desk opportunities that support their career goals and that will enable them to broaden their resume.

- Service desk outsourcing is a common practice for a number of reasons. The relationship between a company and a supplier is a complex partnership aimed at enabling the company to focus on its mission, expand its services, and contain costs. The success and profitability of a supplier is based on the quality of the services the service desk delivers to its customers, so suppliers carefully screen applicants and provide extensive training.

- Companies worldwide are consolidating support services and evolving their help desks into service desks. The number of companies adopting ITIL is fueling this trend. The service desk model challenges managers throughout the company to move transactions that directly involve customers into the service desk. Technology is enabling a further consolidation of support services. The end result is that companies are able to deliver services more efficiently and effectively and increase customer satisfaction.

Key Terms

blended call center—A call center that receives incoming calls and makes outgoing calls.

blog—A journal kept on the Internet; short for web log.

centralized service desk—A single service desk that supports all of the technologies used by its customers.

computer-based training (CBT)—Computer software packages used to train and test people on a wide range of subjects.

contact center—A call center that uses technologies such as email and the web in addition to the telephone.

cost center—A service desk in which the budget items required to run the service desk are considered a cost (expense) to the company.

customer relationship management (CRM)—A program that involves using customer contact and relationship information to generate additional sales and to increase levels of customer service and retention.

decentralized service desks—Multiple service desks, each of which supports specific products or customer communities.

electronic learning (eLearning)—Technology-supported learning and teaching.

escalation (or **escalate**)—To raise an incident from one level to another, such as from level one to level two, to dedicate new or additional resources to the incident.

external service desk—A service desk that supports customers who buy its company's products and services.

follow the sun—A service desk approach that enables an organization to provide 24-hour coverage by scheduling regional service desks to work only during the usual business hours for their location.

inbound call center—A call center that receives telephone calls from customers and may answer questions, take orders, respond to billing inquiries, and provide customer support.

installations, moves, adds, and changes (IMACs)—Activities that include moving equipment, installing and configuring new systems, and upgrading existing systems; also known as *moves, adds, and changes (MACs)*.

internal service desk—A service desk that responds to questions, distributes information, and handles incidents and service requests for its company's employees.

internal service provider—A department or a person within a company that supplies information, products, or services to another department or person within the same company.

Internet-based training (IBT)—A training system that people can access from any device that has an Internet connection and a browser.

large service desk—An internal service desk that has more than 25 people on staff or an external service desk that has as many as several hundred people on staff.

level one—The first point of contact for customers.

level three—The person or group that resolves complex incidents that are beyond the scope of level two.

level two—The person or group that resolves incidents that are beyond the scope or authority (such as system access rights or permissions) of level one.

level zero—Customers solving incidents on their own; see also *self-help*.

local service desk—A service desk that is located close to its customers.

medium service desk—A service desk that has between 10 and 25 people on staff; can take on the characteristics of both small and large service desks.

mission—A description of the customers the service desk serves, the types of services the service desk provides, and how the service desk delivers those services.

moves, adds, and changes (MACs)—Service desk activities that include moving equipment, installing and configuring new systems, and upgrading existing systems; also known as *installations, moves, adds, and changes (IMACs)*.

multi-level support model—A common structure of service desks, where the service desk refers incidents it cannot resolve to the appropriate internal group, external vendor, or subject matter expert.

one-stop shop—A service desk that is fully responsible for resolving all incidents and service requests, even if the solution requires extensive research or even programming changes.

outbound call center—A call center that makes telephone calls to customers, primarily for telemarketing.

out-of-scope service request—A request that is beyond the capabilities of the service desk.

ownership—Tracking an incident to ensure that the customer is kept informed about the status of the incident, that the incident is resolved within the expected time frame, and that the customer is satisfied with the final resolution.

podcast—A method of distributing digital media files over the Internet to personal computers and portable media players.

post-sales support—Helping people who have purchased a company's product or service.

pre-sales support—Answering questions for people who have not yet purchased a company's products or services.

profit center—A service desk that must cover its expenses and perhaps make a profit by charging a fee for support services.

self-help—Customers solving incidents on their own. See also *level zero*.

Service Level Agreement (SLA)—A written document that spells out the services the service desk will provide to the customer, the customer's responsibilities, and how service performance is measured.

social learning—Learning by interacting with other people.

small service desk—A service desk that has one to 10 people on staff.

standard change—A preapproved change that is low risk and follows a procedure.

subject matter expert (SME)—A person who has a high level of experience or knowledge about a particular subject.

telemarketing—The selling of products and services over the telephone.

triage—The process of determining a customer's need and routing him or her to the appropriate support group.

virtual service desk—A service desk that gives the impression of a centralized service desk by using sophisticated telephone systems and the Internet. In reality, the service desk analysts may be located in any number of locations, including their homes.

webinar—A method used to deliver presentations, lectures, workshops or seminars over the web; short for web-based seminar.

wiki—A web site whose users add, modify, or delete its content using a web browser.

Review Questions

1. List and briefly describe the four types of customer service and support organizations described in this chapter.

2. Briefly describe the difference between a help desk and a service desk.

3. Incidents that cannot be resolved at the service desk are referred to the next _____ of support.

4. List the three components of a service desk mission.

5. Why do companies experience higher customer and employee satisfaction when employees understand the company's mission and their department's mission?

6. A service desk that supports a company's employees is a(n) _____ service desk.

7. How can an internal service provider help its company's employees?

8. Define the concept of incident ownership in a service desk setting.

9. List and briefly describe three activities an internal service desk may perform in addition to assisting customers with incidents.

10. Provide at least three examples of service requests.

11. What is an SLA, and how is it different than a contract?

12. Describe two ways that an efficient, effective internal service desk can help reduce costs.

13. Why are internal support organizations more willing to devote funds to technology investments than in the past?

14. A service desk that supports the customers who buy its company's products and services is a(n) _____ service desk.

15. Describe two ways an external service desk helps its company sell and support products and services.

16. What does customer relationship management (CRM) involve, and what are its goals?

17. What two things must companies do to retain today's savvy customers?

18. What three things determine the size of a service desk?

19. What are three reasons some service desks remain small?

20. What challenges are faced by service desks that are people dependent?

21. List at least three benefits of working in a small service desk.

22. What are two ways specialty teams in a large service desk can be oriented?

23. List four benefits of working in a large service desk.

24. What are three benefits of a centralized service desk?

25. How does a virtual service desk give customers the impression of a centralized service desk?

26. Why do some companies establish multiple decentralized service desks?

27. List four factors that may prompt global companies to establish multiple service desks.

28. Describe the service desk approach known as "follow the sun."

29. What are the benefits of combining a single centralized service desk with multiple decentralized service desks?

30. Describe the triage process.

31. What does it mean when a service desk is run as a cost center?

32. Describe how internal and external service desks that run as profit centers determine their service fees.

33. List three reasons why a company might choose not to adopt outsourcing as a business sourcing strategy.

34. List three reasons why a company might adopt outsourcing as a business sourcing strategy.

35. Why must people who work for suppliers keep careful records?

36. How do companies that have outsourced their support services ensure their customers' satisfaction?

37. List three reasons companies adopt the service desk model.

38. List three ways that new technologies enable the service desk to deliver services more efficiently and effectively than in the past.

Hands-On Projects

1. **Consider your options (Part 1).** Think about the two primary service desk types discussed in this chapter: internal service desks and external service desks. At what type of service desk would you like to work? Why? Explain the reasons for your choice.

2. **Consider your options (Part 2).** Think about the two primary service desk sizes discussed in this chapter: small service desks and large service desks. At what size of service desk would you like to work? Why? Explain the reasons for your choice.

3. **Discuss service desk types.** Assemble a team of at least three of your classmates or use your school's online message or discussion board. Discuss the following types of service desk operations:

   - Centralized versus decentralized

   - Cost center versus profit center

   Prepare a list of the advantages and disadvantages that people may experience working at these different types of service desks.

4. **Determine a company's mission.** Visit the web site for a hardware or software company you do business with or are considering doing business with in the future. For example, you could contact the company that manufactured your computer or that published a frequently used software package. From the web site, determine the following:

   - Does the company have a service desk mission statement? If so, what is its mission?

   - Describe the support services offered:

     o For free

     o For a standard fee

     o At an optional (premium) rate

   - Does the service desk provide pre-sales support as well as post-sales support?

   - How does the service desk say it delivers services (for example, professionally, courteously)?

   - Given what you have learned about external service desks in this chapter, what else can you learn about this company's service desk from its web site?

   Critique the company's mission based on the information you found. Write a report that summarizes your findings.

5. **Learn about service desk industry awards.** Visit the web site of either the HDI (*www.thinkhdi.com*, click Membership, and then click Member Awards) or the Technology Services Industry Association (*www.tsia.com*, click Awards & Certification). Review the awards that the organization presents. Prepare a brief paper that answers the following questions:

   - What criteria do these organizations use to select recipients of their "team" excellence awards?

   - What criteria do these organizations use to select recipients of their "individual" excellence awards?

Briefly describe the benefits you believe that companies and individuals derive from being award winners.

6. **Explore how to avoid burnout.** A single-person service desk is a challenging place to work, and its inherent stresses can lead to burnout. Collaborate with at least three of your classmates. Discuss and list the factors that most likely contribute to burnout in this situation. For each factor you identify, explore and describe ways that the burnout can be avoided.

7. **Analyze your school service desk.** Identify all the ways that service desk services are delivered at your school, perhaps by visiting the service desk's web site. If your school doesn't have a service desk, use the service desk at the school or company of one of your friends or family members.

- Are the services centralized?

- Are there multiple decentralized service desks?

- If there are multiple service desks, how do customers determine which one to contact?

- Does the school allow students, faculty members, or administrators to use personal devices to access school systems? If yes:

  o What are the associated policies?

  o What are the customers' responsibilities?

- Do the school service desk(s) provide support when students, faculty, or administrators use personal devices? If yes:

  o What are the associated terms and conditions (for example, best effort, time-specified support)?

- What types of self-help tools does the school service desk(s) provide?

Having discovered how services are delivered, discuss ways the services could be refined to make it easier for customers to obtain support. If you feel the services are being delivered well as they are, explain why. Prepare and present a brief report.

8. **Learn about service desk outsourcing.** Visit the web sites of three of the service desk outsourcing companies mentioned in this chapter. For each company, write a paragraph that describes the following:

- What services do they deliver?

- What do they consider standard services, and what do they offer as optional services?

- How do they distinguish themselves from their competition?

- What do they say about their staff?

- What do they say about their hiring practices?

- What do they say about satisfying their customers?

Case Projects

1. **School Service Desk.** You've been assigned the task of preparing a first draft of a mission for the new virtual service desk to be set up at your school. In addition to supporting students attending classes on campus, this service desk must also accommodate distance learners (students who are taking correspondence courses or web-based classes). Based on your knowledge of your school (review its web site if you need additional information) and your own need for support as a student, draft a mission for the new service desk. Document your answers to the following questions:

   - Who needs support?

   - What kind of support do they need?

   - How should the support be delivered?

   To view the web sites of other colleges and universities, search the web for topics such as "academic computing," "university service desk," and "virtual university service desk."

2. **SmartBusiness.** You've been hired as a consultant by SmartBusiness to help it turn its external service desk into a profit center. SmartBusiness sells a software package that small businesses can use in support of their CRM initiatives. SmartBusiness customers call a toll-free number when they have questions or problems; they have never been charged a fee. The CIO needs to cover the company's costs for delivering service desk services and would like to make a reasonable profit if possible. He asks you to prepare a brief report that outlines what he needs to consider in turning the service desk into a profit center without alienating customers. He also wants you to recommend two ways to expand the service desk services.

CHAPTER 3

The People Component: Service Desk Roles and Responsibilities

In this chapter you will learn:

◎ The principal service desk job categories

◎ The skills required to be a successful front-line service provider

◎ The management opportunities within the service desk

◎ The supporting roles within the service desk

◎ The characteristics of a successful team

The people who work in a service desk play a variety of roles. The principal roles include the front-line service providers and the service desk management personnel who directly support customers and ensure their satisfaction. Additional roles support the front-line staff and provide less direct customer support. Each of these roles is important, and each requires a specific set of skills. People in both these primary and supporting roles must work together as a team to provide quality customer service.

The roles and responsibilities of service desk staff and the advancement opportunities within and beyond the service desk are typically a reflection of the service desk's size and structure. A company's commitment to customer satisfaction and its willingness to invest in the service desk further influence the roles and opportunities that exist. This diversity makes the service desk a rewarding and exciting place for people who want to pursue a career in customer service and support.

To have a successful career in the service desk, you must continuously assess your current skills and develop new ones. Also, it is important that you contribute to the service desk team and that you value other team members' contributions. A sincere desire to satisfy customers and contribute to the service desk's goals will bring you success and enable you to create and pursue a wealth of opportunities.

Principal Job Categories

Two principal job categories are common throughout the support industry. These principal categories, or roles, are the front-line service providers and the management personnel who work in the service desk. Figure 3-1 shows a sample service desk organization chart that reflects these roles.

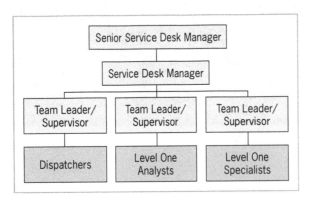

Figure 3-1 Sample service desk organization chart
© Cengage Learning 2014

Front-line service providers and service desk management perform specific roles in the service desk. Each has certain responsibilities and required skills.

Front-Line Service Providers

Front-line service providers are the service desk staff who interact directly with customers. In other words, they serve on the front line between a company or department and its customers. This role is crucial to the success of the service desk. Customers form opinions of the entire company or department based on their interactions with front-line service providers. Figure 3-2 lists the various types of front-line service providers you may find in a service desk.

- Dispatcher
- Level one analyst
- Level one specialist

Figure 3-2   Types of front-line service providers
© Cengage Learning 2014

Dispatcher

Some service desks rely on dispatchers as the first point of contact with customers. A **dispatcher** is the person who initially handles customer contacts, such as questions, incidents, and service requests. The dispatcher logs customer contacts and then routes them to the appropriate level one analyst, specialist, or level two group. Although dispatchers may answer routine questions, they typically resolve a low percentage of the contacts they handle. Their primary job is to log the contact accurately, ensure the customer that the incident or service request will be handled in a timely fashion, and then dispatch it to the correct group. Dispatchers may or may not retain ownership of incidents or service requests they have dispatched. In some organizations, dispatchers route incidents and service requests to a level one analyst who then assumes ownership. In other companies, dispatchers retain ownership of escalated incidents and service requests, in keeping with the service desk's role as customer advocate.

 The dispatcher role may also be called service desk agent, customer care agent, customer service representative, or call screener.

Dispatchers are common in companies such as equipment manufacturers or resellers that provide primarily hardware support. Customers who experience hardware incidents contact the service desk. The dispatcher logs the contact, diagnoses the incident, and, if he or she determines that a hardware failure has occurred, dispatches a field service representative to the customer site. If the dispatcher thinks some other type of incident exists, such as a software incident, he or she may route the incident to a level one analyst or specialist.

When hiring dispatchers, employers look for people with excellent interpersonal skills and an exceptional customer service orientation. On the job, dispatchers are typically measured by their ability to efficiently follow clearly defined procedures and ensure customer satisfaction. People who enjoy helping other people find this role very rewarding. This role can also serve as an excellent training ground for a level one analyst position.

Level One Analyst

Because today's demanding customer is less willing to wait for a solution, and because some service disruptions cause real bottom-line impact, most service desks strive to resolve as many incidents and service requests as possible at the first point of customer contact. Instead of dispatchers, these service desks rely on level one analysts to initially handle customer contacts. These **level one analysts** receive and log contacts, answer questions, and resolve incidents and service requests when possible. When a resolution is not possible, level one analysts provide a workaround where possible, and then escalate the incident or service request to the appropriate level two group along with all available information. To ensure customer satisfaction, the service desk retains ownership of escalated incidents and service requests.

Level one analysts often have titles such as service desk analyst, lead service desk analyst, customer support analyst, or service desk technician.

When hiring level one analysts, employers look for good technical and analytical skills as well as excellent customer service skills. The required technical skills vary, based on customer needs. For example, service desks that support off-the-shelf software usually hire analysts who have experience running and supporting the software packages used by the company. Service desks that support home-grown systems may focus more on a candidate's customer service skills, knowing they will have to train the person on their unique systems. In most cases, the ideal candidate for a level one analyst position has a broad base of technical knowledge, as opposed to extensive knowledge in a single subject area. An ability and willingness to quickly learn new skills is also key. People who enjoy problem solving and helping others solve problems find the level one analyst role rewarding and challenging.

Level one analyst salaries vary based on factors such as quality of work, customer service skills, job responsibilities, industry, geographic region, company size, an individual's education, experience, ability, and so on. According to HDI's *2012 Support Center Practices and Salaries Report*, salaries have risen slightly since 2011 and the average salary for a service desk analyst is between $35,132 and $48,815 per year.

The level one analyst role serves as a great training ground for a level one specialist position or a service desk management position.

Economic conditions prompted some hiring and salary freezes in this industry in 2009, but current conditions are more optimistic. By 2012, 70 percent of companies anticipate expanding their service desks or filling previous frozen roles according to HDI's *2012 Support Center Practices and Salaries Report.*

Level One Specialist

In some organizations, level one analysts refer incidents and service requests they cannot resolve within a predefined period of time to level one specialists. A **level one specialist** researches and resolves complex incidents and handles service requests that require more skill or authority—or, in some cases, more time—than a level one analyst can devote to a single contact. The use of both level one analysts and level one specialists enables an organization to strike the right balance between the need to respond quickly to customer contacts and the need to resolve incidents correctly and permanently.

In organizations that do not have a level one specialist position, level one analysts hand off incidents and service requests they cannot resolve to the appropriate level two person or group. In other organizations, the level one specialists are viewed as level two. In these companies, the various application and technical management support teams are viewed as level three.

Level one specialists often have titles such as service desk specialist, technical support specialist, or customer support specialist.

Level one specialists may be organized into teams that support specific products or services. Some organizations route select customers directly to these specialist teams via telephone options or a web form. For example, customers with a premium service contract, designated customer liaisons, or "super users" may be entitled to bypass the dispatcher or level one analyst roles and interact directly with level one specialists.

In some organizations, level one specialists own all escalated incidents and service requests. This enables level one analysts to focus on handling new contacts. Level one specialists may also represent the service desk on process improvement or project teams. For example, if a new technology is being released, a level one specialist may serve as the service desk liaison to the project team handling the release. This ensures the service desk is involved in planning, testing, and pilot activities and that the service desk is prepared to support the new technology when it is introduced. Level one specialists may also be involved in problem management activities, such as trend and root cause analysis.

When hiring level one specialists, employers value expertise in a specific subject matter, excellent analytical skills, and an exceptional customer service orientation. The required technical skills are based on the customers' needs. The ideal candidate for a level one specialist position is able and willing to continuously learn new skills and share his or her knowledge and experience with other members of the service desk team. This role can serve as an excellent training ground for a service desk management position, a supporting role, or a technical role in another part of the company.

Level one specialist salaries vary based on factors such as quality of work, customer service skills, job responsibilities, industry, geographic region, company size, an individual's education, experience, ability, and so on. According to HDI's *2012 Support Center Practices and Salaries Report*, the average salary for a level one specialist (level two analyst) is between $42,275 and $58,735 per year.

Front-Line Service Provider Responsibilities

Although titles vary from one service desk to the next, level one analysts and specialists often have similar job and professional responsibilities.

Job Responsibilities

The job responsibilities of service desk staff correspond to the responsibilities of the service desk, which are to provide a single point of contact for all support services, deliver value to customers, and capture and distribute information. The responsibilities also correspond to the processes performed by the service desk, such as incident management and request fulfillment. Typically, a front-line service provider:

- Receives customer contacts by telephone, email, the web, and so on.

- Logs each contact by gathering pertinent information about the customer and a description of the incident or service request. This electronic ticket or record typically includes a type or category code and a priority code, and it is updated continuously until that incident or service request is resolved.

- Performs an initial diagnosis of the incident or service request.

- Delivers a solution, when possible, using available tools (such as remote control systems) and procedures (such as troubleshooting procedures).

- Documents the solution thoroughly so that the service desk can reuse it.

- If unable to deliver a solution, determines how quickly the customer needs the incident or service request resolved.

- Communicates to the customer how often he or she will receive status updates or how he or she can obtain status updates, such as by going to the service desk's web site and retrieving the ticket.

- Records all steps taken by both the service desk and the customer to try to resolve the incident or service request and records any additional information the customer provides (such as a shipping address that can be used to send replacement equipment or parts).

- Escalates the incident or service request to the correct level one specialist, level two group, external vendor, or subject matter expert.

- Retains ownership of incidents and service requests that have been escalated to a level two person or group.

- Periodically reports the status of the incident or service request to the customer (such as when the customer can expect a field service engineer to arrive or when ordered equipment or parts should arrive).

- Reviews the resolution to learn how an escalated incident or service request was solved in the event a similar incident or service request is received in the future.

- Follows up with the customer to ensure that he or she is satisfied with the resolution.

- Closes the ticket.

Job descriptions outline the specific responsibilities and tasks assigned to a person. They provide both managers and their employees a clear understanding of the work to be done. The amount of detail companies include in job descriptions ranges from highly specific to quite generic. Some companies even work without job descriptions, but this risky practice often results in employees performing unnecessary work or failing to do necessary work. Also, the lack of a job description may cause an employee and a manager to have mismatched expectations about the service desk job. A well-defined job description provides employees with a clear understanding of work expectations and spells out the employees' professional responsibilities.

Sample job descriptions for the primary service desk roles are provided in Appendix A.

Professional Responsibilities

Professional responsibilities reflect how members of the service desk team are expected to conduct their job responsibilities. Because the service desk is a focal point for their company or department, members of the service desk team must conduct themselves at all times in a professional and ethical manner by:

- Complying with service desk policies and projecting at all times a positive image of themselves, the service desk, and the service desk team.

- Giving customers an honest and accurate estimate of the time it will take to resolve their incident or service request.

- Building confidence and goodwill with customers by keeping commitments and promptly advising customers when commitments cannot be met.

- Communicating in the language of the customer by avoiding confusing terminology and technical jargon.

- Avoiding and discouraging the use of unfriendly language or tone of voice and profanity.

- Encouraging good security practices, such as changing passwords frequently, choosing unique passwords, and not sharing user IDs and passwords.

- Discouraging unethical, illegal, and potentially disruptive computing practices (such as those illustrated by the next three responsibilities) by following security procedures and reporting violations to management.

- Preventing unauthorized access to proprietary and sensitive company data by following procedures and requiring proper authorization prior to granting access.

- Discouraging and reporting **software piracy**, which is the unauthorized use or reproduction of copyrighted or patented software.

- Discouraging and reporting inappropriate and wasteful use of computing resources, such as sending objectionable or harassing emails, printing large unnecessary reports, downloading and playing computer games, and browsing the web unnecessarily.

- Communicating ways to detect, prevent, and eliminate **malicious software (malware)**, which consists of harmful software such as viruses, worms, Trojan horses, spyware, and adware that is designed to damage or disrupt a computer, computer system, or computer network.

- Maintaining current technical skills and using all available knowledge resources, thus avoiding unnecessary escalations to other technical staff.

Trust is an integral part of the service desk's relationships with customers, management, and coworkers. Trust is earned when members of the service desk team consistently behave in an honest and ethical manner. There may be times when service desk analysts are tempted to violate the law or company policies. Consider, for example, a service desk employee who is aware that a customer is using an unauthorized, unlicensed software package. Or, consider a customer who is late in completing an assignment and asks a service desk analyst to reset his or her password without proper authorization. In these and all instances of illegal and unethical behavior, it is the service desk analyst's duty to strictly follow and enforce both the law and the company's policies.

CASE STUDY: Preventing Computer Viruses

Widespread use of email and the Internet has led to a dramatic increase in the number of computer viruses affecting home and business computer users. Although some viruses won't harm an infected system, others are destructive and can damage or destroy data. Some viruses that are attached to files will execute, or run, when the infected file is opened or modified. Other viruses sit in a computer's memory and infect files as the computer opens, modifies, or creates them. One of the best ways to prevent viruses is to use antivirus software that can be purchased from vendors such as McAfee Security (www.mcafee.com) *and Symantec* (www.symantec.com). *For additional virus detection and prevention tips, go to* www.mcafee.com/anti-virus/virus_tips.asp.

Skills Required on the Front Line

Finding people for front-line positions who have the right mix of skills is one of the most difficult challenges facing service desk managers. Strong technicians may lack the empathy skills or the patience required for the service industry, while people-oriented individuals may lack the technical skills required to work in a complex computing environment. Some people prefer a hands-on approach to technical support and become dissatisfied when their position requires them to spend a lot of time on the telephone. The employee and the company benefit when the right skills are matched with the right position.

When hiring people for front-line positions, companies tend to look for people who genuinely enjoy helping other people and who work well with others. Many companies believe that technical skills can be developed more easily than interpersonal skills, so they are willing to hire people with good interpersonal skills and a customer service orientation, knowing they'll need to provide the necessary technical training. This is not to say that technical skills are unimportant. Some companies—particularly those that support highly sophisticated technology—at times hire people with strong technical skills and provide extensive customer service training. The bottom line is that in the current, highly competitive marketplace, both technical and customer service skills are required.

The specific skills a company requires are determined by the company's job description. These skills typically fall into four main categories: business skills, technical skills, soft skills, and self-management skills.

Business Skills

Business skills, such as the ability to understand and speak the language of business and the ability to analyze and solve business problems, are the skills people need to be successful in the business world. When working in a service desk, business skills include the skills that are unique to the industry or profession the service desk supports, such as accounting skills or banking skills. These skills are called *industry knowledge*. Business skills also include skills that are specific to the customer service and support industry, such as understanding the importance of meeting customers' needs and knowing how to manage their expectations. These skills are called *service industry knowledge.*

It is no longer enough for people in the support industry to have only strong technical skills. In addition to supporting technology, technical professionals are being challenged to ensure that a company's technology enables its employees and customers to achieve their business goals. In other words, they must assure that the technology is useful and helps people be productive.

Some business skills are useful in any profession. Your business skills will grow as you acquire education and experience and as you simply observe the activities that occur where you work. The term *business* encompasses a broad range of topics and disciplines. Some basic skills needed include:

- Understanding and speaking the language of business.

- Analyzing and solving business problems.

- Using data, such as service desk data, to analyze trends and quantify improvement opportunities.

- Understanding the importance of developing cost-effective solutions that clearly benefit the company's business goals, not just solutions that take advantage of the latest technology trend.

- Learning to develop and make presentations to market your ideas.

- Communicating the benefits of your ideas in financial terms.

Most employers do not expect individuals in technical professions such as the service desk to have fully developed business skills when they first join the workforce. However, they expect employees to assimilate the role technology plays in a business venture and understand why these skills are important. Even a company that manufactures computer games, a fun use of technology, is in business to make a profit. Technical professionals should know that and understand the role they play in achieving that goal.

Managers are increasingly requiring senior technical professionals to hone and use business skills. For example, senior technical professionals are sometimes required to quantify their proposed projects using techniques such as cost-benefit analysis. **Cost-benefit analysis** compares the costs and benefits of two or more potential solutions to determine an optimum solution. Figure 3-3 shows sample costs and benefits.

Costs	Alternative 1	Alternative 2
Personnel costs such as payroll costs, including overtime benefits and expenses. *Note:* Nonrecurring costs include activities such as project planning and management, solution design, development, and implementation. Recurring costs include end-user education and training, end-user support, and system maintenance activities.	$	$
Hardware costs such as computers, peripheral devices such as printers and scanners, and network devices. *Note:* Hardware costs include the one-time cost of purchasing equipment as well as recurring maintenance and upgrade costs.	$	$
Software costs such as operating system software, application software, productivity tools, and monitoring tools. *Note:* Software costs include the one-time cost of purchasing software as well as recurring maintenance and upgrade costs.	$	$
External services such as outsourcing services, voice and data communication services, cloud computing services, and professional services (consultants). *Note:* External service costs may include the one-time use of consultants as well as recurring services such as outsourcing services.	$	$
Facility costs such as office space, security, and utilities. *Note:* Nonrecurring facility costs may include temporary quarters for the project team as well as recurring costs associated with housing personnel and equipment.	$	$
Total Costs	$	$
Benefits		
Increased profits	$	$
Decreased costs	$	$
Total Benefits	$	$
Net Benefits (Total Benefits – Total Costs)	$	$
Intangible Benefits	**Numeric Value (NV)**	
Increased customer satisfaction	NV	NV
Improved communication	NV	NV
Net Intangible Benefits (Total Numeric Value)	TNV	TNV

Figure 3-3 Sample costs and benefits
© Cengage Learning 2014

Another commonly accepted financial measure used when assessing projects is **return on investment (ROI)**, which measures the total financial benefit derived from an investment—such as a new technology project—and then compares it with the total cost of the project. As shown in Figure 3-4, ROI typically states the return on investment as a percentage.

ROI% = Net Benefits/Project Investment × 100

Figure 3-4   ROI calculation
© Cengage Learning 2014

The absence of business skills may not hinder a technical professional's career. However, the presence of business skills will increase the opportunities available and speed up his or her advancement.

Hundreds of books, ranging from basic to advanced and spanning a broad array of topics, have been written about business. To learn more about business skills, visit your local library or bookstore and search for books, CDs, and videos on topics such as "business," "workplace skills," "business jargon," "finance for nonfinancial professionals," "making presentations," and "project management." You could begin with a business primer and then take a more in-depth look at topics you find interesting or important.

 You can also purchase business-related books, CDs, and videos at web sites such as *www.bizhotline.com*, *www.amanet.org*, and *www.careertrack.com*.

Industry Knowledge

Some service desks seek to hire people who understand the specific industry in which the company is engaged, such as manufacturing, retail, or finance. This knowledge makes it easier for employees to understand the company's goals and contribute accordingly. Many service desks recruit from within the company to find candidates who are already familiar with the company and its goals. These internal candidates sometimes already have a positive working relationship with members of the service desk team and its customers.

Service desks also value candidates who have skills and knowledge that pertain to the product or service being sold. For example, a company that sells accounting software may seek service desk personnel who have an accounting background. Such industry knowledge enables these service desk analysts to understand the customer's needs and appreciate the impact on the customer's business when a product fails to perform properly.

Service Industry Knowledge

When hiring analysts or specialists, many service desks require knowledge of the customer service and support industry. Those that don't require this kind of experience at least consider it highly desirable. Knowledge of or experience with ITSM and quality management frameworks and standards such as ITIL, KCS, and HDI standards may also be viewed as highly desirable. Many employers scan candidates' résumés for previous service experience or job experience that involves helping people. Relevant fields include teaching, sales, social work, and healthcare. People in these fields must be able to recognize that they are delivering a service and that their "customers" look to them for help.

The business skills and knowledge required for a service desk job depend on the company's market niche and the job category (such as level one analyst or level one specialist). People applying for entry-level positions are expected to have little to no business experience, although some basic knowledge and a willingness to learn are viewed as a positive. People applying for management positions are expected to have a great deal of business experience.

Technical Skills

The technical skills required for a service desk position depend on the customers' technical needs. **Technical skills** are the skills people need to use and support the specific products and technologies the service desk supports. At the very least, companies expect people applying for entry-level positions to be computer literate. They must have experience using computers and know how to use common operating systems, such as Microsoft Windows or Mac OS; popular web browsers, such as Google Chrome, Internet Explorer, Mozilla Firefox, and Apple Safari; and popular software packages, such as Microsoft Office. People applying for level one specialist positions are expected to have technical skills and experience in a specific area or with a specific product. For example, a company that provides software support values software literacy. A position in an internal service desk that supports a complex computing environment usually requires a broader base of skills, including experience with network environments, operating systems, applications, and hardware systems.

 The ability to type or keyboard well is an asset in the service desk. With good keyboarding skills, you can enter data quickly and accurately, freeing you to focus on listening to the customer, which is vital in a service desk. Some companies test candidates' keyboarding skills and offer keyboarding classes to improve performance.

Service desks that want to hire people with past support industry experience consider an applicant's knowledge of support technologies—such as telephone systems, incident management systems, and knowledge management systems. Although these skills are not usually required, candidates who demonstrate a level of comfort using support technologies may have the upper hand. Most companies, however, provide training on their specific systems.

When interviewing a potential service desk analyst or specialist, an employer may assess technical skills in a number of ways, including:

- **Education**—Some companies look for candidates who have or are working on an information systems or computer science degree, or who have completed a help desk- or service desk-related diploma program. Often, a specified number of years of related IT experience is accepted in lieu of education.

- **Certification**—Some companies look for candidates who have completed relevant technical certification program(s), such as those offered by vendors like Cisco, CompTIA, Microsoft, and Novell.

Chapter 8 explores the role of certification in the service desk industry.

- **Asking questions**—Some companies have experts prepare a list of questions that assess candidates' knowledge about a particular subject.
- **Testing**—Some employers administer a standardized exam to evaluate candidates' abilities.
- **Problem solving**—Many employers present candidates with a problem (such as a disabled or incorrectly configured system) and evaluate their ability to isolate and fix the problem. Some give candidates a puzzle to solve or ask candidates to write down the steps that they would use to solve a sample problem. As candidates' technical abilities can vary, employers may ask candidates to solve a nontechnical problem, such as why a car won't start, to evaluate the person's ability to analyze and troubleshoot problems in a logical manner.

Soft Skills

Soft skills are the qualities that people need to deliver great service, such as active listening skills, verbal skills, customer service skills, problem-solving skills, temperament, teamwork skills, and writing skills. These skills are recognized as the most basic and important skills that analysts must possess because all the technical skills in the world cannot overcome a lack of soft skills. Knowing how to get along with people and displaying a positive attitude are crucial for success. Soft skills enable companies to be competitive and enable people to be productive. Soft skills also enable people to avoid frustration and to enjoy working in the customer service and support industry.

Active Listening

Listening is frequently ranked as the most important quality that analysts must possess. **Active listening** is when the listener participates in a conversation and gives the speaker a sense of confidence that he or she is being understood. Active listening is particularly important when interacting with customers over the telephone or via the web because they cannot see you nodding your head or making eye contact. Two nonvisual ways to demonstrate listening are to ask clarifying questions and to respond to the customer using a verbal nod of the head through phrases such as "uh-huh," "I see," and "I understand."

Verbal Skills

Because many interactions between a service desk analyst and the customer occur over the telephone, the analyst's ability to communicate verbally is critical. The analyst must be able not only to solve problems, but also to tell others how to solve problems at a level appropriate to each customer. For example, a service desk analyst must use much simpler terminology when talking to a first-time computer user than when talking to an experienced user.

Customer Service Skills

Often referred to as "people" skills, customer service skills include the ability to handle difficult customer situations, such as calming irate or extremely demanding customers or saying "no" to customers without antagonizing them. A person with good customer service skills can gain customer confidence and maintain goodwill, even when the customer's needs cannot be fully met. The art of customer service can be learned through practice, and is explained in the numerous books, CDs, and training programs devoted to the topic.

Problem-Solving Skills

Problem solving is more than just troubleshooting a technical problem. It also involves more than randomly trying things to find an answer or searching a database of solutions. Problem solving involves logical thinking and a methodical approach through which the analyst first determines the probable source of a problem and then decides on a solution. A good problem solver has effective questioning skills. Persistence is also important, as proficient problem solving requires going beyond the "quick fix."

Temperament

The term *temperament* refers to the way a person thinks, behaves, or reacts to situations on a daily basis. Temperament is largely a matter of attitude. In the support industry, a positive attitude—the ability to seek out the good in any situation—is essential. It is also a key to being able to see the good in people and to understand that extraordinary situations sometimes cause even the most reasonable customers to lose patience or become angry. (It happens to the best of us.) A person temperamentally suited to work at a service desk can handle pressure and resists becoming defensive or hostile in difficult situations.

 Continuously step back and objectively assess your soft skills. Good soft skills will serve you well in any career and throughout your life.

Teamwork Skills

Support is an ideal environment for working in teams due to the complexity of the work and the diversity of skills required. Simply working on a team does not, however, make an individual a team player. Rather, a team player is someone who works well with others, shares information and feedback with others, and focuses on the goals of the service desk. Being a team player is a way of life that stems from a desire to accomplish more than you can on your own. Team players understand how they personally contribute to the team and they respect and appreciate others' contributions.

Writing Skills

The ability to write well is an important skill for service desk analysts. This is because analysts have to write to log contacts, document resolutions, develop procedures, and correspond with customers and coworkers. They write using technologies such as word processing software, email, chat, knowledge bases, wikis, and text and instant messaging. Also, many companies now allow customers to directly access the IT organization's incident management system to check the status of outstanding tickets. Other companies use the Internet or their internal company **intranet**—a secured, privately maintained web site that serves employees and that can be accessed only by authorized personnel—to publish the answers to FAQs and allow customers to search online databases for possible solutions. In these situations, a customer's perception of the company is greatly influenced by the clarity and professionalism of the service desk's writing.

Chapter 5 describes the use of wikis in a service desk setting.

Ways to Evaluate Soft Skills

The essential soft skills just described are difficult to assess during an interview. To get a better understanding of a job candidate's soft skills, an employer may use one or more of the following techniques:

- **Role playing**—Some service desks have employees (and sometimes customers) conduct the first interview with candidates over the phone to simulate a real service desk situation and assess applicants' verbal communication skills. Candidates may face a demanding caller or one who continuously interrupts them and questions their skills. The interviewer uses this role playing to determine how candidates handle pressure.

- **Writing samples**—Some service desks ask candidates to bring samples of documents they have prepared, such as procedures, flowcharts, or technical solutions. Alternately, candidates may be asked to solve a problem and then document the solution at the interview.

- **Past experience**—Some service desks encourage candidates to describe specific situations they have handled in the past, along with the actions they took to handle these situations and the results. Candidates may be asked, for example, how they have handled a situation in which a caller was unwilling to answer questions. Alternately, candidates may be asked to describe how they handled a stressful situation at work.

- **Testing**—Some service desks rely on personality tests, such as the Myers-Briggs Type Indicator (MBTI) and the Motivational Appraisal of Personal Potential (MAPP) to learn more about a job candidate. These tests measure qualities such as motivation, temperament, learning style, and people skills.

- **Certification**—Several organizations such as HDI and the Technology Services Industry Association offer certification programs that focus on or at least include soft skills training for service desk professionals, in much the same way the vendor certification programs focus on a candidate's technical skills.

Soft skills affect which service desk job people are most suited for. Some people prefer working alone or find the front line stressful. If that is the case for you, you may want to pursue a job away from the front line. On the other hand, people who enjoy working with customers and helping others solve problems will enjoy working as a service desk dispatcher, level one analyst, or level one specialist.

Self-Management Skills

In addition to business skills, technical skills, and soft skills, service desk personnel need good self-management skills. **Self-management skills**, such as stress and time management, are the skills people need to complete their work effectively, feel job satisfaction, and avoid frustration or burnout. Self-management skills are particularly important in the customer service and support industry because customer service is often ranked as one of the most stressful occupations. Analysts and specialists who can manage their own time and who organize their work enjoy greater job satisfaction. Some of the most important self-management skills include stress management, time management, organization, learning, and knowledge acquisition.

Stress-Management Skills

The term *stress* refers to the adaptation of our bodies and minds to change. Given that change is a constant in the support industry, it is no wonder that people in this industry experience high levels of stress. With stress-management skills, people can minimize stress as much as possible and respond effectively when stressful situations occur. In other words, stress-management skills enable people to work well under pressure. Every person handles change differently and must develop a personal way of coping with stressful events.

Time-Management Skills

The information technology industry and its related support industry are constantly and dramatically changing, leading people to feel they are always behind. Service desk analysts and specialists must effectively manage their limited time to minimize stress and frustration and promote high self-esteem. Time-management techniques, such as establishing priorities and avoiding procrastination (discussed in Chapter 7), enable individuals to gain control over their day and focus on their work.

To manage your time effectively, identify and eliminate the ways you waste time. Next, focus on activities that contribute to both your personal goals and the service desk's goals.

Organizational Skills

Slow, quiet days on a service desk are rare. People who work in the support industry must continually develop the skills needed to handle new technologies, multiple projects, changing policies and procedures, and a somewhat chaotic physical environment. Organization is the key to handling those busy days. Getting and staying organized requires setting up effective paper- and computer-based filing systems and having the personal discipline to maintain those systems on a daily basis.

Learning and Knowledge Acquisition Skills

Learning is the labor of the information age. When discussing learning skills, it is important to distinguish between retrieving information and acquiring knowledge. Retrieving information is the easy part. You can obtain the information you need through textbooks and class notes, knowledge management systems, web sites, online help, manuals and procedure guides, and so on. Good analysts don't try to store all the information they need between their ears. Instead, they determine where to find the information and learn how to get it quickly when they need it. Then, they focus on acquiring knowledge—an understanding of what information means, why information is important, and how information can be used. Acquiring knowledge requires study, analysis, reflection, and a focus on the bigger picture. Getting ahead in the support industry requires the ability to retrieve information and the ability to acquire knowledge. Both require an inherent curiosity and eagerness to learn.

Ways to Evaluate Self-Management Skills

Like soft skills, self-management skills are difficult to assess during an interview. To get a feel for candidates' self-management skills, employers often use some of the same techniques described earlier for assessing soft skills. Like soft skills, self-management skills warrant ongoing self-assessment as there is always room for improvement. The support industry is particularly fast paced, and things are never "normal." People who enjoy a variety of responsibilities and who feel comfortable, and even motivated, when they are faced with challenging problems and situations make perfect candidates for a front-line role.

Continuously step back and objectively assess your soft and self-management skills. These skills will serve you well in any career and throughout your life.

INTERVIEW WITH...

PETE MCGARAHAN
PRESIDENT
MCGARAHAN & ASSOCIATES
YORBA LINDA, CALIFORNIA
www.mcgarahan.com

Courtesy of McGarahan & Associates

In today's rapidly changing business environment, career paths are no longer as predetermined as they used to be. I believe that the roles people play within an organization are becoming very dynamic, and the one thing people can expect is change. The service desk employee has the opportunity to have contact with all of the people in the organization, and that can lead you into any direction you choose to go. The world is an oyster for people in IT support who have a great customer service attitude, technical skills, and business acumen.

It really starts with a great attitude. People like a can-do attitude, an empowered attitude. *I can help you!* Managers today want employees who have a solid work ethic. That means it's up to you to be self-motivated and self-disciplined. Constantly be on the lookout for ways that you can add value. Don't be content to answer the same boring questions day-in and day-out. Be in the problem-prevention business. Recommend ways to eliminate low value-add activities, for example, through automation, and to minimize business impact when technology changes occur. In today's business world, it's not enough to just have great technical skills. It's what you do with your skills. It's all about results.

Service Desk Management Personnel

The size of a service desk determines how many layers of management it requires. Some service desks have front-line staff report directly to a manager. In others, team leaders and perhaps supervisors, handle day-to-day operations so that the service desk manager can focus on more strategic activities such as planning, preparing budgets, and improving service. Larger service desks may assign one or more people to each manager position. In smaller service desks, a single person may take over the duties associated with several management positions. Whether performed by one person or a hierarchy of people, service desk management is critical to the success of the service desk. Figure 3-5 lists the common service desk management roles, although these titles may vary from service desk to service desk.

- Senior service desk manager or director

- Service desk manager

- Service desk supervisor or team leader

Figure 3-5 Common service desk management roles
© Cengage Learning 2014

Senior Service Desk Manager

Typically, a **senior service desk manager** (also called a **service desk director**) establishes the service desk mission and focuses on the service desk's strategic or long-term goals. He or she ensures the service desk's goals are aligned with the goals of the IT organization and the business. He or she approves the service desk budget and acquires (from the larger corporation) the funding needed to make improvements such as hiring additional staff, implementing new processes, acquiring new technologies, and so on. The senior service desk manager actively promotes the value of the service desk to upper management and the entire company, gaining support for the efforts of the service desk and its improvement plans. According to HDI's *2012 Support Center Practices and Salaries Report*, the average yearly salary for a service desk director is between $88,226 and $117,407.

 Top factors that influence salaries for people in management positions include management and leadership skills, quality of work, and the ability to assume increased responsibilities.

Service Desk Manager

The **service desk manager** works closely with the senior service desk manager to prepare the service desk's budget and plan its activities for the coming year. He or she is involved with activities such as preparing reports and analyzing statistics, preparing training plans, establishing and monitoring SLAs, and working with other managers (such as level two and level three managers) to ensure that the service desk's processes and technologies are meeting the company's needs. Working in the service desk manager position can prepare a person for the senior service desk manager role. These management positions also can lead to management opportunities in another part of the company. According to HDI's *2012 Support Center Practices and Salaries Report*, the average yearly salary for a service desk manager is between $68,277 and $88,965.

Service Desk Supervisor or Team Leader

A **service desk supervisor** (also called a **team leader**) oversees the day-to-day operation of the service desk, which includes making sure the service desk is meeting its SLA commitments, monitoring and evaluating the performance of service desk staff, and ensuring that the staff is properly trained. The service desk supervisor and team leader also work closely with service desk managers to hire service desk staff and evaluate their performance.

Many companies turn to their front-line service providers when they need to fill service desk supervisor and team leader roles because these people have in-depth knowledge about the company, the products it uses or sells, and the needs of the service desk. The service desk supervisor or team leader role can also serve as a training ground for people interested in becoming a service desk manager. According to HDI's *2012 Support Center Practices and Salaries Report*, the average yearly salary for a service desk team leader is between $51,909 and $68,339.

Skills Required for Service Desk Management

When hiring service desk managers, employers look for skills related to the particular management position. For example, companies interviewing candidates for a senior service desk manager position usually want someone with a strong background in customer service and support along with long-range planning experience and the ability to manage a budget. Companies interviewing candidates for a service desk manager position often look for people who know how to prepare budgets and plan service desk activities. Experience hiring people, evaluating performance, and coaching and counseling people to maximize their performance is also important. When hiring a service desk supervisor or team leader, companies focus on the candidate's leadership skills and team-building experience. Smaller companies with few layers of management look for people who have all of these skills or the combination of skills needed at that particular company.

Service desk managers need excellent communication skills and the ability to present information and ideas in a manner appropriate for each audience. For example, when communicating with upper levels of management, service desk managers must be able to succinctly present briefings and recommendations using appropriate business terms and supporting statistics. When communicating with their peers—other IT managers—service desk managers must be able to promote a spirit of cooperation and build the rapport needed to work together toward shared goals. When communicating with staff, service desk managers must be able to inspire and motivate while providing clear, firm direction. When communicating with customers, service desk managers must relay empathy and understanding and must excel at managing expectations.

Service desk management personnel need to understand how to manage processes and may be involved in designing and implementing processes. They must understand any process frameworks such as ITIL, standards such as ISO/IEC 20000, or quality improvement programs being utilized in the organization. This is an important skill because process initiatives require management commitment to be successful. Management must demonstrate their commitment through words and deeds. For example, management may announce the benefits of and the need to comply with processes at team meetings. Or, management may ensure analysts' job responsibilities and performance measures reflect process activities. Management also typically directs the creation of procedures that describe how to perform the processes.

Service desk management personnel need technical skills, but they are typically not expected to maintain their skills at the same detailed level as service desk analysts and specialists. Service desk managers need a higher-level understanding of the particular products and systems supported by the service desk. They don't have to know everything, but they must have sufficient knowledge to inform the company about the overall performance of the products and systems the service desk supports. They must also be able to prepare the service desk when new products and systems are being implemented, and they must be able to provide direction when critical problem situations occur. They use their technical knowledge to plan training and evaluate the technical ability of the service desk team and individual analysts within the team.

People leaving front-line positions for management roles often find it difficult to "give up" their technical skills. They are used to being the experts and may enjoy having others look up to them and seek their assistance. In time, however, managers must move from knowing how to *fix* technology to how to *use* technology to achieve business goals. The best managers hire and train good analysts to do the fixing.

Supporting Roles

Front-line service providers and management often rely on others within the service desk or IT department for the tools, processes, and information they need to perform their tasks. In smaller service desks, one person may perform a number of the supporting roles listed in Figure 3-6. Or, a number of people may share these responsibilities. In larger service desks, teams may perform these different roles.

- Knowledge management systerm administration
- Network monitoring
- Service management and improvement
- Technical support
- Training

Figure 3-6   Common supporting roles in a service desk
© Cengage Learning 2014

As companies strive to make the most of the tools and procedures available to the service desk, supporting roles are becoming more important and commonplace. Figure 3-7 shows an organization chart for a larger service desk that includes these supporting roles.

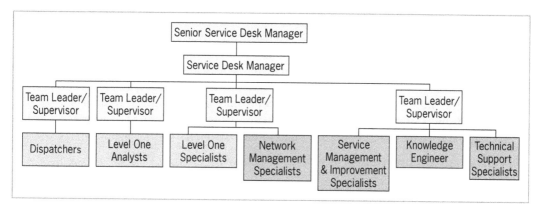

Figure 3-7 Sample service desk organization chart with supporting roles
© Cengage Learning 2014

Supporting roles are also important because they create diverse opportunities in the service desk. Some service desks dedicate people to these positions. Other service desks rotate analysts and specialists through these supporting roles, giving people the opportunity to broaden their base of skills and occasionally step away from the front line. Whether people are dedicated to these supporting positions or rotate through them, these roles help to retain valued people in the service desk.

 Some or all of these supporting roles may be performed by teams other than the service desk. This is often the case in larger organizations.

Knowledge Management System Administration

Many companies maintain knowledge management systems that allow them to consolidate the information sources people need to make decisions and complete their tasks into a single logical system. A **knowledge management system (KMS)** is a set of tools and databases that are used to store, manage, and present information sources, such as customer information, documents, policies and procedures, incident resolutions, and known errors. These databases may be referred to as knowledge bases or known error databases. A **knowledge base** is a logical database that contains data used by a knowledge management system. A **known error** is a problem that has a documented root cause and a workaround. A **known error database (KEDB)** is a database that contains known error records. Known errors are created and managed by the problem management process. Knowledge management systems are created and managed by the knowledge management process.

Chapter 4 explores the problem and knowledge management processes. Chapter 5 explains knowledge management systems in greater detail.

To maintain these systems, many companies designate a knowledge engineer. A **knowledge engineer**, also called a **knowledge base administrator (KBA)**, develops and oversees the knowledge management process and ensures that the information contained in the knowledge management system is accurate, complete, and current. Knowledge management is a critical process because rapid change makes it difficult for companies to provide service desk analysts with as much training as the companies or the analysts would like. As a result, companies must supplement their analysts' skills by providing them with access to effectively managed and maintained knowledge management systems.

A knowledge engineer's responsibilities may include:

- Researching and gathering information sources to include in or remove from the knowledge management system.

- Developing and distributing resolution documentation standards, such as the format and writing style to be used when preparing resolutions.

- Reviewing incident resolutions submitted by service desk analysts and level two and level three service providers.

- Ensuring that information sources (1) are technically valid, (2) are reusable—for example, details relating to a single specific incident, such as names and dates, are removed so other analysts can reuse the source to solve the same incident for a different customer or at a future date, (3) are presented in a clear, consistent, and logical manner, (4) conform to knowledge management standards, and (5) do not duplicate existing information sources.

- Conferring, when necessary, with the author of a resolution or information source to clarify the information and determine where the information should be stored in the knowledge management system.

- Approving or rejecting resolutions and information sources as appropriate.

- Ensuring that analysts can quickly and easily retrieve information added to the knowledge management system.

- Ensuring that the data used to log incidents is consistent with the data used to store information in the knowledge management system so analysts can easily match incidents to resolutions.

- Providing service desk and level two staff with the training they need to create quality information and improve their ability to retrieve information from the knowledge management system.

In smaller companies, a service desk analyst may perform this role on a part-time basis, whereas larger companies may have one or more full-time knowledge engineers. For example, each level two group in larger companies may have an individual who maintains the information sources relative to his or her group's area of expertise. This role is critical as it ensures that the information contained in a company's knowledge management system is accessible, current, accurate, and complete.

Network Monitoring

Network monitoring involves activities that use tools to observe network performance in an effort to minimize the impact of incidents. Network monitoring tools include remote monitoring and network management systems. At some companies, level one analysts and specialists use these tools in their daily work. Other companies establish a separate function and dedicate people to the role of network monitoring. These people may be called network analysts or network management specialists.

CASE STUDY: Establishing an Operations Bridge

Some organizations establish an Operations Bridge to serve as a link or "bridge" between IT Operations Control and the service desk. **IT Operations Control** *is the function within IT that monitors the entire IT infrastructure from a central console or set of consoles. In some organizations, the Operations Bridge covers for the service desk after hours. The Operations Bridge may also be called Network Operations Center (NOC).*

The service desk model is prompting organizations to transition network monitoring from the network management group into the service desk. This transfer of responsibilities enables the service desk to be more proactive and to identify and resolve or escalate incidents more quickly. Network monitoring involves:

- Monitoring the network for signs of degradation.

- Recording network-related incidents.

- Communicating network status to customers.

- Notifying level one analysts and specialists and level two or level three specialists (such as the network management group) when the network is down or likely to be unavailable.

Network monitoring is a logical activity for service desks because it enables them to be proactive. It also enables network management staff to focus on activities such as network configuration, administration, and security. Available network management technologies are making it possible for service desks to extend their reach and more quickly identify and solve incidents.

Service Management and Improvement

Some larger service desks assign one or more people to proactive tasks designed to ensure that the service desk meets its service commitments and continually improves the quality of its services. In smaller service desks, these tasks are performed by service desk management or by service desk staff on a part-time basis. **Service management and improvement** includes activities such as monitoring service desk performance and identifying and overseeing improvements to the service desk. Service management and improvement responsibilities include:

- Developing and distributing management reports that are used by customers, senior IT management, service desk management and staff, and level two and level three managers and staff to monitor metrics, measure performance, analyze trends, and so on.

- Looking for trends, such as an increase in the number of incidents affecting a particular product.

- Executing the problem management process (discussed in Chapter 4) and performing root cause analysis.

- Developing and monitoring service desk performance reports.

- Participating in the negotiation of SLAs and monitoring performance to ensure that the service desk is meeting its commitments.

- Developing, monitoring, and contributing to the continual improvement of service desk processes.

- Soliciting customer feedback and measuring customer satisfaction.

- Identifying ways the service desk can improve and facilitating the implementation of improvements.

- Performing benchmarking activities. **Benchmarking** is the process of comparing the service desk's performance metrics and practices to those of another service desk in an effort to identify improvement opportunities.

Service management and improvement are the hallmark of a world class customer service and support organization. These companies understand the adage "you can't manage what you aren't measuring" and work diligently to ensure that their services are aligned with their customers' needs.

Technical Support

The service desk requires technical support for the tools and technology it uses in the same way that IT customers require support for theirs. In a service desk setting, technical support involves maintaining the hardware and software systems used by front-line service providers and service desk management personnel. In larger service desks, one or more people provide technical support. In smaller service desks, service desk management and staff may perform these tasks on an as-needed basis. In some organizations, level two or level three staff may perform some of these tasks or work jointly with the service desk's technical support staff to perform these tasks.

The technical support function includes activities such as routine maintenance, enhancing and upgrading systems, and providing technology-related training. Technical support may also involve evaluating and selecting new systems, identifying and developing the training needed to implement new systems, and managing the implementation of new systems. Technical support responsibilities may include:

- Evaluating and selecting support technology.

- Developing and delivering training for support technology.

- Creating and maintaining project plans for implementing new technology and associated processes.

- Monitoring and maintaining support systems, such as ensuring that systems are backed up, archiving data when needed, performing database tuning, and so on.

- Resolving incidents related to the technologies used by the service desk.

- Evaluating requests to customize service desk technologies.

- Ensuring that the licenses, warranties, and service contracts for all service desk technologies are up to date.

- Managing the service desk's configuration management system, which is a set of tools and databases used to manage an organization's configuration data.

 Chapter 5 describes configuration management systems.

Technology loses its effectiveness if it is not properly maintained and continuously upgraded to keep pace with its users' needs. Service desk technology is no different. Companies that devote resources to supporting their service desk systems realize this and are willing to do what is required to get the most out of their technology investment.

Training

Although some service desks rely on their company's training department for training, other service desks have a dedicated person or team to oversee the training needs of the service desk team. This is in addition to the cross-training and mentoring that is a daily part of service desk life. The person or team in charge of training focuses on the special needs of the service desk team and ensures that they receive training that addresses the business, technical, soft, and self-management skills that service desk analysts need. This person or team may develop programs, work with other support groups to create programs, or acquire training programs from commercial sources. The responsibilities of a service desk trainer or training group may include:

- Working with service desk management personnel to determine training needs.

- Observing service desk operations and soliciting feedback from service desk staff to determine training needs.

- Developing and delivering training programs.

- Offering relevant certification programs.

- Providing one-on-one training when needed.

- Evaluating and implementing commercially developed training programs (such as computer-based or Internet-based training).

The one sure thing in a service desk setting is that things will change. Because of this, training is essential for a service desk team, and the people who deliver training provide an invaluable service.

 In a service desk, ongoing training is a way of life, and everyone is expected to participate. Even the new person on the team might teach somebody something.

How service desks organize themselves to incorporate these supporting roles varies considerably from one company to the next. Larger service desks have no choice but to dedicate full-time resources to these functions. Smaller service desks may have front-line service providers handle these functions along with their customer support responsibilities. Some service desks have people or teams performing some functions full-time and service desk analysts and specialists perform other functions part-time. Regardless of how these functions are handled, they all add up to customer and employee satisfaction.

Characteristics of a Successful Service Desk Team

You might be tempted to define a team as a group of people doing the same thing, but that's not really true. In a baseball team, for instance, the members of the team all perform different tasks. One plays first base, another specializes in pitching, and so on. Each player has an area of expertise and often performs poorly in areas other than his or her specialty. (Pitchers, for example, are notoriously poor batters.) Each player must also at times be a leader and at other times follow the leader. What makes these people with varying talents a team? The answer is their desire to play together to win the game.

In the modern business world, no single person can know everything about a company's products and systems and provide all the support customers need. The demands are too great. Instead, the members of the service desk need to work together as a team. Each service desk analyst must maintain a high level of knowledge about the products and systems for which he or she is the recognized expert, and at the same time show respect and support for the other team members. In other words, a member of the service desk team who is highly skilled in one particular product cannot discount the efforts of another team member who is unfamiliar with that product. That other team member may be highly experienced in another product or may have business skills, soft skills, or self-management skills that contribute to the team's goals.

The characteristics of a successful team, and of successful team players, include:

- **Ability to collaborate**—When people identify with a team, they want to work well together. Members of a team support each other and do what is best for the team.

- **Effective communication**—When team members interact, information flows freely. People support and trust each other and are willing to share their knowledge and experience.

- **Enhanced capability**—In a team setting, the team performs better than the individual team members alone. The team benefits when it recognizes and uses the talents of each team member. Successful teams capitalize on team members' strengths and compensate for each other's weaknesses.

- **Consensus sought and reached**—Consensus means that all team members work together to make decisions and solve problems that affect the service desk's performance. In the course of reaching consensus, team members come up with more ideas and options than any one person could develop alone.

- **Sense of commitment**—People feel a responsibility to the team and its members and don't want to let them down. People understand that they must do their fair share of the work and that they must continually look for more efficient and effective ways to do their work.

Most people who work on a service desk value the fact that they are part of a team. They rely on others for their knowledge, experience, and support, and in turn, they want their coworkers to appreciate and respect them. The most successful teams rise up and meet the most demanding performance challenges. In fact, a common performance goal is more important to a team than a great leader or special incentives. In the support industry, the performance goal is clear: satisfy the customer.

Chapter Summary

- The service desk is a rewarding and exciting place for people who want to pursue a career in customer service and support. A variety of roles in the service desk industry provide potential and existing service desk employees with many opportunities. These roles include the front-line service providers (such as dispatchers, level one analysts, and level one specialists) and service desk management personnel (such as managers, supervisors, and team leaders) who directly support customers and ensure their satisfaction. Additional people support the front-line staff and provide indirect customer support.

- The primary responsibilities of a service desk are to provide a single point of contact for all support services, deliver value to customers, and capture and distribute information. The job responsibilities of service desk dispatchers, analysts, and specialists correspond to those responsibilities. The professional responsibilities of service desk staff involve conducting themselves at all times in a professional and ethical manner. In instances of illegal and unethical behavior, it is the service desk analyst's duty to strictly follow and enforce both the law and the company's policies.

- Each of the service desk roles requires a specific set of skills. Front-line service providers need the right mix of business skills (including industry and service industry knowledge), technical skills (expertise with the products and technologies the service desk supports), soft skills (such as active listening, verbal, customer service, problem-solving, temperament, teamwork, and writing skills), and self-management skills (such as stress and time management, organizational, and learning and knowledge acquisition skills). Soft skills are the most important because people need them to deliver great service and to enjoy working in the customer service and support industry.

- The size of a service desk determines how many layers of management it requires. Management roles may include senior service desk manager, service desk manager, and service desk supervisor or team leader. Whether performed by one person or a hierarchy of people, service desk management is critical to the organization's success. The service desk can continuously improve through management activities such as strategic planning, preparing budgets, and monitoring and evaluating performance.

- Front-line service providers and service desk managers often rely on others within the service desk for the tools, processes, and information they need to perform their tasks. As a result, supporting roles such as knowledge management system administration, network monitoring, service management and improvement, technical support, and training are growing in importance. These roles enable companies to make the most of the tools and procedures available to the service desk, create diverse opportunities in the service desk, and enable the service desk to retain valued people.

- Members of a service desk need to work together as a team because no single person can know it all or do it all. Most people who work on a service desk value being part of a team. They know they can rely on their coworkers for their knowledge, experience, and support and that their teammates appreciate and respect them in turn. The most successful teams rise up and meet the most demanding performance challenges. In the support industry, the primary performance goal is clear: satisfy the customer.

Key Terms

active listening—Listening in which the listener participates in a conversation and gives the speaker a sense of confidence that he or she is being understood.

benchmarking—The process of comparing the service desk's performance metrics and practices to those of another service desk in an effort to identify improvement opportunities.

business skills—The skills people need to work successfully in the business world, such as the ability to understand and speak the language of business; the skills that are unique to the industry or profession the service desk supports, such as accounting skills or banking skills (industry knowledge); and the skills that are specific to the customer service and support industry, such as understanding the importance of meeting customers' needs and knowing how to manage their expectations (service industry knowledge).

cost-benefit analysis—A business calculation that compares the costs and benefits of two or more potential solutions in order to determine an optimum solution.

dispatcher—The person who initially handles customer contacts; also called a service desk agent, customer care agent, customer service representative, or call screener.

front-line service provider—Service desk staff who interacts directly with customers.

intranet—A secured, privately maintained web site that serves employees and that can be accessed only by authorized personnel.

IT Operations Control—The function within IT that monitors the entire IT infrastructure from a central console or set of consoles.

knowledge base—A logical database that contains data used by a knowledge management system. See also *knowledge management system (KMS)*.

knowledge base administrator (KBA)—Another name for a *knowledge engineer*.

knowledge engineer—The person who develops and oversees the knowledge management process and ensures that the information contained in the knowledge management system is accurate, complete, and current; also called a *knowledge base administrator (KBA)*.

knowledge management system (KMS)—A set of tools and databases that are used to store, manage, and present information sources such as customer information, documents, policies and procedures, incident resolutions, and known errors.

known error—A problem that has a documented root cause and a workaround.

known error database (KEDB)—A database that contains known error records. See also *knowledge management system (KMS)*.

level one analyst—A person who receives and logs contacts, answers questions, and resolves incidents and service requests when possible; also called service desk analyst, customer support analyst, or service desk technician.

level one specialist—A person who researches complex incidents and handles service requests that require more skill or authority—or, in some cases, more time—than a level one analyst can devote to a single contact; also called service desk specialist, technical support specialist, or customer support specialist.

malicious software (malware)—Harmful software such as viruses, worms, Trojan horses, spyware, and adware that is designed to damage or disrupt a computer, computer system, or computer network.

network monitoring—Activities that use tools to observe network performance in an effort to minimize the impact of incidents.

return on investment (ROI)—A business calculation that measures the total financial benefit derived from an investment—such as a new technology project—and then compares it with the total cost of the project.

self-management skills—The skills, such as stress and time management, that people need to complete their work effectively, feel job satisfaction, and avoid frustration or burnout.

senior service desk manager—The person who typically establishes the service desk mission and focuses on the service desk's strategic or long-term goals; also called a *service desk director*.

service desk director—Another name for the *senior service desk manager*.

service desk manager—The person who works closely with the senior service desk manager to prepare the service desk's budget and plan its activities for the coming year.

service desk supervisor—The person who oversees the day-to-day operation of the service desk, which includes making sure the service desk is meeting its SLA commitments, monitoring and evaluating the performance of service desk staff, and ensuring that the staff is properly trained; also called *team leader*.

service management and improvement—Activities such as monitoring service desk performance and identifying and overseeing improvements to the service desk.

soft skills—The qualities that people need to deliver great service, such as active listening skills, verbal skills, customer service skills, problem-solving skills, temperament, teamwork skills, and writing skills.

software piracy—The unauthorized use or reproduction of copyrighted or patented software.

team leader—Another name for the *service desk supervisor*.

technical skills—The skills people need to use and support the specific products and technologies the service desk supports.

Review Questions

1. What two principal job categories exist within a typical service desk?

2. What factors determine the variety of roles and advancement opportunities found in a service desk?

3. What role do front-line service providers play in a service desk?

4. Why is the role of front-line service provider crucial?

5. Describe the primary difference between the dispatcher role and the level one analyst role.

6. What do dispatchers and level one analysts have in common?

7. Briefly list the skills that companies look for when hiring people for the following front-line roles:

   - Dispatcher

   - Level one analyst

   - Level one specialist

8. What are the three primary responsibilities of a typical service desk?

9. List two specific tasks performed at the service desk that correlate to the service desk's three primary job responsibilities.

10. How are members of the service desk team expected to conduct themselves?

11. List three ways that service desk team members can exhibit professional and ethical behavior.

12. When hiring people for front-line positions, what kind of people do companies look for?

13. List the four main skill categories necessary for working in a service desk.

14. Describe the various business skills that are often required to work in a service desk.

15. Define the term *cost-benefit analysis* and describe how it is used.

16. What determines the technical skills required for a service desk position?

17. What are the minimum technical skills that most companies require in a service desk analyst?

18. Describe two ways that companies assess a job candidate's technical skills.

19. Can technical skills compensate for a lack of soft skills? Explain your answer.

20. What is the most important soft skill that analysts must possess?

21. What are two ways a customer knows an analyst is listening when he or she is speaking over the telephone?

22. Describe the characteristics of problem solving.

23. Why is writing an important soft skill for service desk analysts?

24. Describe two ways that companies assess a job candidate's soft skills.

25. Why are self-management skills important?

26. What two skill categories warrant ongoing self-assessment? Why?

27. List one responsibility for each of the three service desk management categories discussed in this chapter.

28. How do managers need to present information and ideas? Explain your answer with two examples.

29. How must people learn to use their technical skills when moving into a management position?

30. What supporting role plays a critical role in maintain a company's information sources? Why is this role important in a service desk setting?

31. Why is training essential in a service desk setting?

32. Why does it make sense to manage the service desk as a team?

33. What single factor is more important to a service desk team than any other?

Hands-On Projects

1. **Investigate service desk job opportunities and salaries.** Look at the Sunday newspaper or search the web for service desk want ads. On the web, search for topics such as "service desk jobs" or visit one or more of the following sites: *www.justtechjobs.com* or *www.monster.com*. Also, obtain salary information at these sites or by going to sites such as *www.salary.com*. Locate want ads for each of the primary job categories described in this chapter. Prepare a table or report that contains your answers to the following questions:

   - What business skills are required for each job category?

   - What technical skills are required for each job category?

   - What soft skills are required for each job category?

   - What self-management skills are required for each job category?

   - What is an average salary for each job category?

   Summarize your findings by answering the following questions:

   - Generally speaking, what do these want ads tell you about the service desk profession?

   - Generally speaking, what do these want ads tell you about the skills required in the service desk profession?

2. **Assess your business skills.** Prepare a list of the business skills discussed in this chapter. Then assess your own business skills by answering the following questions:

   - In what areas are your business skills strong?

   - In what areas can you improve your business skills?

   - What steps can you take to improve your business skills?

   - Given what you have learned in this chapter, what conclusions can you draw about your business skills?

3. **Perform a cost-benefit analysis.** Many people who perform cost-benefit analyses tend to call it "shopping around." Think of an acquisition you have been considering. For example, you may be thinking about buying a digital camera, a smartphone, or a fairly expensive gift for a friend or family member. Complete the following steps:

   - Document the goal you are trying to achieve.

   - Produce a table that shows all of the costs (purchase price, monthly service fee, time to set up, and so forth) and that lists benefits of two or more of the products you want to purchase.

   - Analyze the costs and benefits and select a product.

   - Document the reason for your decision.

4. **Assess your soft skills.** Prepare a list of the soft skills discussed in this chapter. Then assess your own soft skills by answering the following questions:

   - In what areas are your soft skills strong?

   - In what areas can you improve your soft skills?

   - What steps can you take to improve your soft skills?

   - Given what you have learned in this chapter, what conclusions can you draw about your soft skills?

5. **Create a writing sample.** Many companies require candidates for service desk roles to submit a writing sample or answer an essay question during the interview process.

   a. On the web, search for topics such as "preparing a writing sample for a job interview," and prepare a list of three to five tips to consider.

   b. Prepare a one-page writing sample that includes the following:

      - Describe how you would handle a situation in which a customer is angry.

      - Describe the steps you would take to determine why your car won't start.

      - Describe the steps you would take if you receive a call at the service desk that exceeds your technical ability.

6. **Assess your self-management skills.** Prepare a list of the self-management skills discussed in this chapter. Then assess your own self-management skills by answering the following questions:

   - In what areas are your self-management skills strong?

   - In what areas can you improve your self-management skills?

   - What steps can you take to improve your self-management skills?

   - Given what you have learned in this chapter, what conclusions can you draw about your self-management skills?

7. **Become a better listener.** Assemble a team of three to five classmates or use your school's online message or discussion board. As a team, discuss things that get in the way of being a good listener. Identify at least five obstacles to good listening. Determine whether each of those obstacles is self-imposed or is caused by what is happening around us. Next, identify ways to remove or overcome each of these obstacles. Present your findings to the class.

8. **Learn about balancing technical and management skills.** Interview an acquaintance, family member, or coworker who manages a team of people who perform technical jobs. For example, the person might manage people who provide

technical support, develop computer programs, or install or repair technology or equipment. Write a short paper that answers the following questions:

- What level of technical skill does this person think he or she must maintain to be an effective manager?

- How does this person balance the need to maintain his or her technical skills while at the same time developing managerial skills?

- What satisfaction does this person derive by being a manager as opposed to a technician?

9. **Learn about working in a team.** Talk to at least three people (friends, family members, or classmates) who work in a team setting or play on a sports team. Write your answers to the following questions:

- What is the common goal of their teams?

- How does each member personally benefit from being a member of a team?

- In what ways do they feel they contribute to their team?

- Given what you have learned in this chapter, what conclusions can you draw about each of their experiences?

10. **Discuss what it means to be a team leader.** Go to the library and research the subject of leadership and what it takes to be a team leader. List the three qualities you think are most important, describe them, and explain why each is important. Assemble a team of at least three of your classmates or use your school's online message or discussion board. Have each member describe the three qualities he or she believes are most important and explain why. As a team, compile a list of all the qualities mentioned and then determine which are the top three qualities identified.

Case Projects

1. **Ethical Dilemma.** You work for the service desk at a law office. A young lawyer who is always pleasant when he contacts the service desk has asked you to provide him a copy of the firm's standard word processing software so that he can install it on his home computer. He has a big case coming up and he wants to put in some extra hours. Your company's software licensing agreement with the vendor is machine specific, and home computers are not covered in the agreement. Also, due to the confidential nature of client information, it is against the firm's computing policy for associates to store client information on computers that are not connected to the firm's network. You really like this guy and want to help him out. Write a short paper describing the possible ramifications of providing the software and explain what you would do. Would you provide him a copy of the software? Would you notify management? What other steps could you take to address this situation?

2. **Email and Text Messaging Tips.** As service desk team leader, you've noticed that your staff tends to be very informal in its approach to handling emails and sending text messages, whether they are sending them to coworkers or customers. You want the team to present a more professional image with their written correspondences. Search the web or visit the library for ideas about "managing email," "business email etiquette," "business text messaging etiquette," and "sending a professional email or text message." Prepare a memo that describes the following:

- 10 tips for managing email
- 10 tips for writing professional emails
- 10 tips for writing professional text messages

CHAPTER 4

The Process Component: Service Desk Processes and Procedures

In this chapter you will learn:[1]

- ◎ The anatomy and evolution of processes
- ◎ How to use process frameworks and standards
- ◎ The leading quality management frameworks and standards
- ◎ The leading IT service management frameworks and standards
- ◎ The most common processes used in service desks
- ◎ Processes that support the service desk and enable quality improvement
- ◎ Why processes are important

[1]All ITIL definitions © Crown copyright 2014. All rights reserved. Material is reproduced with the permission of the Cabinet Office under delegated authority from the Controller of HMSO.

Processes enable people to know the expected results of their efforts and ensure that their efforts are tied to business goals. By understanding an overall process—all of the tasks that must be performed to produce a result—people can better understand the importance of completing a single task. People who understand processes know that the work they are doing is necessary and valued. In other words, they know *why* they are doing that work. Procedures describe *how* to do tasks. Processes and procedures help to produce consistent results because people know *what* needs to be done and *how* to do it.

Processes and procedures are an integral component of every service desk. For example, the processes of solving incidents and handling service requests can involve numerous procedures. Clearly defined procedures ensure that incidents are solved and that service requests are handled quickly and correctly. When multiple groups are involved in solving an incident or service request, processes and procedures provide guidelines that enable each group to understand its role and responsibilities.

This chapter explores some of the most common processes used by people working in service desks. Be aware that the terminology and exact procedures for each process differ from company to company. The degree of formality with which the processes are defined and executed also varies. Regardless of the terminology and formality, if you understand the objectives of these processes, you can produce the intended results at any service desk. Delivering these results will enable you to satisfy your customers and managers and promote your career. You will also have the personal satisfaction that comes from helping and working with others.

The Anatomy of Processes

Processes and procedures exist in every service desk and in every business. A process is a collection of interrelated work activities that take a set of specific inputs and produce a set of specific outputs that are of value to a customer. A procedure is a step-by-step, detailed set of instructions that describes how to perform the tasks in a process. Each task in a process has a procedure that describes how to do that task. In other words, processes define *what* tasks to do, whereas procedures describe *how* to do the tasks.

Every worker is responsible for a process at some level. Furthermore, every worker is simultaneously a supplier (or creator) of input and a customer (or recipient) of output. Figure 4-1 illustrates how workers follow procedures that both take input and create the output needed to complete a process.

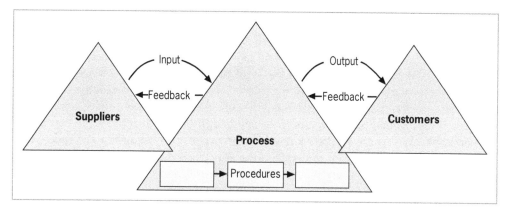

Figure 4-1 Components of a process
© Cengage Learning 2014

Flowcharts are often used in business to outline processes. A **flowchart** is a diagram that shows the sequence of tasks that occur in a process. Table 4-1 describes the purpose of each symbol used in flowcharts. Flowcharts are useful because they show how all the tasks involved in a process are interconnected.

Symbol	Name	Purpose
A	On Page Connector	Represents an exit to, or entry from, another part of the same flowchart.
Task	Task	Shows a single task or operation.
Predefined Process	Predefined process	Represents another process that provides input or receives output from the current process.
Decision	Decision	Represents a decision point and typically has a "yes" branch and a "no" branch.
—No→	No result	Used in conjunction with a decision to show the next task or decision following a "no" result.
Yes	Yes result	Used in conjunction with a decision to show the next task or decision following a "yes" result.
Start/Stop	Start/Stop	Shows the starting or stopping point of a process.

Table 4-1 Flowchart symbols
© Cengage Learning 2014

Evolution of Processes

The concept of processes and procedures used by service desks, and by business in general, originated in 1776 when philosopher and economist Adam Smith introduced his principle of the division of labor. Smith believed that the same number of workers is more efficient and productive when each performs one simple, specialized task rather than all the tasks in a process. Because each person performed only a single task, businesses needed complex processes to pull together and integrate these specialized tasks and achieve the expected output or result. As a result, workers knew only the procedures required to complete their portion of a process; they did not understand the entire process. It was the supervisor's responsibility to ensure that every person performed his or her tasks properly and on time, and then handed the results to the next person in the process.

Given the lack of education and training most workers received at the time, Smith's principle was embraced widely. Many companies still operate on this division of labor principle today. Think about going to the movies: one person sells you a ticket, a different person collects your ticket, another person takes your snack order, and someone else prepares and gives you your snack. Although some division of labor makes sense, we can all think of frustrating situations where one person is doing nothing while another—the one you're waiting for—is overloaded with work.

Today's workers are far more educated and self-motivated than those Adam Smith observed in the 1700s. To accommodate this change in workers, companies assign people greater responsibilities and empower them to make decisions about how to do their work. Rather than completing one simple task and handing off the result to another worker, today's workers complete all or many of the procedures required to perform a process. At a minimum, they understand what procedures are required to perform a process.

When employees understand an entire process and clearly understand the expected result, they see where their jobs fit into the process and how their contributions work with others to produce that result. Because they understand the expected result, employees can eliminate bottlenecks and unnecessary tasks that may stand in their way or slow them down. Also, because employees are continuously identifying new customer requirements, employees who understand an entire process can respond quickly to changing customer needs.

Because today's workers have a better understanding of processes, they can see that changing one procedure within a process may affect the next procedure as well. When a single procedure changes, its effect on the entire process must be analyzed. Employees can perform that analysis only if they understand the entire process. This greater understanding of processes also means that companies can use simpler processes. Simpler processes can be used because, for example, companies can reduce handoffs or eliminate check points and reviews that may have been put in place to compensate for the fact that workers understood only their own specialized task.

Simpler processes are more efficient, less prone to error, and less expensive. Simpler processes also enable companies to eliminate management layers by allowing workers or teams of workers to make their own decisions, instead of waiting for management approval or direction. In a service desk setting, for example, analysts in some organizations are authorized to complete certain service requests, such as setting up a new user account, rather than referring those requests to a level two support group.

A strong business trend is to use business process management programs to achieve simpler, more efficient, and more effective processes. **Business process management (BPM)** is a systematic approach to improving an organization's business processes. BPM involves designing, measuring, and improving processes in an effort to ensure processes are aligned with customer needs. Processes may include the core processes used by a company to deliver products and services (such as manufacturing or financial services processes) or processes that support business activities (such as accounting, human resource management, and IT service management processes).

117

Common factors that prompt organizations to focus on business process improvement include:

- Reducing costs

- Increasing efficiency, effectiveness, productivity, and profitability

- Attracting new customers and retaining existing customers

- Attracting and retaining an effective workforce

- Supporting the delivery of new products and services (innovation)

- Maintaining a competitive advantage in the marketplace

- Complying with legal and regulatory controls

BPM programs may be triggered by changes in the way we live and work and by the introduction of new technologies. For example, web-based mobile and social technologies have created tremendous opportunities for companies to rethink how they interact with customers; attract and retain employees; and manage data, information, and knowledge. Simply implementing such technologies does not, however, guarantee success. Companies must revise existing or design new processes that take advantage of those technologies in way that supports the company's mission, goals, and priorities. BPM programs may also be triggered by the maturation of the organization and its understanding of processes and process improvement. Some processes are too simple when first implemented; or they may be too complex. As the organization matures and gains a better understanding of processes and how to design and improve them, the processes themselves can be refined to better match the organization's capabilities and resources.

Whether simple or complex, processes must be continually improved to remain effective. This is because customer expectations about the products and services that companies deliver are constantly changing, just as customer expectations about the services that the service desk delivers are constantly changing. Companies that are committed to continually improving their processes often use existing frameworks and standards.

Using Process Frameworks and Standards

Although it is possible to start with a clean sheet of paper when designing or improving a process, it is much more efficient to use an existing framework or standard as a starting point. A **framework** is a structure designed to enclose something. For example, an outline is a framework for a book. A framework may also describe concepts that can be used to solve or address complex issues. A process framework—such as ITIL—describes best practices that can be used to define and continually improve a given set of processes. Frameworks also provide a common vocabulary that organizations can use when describing and executing processes.

A **standard** is a document that contains an agreed-upon, repeatable way of doing something. A standard contains a formal specification and lists mandatory controls or rules that an organization must have in place to be certified.

Because a framework is not a standard, organizations can choose to adopt some practices and not others. This is an important distinction, as organizations often lack the resources required to adopt all of the practices described in a framework, at least initially. For example, ITIL describes more than 25 processes and hundreds of best practices. Few organizations have the resources to focus on all of these processes at once. Instead, most organizations initially adopt a basic set of practices for a small subset of processes and expand their use of the framework over time.

 ITIL does not prescribe a set order in which to implement processes. However, organizations often view incident management as a top priority and starting point given the role it plays in overall customer satisfaction.

The term *compliant* is sometimes erroneously used when discussing frameworks; for example, an organization may say that it is "ITIL-compliant." A framework is not a standard and thus lacks the mandatory controls needed for an organization to demonstrate compliance. Those mandatory controls are found in standards.

The world's largest developer and publisher of international standards is the **International Organization for Standardization**, also known as ISO. ISO is a network of the national standards institutes of 164 countries, with one member per country. The organization has a Central Secretariat in Geneva, Switzerland.

ISO standards are created by committees of experts who discuss and debate requirements until a consensus is reached on a draft agreement. Draft agreements are published for public review, and committee members use the feedback they receive to formulate a revised agreement. For an agreement to be accepted as an international standard, it must be voted on and approved by the ISO national members.

ISO standards are voluntary, and organizations can choose to comply with the standards—or not. However, to be certified as compliant with a standard, an organization must produce evidence that it has put in place *all* of the mandatory controls specified in the standard. This evidence must be presented to a third-party organization known as a registered certification body (RCB) during an independent audit.

Achieving ISO certification can cost an organization tens of thousands of dollars and can take months of effort. Companies that seek ISO certification typically do so to provide their customers assurance that quality processes are used to produce their products and services. ISO certification also gives companies a competitive advantage and helps attract customers. Some organizations are required to achieve ISO certification if they choose to do business with a particular customer or compete in a particular marketplace. Table 4-2 compares the characteristics of frameworks and standards.

Frameworks	Standards
Describe best practices	Define an agreed-upon, repeatable way of doing something
Provide guidance and suggestions	Define a formal specification
Support organizations' efforts to design and continually improve processes	Prescribe a minimum set of practices organizations must have in place to assure quality processes
Lack the mandatory controls needed for an organization to demonstrate compliance	List mandatory controls that an organization must have to be certified

Table 4-2   Characteristics of frameworks and standards

© Cengage Learning 2014

Many frameworks and ISO standards exist that enable IT organizations to manage and support information technology and continually improve the quality of their services. These frameworks and ISO standards fall into the following general categories:

 Frameworks and standards also exist that enable IT organizations to design and develop information technology—activities that are outside the scope of this book.

- **Quality management and improvement**—Focus on the ongoing management and improvement of an organization's processes and performance and its ability to satisfy customer requirements. Examples include Total Quality Management (TQM) and ISO 9000.

- **IT service management**—Focus on the management of IT services and on ensuring the quality of those services. Examples include ITIL and ISO/IEC 20000.

- **IT governance**—Focus on ensuring the investments an organization makes in information technology generate business value and on mitigating the risks that are associated with information technology. Examples include Control Objectives for Information and related Technology (COBIT) and ISO 38500.

- **Project management**—Focus on the management of projects and programs. A **project** is a temporary endeavor undertaken to complete a unique product, service, or result. A **program** may be used to manage one or more interdependent projects. Examples include Projects IN Controlled Environments, Version 2 (PRINCE2) and Project Management Body of Knowledge (PMBOK) and ISO 21500.

The service desk is not typically the primary group within IT responsible for IT governance and project management. For example, a company's board of directors and management team are ultimately responsible for IT governance. Project managers and, in some organizations, a Program Management Office (PMO) are responsible for project management.

However, the service desk does play an important role in quality management and IT service management. The following sections describe these frameworks and standards in greater detail.

Quality Management and Improvement Frameworks and Standards

Quality management and improvement frameworks and standards focus on the ongoing management and improvement of an organization's processes and performance, as well as its ability to satisfy customer requirements. A **requirement** is something that is necessary or essential. New requirements surface constantly. As a result, companies must continually assess the quality of their products and services, just as service desks must continually assess the quality of their services. **Quality** is a characteristic that measures how well products or services meet customer requirements.

Companies that have a quality program in place typically dedicate resources to activities such as developing, documenting, and improving processes. Some companies that establish quality programs are simply striving to use processes to continually improve. Other companies are striving to improve their business opportunities or to receive awards. Figure 4-2 lists the most common quality management and improvement frameworks and standards you may encounter when working in a service desk.

- Total Quality Management (TQM)

- Six Sigma

- ISO 9000 – International Standard for Quality Management Systems

---

Figure 4-2   Quality management and improvement frameworks and standards
© Cengage Learning 2014

Total Quality Management (TQM)

In the 1950s, Japan developed a system known as **Total Quality Control (TQC)** to implement *Kaizen* in the workplace. ***Kaizen*** means continuing improvement that involves everyone—managers and workers alike. TQC is based on the teachings of Dr. W. Edwards Deming, an American consultant who specialized in statistical studies. Dr. Deming was invited to Japan by the Union of Japanese Scientists and Engineers (JUSE) to present a series of lectures on the basic principles of statistical quality control. His teachings made a deep impression on the participants—executives, managers, and engineers of Japanese industries—and led to the development of TQC in Japan.

Although its roots are in Total Quality Control, today Total Quality Management is the term used more commonly. **Total Quality Management (TQM)** is a management approach to long-term success through customer satisfaction. TQM was initially coined by the United States Naval Air Systems Command to describe its Japanese-style management approach to quality improvement. Since then, TQM has taken on many meanings. For the most part, however, Total Quality Management relies on a single fundamental principle, which in today's competitive business climate very often serves as the core mission of any business: Maximize productivity while minimizing costs.

Productivity is an efficiency measure that relates output (goods and services produced) to input (the number of hours worked). Companies and departments that produce information and services sometimes have a hard time quantifying output because their results are less obvious than, for example, a manufacturing company whose products can be easily counted. **Costs** are the amounts paid to produce a product, such as workers' wages, salaries, and benefits; the facilities and equipment that workers use; and any materials and supplies they consume. When companies are able to maximize productivity while minimizing costs, they can expand their business, develop and introduce new products, increase the salaries and benefits they pay to workers, and so on.

For TQM to work, management must empower employees to continually gather information before taking action and to check the results of their actions to ensure that those actions achieve the desired results. This iterative cycle, illustrated in Figure 4-3, includes the steps Plan, Do, Check, and Act (PDCA). Popularized by Dr. W. Edwards Deming and known as the Deming Cycle, this cycle of quality improvement and control is widely used in business. Its philosophy of checking results or using performance measures to gauge needed improvements is found, in some form, in all other quality improvement programs.

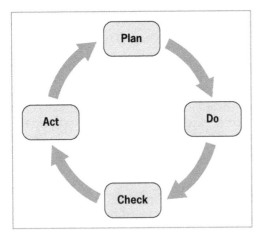

Figure 4-3 Deming Cycle
© Cengage Learning 2014

Six Sigma

Six Sigma is a disciplined, data-driven approach for eliminating defects in any process. The basic difference between TQM and Six Sigma is the approach. TQM views quality as conformance to requirements, whereas Six Sigma focuses on improving quality by reducing defects. Six Sigma was developed by Motorola engineers in the late 1970s and was popularized in the mid-1980s. The measurement-based strategy has enabled companies such as Motorola, GE, and AlliedSignal to save billions of dollars by focusing on process improvement. Leading (typically larger) companies that seek to increase profits by reducing the cost of poor quality often adopt Six Sigma.

 Lean Six Sigma combines the concepts of Lean Manufacturing and Six Sigma. Lean Manufacturing focuses on removing *waste* and improving the flow of processes and procedures. Six Sigma focuses on reducing *defects* by measuring standard deviations from an expected norm.

Organizations of all sizes can benefit from Six Sigma. However, adopting Six Sigma can itself be costly because capturing the data required to execute the Six Sigma processes can be quite labor intensive. Acquiring the skill needed to analyze that data can also be costly. Six Sigma processes are typically executed by certified professionals who hold distinctions such as Six Sigma Green Belts and Six Sigma Black Belts. Six Sigma Master Black Belts oversee process execution activities. An integral, interconnected set of Six Sigma activities is called DMAIC, which is the acronym for Define, Measure, Analyze, Improve, and Control.

 TQM, Six Sigma, and ISO 9000 are usually corporate-wide initiatives rather than efforts undertaken by individual departments or divisions on their own.

ISO 9000

ISO 9000 is a set of international standards for quality management. The first standard in the set, also called ISO 9000, establishes a starting point for understanding the set of standards and covers the basic concepts and vocabulary terms used in the ISO 9000 family. The second standard in the set, ISO 9001, is the most comprehensive of the standards. It applies to all types of industries and is as applicable to companies that deliver services such as financial or communication services, as it is to companies that manufacture products such as equipment or buildings. ISO 9001 contains the specifications that companies use to assess their ability to meet customer and applicable regulatory requirements. The remaining standards provide guidance that companies can use to manage their quality programs.

ISO 9000 certification provides companies doing business in today's global economy a way to demonstrate that they are committed to continually improving the processes used to produce their products and services. Many companies require their suppliers to become certified for the same reason.

To become certified, companies must document and distribute their processes in a manner that conforms to the ISO standards. Companies must train their employees in the documented processes and must be able to demonstrate through a series of quality audits that they are performing the processes as documented. These audits go beyond simply assessing the end result of a process—they also inspect the company's efforts to monitor and continually improve its processes through the use of performance measures. The standard also requires company executives to demonstrate their commitment to quality rather than simply delegate quality functions to junior administrators. This requirement that companies demonstrate continual improvement addresses past criticism that the focus of ISO 9000 was on documenting processes and not on quality performance.

Although becoming ISO 9000 certified is hard work, the focus on continual process improvement has enabled ISO 9000 certified companies to achieve dramatic reductions in customer complaints, significant reductions in operating costs, and increased demand for their products and services. As a result, ISO 9000 quality standards are accepted and employed by a wide variety of organizations worldwide.

IT Service Management Frameworks and Standards

IT service management frameworks and standards focus on the management of IT services and on ensuring the quality of those services. These frameworks and standards are unique to IT departments and companies that deliver IT-related services, so they include processes that are performed by the service desk. Figure 4-4 lists the most common IT service management frameworks and standards you may encounter when working in a service desk.

- Information Technology Infrastructure Library (ITIL)

- Microsoft Operations Framework (MOF)

- ISO/IEC 20000 – International Standard for IT Service Management

Figure 4-4   IT service management frameworks and standards
© Cengage Learning 2014

Information Technology Infrastructure Library (ITIL)

The best practice framework most commonly used to improve the quality of IT services is ITIL. A fundamental premise of ITIL is that IT organizations must adopt a service-oriented approach to managing IT services, versus the traditional product- or technology-centric approaches. In other words, IT organizations must recognize their role as service providers and strive to satisfy their customers' requirements. This philosophy applies whether IT serves internal customers, such as other departments or divisions within the same company, or external customers. The current version of ITIL, published in July 2011, provides guidance that IT organizations can use to meet customer needs by managing IT services as efficiently and effectively as possible. ITIL consists of the following five books that provide guidance on the various stages of a service lifecycle:

- *ITIL® Service Strategy*—Provides guidance on how to define and execute a service strategy within a service provider organization that meets the current and future requirements of its customers.

- *ITIL® Service Design*—Provides guidance for the design and development of services and service management processes.

- *ITIL® Service Transition*—Provides guidance for the transition of new and changed services into operations.

- *ITIL® Service Operation*—Provides guidance on achieving efficiency and effectiveness in the delivery and support of services.

- *ITIL® Continual Service Improvement*—Provides guidance in creating and maintaining value for customers through better design, introduction, and operation of services.

Together, these five books cover more than 25 processes that are responsible for the provision and management of effective IT services. These books also describe the teams or functions within IT that execute those processes. One of the teams described in detail in the *ITIL® Service Operation* book is the service desk.

ITIL is used by organizations of all types and sizes and is enabling organizations to recognize millions of dollars in cost savings. For example, Procter & Gamble has publicly attributed nearly $125 million in annual IT cost savings to its adoption of ITIL. Other companies using ITIL include British Airways, Microsoft, Hewlett-Packard, IBM, Walmart, Target, Sony, Disney, Citi, Bank of America, Barclay's, Boeing, and Toyota. ITIL is also being used by numerous government agencies and academic institutions worldwide. Many vendors that publish IT service management solutions have made their products consistent with the ITIL vocabulary and best practices. As a result, its guidance, vocabulary, and service lifecycle have become familiar to service desk management and staff.

Due to the considerable culture change ITIL requires, adopting it can be difficult. Adopting all or most of the processes described in ITIL often takes an organization several years. The most successful companies take their time and recognize that incremental improvement is essential. These companies implement only those processes that support the organization's mission, goals, and priorities, and implement those processes only to the extent that benefits the organization. In other words, the processes do not have to be "perfect." Rather, they must reflect the organization's current capabilities and needs. The Deming Cycle and other continual improvement methods and techniques can then be used to improve the processes over time.

The most successful organizations provide training to their management teams and staff when adopting a framework such as ITIL. Many organizations use the ITIL qualification scheme to certify key individuals and ensure they have the knowledge needed to contribute to the organization's improvement efforts.

 Learn more about ITIL and the ITIL qualification scheme at *www.best-management-practice.com*. View an illustration of the ITIL service lifecycle at *www.best-management-practice.com/serviceOperation2011_demo*.

Microsoft Operations Framework (MOF)

Another widely used IT service management framework is **Microsoft Operations Framework (MOF)**, which is a collection of best practices, principles, and models that offers guidance to IT organizations for managing their IT services. Originally introduced by Microsoft in 1999 and based on ITIL, the framework has evolved into MOF 4.0, which was introduced in July 2008. MOF offers practical, question-based advice and is generally viewed as more prescriptive than ITIL. For this reason, many organizations use MOF in conjunction with ITIL, turning to MOF when they want to understand *how* to achieve a best practice that may be described in ITIL.

The guidance in MOF encompasses all of the activities and processes involved in managing an IT service: its conception, development, operation, maintenance, and retirement. MOF organizes these activities and processes into Service Management Functions (SMFs), which are grouped together in phases that mirror the IT service lifecycle.

The MOF IT service lifecycle is composed of three ongoing phases and one foundational layer that operates throughout all of the other phases. The three ongoing phases and the foundational layer are:

- **Plan**—Planning and optimizing the IT service to align with the business strategy.
- **Deliver**—Designing and delivering the IT service.

- **Operate**—Ongoing operation and support.
- **Manage**—Underlying foundation of IT governance, risk management, compliance, team organization, and change management.

Learn more about MOF and download it for free at *www.microsoft.com/mof.*

Many organizations use a combination of frameworks such as ITIL and MOF to achieve ISO/IEC 20000 certification.

ISO/IEC 20000

ISO/IEC 20000 is an international standard for IT service management. ISO/IEC 20000 promotes an integrated process approach that companies can use to deliver IT services that meet business and customer requirements. Figure 4-5 illustrates the processes that are included in the ISO/IEC 20000 standard. These processes are performed by all of the various groups within IT. Only some, such as incident and problem management, are performed by the service desk.

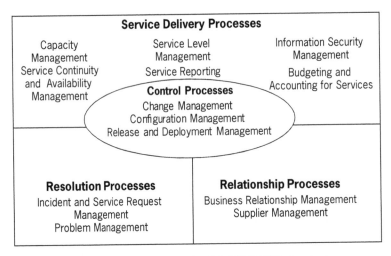

Figure 4-5   Processes included in the ISO/IEC 20000 standard

Initially introduced in December 2005 and recently updated, ISO/IEC 20000 consists of two parts:

- **ISO/IEC 20000-1: 2011** —The requirements—"shalls"—for a service provider to plan, establish, implement, operate, monitor, review, maintain, and improve a service management system (SMS).

- **ISO/IEC 20000-2: 2012** —The guidance—"shoulds"— for service management processes within the scope of ISO/IEC 20000-1.

In any ISO standard, "shall" statements represent what organizations *must* do to be in compliance with the standard and realize its objectives. The "should" statements provide examples and suggestions that organizations can use to interpret the requirements and apply them effectively.

For example, ISO/IEC 20000-1 states that there *shall* (must) be a documented procedure for recording all incidents. The standard does not say *how* incidents must be recorded. It just says that organizations seeking certification must be prepared to show evidence that incidents are being recorded in a manner that complies with the documented procedure. Evidence may include policies and procedures directing employees to log incidents, training programs describing how to log incidents, and an incident management system where incidents are logged. ISO/IEC 20000-2 suggests that incidents should be handled consistently and that incident data should be stored in a medium that is suitable for the size or complexity of the organization.

ISO/IEC 20000 was originally developed using ITIL as a starting point; however, ISO/IEC 20000 is not a formal ITIL certification. The ISO/IEC 20000 standard is much more specific and succinct than ITIL. ISO/IEC 20000 describes what organizations must do to prove that they are complying with an internationally recognized IT service management standard.

To achieve ISO/IEC 20000 certification, organizations must be audited by a registered certification body and provide evidence of compliance with the requirements reflected in the standard. In other words, they must provide evidence of compliance with the *shall* statements specified in the standard. Hundreds of organizations worldwide have achieved ISO/IEC 20000 certification, including managed service providers, financial institutions, government agencies, and academic institutions.

Not all companies that use the ISO/IEC 20000 standard seek certification. Achieving certification can be costly and requires a concerted effort on the part of both the IT organization and its customers. Because the standard is voluntary, some organizations simply use the standard to benchmark their performance. In other words, they compare their practices to those reflected in the standard without incurring the cost of an independent audit. Such a technique can be particularly effective for organizations that lack the resources needed to adopt all of the guidance provided in a framework such as ITIL. Because the standard is relatively succinct, these organizations can focus on those practices viewed as mandatory by the standard.

Learn more about ISO/IEC 20000 and about organizations that have achieved certification at *www.isoiec20000certification.com*.

Like ITIL, certification courses are available that enable individuals within an organization to acquire the knowledge needed to understand the standard and contribute to benchmarking or certification efforts.

Common Process Characteristics

Many companies use techniques from each of these frameworks and standards to develop their own approach to designing and continually improving processes. According to a 2011 study conducted by *InformationWeek* and HDI, more than 50 percent of the support organizations polled already are working with ITIL and an additional 20 percent of organizations are planning to implement ITIL (*State of the IT Service Desk*, InformationWeek/HDI, June 2011). In the same survey, many of these companies also reported using one or more other frameworks and standards. For example, 44 percent reported using Six Sigma or Lean Six Sigma, 40 percent have quality management/TQM programs in place, 36 percent use ISO standards, and 19 percent use Microsoft Operation Framework.

It is possible to use multiple frameworks and standards because the vocabularies are fairly consistent and the process maturity lifecycle represented by each is essentially the same. Processes must be:

- **Defined**—The processes' purpose, objectives, and goals must be clearly stated.

- **Documented**—The processes' associated procedures and vocabulary must be published.

- **Managed via performance metrics**—The processes must be monitored and measured to ensure conformance to requirements.

- **Continually improved**—The processes must be continually refined to meet new and changing requirements.

Learn more about the Certified Process Design Engineer (CPDE) certification, which imparts best practices in designing and improving IT service management processes, at *www.best-management-practice.com*.

To be successful, employees must understand how these quality improvement frameworks and standards help companies to produce quality products and services. For example, understanding the vocabularies associated with these frameworks and standards enables employees to communicate more effectively with customers, coworkers, and management as a consistent vocabulary is being used. Understanding the importance of processes and the processes being performed within an organization enables employees to help identify opportunities to improve those processes. Anyone interested in pursuing a career in IT benefits from having knowledge of and holding certifications in these frameworks and standards.

Common Processes Used in Service Desks

Processes and procedures are particularly important in the fast-paced service desk setting, where the bottom line is always to meet or exceed customer expectations. A successful service desk must perform several tightly integrated processes to achieve customer satisfaction. These processes are integrated because the output produced by one process might be used as input to another process. Figure 4-6 lists the IT service management processes most commonly found in a service desk. These processes are all defined in ITIL and most are defined in ISO/IEC 20000. These processes are needed to manage and support IT services and ensure customer satisfaction. These processes also enable the service desk to work more efficiently and effectively.

- **Incident management**—The process responsible for managing the lifecycle of incidents.

- **Problem management**—The process responsible for managing the lifecycle of problems.

- **Request fulfillment**—The process responsible for managing the lifecycle of service requests.

- **Knowledge management**—The process responsible for gathering, storing, and sharing information and knowledge within an organization.

- **Change management**—The process responsible for controlling the lifecycle of changes, enabling beneficial changes to be made with minimal disruption to IT services.

- **Service asset and configuration management (SACM)**—The process responsible for ensuring that the assets required to deliver services are properly controlled, and that accurate and reliable information about those assets is available when and where it is needed.

Figure 4-6 Processes commonly found in a service desk
© Cengage Learning 2014

The service desk plays an important role in each of these processes, which are vital to the success of an IT organization. Incident management, request fulfillment, problem management, and knowledge management are essential to achieving customer satisfaction—the main goal of a service desk. Change management and service asset and configuration management (SACM) are just as important. Change management allows changes to occur as quickly as possible with the optimal amount of risk and impact (and the fewest number of incidents). SACM facilitates the capture and maintenance of information about the products and services that the IT organization delivers and supports. The service desk and others involved in support use this information to diagnose incidents more quickly and to determine the potential impact of incidents and changes. For example, analysts who perform the incident management process often use the information collected through the SACM process to determine where a failing hardware device is located or what software is installed on a customer's laptop. The service desk and others involved in problem management also use this information to proactively prevent incidents and problems.

These processes may not exist in some companies, or they may be defined differently from one company to the next. For example, some companies do not treat incident and request fulfillment as separate processes. Some companies adopt the philosophy that any time a customer cannot do something he or she wants to do, it is an incident. Other companies view any customer contact as a request for service, even when that request for service involves fixing an incident. Problem management may not exist in companies that lack the skilled resources needed to perform the process. Other companies combine some aspects of problem management with incident management by, for example, ensuring that problem management is always involved in investigating the root cause of major incidents. Knowledge management may not exist because it is difficult to implement and some companies lack the technology needed to maintain this process successfully. The change management and SACM processes, although necessary, may not exist in some companies because they do not have the resources to perform these processes or they simply do not recognize the importance of these processes. Some companies may handle the change management, knowledge management, and SACM processes informally, or may use a disparate set of tools to support these processes.

A clearly defined process ensures that people focus their efforts on tasks that produce the intended result. In a service desk setting, this means satisfying customers.

Incident Management Process

ITIL defines **incident management** as the process responsible for managing the life cycle of incidents. The objective of incident management is to restore service as quickly as possible in an effort to minimize the impact of incidents on business activities.

Common incidents include a broken device, an error message, and a system outage.

Incidents can be detected by people using technology who contact the service desk after encountering an unplanned or unexpected interruption to an IT service. Incidents can also be detected by technologies such as monitoring systems that automatically detect events in the infrastructure. ITIL defines an **event** as a change of state that has significance for the management of an IT service or other configuration item. ITIL defines a **configuration item (CI)** as any component or other service asset that needs to be managed in order to deliver an IT service. Examples of CIs include services, hardware, software, formal documents such as SLAs, people, and buildings. In some organizations, a separate process called **event management** captures and logs events, analyzes them, and determines an appropriate action. Actions can include taking steps to avoid incidents, such as automatically archiving data to prevent a storage disk from filling to capacity, or triggering a standard change to add additional capacity. Actions can also include triggering an incident, which is then handled by the service desk.

In some organizations, incident management includes answering customers' questions and inquiries. **Questions**, such as "How do I . . . ?," are customer requests for instruction on how to use a product. Questions occur not when a product is broken, but when the customer simply needs help using it. **Inquiries**, such as "When will the new release of software arrive?," are customer requests for information. Inquiries, like questions, typically occur not when the product is broken, but when the customer wants a current status report. Many companies distinguish among incidents, questions, and inquiries because they represent varying degrees of impact and speak differently to product and company performance. For example, a customer calling to inquire about the date for the next release of a software package may not be dissatisfied with the current product; instead he or she is eagerly looking forward to the new version. On the other hand, a customer who gets error messages or loses data when trying to use a software package clearly is dissatisfied, and the company must try to resolve the incident quickly or risk losing that customer. Distinguishing among incidents, questions, and inquiries also makes it possible for companies to determine, when applicable, the best way to enable self-help. For example, some companies provide solutions to known errors in an online knowledge base. "How do I...?" questions might also be answered in an online knowledge base or via a discussion forum. Some companies provide information about upcoming releases on an announcements page on their web site or in press releases sent via email.

 Some service desks handle questions and inquiries via the request fulfillment process. Others use a code to distinguish among incidents, questions, inquiries, and service requests in their incident management system.

Incident management involves a series of activities that can occur consecutively, simultaneously, or not at all. These activities include:

- **Incident identification**—Detecting and identifying incidents or potential incidents through the monitoring of events, trend analysis, and observation; also called incident recognition.

- **Incident logging**—Notifying a central point such as the service desk about an incident and logging information about the incident, typically in an incident management system. Incident logging includes categorizing the incident and assigning a priority (discussed below).

- **Initial diagnosis**—Using available resources to determine what service or configuration item has failed or is being impacted and how to correct it. Initial diagnosis is typically performed by the service desk and may involve using diagnostic scripts, known errors, workarounds, and information found in a knowledge management system. A **workaround** involves temporarily circumventing or minimizing the impact of an incident. Workarounds such as rebooting a PC or temporarily disabling a software feature can make the failing component usable again, even if only partially, thus restoring service to the customer.

- **Incident escalation**—Adding new or additional resources as needed to resolve an incident. Incident escalation may involve raising an incident from one level of support to the next or it may involve engaging or notifying management.

- **Investigation and diagnosis**—Using available resources on an ongoing basis to determine what has gone wrong and how to correct it.

- **Resolution and recovery**—Performing the corrective action that restores service to the customer's satisfaction by repairing, replacing, or modifying the affected service or configuration item. The fix to an incident may be a workaround that restores service by temporarily modifying the source of the incident. The fix may also involve a more permanent resolution aimed at eliminating the root cause of the incident. The root cause of an incident is typically identified by problem management. Permanent resolutions are typically applied under the control of change management.

- **Incident closure**—Verifying that the incident is resolved, the customer is satisfied, and all incident details are recorded accurately and completely. This may include recording the suspected or possible root cause.

- **Management review**—Evaluating the efficiency and effectiveness of the incident management process and the associated reporting system.

The management review task differentiates incident "tracking" from incident "management." **Incident tracking** follows *one* incident from identification to closure. Incident management involves reviewing *all* incidents to help ensure that they have been resolved in a timely fashion. Incident management also captures the data needed by problem management to prevent similar incidents in the future. Tracking a single incident through to closure is important because it ensures the customer's satisfaction. Looking at all incidents that have occurred allows the service desk to identify related or recurring incidents, trends, and incident-prevention opportunities.

 Service desks resolve a higher percentage of incidents when effective processes and procedures are in place and when analysts have the needed technical skills, tools, and information.

The flowchart in Figure 4-7 shows how responsibility for specific tasks changes as an incident moves from identification to closure in the incident management process. Each level tries to resolve the customer's incident before handing it off to the next level. After the incident is resolved and any necessary change is implemented, the incident owner contacts the customer to make sure the customer is satisfied with the solution before formally closing the incident record.

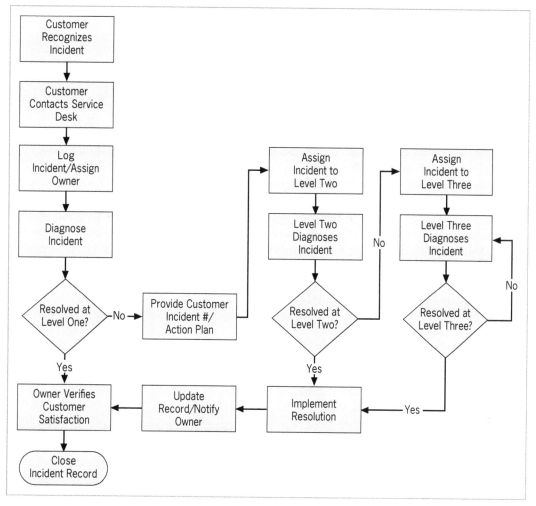

Figure 4-7 Incident management process
© Cengage Learning 2014

This flowchart is a fairly simple representation of how the incident management process may work within a company. The process varies from one company to the next and is refined continually. Once the overall process is defined or refined, a company develops procedures so that everyone involved in the process of solving incidents understands exactly who needs to do what to satisfy customers. These procedures, along with the company's policies, clearly define how to perform each step in the process. A **policy** is a formal document that describes the intentions and expectations of management. Companies may define policies with regard to issues such as:

- Customer entitlement

- Incident categorization and prioritization

- Incident escalation

- Incident ownership

- Incident notification

The following sections provide a brief description of each of these issues.

Customer Entitlement

While the service desk is logging an incident and before trying to resolve the incident, it may check **customer entitlement**, which is the determination of whether the customer is authorized to receive support, and if so, the level of support the customer should receive. Some companies don't need to determine entitlement. For example, internal service desks that provide "free" support to the company's employees rarely determine entitlement. Companies that charge for all or some service desk services (such as after-hours support and premium support) verify that a customer's service contract is current or that the customer is entitled to the level of support being requested. In many companies, entitlement consists simply of asking the customer for a product key, customer ID or contract number, or personal identification number (PIN).

Incident Categorization and Prioritization

After entitlement is verified, the service desk continues logging the incident by isolating the affected service or configuration item and recording its category. It also must determine the incident's impact and urgency and record its priority.

Categorizing an incident is an important step. **Categorization** involves recording the type of incident being reported. Most incident management systems provide a multi-level approach to categorization. These category levels may also be referred to as an organization's subject tree. Figure 4-8 shows sample incident category levels.

 The same category or subject tree used to record incidents is often also used to record problems, service requests, and changes.

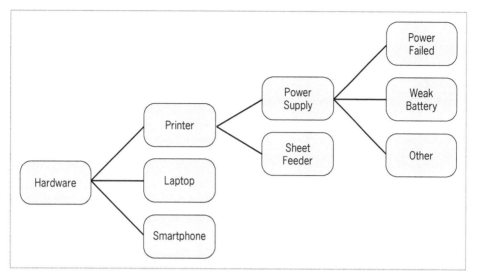

Figure 4-8 Sample incident category levels
© Cengage Learning 2014

Identifying the correct category is critical because the category field is used in a variety of ways, including:

- Managing workflow (such as for escalations)
- Navigating decision tree logic (such as for diagnostic scripts)
- Identifying SLAs and determining targets
- Defining priorities
- Searching knowledge bases
- Analyzing trends
- Performing root cause analysis
- Producing metrics and reports
- Reporting on SLA achievements

The specific incident categories vary among organizations because they are based on each organization's services, systems, networks, and products. They are also based on each organization's requirements for retrieving data by searching the incident management or knowledge management systems or by producing reports. A common technique can be used, however, to define categories and to determine the number of subsequent category levels required. Generally, the first level includes a limited number of broad categories that become more specific in subsequent levels. These levels are often broken down as follows:

- Category (High level)
  - Start with broad categories (10 or fewer)
  - Examples include hardware, software, application, network, database, and security
  - Examples of service-oriented categories include accounts and passwords, connectivity services, desktop services, printing services, and security services
- Subcategory (More specific)
  - Further defines categories
  - Example subcategories for the "hardware" category may include printer, laptop, and smartphone
- Item (Most specific)
  - Further defines subcategories
  - Example items for a "printer" may include power supply and sheet feeder
- Symptom (Customer perspective)
  - Error or symptom being experienced by customer
  - Example symptoms include a specific error message appearing on the printer display such as paper jam or printer ink low

The category field is often composed of a series of drop-down menus that aid data entry by guiding the analyst through the category levels. For example, once "hardware" is selected as a category, only hardware-related subcategories are displayed. Or, once a service is selected, only options related to that service are displayed.

An "other" option is often included for when the correct category, subcategory, or item is unclear. Having an "other" option is useful as without it, analysts have no choice but to select a category, subcategory, or item that they know is incorrect. This may then trigger an inappropriate workflow, decision tree, or SLA. However, the "other" option can be misused. To prevent misuse, a service desk team leader or member of the technical support team should monitor the "other" option to determine if analysts need training or if a new category, subcategory, or item value is needed.

Prioritizing the incident is equally important. ITIL defines **priority** as a category used to identify the relative importance of an incident, problem, or change and is based on impact and urgency. In other words, priority determines the order in which incidents, problems, or changes are handled, and can also be used to determine the order in which service requests are handled. Although first-come, first-served may sound fair, it is ultimately not in the best interest of the business. For example, incidents that have a high impact on the business, such as an incident affecting the company's revenue-generating web site, must be resolved more quickly than minor or inconvenient incidents. Figure 4-9 shows a sample matrix that uses impact and urgency to define a priority code.

	Impact		
Urgency	**High**	**Medium**	**Low**
High	1	2	3
Medium	2	3	4
Low	3	4	4

Figure 4-9 Sample priority code matrix
© Cengage Learning 2014

ITIL defines **impact** as the effect an incident, problem, or change is having on business processes. For example, an incident that affects many customers is typically considered to have a higher impact than an incident that affects one customer. Other factors that influence impact include risk to life or limb, potential financial loss or regulatory breach, and the role of the customer. For example, incidents affecting very important people (VIPs) such as executives or high-ranking politicians are often assigned a higher impact. Many organizations define a separate set of procedures for handling **major incidents** that are causing significant business impact. The service desk plays an important role in major incidents by ensuring that all activities are recorded and that users are kept fully informed of incident status.

Some organizations use the term **severity** to communicate the impact incidents are having on the business.

ITIL defines **urgency** as a measure of how long it will be until an incident, problem, or change has a significant impact on the business. Impact and urgency combine to determine priority. Criteria for determining impact, urgency, priority, and target resolution time are typically defined in SLAs or, in the absence of SLAs, an organization's policies and procedures. **Target resolution time** is the time frame within which the support organization is expected to resolve the incident. As shown in Table 4-3, each priority code has a target resolution time. Also, some companies establish guidelines for **target response time**, the time frame within which the service desk or level two group acknowledges the incident, diagnoses the incident, and provides the customer with an estimated target resolution time. Target response time guidelines ensure that incidents, particularly incidents that are submitted or escalated electronically, are acknowledged and that sufficient diagnosis is performed to determine the impact and urgency, and therefore priority, of the incident. Target response time guidelines also ensure customers know that their incidents have been received and prioritized and will be handled in a timeframe in keeping with the priority.

Priority	Definition	Examples
1	• Service, system or device down • Critical business impact • No workaround available • Begin resolution activities immediately • Bypass/recover within four hours • Resolve within 24 hours	• A network device is not working and many customers are affected • The only printer that can print checks or special forms is malfunctioning • A real-time critical application, such as payroll or the company's web site, is down
2	• Service, system or device down or level of service degraded • Potential business impact • Alternative or workaround available • Resolve within 48 hours	• A slow response time on the network is severely affecting a large number of customers • The network is down, but customers can temporarily work offline • A product is usable, but its use is restricted due to memory constraints
3	• Not critical • Customer can wait • A workaround is possible • Resolve within 72 hours	• A printer is down, but customers can route their output to a similar printer down the hall • One of many registers in a retail store is down at a slow time of the month
4	• Not critical • Customer can wait • A workaround is possible with no operational impact • Time to resolve negotiated with customer	• Intermittent errors that the customer can work around • Laptop fan is noisy and stays on for an extended period of time

Table 4-3   Sample priority definitions

© Cengage Learning 2014

Determining incident priority can be a difficult challenge for service desk analysts. Customers often insist their incidents are critical when they may be relatively minor compared to other incidents. To combat this, many companies publish definitions with specific examples of each incident priority so that both customers and the service desk define priority in the same way.

Incident priority typically remains the same throughout the life of an incident. This ensures that an incident is resolved in the proper time frame and that it is not forgotten or neglected. It also ensures that ad hoc, daily, weekly, and month-end reports accurately reflect the priority of all outstanding incidents. However, obtaining new or additional information, such as a higher impact or decreased urgency, could prompt a change in the priority.

Make sure you understand your company's priorities and target resolution times so you can give customers an honest estimate of when to expect a resolution or status update. Promising a swift resolution that can't be delivered creates dissatisfaction.

Also, in some organizations, the incident priority increases if an incident is not resolved within its target resolution time, the customer's down time is excessive, the incident recurs, or management directs it. Management may increase the priority of an incident when, for example, the customer affected is a VIP, the customer previously had a similar incident that was not resolved to the customer's satisfaction, or management simply makes a judgment call and prioritizes one incident over another.

Incident Escalation

Sometimes, the service desk is unable to resolve an incident or may lack the authority needed to resolve the incident. In other cases, the service desk may be unable to find a workaround during initial diagnosis. For those cases, the service desk needs clearly defined escalation procedures for each type of potential incident. **Escalation** (or escalate) means to raise an incident from one level to another, such as from level one to level two, to dedicate new or additional resources to the incident. The incident's priority influences how quickly the service desk escalates the incident from one level to the next. For example, a company's incident management policies may dictate that the service desk escalates high-priority incidents quickly to level two and, if necessary, to level three. Escalation ensures that the support organization resolves incidents in the most efficient and cost-effective manner possible—whether the service desk, a level two group, or a level three group resolves them. Escalation also ensures that appropriate incident notification activities occur until the incident is resolved.

ITIL defines two types of escalation. **Functional escalation** transfers an incident from one line of support to the next. Functional escalation occurs when greater knowledge or authority is required to resolve an incident or a target time frame has been exceeded. In ITIL, incident ownership remains with the service desk regardless of where the incident is escalated. **Hierarchic escalation** occurs when management is involved in the incident management process, even if only for information purposes. Hierarchic escalation occurs when steps are taking too long, there is contention about assignments, or additional resources are needed (such as vendor resources) to resolve an incident. In such cases, the company's policies define how and when the individual handling the incident or a member of the service desk should engage management.

Customers sometimes perceive that the service desk escalates an incident because it does not have the knowledge or ability to solve the incident. Although this is true in some cases, the service desk often escalates incidents based on a **target escalation time**, a time constraint placed on each level that ensures that incident resolution activities are proceeding at an appropriate pace. For example, a company might establish the guideline that if level one doesn't find a solution within 30 minutes, it escalates the incident to level two. The service desk might also escalate an incident because of a security consideration or to involve a resource that is closer to the incident (such as an on-site field service representative). Figure 4-10 shows how a PC hardware incident might be escalated.

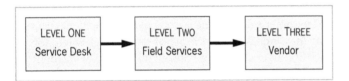

Figure 4-10 Sample escalation sequence for a PC hardware incident
© Cengage Learning 2014

The ultimate goal is to resolve most incidents at level one and to escalate only a small percentage of incidents to level three. Escalating an incident from level one does not always indicate lack of skill at the service desk. For example, the service desk may have to hand off the incident to field services simply because it doesn't have the tools to diagnose the incident remotely and must send someone to the site. As incidents escalate, each level must document its efforts to resolve the incident, including communications with the customer, and pass along as much information as possible to the next level. This enables analysts at each level to learn how they can handle similar incidents in the future. This also enables anyone who inquires to determine the current status including the incident owner, the customer, IT management, and IT staff.

Each level has specific responsibilities and activities. Level one is the initial point of contact for customers when they have an incident. For example, a customer experiencing an error message while using a software application contacts the service desk to report the incident. The customer reaches a level one analyst, who then performs the following activities:

- Gathers data about the incident—including its category and priority—and creates an incident ticket.

- Provides the customer an incident number.

- Diagnoses the incident and resolves it, if possible, using available tools and procedures.

- Escalates the incident to level two as necessary.

- Documents the incident's current status, along with all steps taken to diagnose or resolve the incident.

- Retains ownership of escalated incidents in an effort to ensure timely resolution.

- Ensures that the customer has an up-to-date status.

- Ensures that the customer is satisfied after the incident is resolved.

- Closes the incident ticket.

If the level one analyst cannot resolve the customer's incident, then the incident escalates to a level two person or group. Level two might be a software development group or a network support group that has greater authority (such as system access rights or permissions) than level one. Level two might also be a subject matter expert who has specialized knowledge. Continuing the earlier example, the level one analyst contacts the application support group responsible for the software application that is generating the error message. The person or group at level two performs the following activities:

- Acknowledges the assignment from level one.

- Reviews the data provided by level one.

- Uses specialized tools or contacts the customer as needed to gather additional data.

- Resolves the incident within the time frame required by the incident's priority.

- Provides the customer and other interested parties, such as the incident owner and management, with ongoing communication regarding the incident's status; this communication typically occurs via the incident management system.

- Reassigns the incident when appropriate (for example, to other level two service providers if the diagnosis determines that another group's skills are needed).

- Documents the incident's current status, along with all steps taken to diagnose or resolve the incident.

- Escalates the incident to level three when necessary.

 The groups designated as level two and level three vary from one organization to the next.

If level two cannot resolve the customer's incident, the incident then escalates to level three. Level three is the person or group that resolves complex incidents that are beyond the scope of level two. This level might involve multiple technical areas (for example, the network architecture group and the application development group may work together to solve an incident), hardware or software vendors, consultants, or a subject matter expert. Continuing the example, the application support group may find it necessary to contact the developer or software publisher of the product that is producing the error. The person or group at level three performs the following activities:

- Acknowledges the assignment from level two.

- Reviews the data provided by levels one and two.

- Uses specialized tools or contacts the customer as needed to gather additional data.

- Provides the customer and other interested parties, such as the incident owner and management, with ongoing communication regarding the incident's status; this communication typically occurs via the incident management system.

- Resolves the incident within the time frame required by the incident's priority.

- Oversees resolution activities that require multiple technical areas, a third-party vendor, or a consultant.

- Documents the incident's current status, along with all steps taken to diagnose or resolve the incident.

After an incident is escalated to level three, any and all resources needed to solve the incident are engaged and work together until the incident is resolved. Occasionally, incidents cannot be resolved. For example, the solution to an incident may require that the software publisher change the software in a way the publisher is not willing to do. In that type of situation, the vendor's response is communicated to the customer—the person or group who relays the information to the customer varies from one situation to the next—and efforts are made to provide the customer an acceptable workaround. A high percentage of incidents can, however, be solved to the customer's satisfaction at level one, and only the most complex incidents escalate through level two to level three. Again, the goal is to solve as many incidents as possible at level one.

INTERVIEW WITH...

Courtesy of Fry-Consultants

Malcolm Fry
President
Fry-Consultants
United Kingdom
www.theitillitebook.com

In the past 10 years, service desks have gotten very good at first level incident resolution. They've had to in some respects because service and support is being looked at in a different way. Once considered a back office role, the service desk is now part of the front office and the impact of incident management is hugely magnified. Consider a retailer with an online store. If the company's web site is down, the CEO may now have a direct line to the service desk to ask, "Why is our biggest store down?"

People entering the service desk field today are joining an industry that is increasingly important, and the level of professional opportunity is proportional. You could say that, in the last 10 years, the service desk has gone from being simply a job to being a profession with career prospects, qualifications, and recognition. Working in a service desk will enable you to hone your problem-solving skills and, more importantly in the coming years, your problem-elimination skills. Going into the future, service desks must get better at problem elimination, which can be accelerated by adopting a best practice framework such as ITIL. They must integrate their processes, use good processes to expose bad processes, and get better at harnessing technology—all in an effort to prevent incidents, rather than simply fixing them quickly. If people want to be exposed to how a business works and how they can impact a company's bottom line, there is no better place to start than the service desk.

Incident Ownership

The concept of **incident ownership** ensures that, when the service desk analyst cannot resolve an incident during the first contact or escalates the incident to a person or group outside of the service desk, an incident owner is designated. The **incident owner** is an employee of the support organization who acts as a customer advocate and proactively ensures that an incident is resolved to the customer's satisfaction. When an incident owner is designated, the customer shouldn't have to initiate another call. Nor should the customer have to call the different groups involved in solving the incident to find out the incident's status or progress. The incident owner maintains contact with the customer. In addition, the incident owner:

- Tracks the current status of the incident, including who is working on the incident and where the incident is in the process.

- When possible, identifies related incidents.

- Ensures that the incident is assigned correctly and not passed along from level to level or group to group without any effort being made to identify a resolution.

- Ensures that appropriate notification activities occur when the incident is reported, escalated, and resolved.

- Before closing an incident, verifies that all steps taken to resolve the incident are documented and that the customer is satisfied with the resolution.

- Closes the incident ticket.

In many companies, the incident management system automates many of these activities and makes it possible for anyone in the service desk to serve as the incident owner. These tools use business rules to trigger alerts when an incident requires follow up. ITIL best practice guidance suggests that only the incident owner (service desk) can close the incident and does so only after verifying that the customer is satisfied. Figure 4-11 shows a sample escalation sequence where the level one analyst and the incident owner are the same person.

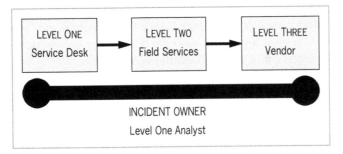

Figure 4-11 Sample escalation sequence with incident owner
© Cengage Learning 2014

In some companies, the incident owner changes as incidents are escalated from one level to the next. The person designated to work on the incident must accept responsibility for the incident and agree to assume ownership before the previous incident owner transfers responsibility for the incident (ownership) to the new owner. This approach works only when managers in the organization hold the individuals designated as incident owners accountable to the policies and targets specified in the incident management process. When managers do not hold incident owners accountable to the process, it is common to see incidents transferred from one support group to another with little effort being made to seek a resolution and little contact with the customer. This often occurs because the individuals who work in level two and level three support groups do not view satisfying customers as part of their job description. For this reason, a best practice remedy is to have the service desk assume ownership of all incidents.

Incident management is often known as a "closed loop process" because before the incident lifecycle is considered complete, the customer who reports an incident must accept the solution (i.e., close the loop).

Ownership is critical to the incident management process. Without it, customer dissatisfaction invariably occurs. Ownership forces everyone involved in the incident management process to stay focused on the customer's need to have the incident solved in a timely fashion and to be informed when the incident requires more than the expected time to resolve.

Incident Notification

An extremely important part of incident management is promoting awareness that an incident has occurred and regularly communicating its status. These activities are known as incident notification. **Notification** informs all of the stakeholders in the incident management process (including management, the customer, and service desk analysts) about the status of outstanding incidents. Notification can occur when an incident is reported or escalated, when an incident is nearing or has exceeded a predefined threshold (such as its target resolution time), or when an incident is resolved.

Notification to each of the stakeholders occurs at different points and has different goals. For example, *management* notification is appropriate when:

- The incident is high priority (e.g., a critical service or a VIP is being impacted).
- The incident priority has changed.
- The target resolution time has been or is about to be reached.
- Required resources are not available to determine or implement a solution.
- The incident has been transferred repeatedly from one level two or level three group to another without a resolution.
- The customer expresses dissatisfaction.

In each of these cases, notification keeps management aware of incidents that might require management intervention. The goals of management notification are to ensure that:

- Management knows the current status of high priority incidents.
- Management knows the current status of incidents that are nearing or have exceeded a predefined threshold. For example, the target resolution time has been exceeded or a level two group is not acknowledging an incident that has been assigned to them.
- Management has sufficient information to make decisions (such as add more resources, determine what group an incident should be assigned to, or reassign responsibilities), follow up with the customer, or call in other management.
- Management actions are recorded in the incident record so that everyone affected by or involved in solving the incident knows what decisions management has made or what steps they have taken to follow up with the customer or involve other management.

These goals make sure that the customer's incident is being addressed and responded to in an appropriate time and way.

Like management notification, *customer* notification is appropriate in specific situations, such as when:

- The incident priority has changed.
- The target resolution time will not be met.
- Customer resources are required to implement a solution.
- The incident is a high priority and justifies frequent status updates.
- The customer has been promised status updates at certain times.
- The customer was dissatisfied with earlier solutions.
- The incident is resolved.

Customer notification keeps the customer informed about the progress of incident resolution activities. The goals of customer notification are to ensure that:

- The customer knows the current status of the incident.
- Customer comments or concerns are recorded in the incident record and addressed.
- The customer's satisfaction with a resolution is verified before the incident is closed.

These goals make sure that the customer knows that the incident is being addressed and responded to in an appropriate time and way.

Service desks deliver value by: (1) making it easy for customers to report incidents; (2) delivering solutions; and (3) ensuring that incidents that cannot be resolved immediately are addressed in the required time frame. One of the most common customer complaints is that the service desk did not keep him or her informed. Remember, even bad news is better than no news at all. The service desk must contact customers when the target resolution time cannot be met and explain the reason for delays (such as waiting for parts to arrive).

> Keep the customer informed. . . keep the customer!

The service desk can notify management, customers, and others by telephone or in person, with an email or text message, or automatically by the incident management system. How notification occurs and who is notified varies based on conditions such as the incident's priority, who is affected by the incident, and when the incident occurs. Many companies have documented procedures that spell out who to notify and how to do so. Figure 4-12 shows a sample incident notification procedure.

	Incident Identification	Based on Priority												Incident Resolution
		1			**2**			**3**			**4**			
		50	75	100	50	75	100	50	75	100	50	75	100	
Customer	V		V	V		V	V		D	D		D	D	D
Incident Owner	V	A	A	A	A	A	A		A	A		A	A	A
Level Two	A		A	A	A	A	A	A		A	A		A	D
Management	D	T	T	T		T	T		E	E			E	D
Senior Management	D		T	T			T							D

Legend:

A – Automatic notification (via the incident management system)
D – Notification requirements are determined by the incident owner
E – Email notification
T – Text notification
V – Verbal notification

50 – 50% of the target resolution time has passed
75 – 75% of the target resolution time has passed
100 – 100% of the target resolution time has passed

Figure 4-12 Sample incident notification procedure
© Cengage Learning 2014

To see how this procedure works, consider a priority 1 incident, such as a server going down. The service desk staff follows the documented procedures and immediately notifies affected customers and management as well as the appropriate level two group in case they are unaware. Customers are notified verbally or via a text message. Level two automatically receives notification through the incident management system when the incident ticket is assigned to them. Such notifications are often forwarded to incident management system users via an email or text message. The incident owner determines whether to notify management and senior management immediately. After the incident has exceeded 50 percent of its target resolution time, the incident owner receives an alert from the incident management system, which prompts the owner to follow up and provide a status to management. Management is informed about the incident status via a text message.

 During a high priority incident, ongoing status updates are typically posted on the service desk's web site, announced via the service desk's telephone system, or communicated via social media such as Twitter or Facebook.

Now consider a priority 4 incident, such as a customer calling to say a printer is chronically jamming. In this case, management would not be notified until this incident had exceeded its target resolution time, and then they would receive that notification by email.

Incident notification procedures are designed to ensure that all involved parties are kept fully informed when high-impact incidents occur and are informed only when noncritical incidents exceed predefined thresholds. The procedures also ensure that uninvolved parties are not impacted by unnecessary notification activities. The ultimate goal is to ensure that notification occurs *before* the target resolution time is exceeded so that the support organization can set and meet the customer's expectation.

The service desk cannot be held solely responsible for effective incident management. The company must commit the resources necessary to design, implement, and maintain an incident management process that ensures all levels of support handle incidents in a manner that reflects the impact of those incidents on the business. The company also must capture the data needed to determine the root cause of incidents via the problem management process.

Problem Management Process

ITIL defines **problem management** as the process responsible for managing the lifecycle of problems. The objectives of problem management are to minimize the impact of incidents, eliminate recurring incidents, and prevent problems and their resulting incidents from occurring. These objectives are achieved by such activities as logging problems and maintaining information about their status, analyzing their root cause, and determining both temporary and permanent resolutions that work around or eliminate the root cause. **Root cause** is the most basic reason for an undesirable condition or problem, which if eliminated or corrected, would prevent the undesirable condition or problem from existing or occurring. **Root cause analysis** is a methodical way of determining why problems occur and identifying ways to prevent them.

Common problems include chronic hardware failures, corrupt files, software errors or bugs, and human error.

ITIL views the incident and problem management processes as separate and distinct. One reason is that performing root cause analysis often prolongs the restoration of service. In this day and age when outages can cost companies millions of dollars, most organizations strive to first restore services—via incident management—and then later determine the root cause. This is like a fire fighter who first puts out a fire and then calls for an arson inspector to determine the root cause. Another reason to keep the two processes separate is that not all incidents require root cause analysis. In some cases, the root cause is obvious, such as in the case of a laptop that was dropped or damaged. In other cases, root cause analysis may not be justified, such as in a situation where an easy to use and viable workaround exists.

Problem management includes a series of activities that can occur consecutively, simultaneously, or not at all. These activities include:

- **Problem detection**—Detecting a problem when a definitive cause cannot be determined for one or more incidents. Problems may be detected by the service desk or other technical support groups, by a vendor or contractor, or by an automated system such as a remote monitoring system.

- **Problem logging**—Notifying the problem management process about a problem and logging information about the problem, typically in an integrated IT service management tool. Problem logging includes categorizing the problem—often using the same categories used to log incidents—and assigning a priority. As with incidents, the priority of a problem is based on its impact and urgency. The criteria used to define impact and urgency of a problem will typically be slightly different than those used to define incidents. The target resolution time also tends to be longer to allow time for a thorough investigation.

- **Problem investigation and diagnosis**—Using available resources to analyze and determine the root cause of the problem using proven problem-solving techniques.

- **Problem resolution**—Performing the corrective action that eliminates the problem, typically via the change management process. In the event a permanent solution cannot be justified, a workaround is used to quickly resolve related incidents.

- **Problem closure**—Verifying that the change has been implemented and successfully reviewed, that the problem is resolved, and that all problem details are recorded accurately and completely.

- **Management review**—Evaluating the efficiency and effectiveness of the problem management process and associated reporting system.

The flowchart in Figure 4-13 shows the tasks that occur as a problem moves from detection to closure in the problem management process.

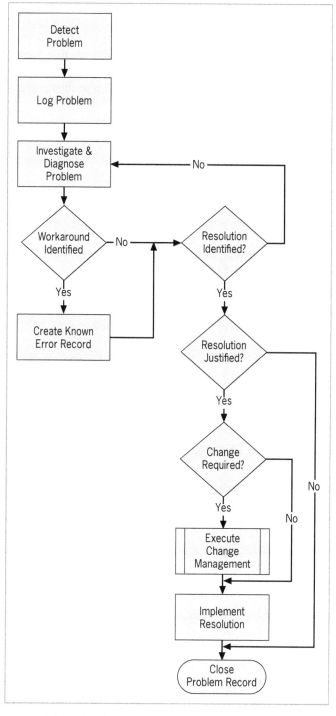

Figure 4-13 Problem management process
© Cengage Learning 2014

A primary responsibility of the service desk is to focus on incident management, so the service desk typically contributes to and uses problem management through its integration with the incident management process. For example, many problems are detected by the service desk in the course of handling incidents and are reported to the problem management process. Problem management uses incident-related data—much of which is captured by the service desk—when investigating and diagnosing the root cause. In return, problem management identifies known errors and workarounds that the service desk can use to resolve and reduce the impact of incidents.

Known errors and workarounds are commonly stored as separate records and referred to as "known error records." The records are stored in a known error database or knowledge base that integrates with other systems, such as the incident management system and the knowledge management system.

Regardless of where the known error is stored, the known error should be recorded as soon as it becomes useful to do so, even if only for information purposes. In other words, if a workaround has been identified but the root cause has not, a known error record is still recorded, making the workaround available for use in resolving incidents.

Problem management maintains the known error database and also helps to ensure that known errors that are detected but not resolved during the development, testing, and deployment of new services, systems, networks, and products are captured and made available to the service desk and other support groups. Doing so enables the service desk to contribute to the successful implementation of changes to the production environment by being prepared when new services are introduced.

Problem Investigation and Diagnosis

Although senior service desk analysts may participate, problems are usually investigated and diagnosed by the technical specialists, vendors, and contractors who are subject matter experts in a company's systems, networks, and applications. In the case of particularly complex problems, a team of experts work together under a problem manager. A **problem manager** coordinates all problem management activities and ensures problems are resolved within SLA targets. The problem manager makes sure the needed resources are available to analyze problems and to determine their root cause so that the company can take steps to prevent similar problems from occurring in the future.

Common techniques used to diagnose problems include:

- **Brainstorming**—A technique performed by a group of people and designed to generate a large number of ideas for solving a problem. Keys to successful brainstorming include avoiding criticism, encouraging unusual ideas, and compounding or combining ideas. Once a complete list of ideas is generated, analysis can begin.

- **Five Whys**—A technique that involves repeatedly asking the question "Why?" until the root cause of a problem is determined. For example, "Why do printers jam?" If the answer is that the paper does not feed properly, ask "Why" that is, and so on. The answer to one question leads to another question and eventually to the root cause. You may be able to ask fewer than five questions to determine the root cause.

- **Cause and effect analysis**—A technique used to generate the possible problem causes and their effect. This technique involves producing an Ishikawa diagram, which is a cause and effect diagram that visually displays the many potential causes for a specific problem or effect. Because of its shape, the cause and effect diagram is sometimes called a fishbone diagram. This diagram was originally proposed in the 1950s by Kaoru Ishikawa, a Japanese professor. Figure 4-14 shows a sample cause and effect diagram. In Figure 4-14, the effect being diagnosed is hardware failures. The vertical lines or "bones" of the diagram represent the major categories of problem causes. The horizontal lines are used to record the possible causes for each category. The possible causes may be determined by brainstorming, performing the Five Whys, or performing trend or root cause analysis. An effective technique is to transfer the identified causes to a Pareto chart for further analysis.

151

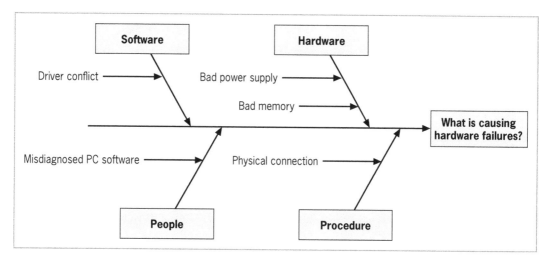

Figure 4-14 Sample cause and effect diagram
© Cengage Learning 2014

- **Pareto analysis**—A technique for determining the most significant causes from a list of many possible causes of a problem. Pareto analysis can be combined with the results produced from techniques such as brainstorming, Five Whys, and cause and effect analysis. This technique involves producing a bar chart that displays by frequency, in descending order, the possible causes of a problem—making it possible to identify the most significant of those causes. Figure 4-15 shows a sample Pareto chart. The left vertical axis of the chart represents the number of incidents the problems caused. The line graph shows the cumulative percentage associated with each problem cause. For example, Figure 4-15 shows that more than 84 percent of hardware incidents are caused by bad power supplies or bad memory. Conclusions that could be drawn from this chart include selecting vendors that provide higher quality components, or ensuring power supplies and memory are kept in stock to minimize the time required to correct these failures. Providing training and diagnostic scripts to the service desk staff is also important so these incidents are quickly diagnosed and resolved.

Pareto analysis reflects the Pareto Principle, also known as the 80/20 Rule, which, relative to problem management, means that 20 percent of the defects or failures that occur cause 80 percent of the problems.

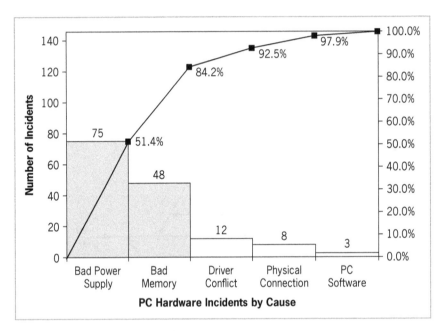

Figure 4-15 Sample Pareto chart
© Cengage Learning 2014

- **Kepner-Tregoe problem analysis**—A proprietary problem analysis technique developed by Charles Kepner and Ben Tregoe. This technique involves defining and describing the problem, establishing possible causes, testing the most probable cause, and verifying the true cause.

Charles Kepner collaborated with Mat-thys Fourie on thinking approaches—one of which is the Kepner and Fourie IT root cause analysis approach—that are also widely used.

Figure 4-16 lists common root cause codes for technology-related problems. Notice that many of the root cause codes listed are not related specifically to hardware products or software systems. They are related to how people are implementing or using the technology. In many companies, the technology itself is actually quite stable. The bulk of the problems are caused by changes made to the technology, attempts to integrate technologies, or factors such as inadequate training and insufficient documentation.

Code	Description
Communications Failure	For example, network or telephone line down
Configuration Error	PC/System configured incorrectly
Database Problem	For example, database full or generating errors
Environment	For example, power outage
Hardware Failure	Hardware malfunction
Human Error	Problem caused by human error
Incorrect Data	Incorrect input produced incorrect output
Incorrect Documentation/Procedures	Inaccurate or incomplete documentation/procedures
Incompatible Hardware	Incompatible/nonstandard hardware
Incompatible Software	Incompatible/nonstandard software
Installation Error	Hardware/Software installed incorrectly
Insufficient Resources	For example, memory
Lack of Training	For example, for use with "how-to" type inquiries
Other	For use when no other response is appropriate
Planned Outage	For example, customer is unable to access a system due to a planned outage
Procedure Not Followed	Complete and accurate procedure not followed
Result of Change	Problem caused by a change to the system/device
Request for Information	For example, for use with inquiries
Software Bug	Incorrect software code
Unknown	Problem could not be duplicated

Figure 4-16 Sample root cause codes
© Cengage Learning 2014

Without the data captured by service desk analysts, problem management is not possible. When problem management is not performed, it is likely that resulting incidents will recur and that new incidents will appear. When problem management is performed, the organization is able to identify, eliminate, and ultimately predict and prevent problem causes.

Given the rapid pace at which technology changes, it is unlikely that problem management will enable a company to prevent *all* problems. However, problem management will enable the elimination of common problems and the associated recurring incidents. As a result, service desk analysts are freed to pursue new skills, work on more complex incidents, and handle service requests.

Request Fulfillment Process

ITIL defines **request fulfillment** as the process responsible for managing the lifecycle of service requests. The objective of request fulfillment is to provide technology users a channel to request and receive standard services. ITIL makes a clear distinction between a request for "standard" services—that is, a service request—and a request for change. A service request must meet predefined prerequisites, such as: it must be low risk, it must be preapproved, and it must have documented procedures. Larger, higher-risk, or infrequent changes must go through a formal change management process.

 Common service requests include reset a password, install pre-approved software, set up a new employee within an organization, or provide access to an IT service.

The request fulfillment process integrates closely with the access management process. **Access management** is the process responsible for granting authorized users the right to use a service in accordance with the company's security policies while preventing access to nonauthorized users. Although the role of the service desk varies from one organization to the next, typical access management activities performed by the service desk include receiving and validating access requests, granting access, and detecting access-related incidents. Access-related incidents may include attempts to obtain access without the proper approvals and repeated and regular (e.g., daily) password reset requests. Such requests may indicate unauthorized password sharing or access attempts.

Like incident management, request fulfillment ensures that customers have access to the services, systems, products, and networks they need to do their work. The difference between incident management and request fulfillment is that when customers have a request, they are not reporting a failure. Rather, they are asking for a service they have never had or they are asking for additional information about an existing service. However, when customers contact the service desk with an incident, that incident is preventing them from gaining access to a service that they were previously able to use.

Like incident management, request fulfillment includes a series of activities that can occur consecutively, simultaneously, or not at all. Request fulfillment activities include:

- **Request entry**—Submitting to a central point such as the service desk the initial service request and logging information about the request.

- **Approval**—Ensuring that appropriate approvals, such as financial approval or business management approval, are obtained.

- **Fulfillment**—Performing the actual steps required to satisfy the request. These activities depend on the nature of the request.

- **Request closure**—Verifying that the request is complete, the customer is satisfied, and all request-related details are recorded accurately and completely.

- **Management review**—Evaluating the efficiency and effectiveness of the request fulfillment process and associated reporting system.

The flowchart in Figure 4-17 shows how responsibility for a specific task changes as a request moves from request entry to closure.

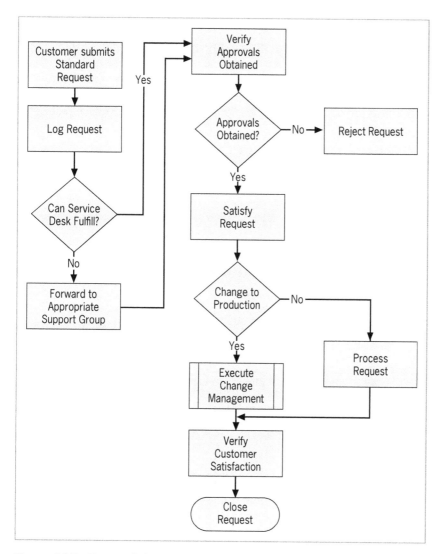

Figure 4-17 Request fulfillment process
© Cengage Learning 2014

Requests can vary considerably in complexity. A simple request, such as setting up a new user account, might be completed within hours of the request. A more complex request, such as setting up a new employee, can involve many different support groups and result in the deployment of many different services. For example, a new employee typically requires, at a minimum, a workstation, a telephone, an email account, access to standard services such as the network, and access to specific services based on his or her role in the organization.

Users may initiate requests by calling the service desk or completing a form such as a self-help web-based form selected from a predefined menu of request types.

The role of the service desk in the request fulfillment process can vary from one company to the next and even within a company based on the type of request. For example, the service desk may be involved actively with a request to set up a new employee by coordinating the efforts of groups such as facilities (who readies the person's cubicle), desktop support (who sets up the workstation), and so on. Or, the service desk may simply log a service request and hand it off to the appropriate support group.

Typically, the service desk performs the following activities in the request fulfillment process:

- Gathers data and creates a request ticket.

- Provides the customer a request number.

- Satisfies the request when possible.

- Documents the resolution.

- Forwards the request to the appropriate service provider when necessary.

- Retains ownership of the outstanding request.

- Ensures that the customer has an up-to-date status.

- Confirms that the customer is satisfied once the request is resolved.

- Closes the request ticket.

Like incidents, service requests are prioritized to ensure that they are resolved in a timely manner and in an order that meets business needs. Also like incidents, the service desk retains ownership and verifies customer satisfaction before closing service requests.

Distinguishing Incident Management and Request Fulfillment

Although it may seem that the service desk could use the same process to manage incidents and service requests—and some do—many companies find sufficient differences to warrant separate processes. For example:

- Management approval is typically not needed to resolve incidents, whereas management approval—such as financial approval—is required before work begins on a service request.

- Incidents are often prioritized differently from service requests because customers typically view restoring service—that is, resolving incidents—as more important than adding new service.

- Companies want to be able to accurately report their performance and the impact of their actions to customers. For example, an unscheduled outage that occurs as a result of an incident often has a greater impact than a scheduled outage that occurs so that a service request can be implemented. In the case of the scheduled outage, customers can prepare for the impact, whereas with unscheduled incidents, they cannot.

Both the incident management and request fulfillment process provide input to and receive output from the knowledge management process.

The incident management, problem management, and request fulfillment processes are described in greater detail in the *ITIL® Service Operation* publication.

Knowledge Management Process

Knowledge management is the process responsible for gathering, storing, and sharing information and knowledge within an organization. The objective of knowledge management is to enable organizations to be more efficient and improve the quality of decision making by providing access to reliable and secure data, information, and knowledge. For example, in a service desk setting, many technology incidents and service requests are recurring, meaning that they happen over and over. Because of this, many companies enter the information needed to resolve incidents and service requests into a knowledge management system. Other information includes known errors, workarounds, and answers to FAQs.

Knowledge-Centered Support (KCS) is a knowledge management strategy for service and support organizations developed by the Consortium for Service Innovation (*www.serviceinnovation.org*). KCS is a set of practices and processes that focuses on knowledge as a key asset of the support organization.

Knowledge management activities include:

- **Knowledge capture**—Submitting to a central point, such as the knowledge engineer, reusable information and logging that information in a knowledge management system.

- **Knowledge review**—Evaluating the information to make sure it is accurate and conforms to predefined standards.

- **Knowledge revision**—Refining the information as needed to improve its accuracy and ensure that it conforms to standards.

- **Knowledge approval**—Evaluating the refinements made during the knowledge revision phase followed by the knowledge engineer's acceptance or rejection of the information.

- **Management review**—Evaluating the efficiency and effectiveness of the knowledge management process and associated reporting system.

As these activities indicate, a formalized knowledge management process is needed to ensure the information captured is accurate, complete, and current.

The rapid pace of change makes it difficult for people to maintain their skills through training alone. They must be able to learn quickly and avoid diagnosing and solving incidents that have been solved before. To avoid "reinventing the wheel," anyone who solves an incident or successfully handles a service request must document the resolution and submit it to the knowledge engineer for inclusion in the knowledge management system.

The flowchart in Figure 4-18 shows how information flows through the knowledge management process and reflects the responsibilities of people involved in the process.

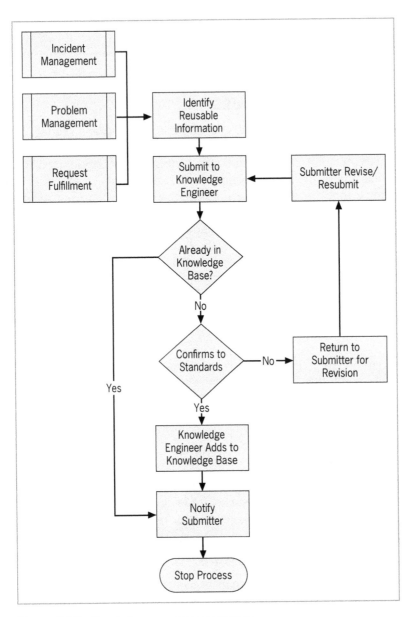

Figure 4-18 Knowledge management process
© Cengage Learning 2014

The knowledge engineer approves or rejects information as appropriate and ensures that analysts can quickly and easily retrieve information and resolutions from the knowledge management system. An effective knowledge management process enables service desk analysts to solve a greater number of incidents and service requests quickly and accurately.

The service desk is an important part of the knowledge management process. Not only does it use the information collected, it also helps compile the information and encourages use of the knowledge management system. Specifically, the service desk:

- Uses the knowledge management system to resolve incidents, problems, and service requests.

- Documents resolutions, procedures, and so on, and submits them to the knowledge engineer for review and approval.

- Makes suggestions to the knowledge engineer about information to add to the knowledge management system.

- Promotes awareness of the knowledge management system to others who may benefit from using it, such as customers, level two staff, and level three staff.

The widescale proliferation of web-based and social technologies have dramatically changed the way companies view the knowledge management process. Because web-based and social technologies make it so easy for users to access information 24 hours a day, 7 days a week, companies must diligently capture knowledge and make it available for reuse.

The knowledge management process described here represents a formalized approach and can represent a significant culture change for some organizations. This is because it can be difficult to:

- Determine what knowledge is critical to the ongoing success of the organization

- Determine where the knowledge resides (e.g., in databases and knowledge bases, in peoples' heads, in documents)

- Create a culture that encourages knowledge sharing

A knowledge management strategy is needed that defines the scope of the knowledge management system and that ensures clear policies are defined. Such a strategy must also ensure that resources are allocated including human, financial, and technological resources.

An effective knowledge management strategy also acknowledges that informal knowledge sharing and collaboration are essential in today's fast-paced business environment. Informal approaches to knowledge sharing may include:

- **Communities of practice (CoPs)**—A **community of practice (CoP)** is a group of people who are bound together by similar interests and expertise. CoP members are active practitioners who come together to share information, experiences, tips, and best practices. Members provide support for each other to avoid reinventing the wheel, and look for innovative ways to overcome challenges and achieve common goals. To be successful, all community members must participate, contribute and show a true willingness to collaborate.

- **Mentoring programs**—Programs that enable a less experienced or less knowledgeable person to receive guidance or advice from a more experienced or knowledgeable person.

- **Webinars, wikis, blogs, social media**—Technology-driven ways to facilitate knowledge sharing.

Whether users access knowledge and information via a formal knowledge management system or in a less formal way, they will value that knowledge and information only if it is accurate, current, and presented clearly. Companies that are serious about capturing and leveraging knowledge reward people who willingly share what they know and understand how important knowledge management is to the company's growth and success.

Change Management Process

ITIL defines **change management** as the process responsible for controlling the lifecycle of changes, enabling beneficial changes to be made with minimal disruption to IT services. The objective of change management is to ensure that changes made to IT services balance risk, resource effectiveness, and potential disruption to business activities. Before they are moved into the production environment, new services or components, and upgrades to existing services or components, typically are installed, developed or configured, and tested in a development environment. A development environment is used so that any risks associated with installing, for example, a new version of an operating system can be assessed and minimized before the software is distributed or deployed to customers, minimizing service disruptions. Once in the production environment, customers can access and use them.

The ITIL release and deployment management process integrates with change management and is responsible for planning and managing the rollout of significant changes—such as a new operating system—across an organization.

Programmers, technicians such as network technicians, vendors, and occasionally service desk analysts may develop or test these new or upgraded components. They must then complete the activities specified by the change management process to install the component in the production environment. In other words, change management is the "control" process used to manage the transition of new or upgraded services or hardware, software, network, and application components from development to production.

Change management activities include:

- **Change recording and review**—Submitting to the change management process a **request for change (RFC)**, which is a request to change the production environment. RFCs are typically logged in an integrated service management tool. This activity also includes reviewing the RFC and rejecting any changes that are impractical or that require further justification. For example, if a customer requests a piece of equipment that does not conform to the company's standard, the RFC will be rejected unless the purchase can be justified by the customer.

- **Assessment and evaluation**—Assessing the potential impact and risk of the change as well as the proposed benefits of the change and evaluating whether the change should be approved.

- **Change authorization**—Authorizing the change and planning the activities required to build the change.

- **Coordinating change implementation**—Coordinating the work being done by technical groups to build, test, and implement the change. This includes the communication, preparation, and training needed to ensure the change is a success.

- **Change review and closure**—Conducting a change review, also known as a post-implementation review (PIR), to verify that the customer is satisfied with the change and that no unexpected side effects occurred. Change review includes reviewing incidents caused by the change and ensuring those incidents have been resolved via the incident management process, before the change is closed.

- **Management review**—Evaluating the efficiency and effectiveness of the change management process and associated reporting system.

These activities work together to provide an effective way to manage changes. The flowchart in Figure 4-19 provides an overview of the activities in the change management process.

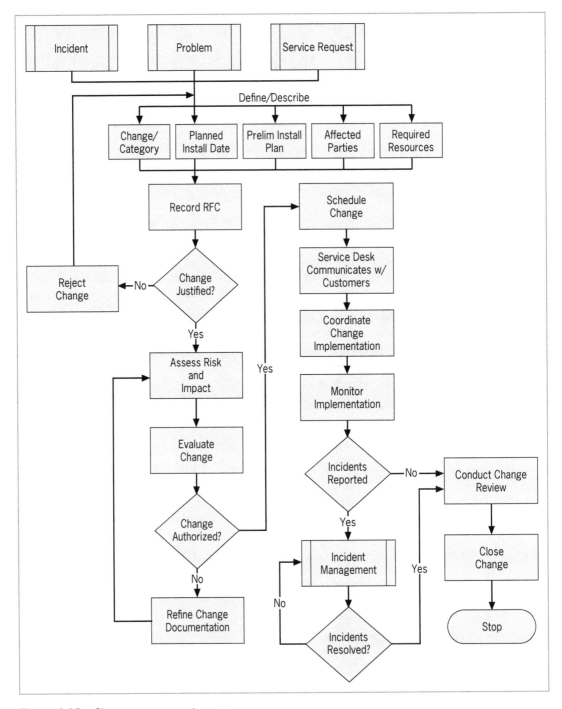

Figure 4-19 Change management process
© Cengage Learning 2014

Some companies have a very formal change management process. For example, some have a separate group known as a **change advisory board (CAB)** that (as defined in ITIL) supports the assessment, prioritization, authorization, and scheduling of changes. In the case of standard—low-risk—changes, these assessment and subsequent approval activities will be delegated to managers or perhaps even the service desk. Many companies hold regular CAB meetings to discuss nonstandard changes scheduled for the coming week, month, and so on, along with high-impact changes scheduled for the longer-term future. All affected stakeholders, including representatives from the service desk, involved level two and three groups, and the customer community, attend these meetings. In an effort to prevent incidents, the attendees discuss each change and provide advice to the change manager about its technical readiness, proposed implementation date, and assessed risk and impact. The **change manager** coordinates all change management activities and ensures approved changes represent an acceptable level of possible and probable risk and impact.

Some companies designate certain days of the week or month for changes. For example, a company may state that, unless it is an emergency, changes can be made only on Saturdays and Wednesdays, assuming they have been approved by the CAB. Or, all changes affecting the accounting department are made the second week of the month. The day or days of the week or month selected correspond to the needs of the business. For example, companies that experience heavy workloads on Mondays and Fridays tend not to make changes on Sundays and Thursdays in an effort to avoid service disruptions on their busiest days.

Many organizations define a separate set of procedures for **emergency changes**, which must be introduced as soon as possible to repair errors in an IT service that have a high impact on the business. Such changes are often linked to major incidents being handled by the service desk.

Although the service desk does not usually have primary responsibility for this process, in companies that have a formal change management process the service desk plays an important role. For example, the service desk typically participates in CAB meetings and then posts the change schedule for the coming week on the service desk's web site. In companies that do not have a formal change management process, the service desk simply does its best to stay on top of changes that developers, technicians, vendors, and so on may make with little advance communication. One of the best ways they can do this is to log all incidents so that incidents caused by change can be tracked and ultimately prevented when similar changes are made in the future.

Change management enables the service desk to be proactive because it knows what changes are coming and can prepare for them. For example, the service desk can determine what training analysts need to support the new services, systems, networks, or products being released. Or, the service desk can hire people with specialized knowledge to cross-train existing staff. The service desk also may need to adjust its incident handling procedures. For example, the service desk may need to extend its hours of operation or provide web-based support after hours. Some changes may prompt the service desk to install new support systems, such as more advanced remote diagnostic equipment. The service desk also tracks and analyzes incidents that result from change to determine how to perform changes better in the future.

The service desk's role in the change management process may include the following activities:

- Participates in CAB meetings, often serving as the customer advocate.

- Determines if service desk staffing levels, skills, processes, or technologies need to be refined to accommodate the scheduled change.

- Approves changes for which it has been delegated the authority.

- Communicates the calendar of upcoming changes and planned outages.

- Logs standard changes submitted as service requests and manages those service requests (standard changes) throughout their lifecycle.

- Implements standard changes for which it is responsible.

- Follows up with affected parties to ensure satisfaction with the change when appropriate.

- Tracks incidents caused by change via the incident management process.

The change management process is very important because it enables the service desk to prepare for upcoming changes. However, the service desk's involvement in change management may not be limited to simply getting prepared. The service desk also may act as a testing site for new services, systems, and products; help develop the installation procedures; and prepare answers to FAQs. In some cases, the service desk may even perform the actual change, such as electronically distributing new software. The more actively the service desk is involved in the change management process, the more value it adds to its company and customers.

Service Asset and Configuration Management Process

Service asset and configuration management (SACM) is defined by ITIL as the process responsible for ensuring that the assets required to deliver services are properly controlled, and that accurate and reliable information about those assets is available when and where it is needed. The objectives of the SACM process are to identify and manage assets that are under the control of the IT organization. Such assets include financial capital, people, processes, technology, knowledge, and information.

The type and amount of information captured by the SACM process varies from one organization to the next. Typically, the SACM process captures financial information about assets; particularly assets that represent a significant investment. For example, SACM might collect and maintain the cost of the asset, who owns it, its current value, and other associated costs such as license and warranty information. The SACM process also captures nonfinancial information about IT assets, along with how the assets are related or configured. For example, SACM might collect and maintain a record of all servers, where they are installed, their model and serial numbers, what applications are installed on those servers, and how they are, or can be, connected to other devices on the company's network. Most importantly, SACM collects and maintains information about what business services those servers and applications support, so that the impact of changes to or incidents affecting those servers and applications is understood.

Service asset and configuration management may also be called inventory management; however, **inventory management** typically focuses only on collecting and maintaining information about IT assets, not the relationships that exist among those assets.

When the entire support organization has access to information about the assets used to deliver IT services, incidents and problems can be diagnosed more quickly, the impact of changes assessed more accurately, and a company's financial investment managed more effectively. The SACM process provides and is supported by a central repository of data and information known as a configuration management system. A **configuration management system (CMS)** is a set of tools and databases for managing information about configuration items and linking that information to related incidents, problems, known errors, changes, and releases. The CMS provides the ability to view historical information about CIs, the current state of CIs, and planned changes to CIs.

The SACM process maintains information about changes to CIs. The actual changes are managed via the change management process.

In many companies, the CMS is a logical entity, rather than a physical entity. In other words, the data and information that composes the CMS may reside in a number of physical databases known as configuration management databases, rather than one large physical database. ITIL defines a **configuration management database (CMDB)** as a database used to store configuration records throughout their lifecycle. ITIL defines a **configuration record** as a record containing details of a configuration item. For example, network-related configuration records may be housed in one CMDB, data center hardware and software configuration records in another, configuration records related to cloud-based services in another, and so on.

SACM activities include:

- **Configuration identification**—Identifying a CI and recording information about it in the CMDB.

- **Configuration control**—Maintaining a record of changes to CIs.

- **Status accounting and reporting**—Maintaining and reporting on the status of CIs throughout their lifecycle; for example, under development, in test, live, or retired.

- **Verification and audit**—Reviewing and auditing the CMS and verifying that it matches the physical environment.

The flowchart in Figure 4-20 shows how these activities progress in the SACM process.

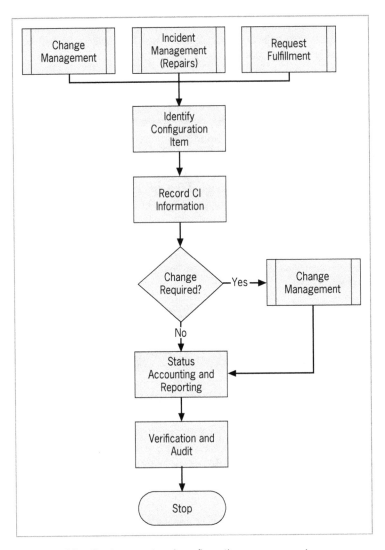

Figure 4-20   Service asset and configuration management process
© Cengage Learning 2014

The service desk does not usually have primary responsibility for this process, although it may in a smaller company. In larger support organizations, the groups responsible for setting up and installing new services, systems, and products usually maintain the CMS. The service desk then uses the CMS and may help with verification and audit activities. For example, when logging an incident, the service desk may verify that the information in the CMS is up to date and report any inaccuracies to the appropriate group.

Table 4-4 lists the groups that typically oversee the day-to-day maintenance of the CMS. The information these groups keep about assets includes a physical description of each item, location information, financial information including licensing information, warranty and service contract details, and any other details that are important to the group.

Group	Data Area Maintained
Desktop and Mobile Device Support	PC-related components (within the confines of a workstation) and mobile devices such as laptops, tablets, and smartphones
Network Management	Non-PC-related components/network components (voice and data)
Computer Operations	Data center hardware and software
Purchasing	Contracts or service and license agreements

Table 4-4   Sample of groups that maintain service asset and configuration management data
© Cengage Learning 2014

The CMS provides essential information to a number of processes, including incident, problem, knowledge, and change management, and request fulfillment. In turn, these processes provide information that ensures that the information stored in the CMS remains accurate and complete. Figure 4-21 shows how these processes are integrated via the CMS.

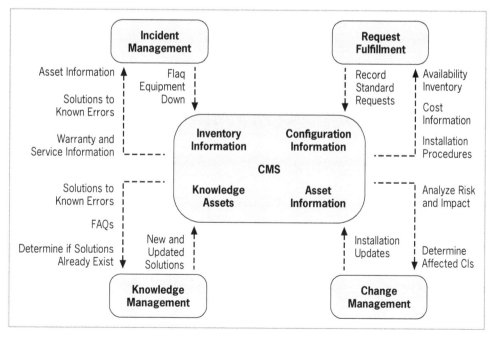

Figure 4-21   Process integration via the CMS
© Cengage Learning 2014

Having access to information housed in the CMS increases the efficiency and effectiveness of the service desk considerably. For example, when a customer calls to say "it" broke, a level one analyst can search the CMS to determine what "it" the customer is using. The analyst is then able to view the history of the failing component and also assess the impact of the incident based on the relationship the component has with other components in the infrastructure. For example, a failed printer that is the only printer in the office may be given a higher priority than a failed printer that is one of many on the same floor.

In addition, when the CMS is linked to the incident management system, the service desk staff has less data to enter and is able to enter more accurate data. For example, if the service desk analyst types a serial number into an incident record, related information stored in the CMS (such as device type and version) may appear. The customer also benefits because the service desk can create the incident record more quickly. The service desk can also use the contract data stored in the CMS to determine a product's warranty and service status prior to contacting a vendor.

> The knowledge management, change management, and SACM processes are described in greater detail in the *ITIL® Service Transition* publication.

Integrating the Service Desk Processes

The incident, problem, knowledge, change, and service asset and configuration management, and request fulfillment processes are key to the success of the service desk. These processes are all important and they are very tightly integrated. Figure 4-22 illustrates how these processes interconnect.

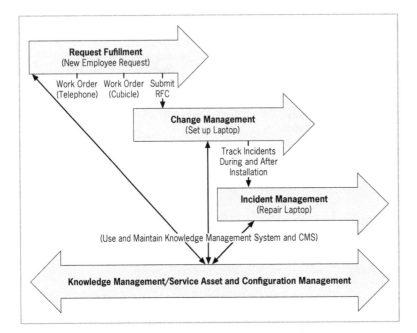

Figure 4-22   Integration of key service desk processes
© Cengage Learning 2014

This illustration begins with a service request submitted via the request fulfillment process to set up a new employee. Work orders may be used to set up the new employee's cubicle and telephone. An RFC is submitted for the employee's new laptop. The purchase of the laptop is authorized via the change management process. The change is assessed for impact and risk, approved, and scheduled for installation. After the laptop is set up, any incidents are handled via the incident management process until the laptop is removed from the production environment. The request fulfillment, change, and incident management processes all use information that is housed in the company's knowledge management system and CMS. These processes also contribute information to those systems via the knowledge management and SACM processes.

Relationship management and quality improvement processes use the information produced by all of these processes.

Relationship Management and Quality Improvement Processes

Several processes analyze the data and information captured by both the service desk and other parts of the IT organization and use that data and information to help manage the relationship the IT organization has with its customers. This data and information can also be used to maximize customer satisfaction with the IT organization's services and ensure that the IT organization is delivering value to the company and its customers. Figure 4-23 lists the relationship management and quality improvement processes that most directly interface with the service desk.

- Service level management

- Business relationship management

- Trend analysis

Figure 4-23 Relationship management and quality improvement processes
© Cengage Learning 2014

Front-line analysts typically do not perform these processes, although they may in some service desks. Front-line analysts do, however, perform activities that are used as input to these processes such as logging incidents and service requests and conducting customer satisfaction surveys. This data and information can be used to improve service desk efficiency and effectiveness. It can also be used to measure and improve the overall quality of IT services and customers' perception of those services and the entire IT organization.

The service level management and business relationship management processes are tightly integrated and both play important roles in terms of managing the relationship an IT organization and the service desk has with its customers.

Service Level Management

Service level management is the process of negotiating and managing customer expectations by establishing SLAs, which spell out the services the IT organization—including the service desk—provides to the customer, the customer's responsibilities, and how service performance is measured. SLAs help ensure that both the service provider and customer have the same level of expectation about the services the provider will deliver.

SLAs are explored in more detail in Chapter 6.

SLAs also provide performance objectives and identify reports to create regularly that monitor how well the IT organization is achieving its targeted objectives. Within the service desk, a service desk manager, supervisor, or team leader uses these SLA performance reports to perform trend analysis as well as to develop and execute action plans that improve performance. In addition, analysis of SLA performance reports may reveal changes in the service environment that signal the need to adjust or renegotiate the SLA. The analysis of SLA performance reports related to specific customer communities is sometimes assigned to dedicated business relationship managers.

Service level management focuses on ensuring a service provider is delivering the agreed upon levels of service.

Business Relationship Management

Customer relationships are complex and must be constantly monitored and maintained. One of the reasons most frequently cited by customers who stopped doing business with a company is that they felt an attitude of indifference. To combat this problem, some companies establish a business relationship management or an account management function to ensure that customers' needs are being met. ITIL defines **business relationship management** as the process responsible for maintaining a positive relationship between a service provider and its customers. A **business relationship manager** is an employee who has in-depth knowledge of a specific customer community and is responsible for maintaining the relationship with that customer. Business relationship managers may also be known as account managers. In a service desk setting, business relationship managers or account managers take the lead when a customer's incidents (particularly major incidents), problems, or service requests require special attention. Also, business relationship managers review reports related to their assigned customer communities, monitor their customer's satisfaction, and ensure that complaints related to the overall quality and relevance of services are being analyzed and addressed. In some companies, such as companies that provide service desk outsourcing services, a service desk team leader or senior staff member might serve as a business relationship manager.

Business relationship management focuses on ensuring a service provider is delivering the right set of services needed to meet customers' current and future needs.

Trend Analysis

Trend analysis is a methodical way of determining and, when possible, forecasting service trends. Trends can be positive, such as a reduction in the number of "how to" questions the service desk receives after an improved training program. Or, trends can be negative, such as a dramatic increase in contact volume after a new product is introduced into the market.

Trend analysis works hand in hand with root cause analysis. They can be used together reactively to solve incidents and problems or proactively to identify improvement areas. Root cause analysis—performed via the problem management process—is the more difficult of the two disciplines, so not all companies determine and document root cause. These companies fail to take the extra time needed to determine *why* an incident occurred once they have "fixed" it. Unfortunately, by not capturing and then eliminating the root cause, these companies put themselves at risk that the same or similar incidents will happen again.

Some IT organizations have highly skilled statisticians who perform trend and root cause analysis. These individuals may, for example, be part of a problem management team. However, any or all members of the service desk team can perform trend analysis. Very often, the front-line staff can identify trends simply by considering the contacts they are receiving. For example, the service desk might notice that it is receiving a lot of contacts about a certain system or product, or from a certain customer community, and bring that fact to management's attention. A trend report can then be created to validate statistically the service desk's "hunch."

Without the data captured by the service desk, trend analysis and root cause analysis are impossible. Trend analysis and root cause analysis enable a service desk to minimize the impact of incidents, and ultimately, to prevent incidents. As a result, the service desk enhances its productivity, its customers' productivity, and its customers' satisfaction.

By combining the data captured by the service desk with data captured by other parts of the IT organization, a service provider can improve the overall quality of its services.

Why Processes Are Important

All of the processes discussed in this chapter are designed to define clearly the work to be done, clarify roles and responsibilities, ensure that data is captured, and generate information. The most successful companies understand that processes are not static. Instead, they must be treated as living, breathing organisms that need care and feeding. Because customer requirements change constantly, processes must be continually improved and occasionally redesigned or they will cease to be effective.

Companies in today's competitive business climate cannot afford to waste resources. They have to maximize their resources, especially their precious human resources, and accomplish more with them than was ever possible. With processes, roles and responsibilities are clearly defined and people understand what they are expected to do. People who understand the expected result can determine the most efficient and effective way to achieve it. What's most important is that, with processes, required information is captured in a meaningful and useful way. Through analysis and understanding, this information becomes knowledge. Knowledge enables service desk staff to be proactive because they can foresee potential problems, identify preventative measures, and ultimately, enhance customer satisfaction as well as their own job satisfaction.

Chapter Summary

- Processes and procedures are an integral component of every service desk because they represent the work to be done such as solving incidents and handling service requests. Processes define *what* tasks to do, whereas procedures describe *how* to do the tasks. When processes are understood, people know *why* they are doing the tasks. When multiple groups are involved in solving an incident or satisfying a service request, processes and procedures provide the guidelines that enable each group to understand its role, responsibilities, and the expected results of its efforts.

- Many companies use existing frameworks and standards when designing and improving processes. Frameworks describe best practices that can be used to define and continually improve a given set of processes. Standards contain a formal specification and list mandatory controls that an organization must have in place to be certified. Quality management and improvement frameworks and standards include TQM, Six Sigma, and ISO 9000. IT service management frameworks and standards include ITIL, MOF, and ISO/IEC 20000.

- A successful service desk must manage several tightly integrated processes to achieve customer satisfaction. Two processes that are vital to the success of a service desk are incident management and request fulfillment. Incident management involves determining the priority of an incident—such as a broken device or error message—based on its impact and urgency, and then determining when and how to solve it. Request fulfillment provides a channel for users to submit service requests—such as reset a password or install preapproved software—as well as verify that appropriate approvals are obtained and satisfy the requests.

- The service desk cannot always resolve incidents and service requests during the initial contact. When incidents and service requests are assigned to groups outside of the service desk, the service desk is the owner and customer advocate. As owner, the service desk ensures that the incident or service request is handled to the customer's satisfaction. The owner also sees that appropriate notification activities occur (such as management and customer notification) when necessary.

- Other processes important to the service desk include problem and knowledge management. Problem management helps to minimize the impact of and eliminate incidents by determining their root cause and by identifying both temporary and permanent resolutions. Problem management also captures information about known errors and workarounds in a known error database or knowledge base. Knowledge management enables organizations to be more efficient and to improve the quality of decision making by providing access to reliable and secure data, information, and knowledge in a knowledge management system.

- Change management and service asset and configuration management are also important to people working in a service desk. Change management allows changes to occur as quickly as possible with the optimal amount of risk and impact (and the fewest incidents). Service asset and configuration management facilitates the capture and maintenance of information about the assets underpinning IT services. The service desk and others involved in support use this information to diagnose and resolve incidents and problems more quickly and to determine the potential impact of incidents and changes.

- Relationship management and quality improvement processes, such as service level management, business relationship management, and trend analysis, use the information produced by all of these processes. Quality improvement processes analyze the data captured by service desk analysts and help maximize customer satisfaction, improve service desk efficiency and effectiveness, and contribute value to the company and its customers.

- The most successful companies understand that processes and procedures are not static. They must be treated as living, breathing organisms that need care and feeding. Because customer requirements are constantly changing, processes and procedures must be continually improved and occasionally redesigned, or they will cease to be effective. Processes and procedures enable people to understand what they are expected to do. People who understand the expected result can determine the most efficient and effective way to achieve it.

Key Terms

access management—The process responsible for granting authorized users the right to use a service in accordance with the company's security policies while preventing access to nonauthorized users.

brainstorming—A technique performed by a group of people and designed to generate a large number of ideas for solving a problem.

business process management (BPM)—A systematic approach to improving an organization's business processes.

business relationship management—The process responsible for maintaining a positive relationship between a service provider and its customers. (ITIL definition)

business relationship manager—An employee who has in-depth knowledge of a specific customer community and is responsible for maintaining the relationship with that customer.

categorization—Recording the type of incident being reported. Categorization also involves recording the type of problem, service request, or change being reported.

cause and effect analysis—A technique used to generate the possible problem causes and their effect.

change advisory board (CAB)—A group or a committee that supports the assessment, prioritization, authorization, and scheduling of changes. (ITIL definition)

change management—The process responsible for controlling the lifecycle of changes, enabling beneficial changes to be made with minimal disruption to IT services. (ITIL definition)

change manager—The person who coordinates all change management activities and ensures approved changes represent an acceptable level of possible and probable risk and impact.

community of practice (CoP)—A group of people who are bound together by similar interests and expertise.

configuration item (CI)—Any component or other service asset that needs to be managed in order to deliver an IT service. (ITIL definition)

configuration management database (CMDB)—A database that is used to store configuration records throughout their lifecycle. (ITIL definition)

configuration management system (CMS)—A set of tools and databases for managing IT asset information and linking that information to related incidents, problems, known errors, changes, and releases.

configuration record—A record containing details of a configuration item. (ITIL definition)

costs—The amounts paid to produce a product, such as workers' wages, salaries and benefits; the facilities and equipment workers use; and any materials and supplies they consume.

customer entitlement—The determination of whether the customer is authorized to receive support, and if so, the level of support the customer should receive.

emergency change—A change that must be introduced as soon as possible to repair an error in an IT service that has a high impact on the business.

escalation (or escalate)—To raise an incident from one level to another, such as from level one to level two, to dedicate new or additional resources to the incident.

event—A change of state that has significance for the management of an IT service or other configuration item. (ITIL definition)

event management—A process that captures and logs events, analyzes them, and determines an appropriate action.

Five Whys—A technique that involves repeatedly asking the question "Why?" until the root cause of a problem is determined.

flowchart—A diagram that shows the sequence of tasks that occur in a process.

framework—A structure designed to enclose something.

functional escalation—Escalation that transfers an incident from one line of support to the next; occurs when greater knowledge or authority is required to resolve an incident or a target time frame is approaching or has been exceeded.

hierarchic escalation—Escalation that occurs when management is involved in the incident management process, even if only for information purposes; occurs when steps are taking too long, there is contention about assignments, or additional resources are needed to resolve a incident.

impact—A measure of the effect an incident, problem, or change is having on business processes. (ITIL definition)

incident management—The process responsible for managing the lifecycle of incidents. (ITIL definition)

incident owner—An employee of the support organization who acts as a customer advocate and proactively ensures that an incident is resolved to the customer's satisfaction.

incident ownership—A practice that ensures that, when the service desk analyst cannot resolve an incident during the first contact or escalates the incident to a person or group outside of the service desk, an incident owner is designated.

incident tracking—The practice of following *one* incident from identification to closure.

inquiry—A customer request for information, such as "When will the new release of software arrive?"

International Organization for Standardization—A network of the national standards institutes of 164 countries; also known as ISO.

inventory management—A process that focuses only on collecting and maintaining information about IT assets, not the relationships that exist among those assets. See also *service asset and configuration management*.

ISO 9000—A set of international standards for quality management.

ISO/IEC 20000—An international standard for IT service management.

Kaizen—A Japanese term that, when applied to the workplace, means continuing improvement involving everyone—managers and workers alike.

Kepner-Tregoe problem analysis—A proprietary problem analysis technique developed by Charles Kepner and Ben Tregoe that involves defining and describing the problem, establishing possible causes, testing the most probable cause, and verifying the true cause.

knowledge management—The process responsible for gathering, storing, and sharing information and knowledge within an organization.

Lean Six Sigma—A process improvement approach that combines the concepts of Lean Manufacturing (removing waste) and Six Sigma (reducing defects).

major incident—An incident that is causing significant business impact.

mentoring program—A program that enables a less experienced or less knowledgeable person to receive guidance or advice from a more experienced or knowledgeable person.

Microsoft Operations Framework (MOF)—A collection of best practices, principles, and models that offers guidance to IT organizations for managing their IT services.

notification—The activities that inform all of the stakeholders in the incident management process (including management, the customer, and service desk analysts) about the status of outstanding incidents.

Pareto analysis—A technique for determining the most significant causes from a list of many possible causes of a problem.

policy—A formal document that describes the intentions and expectations of management.

priority—A category that defines the relative importance of an incident, problem, or change and is based on impact and urgency. (ITIL definition)

problem management—The process responsible for managing the lifecycle of problems. (ITIL definition)

problem manager—An employee of the support organization who coordinates all problem management activities and ensures problems are resolved within SLA targets.

productivity—An efficiency measure that relates output (goods and services produced) to input (the number of hours worked).

program—An approach used to manage one or more interdependent projects.

project—A temporary endeavor undertaken to complete a unique product, service, or result.

quality—A characteristic that measures how well products or services meet customer requirements.

question—A customer request for instruction on how to use a product, such as "How do I . . . ?"

request for change (RFC)—A request to change the production environment.

request fulfillment—The process responsible for managing the lifecycle of service requests. (ITIL definition)

requirement—Something that is necessary or essential.

root cause—The most basic reason for an undesirable condition or problem, which if eliminated or corrected, would prevent the undesirable condition or problem from existing or occurring.

root cause analysis—A methodical way of determining why problems occur and identifying ways to prevent them.

service asset and configuration management (SACM)—The process responsible for ensuring that the assets required to deliver services are properly controlled, and that accurate and reliable information about those assets is available when and where it is needed. (ITIL definition)

service level management—The process of negotiating and managing customer expectations by establishing SLAs, which spell out the services the IT organization—including the service desk—provides to the customer, the customer's responsibilities, and how service performance is measured.

severity—The impact an incident is having on the business.

Six Sigma—A disciplined, data-driven approach for eliminating defects in any process.

standard—A document that contains an agreed-upon, repeatable way of doing something.

target escalation time—A time constraint placed on each level that ensures that incident resolution activities are proceeding at an appropriate pace.

target resolution time—The time frame within which the support organization is expected to resolve an incident.

target response time—The time frame within which the service desk or level two acknowledges the incident, diagnoses the incident, and provides the customer with an estimated target resolution time.

Total Quality Control (TQC)—The system that Japan developed to implement *Kaizen*, or continuing improvement.

Total Quality Management (TQM)—A management approach to long-term success through customer satisfaction.

trend analysis—A methodical way of determining and, when possible, forecasting service trends.

urgency—A measure of how long it will be until an incident, problem, or change has a significant impact on the business. (ITIL definition)

workaround—A temporary way to circumvent or minimize the impact of an incident.

Review Questions

1. Define the terms *process* and *procedure*.

2. Explain the relationship between processes and procedures.

3. How are flowcharts used in business?

4. Describe the benefits of establishing simpler business processes.

5. Describe the difference between a framework and a standard, and provide an example of each.

6. True or False. ITIL is a framework that can be used to design and develop new IT services. Explain your answer.

7. How do TQM and Six Sigma differ in approach?

8. What is ISO/IEC 20000?

9. What four characteristics do all process frameworks and standards have in common?

10. What is the objective of the incident management process?

11. What are questions and inquiries, and how are they different than incidents?

12. Provide two examples of a workaround.

13. Describe the difference between incident tracking and incident management.

14. What two criteria determine an incident's priority?

15. Define the term *escalation*.

16. List three reasons why incidents might be escalated from level one to level two.

17. Describe the responsibilities of an incident owner.

18. Why is incident management referred to as a "closed loop process"?

19. What is the purpose of incident notification?

20. What are the objectives of the problem management process?

21. Define the term *root cause*.

22. List at least two reasons why companies differentiate between incidents and problems.

23. Why is it important to determine the root cause of problems?

24. What is the objective of the request fulfillment process?

25. List at least two reasons why companies differentiate between incidents and service requests.

26. List at least two ways the incident management and request fulfillment processes are similar.

27. Provide two examples of information stored in a knowledge management system.

28. What two types of technologies have dramatically changed the way companies view the knowledge management process?

29. What brings together members of a community of practice?

30. Why is it important to test new technologies before they are moved into the production environment?

31. What are two ways the service desk may participate in the change management process?

32. If no formal change management process is in place in the company, what can service desk management and staff do to stay on top of upcoming changes?

33. How does the change management process enable the service desk to be proactive?

34. What is the difference between inventory and service asset and configuration management?

35. Describe a scenario wherein the CMS integrates with the incident management process.

36. Describe a scenario wherein the CMS integrates with the request fulfillment process.

37. Provide three examples of items described in SLAs.

38. How do SLAs influence service desk and customer expectations?

39. Describe three tasks that a business relationship manager performs.

40. What makes it possible for the service desk to perform trend analysis?

Hands-On Projects

1. **Discuss Adam Smith's principle.** Assemble a team of at least three of your classmates and discuss Adam Smith's principle of the division of labor. Think of business examples in which you still see this principle in action, and then select one example that everyone in your group has experienced. Write a brief description of the example you have selected, and then document your answers to the following questions:

   What are the pros and cons of assigning specialized tasks to the workers at this business?

   How could this business potentially streamline its business processes?

   How would customers benefit from streamlined business processes?

   What factors may hinder the business's ability to implement the streamlined business processes?

2. **Develop a process flowchart.** Assemble a team of three to five classmates. Develop a flowchart that shows all the steps for having a pizza delivered that contains the toppings the entire team agrees upon.

   a. Begin the process with the decision to order a pizza, and end the process by throwing the pizza box in the recycling bin.

   b. If you have access to flowcharting software, use it to construct and print your flowchart. The most popular flowcharting software is Microsoft Visio (*www.microsoft.com/office/visio*). SmartDraw (*www.smartdraw.com*) and bizagi (*www.bizagi.com*) also offer flowcharting software that you can download free of charge.

   c. Develop procedures for at least two of the steps in your process.

3. **Distinguish record types.** Working as a class, consider the various types of records discussed in this chapter such as incidents, questions, inquiries, service requests, and changes. In the context of a service desk that supports a standard PC environment and uses Microsoft software products, list three examples of each record type.

4. **Determine an incident's priority.** Working with a group of two or three classmates, discuss the following incident scenarios. Document the priority the team would assign to each incident and why. You must make some assumptions to determine the priority; document your assumptions.

   a. The company president calls with a question about how to use an advanced spreadsheet feature.

   b. An administrative assistant calls to report that one of the five computers in her area is not working.

   c. An angry customer calls and insists that someone come to his department immediately to change the toner in his printer.

   d. A customer calls to indicate that neither she nor her coworkers can log on to the system through the network. She can, however, use a software package installed on her PC.

5. **Identify and prevent root causes.** Using your school's online message or discussion board, or working together as a class, use the brainstorming, Five Whys, or cause and effect analysis technique to determine and document the root cause of and ways to prevent the following problem: You are on your way to school and your car sputters to a stop on the side of the road. Why did your car stop?

6. **Learn about knowledge management.** Knowledge management is recognized as a very important service desk process. Cross-generational knowledge transfer is a particularly important consideration as millions of baby boomers prepare to retire. Search the Internet for articles that describe:

   - How Gen Y and Millennial workers view the topic of knowledge management and information sharing

   - How organizations are handling cross-generational knowledge transfer.

Write a brief report that outlines how these different generations view knowledge sharing and that lists five steps that can be taken to enable effective cross-generational knowledge sharing.

7. **Identify the tasks required to complete a service request.** Either alone or with a small group of classmates, consider all of the tasks that are required to log a service request for setting up an office for a new employee. Prepare a list of all the tasks that must be completed to provide the new employee with the office setup you would expect to have when starting work at a new company.

8. **Assess the impact of a change.** Imagine that you are the change manager for a company that does business entirely via the Internet. The head development engineer calls to indicate he wants to make a small change to one of the programs that controls the shopping cart application that is used to conduct e-commerce. He indicates that he has tested the change on his system and it worked fine. Using a scale of low to high, write a report explaining what risk and impact you would assign to this change and why.

9. **Learn about service asset and configuration management.** Interview an acquaintance, family member, or coworker who works in an IT department. Write a short paper that answers the following questions:

   • Does this person have access to a CMS or CMDB (even if it is called something different)?

   • If so, what data or information can this person derive from the repository? How often does this person use the repository? Does this person consider the repository a useful tool? Please explain.

   • If not, would this person benefit if a CMS or CMDB were established? Please explain.

   • Does this person ever experience a situation where the same data is stored in more than one repository?

   • If so, what problems arise with maintaining the data or with knowing which repository should be viewed as the definitive source?

Case Projects

1. **Minimize Customer Dissatisfaction.** A level two service provider has just informed you that because another incident he is working on is taking longer than expected, he will not meet the target resolution time for an incident that you own. The only other person who could work on the incident is on vacation this week. Briefly describe who you would notify and how you would minimize customer dissatisfaction in this situation.

2. **Customer Responsibilities in SLAs.** You have been chosen to work on a committee that is drafting an SLA to be used during negotiations with service desk customers. For the first meeting, each attendee has been asked to prepare a list of suggested customer responsibilities. Prepare for the meeting by listing your recommendations. Think through any service encounters you have been involved in (such as calling a software publisher or hardware vendor) when preparing your list and determine what you feel was reasonable for vendors to ask you to do.

CHAPTER 5

The Technology Component: Service Desk Tools and Technologies

In this chapter you will learn:[1]

- ◎ How technology benefits the service desk
- ◎ Common technologies found in service desks
- ◎ The tools used by service desk managers
- ◎ The relationship between processes and technology
- ◎ The steps involved in selecting service desk technology

[1] All ITIL definitions © Crown copyright 2014. All rights reserved. Material is reproduced with the permission of the Cabinet Office under delegated authority from the Controller of HMSO.

The service desk uses a wide array of tools and technologies—collectively referred to as technology—to do its work. A **tool** is a product or device that automates or facilitates a person's work. **Technologies** are inventions, processes, or methods that enable the creation and enhancement of tools. For example, advances in wireless technology have led to a rise in mobile computing. Tools and technologies allow the service desk to handle customer contacts such as telephone calls, emails, text messages, and chats; log and resolve incidents and service requests; and manage information. Service desk tools range from simple email and voice mail to more complex and sophisticated telephone systems, incident management systems, and knowledge management systems. These tools enable service desk staff to work more efficiently and effectively. As a result, the service desk can reduce or maintain costs while increasing productivity.

Service desks often combine or integrate tools and technologies to quickly transfer data between systems and to automate routine tasks. The tools and technologies a service desk uses depend on the funding it has available and on the number and complexity of the processes being supported—such as incident management, problem management, knowledge management, change management, service asset and configuration management, and request fulfillment. Very small or new service desks often rely on the telephone or email and a simple web- or PC-based tracking system. Larger service desks use a wide variety of tools in an effort to address incidents and service requests efficiently and effectively.

Tools and technologies are part of the service desk job whether you work in a small, growing service desk or a large, established one. Although the variety of tools and technologies used vary from one company to the next, the intent and benefits of them typically do not. Understanding the advantages of these tools and technologies will help you to adapt quickly when new technologies are introduced and will also help you use tools to be more self-sufficient and productive.

How Technology Benefits the Service Desk

The number of incidents that service desks handle is on the rise, as is the number of customers that service desks support, the number of devices and application components that service desks support, and peoples' dependence on those devices and applications. This increase, coupled with management pressure to do more with less, induces many companies to use technology to maximize their resources.

A service desk can use technology to:

- Offer customers a variety of support channels such as the telephone, email, web forms and online chat.

- Increase the efficiency with which incidents and service requests are handled by, for example, using remote control and diagnostics systems and knowledge management systems.

- Proactively avoid or minimize the impact of incidents through the use of monitoring systems.

- Communicate and collaborate with others via social media.

- Gather, organize, and use information about its customers, which improves decision making and reduces the number of recurring incidents.

- Gather, organize, and use information about IT assets and how they are configured, which improves the service desk's ability to assess the impact of incidents and service requests and assign priorities.

- Gather, organize, and use the information needed to charge customers—when applicable—for services, which ensures the costs associated with the service desk are accounted for, recovered, and in keeping with business requirements.

- Monitor critical hardware, software, network, and application components and proactively detect incidents, which speeds the resolution of incidents and reduces their impact.

- Eliminate manual, repetitive functions (such as password resets), which frees service desk staff to work on complex incidents and special projects.

- Empower customers to identify and potentially solve routine incidents, or electronically submit service requests, which frees service desk staff to develop even more self-help services.

- Manage costs, optimize staffing levels, and most importantly, provide excellent customer service, which leads to management and customer satisfaction.

Technology enables a service desk to handle more incidents and service requests, resolve them in a prioritized and timely manner, offer more ways for customers to request services, and optimize the efficiency and effectiveness of service desk staff. Technology enables service desk staff to focus on more complex and challenging incidents, rather than routine and recurring incidents. It also enables service desk staff to work on projects that offer the opportunity to learn new skills.

However, technology can be costly and can be a detriment when it is implemented without the benefit of well-designed processes and well-trained staff. Technology costs include both one-time costs and ongoing costs.

One-time costs that may be incurred include:

- Consulting fees

- Requirements definition, design, and development activities

- Hardware and software purchases, including licensing fees

- Education, awareness, and training programs

- Additional staff—such as technical support staff—recruiting, training, salaries, and accommodations

Ongoing costs may include:

- Maintenance fees

- Upgrades and enhancements

- Consulting fees, such as for ongoing improvements

- Ongoing education, awareness, and training

- Ongoing system administration and support

- System integration activities

System integration involves physically or functionally linking together different computer systems and applications. System integration is critical in a service desk setting, as it allows analysts to view and use data from multiple systems without having to log on and off of those systems individually. Instead, analysts can create and use data and information from diverse systems via a single integrated system such as a web site.

Organizations often fail to recognize all of the costs—particularly the ongoing costs—associated with service desk technology. Or, they implement multiple systems over time without recognizing the impact those systems are having on the service desk and its customers.

Poorly implemented technology can reduce, rather than increase, the productivity of service desk analysts. For example, analysts may be required to manually rekey data from one system to another due to a lack of integration. Or, system performance and response time may suffer because ongoing maintenance activities, such as installing upgrades and additional memory and disk space, are not performed in a timely fashion. Inadequate training can also reduce analysts' ability to fully reap the benefits of technology.

Poorly implemented technology can also reduce, rather than increase, customer satisfaction. Some organizations implement so much technology that customers view it as a barrier to service. Other organizations implement technology that fails to consider the skills and preferences of their customers. For example, they might have a sophisticated telephone system, but have customers who prefer to use the web. Or, they have a sophisticated web site, but their customers prefer to—or sometimes need to—speak with someone over the telephone.

Care must be taken when implementing technology to ensure the costs do not outweigh the benefits. It is also important to first clearly define the roles and responsibilities of the people who will be using the technology, along with the processes the technology is being implemented to support. Technology should match and support processes and not the other way around.

Selecting and Implementing Service Desk Technologies

Each service desk chooses its tools based on its size, company goals, the nature of the business it is in, and customer expectations. For example, very small service desks tend to use a small set of fairly simple tools. As service desks grow, they rely on increasingly sophisticated and complex technology. Some companies are committed to maximizing their use of technology and are willing to take risks and quickly adopt new technologies. Other companies take a more conservative approach and introduce technology only when the technology is proven and there is a clear business benefit.

All service desks can benefit from technology. Small service desks sometimes mistakenly believe that they don't need technology, or they lack the time to implement and use technology. As a service desk grows and becomes busier, it becomes increasingly difficult to implement technology, and so the service desk becomes overwhelmed. A better approach is to implement technology—even if only simple technology—while the service desk is small. Then more sophisticated technology can be implemented as the service desk grows. With this approach, analysts become comfortable using technology to do their jobs, and the service desk needs less time to adopt new technologies.

The nature of the company's business and customer expectations also influences a service desk's tool selection. For example, customers expect companies in high-technology industries to use state-of-the-art support technology. Customers would be surprised if companies such as Microsoft and Apple didn't have web sites that offer robust support services, such as online tutorials and knowledge bases, as well as a variety of channels that can be used to obtain support. On the other hand, customers do not expect industries and companies that are less technology-oriented to use sophisticated systems. However, customers do expect even less technology-oriented companies to offer basic support services such as answers to FAQs and the ability to submit inquiries via email.

Some tools and technologies are used in most service desks. Nearly all companies have a telephone number that customers can call to report incidents and submit service requests. Telephone technologies range from simple voice mailboxes to highly complex, automated systems. Some companies also provide customers with the ability to submit incidents and service requests through email, fax, and web-based systems.

Service desks must carefully manage customer expectations of target response times for contact channels such as the telephone, voice mail, and email. Unless informed otherwise, customers expect to receive immediate, real-time responses. Many companies specify target response times for all contact channels in their SLAs or when communicating their services to customers. For example, a service desk may indicate that telephone calls will be answered within 60 seconds, voice mail messages will be answered within 15 minutes, and email messages will be answered within 30 minutes.

Target response time reflects how long the service desk will take to acknowledge the customer's contact, not how quickly it will resolve the incident or service request.

Most companies also use tools to record customers' incidents and service requests in some way. Some companies use paper forms to record incidents. However, pressure from customers and from management to deliver services faster, cheaper, and better prompts even very small service desks to implement an incident management system. According to HDI's *2012 Support Center Practices and Salary Report*, 89 percent of companies have implemented a system to enable their service desks to log and manage incidents and service requests. An additional 3 percent of the companies surveyed plan to add an incident management system within 12 months. Often, these companies are integrating their incident management systems with knowledge management systems so they can capture and reuse known errors and solutions.

The sections that follow describe in greater detail the technologies most commonly found in service desks.

Telephone Technologies and Services

The telephone is the primary way that most service desks communicate with their customers. According to HDI's *2012 Support Center Practices and Salary Report,* more than 95 percent of its members indicated that customers request services via the telephone. Although many companies also use technologies such as email and the web to deliver support services, the telephone will always play a role in customer service. This is for a variety of reasons: some customers do not have access to email or the web, some may be temporarily unable to access email or the web, while others simply prefer to interact with a human being, particularly when they are having a problem. During a typical telephone call, a service desk analyst talks to a customer, asks questions, enters responses into a computer, and assists the customer, often using information from a computer system. Telephone technology automates many of these functions.

Telephone Technologies

Service desks depend on and benefit from a number of telephone technologies. Figure 5-1 lists the telephone technologies most commonly used in service desks.

- Voice over Internet Protocol
- Voice mail
- Fax
- Announcement systems
- Automatic call distributor
- Voice response unit
- Computer telephony integration
- Recording systems

Figure 5-1 Telephone technologies commonly used at service desks
© Cengage Learning 2014

Because telephone technologies tend to be tightly integrated, it can be difficult to tell where one technology ends and another begins.

Voice Over Internet Protocol

Voice over Internet Protocol (VoIP) systems translate voice communications into data and then transmit that data across an Internet connection or network. At the other end, the data is converted back into its original voice form and emerges like a regular phone call. In other words, VoIP transmits voice communications in the same way that email and instant messaging systems send messages across the Internet. A benefit of VoIP in a service desk setting is that an organization can reduce its costs by using its existing data network to route phone calls. Cost reductions include the ability to reduce telephone company fees, long distance charges, and costs associated with supporting and maintaining both a voice and data network. Other benefits include integration with existing data systems and analyst mobility. For example, VoIP systems enable many of the computer telephony integration features offered by traditional telephone systems such as screen pops (discussed below). VoIP also makes it easy for companies to link local service desks and analysts working at home.

 Popular VoIP providers include Skype and Vonage.

One obstacle to VoIP is that companies using traditional telephone systems need to invest in significant upgrades to their data network in order to support VoIP traffic and to guarantee both call quality and network reliability. Without such upgrades, a network-related incident could result in poor call quality, and a network-related outage could result in all channels used to contact the service desk being unavailable. Despite these concerns, most companies are moving to VoIP rather than upgrading or replacing their existing telephone systems when those become obsolete. New call centers and service desks are likely to be VoIP only.

Voice Mail

Voice mail is an automated form of taking messages from callers. Companies often combine voice mail with automatic call distributors and voice response units, enabling customers to choose between waiting in a queue or leaving a message. More than 54 percent of companies use voice mail to take after-hours calls, according to HDI's *2012 Support Center Practices and Salary Report*. Customers can perceive voice mail negatively if, for example, a previous voice mail message was not returned or if they are not given an idea of when the call will be returned. The best companies set and manage voice mail response times and promptly return all customer calls, even if only to let the customer know the call was received, logged, and is being handled.

Fax

A **fax**, short for facsimile, is an image of a document that is electronically transmitted to a telephone number connected to a printer or other output device. Faxes can be sent and received via fax machines, multi-function printers, or computers. Faxes can also be sent and received via email. Some companies allow customers to fill out forms requesting service and then fax the form to the service desk. According to HDI's *2012 Support Center Practices and Salary Report*, slightly more than 10 percent of its members receive incidents via fax, down from 25 percent in 2008. Some service desks also ask customers to fax reports that contain error messages, for example, so an analyst can see the report and better diagnose the incident. Faxed incidents and service requests typically are logged the same way as a telephone call.

Announcement Systems

An **announcement system** greets callers when all service desk analysts are busy and can provide valuable information as customers wait on hold. For example, companies often use an announcement system to let customers know about a major incident such as a computer virus that is affecting a high number of customers. Or, companies may use an announcement system to announce the release of a new product. Customers then can obtain additional information by visiting the company's web site. Often, announcement systems are integrated with automatic call distributors and voice response units.

Automatic Call Distributor

An **automatic call distributor (ACD)** answers a call and routes, or distributes, it to the next available analyst. If all analysts are busy, the ACD places the call in a queue and plays a recorded message, such as, "We're sorry, all of our service representatives are currently assisting other customers; your call will be answered in the order it has been received." ACDs are very common in medium and large service desks that handle a high volume of calls. They are also increasingly found in small service desks that are experiencing a growing call volume. According to HDI's *2012 Support Center Practices and Salary Report,* 67 percent of its members use automatic call distributors. Another 6 percent plan to add ACDs within 12 months.

A **queue** is simply a line. The term *queue* can be used to refer to a list of calls, tickets, or email messages waiting to be processed.

ACD software determines what calls an analyst receives and how quickly the analyst receives those calls. Analysts use an ACD console such as the one shown in Figure 5-2 to perform ACD functions.

Figure 5-2 Sample ACD console
Courtesy of American Telebrokers, Inc.

An ACD console enables analysts at their desks to:

- Log on at the start of a scheduled shift each day and place the telephone in an available state. An **available state** means the analyst is ready to take calls.

- Log off any time they leave their desks for an extended period of time and log on when they return.

- Log off at the end of a scheduled shift each day.

- Answer each call routed to them within a certain number of rings, as specified by service desk policy, to avoid an idle state. An **idle state** means the analyst is logged on to the ACD but is not accepting calls. For example, the analyst may be speaking with someone who has arrived at the analyst's desk. When an idle state occurs, the ACD transfers the call to the next available analyst.

- Correctly use **wrap-up mode**, a feature that prevents the ACD from routing a new inbound call to an analyst's extension. Analysts use this wrap-up time to finish documenting the customer's request after they have hung up, to escalate a call, and to prepare for the next call. Many companies establish guidelines for how long analysts can stay in wrap-up mode before making themselves available to take the next call.

The terminology used to describe ACD functions and states differs slightly from one ACD system to the next.

ACDs provide a wealth of statistical information that the service desk can use to measure its performance, such as the number, duration, and time of calls received and how quickly calls are answered. Chapter 6 discusses these performance measures.

ACDs can integrate with and use other technologies to deliver information to analysts and customers. For example, when integrated with an announcement system, an ACD can inform customers about the status of a system that is down. Or, the ACD can use caller ID data to provide the analyst with the name of the caller. ACDs also can use the caller's telephone number or information collected from the caller to route the call. This information can be captured in a number of different ways, including via an automated attendant.

ACDs may also come with advanced features. Two common ACD advanced features are automated attendant and skills-based routing.

An **automated attendant** is an ACD feature that routes calls based on input provided by the caller through a touch-tone telephone. Some systems have speech-recognition capability that allows customers to speak their input rather than key it in through their telephone keypad. A basic automated attendant prompts the caller to select from a list of options or enter information, such as the extension of the party the caller wants to reach, and then routes the call based on the caller's input. Automated attendants can be much more sophisticated. They can also be integrated with other technologies to enhance functionality. For example, automated attendants can use caller ID to identify the customer and then route the caller to an appropriate analyst or group of analysts.

Skills-based routing (SBR) is an ACD feature that matches the requirements of an incoming call to the skill sets of available analysts or analyst groups. The ACD then distributes the call to the next available, appropriately qualified analyst. Skills-based routing determines the call requirements from the customer's telephone number or information collected from the customer or a database. The call requirements can also come from information the caller provides by selecting or speaking options via a voice response unit. Companies that use SBR require analysts to create and maintain a skills inventory that correlates the products, systems, and services supported by the service desk to each analyst's level of skill. Then, calls can be routed to an analyst who has the skill needed to handle the customer's incident or service request. For example, with SBR, a call about a spreadsheet application can be routed to an analyst who has experience supporting spreadsheets.

Chapter 6 discusses creating a skills inventory in more detail.

Voice Response Unit

Also called an interactive voice response unit (IVRU), a **voice response unit (VRU)** integrates with another technology, such as a database or a network management system, to obtain information or to perform a function. Like an automated attendant, a VRU obtains information by having the caller press keys on his or her touch-tone telephone or, when speech recognition is available, speak his or her input into the telephone. For example, a VRU can collect a customer's personal identification number (PIN) or product ID number and then use it to handle the customer's request or verify that the customer is entitled to service. Companies also use a VRU to automate self-help tasks, such as changing a password, checking the status of an order, or obtaining information such as the service desk's hours of operation. Other companies use a VRU to provide access to a predefined, typically reduced set of service desk services during nonbusiness hours. For example, customers may be able to obtain system status information or request emergency service.

When poorly implemented, voice response technology can lead to customer frustration and may be perceived negatively. For example, some companies offer long menus with a number of confusing options. Others may not offer any way to reach a human being who can help callers determine which option to choose.

To increase customer acceptance, the optimum number of choices for a VRU menu is four options that lead to no more than four additional options. Optimally, one of the options enables customers to speak with an analyst. To avoid confusion and frustration, VRUs should also be programmed to allow callers to repeat the menu options, return to the main menu, and cancel input. A well-designed VRU leaves callers feeling that they are in control of calls and have options, not that the company is trying to avoid human interaction.

Computer Telephony Integration

Computer telephony integration (CTI) links computing technology with telephone technology to exchange information and increase productivity. Companies use CTI at the service desk to perform functions such as screen pops and simultaneous screen transfers. CTI also can facilitate outgoing calls.

A **screen pop** refers to a CTI function that enables information about the caller to appear or "pop" up on the analyst's monitor and is based on caller information captured by the telephone system and passed to a computer system. Figure 5-3 illustrates how the telephone system can use caller ID to determine the caller's telephone number and how the computer system can look up the telephone number in the company's customer database to find additional information about the caller, such as the caller's name and address. The computer can add this information to the telephone number and create a new ticket that pops up on the screen of the analyst taking the call. The analyst can quickly verify the customer information and then ask questions and add details of the customer's incident to the ticket.

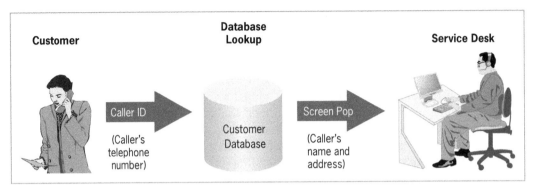

Figure 5-3 Computer telephony integration
© Cengage Learning 2014

If the service desk analyst realizes that the customer should be transferred to another support group, he or she can perform a **simultaneous screen transfer**, a function that transfers the call as well as all the information collected in the ticket up to that point. The ticket pops up on the screen of the analyst receiving the transferred call as the customer comes on the line. Customers greatly appreciate this function because they do not have to repeat details they already provided to the first analyst.

Recording Systems

Recording systems record and play back telephone calls. These systems enable a company to monitor and evaluate analyst performance or record calls for security purposes. Companies that use this technology often inform customers about the recording system by playing a message such as, "Please be advised that this call may be monitored or recorded for quality purposes."

Telephone Services

Telephone technologies are even more effective when combined with certain services provided by local and long-distance carriers. These telephone services deliver information that the telephone technologies use to process calls. This information can considerably increase the efficiency with which analysts handle calls. Customer satisfaction increases as well because customers do not have to provide as much preliminary information, such as their name and address, when their call is answered or transferred to another analyst. Instead, they can focus on describing their incident or service request. Figure 5-4 lists the most common telephone services used in conjunction with telephone technologies at service desks.

- Automatic number identification
- Caller identification
- Dialed number identification service
- Information indicator digits

Figure 5-4 Common telephone services
© Cengage Learning 2014

Automatic Number Identification

Automatic number identification (ANI) is a service provided by a *long-distance* service provider that delivers the telephone number of the person calling.

Caller Identification

Caller identification (caller ID) is a service provided by a *local* telephone company that delivers the telephone number of the person calling. Where available, caller ID can also provide a name associated with the calling telephone number.

Dialed Number Identification Service

Dialed number identification service (DNIS) provides the number the person called when the call is made using a toll-free number or a 1-900 service. A popular use of DNIS is to direct customers to specialized support groups without requiring the caller to select from a telephone menu. For example, a software publisher may assign different toll-free numbers to its various products. With DNIS, the company can determine which toll-free number the customer dialed and then route the call to analysts familiar with the associated product.

Information Indicator Digits

Information indicator digits (IID) identify the origin of a call from the type or location of the telephone being used to place the call, such as a public phone, cell phone, or hotel phone. Some service desks that support a remote workforce have begun using this service so they can adjust their call handling procedures based on where the customer is calling from. For example, if a customer calls from the corporate office, his or her telephone number, automatically obtained with caller ID, can be used to do a CTI lookup. If that same customer calls from a public or cell phone, he or she may be prompted to enter a PIN so the CTI lookup can be performed.

In a business setting, a company's telephone system typically also provides features such as the ability to place calls on hold, establish conference calls with multiple people, and transfer calls to other telephone numbers or extensions. Most service desks have policies regarding the use of these features, because the features can be very frustrating to customers when used improperly. These features should be employed sparingly and with the customer's consent.

When telephone technologies are implemented properly, customers are unaware that these services are being used. They just know that their call is being routed efficiently to the analyst who has the skills needed to provide assistance. Or, they are being given alternate ways to request support, such as voice mail, email, or the web. Analysts benefit from these technologies because calls suited to their skills are routed to them in an orderly manner and arrive with information that analysts can use to immediately begin supporting the customer. Companies also benefit, as they have a wealth of data and information that can be used to understand customer calling patterns, optimize a service desk's staffing levels and measure its performance, and when applicable, charge for its services.

Email

Most service desks—just under 87 percent according to HDI—use email in some way to communicate internally, with other support groups, and with their customers (*2012 Support Center Practices and Salary Report*, HDI). For example, email can be used within the service desk to communicate schedule changes, promote awareness of process or procedure changes, and notify staff of upcoming system changes. Service desk analysts and managers may use email to communicate with other support groups about the status of projects or about changes to existing procedures. Some companies use email to communicate with customers.

Using Email to Communicate with Customers

Email is an easy way to communicate with customers. For example, many companies integrate their email, incident management, and knowledge management systems. They can then email status updates, solutions, and workarounds from their incident and knowledge management systems.

Most service desks use email to conduct customer satisfaction surveys. Customers are sent a form to complete and return or they are sent a link to a form on the service desk's web site that they can fill out and submit. The responses are typically stored in a database that service desk managers can use to run reports and analyze service desk performance.

It is also common for companies to use email to distribute the service desk's newsletter or to announce upcoming changes that might affect customers. These emails often refer customers to the service desk's web site for additional information. Sending the email ensures that customers who are not in the habit of regularly checking the service desk's web site receive the information they need.

It is less common for service desks to view email as a primary way of communicating with customers for a number of reasons. First, email can be perceived as impersonal and typically doesn't provide the immediate, interactive feedback that customers want, particularly when they are confused or upset. Second, email does not provide many of the capabilities that an incident management system provides. For example, email cannot be used to automatically create trend reports, and it cannot be used as a knowledge management system. As a result, service desk analysts are usually required to log all email incidents and service requests from customers in their company's incident management system. Analysts are then able to record all status updates related to a customer's incident or service request in the incident management system, not in email messages that may be lost or forgotten. Third, analysts sometimes find that using email prolongs the problem-solving process. For example, if the service desk receives an email that does not contain sufficient information, the analyst must either try to contact the customer by telephone or send an email message back to the customer requesting the needed details. The analyst must then wait for a reply before being able to solve the incident. According to HDI, 43 percent of emails require two exchanges to resolve an incident (an exchange is one received and one sent email) and an additional 23 percent of emails require three exchanges (*2011 Support Center Practices and Salary Report*, HDI).

Email exchanges are conversations with another person. Think about and acknowledge that person just as you would if you were interacting face to face or over the telephone. Include only things you would say if that person were standing in front of you or with a group of people.

Service desks are using a number of techniques to ensure that email communications are handled efficiently and effectively. These techniques include:

- Providing analysts with email etiquette training and guidance

- Integrating email packages and incident management systems

- Using forms and templates

- Using email management systems

The next sections explore each of these techniques.

Providing Analysts with Email Etiquette Training and Guidance

A growing number of service desks provide analysts with training and guidance to ensure that they use common sense, courtesy, and best practices when using email to communicate with customers. Email best practices include making sure all of a customer's questions and concerns are addressed; avoiding lengthy discussions and debates; and using correct grammar, punctuation, and spelling, to name just a few. Some companies recommend that analysts have a coworker or a supervisor review important or complicated emails before they are sent to customers.

To learn more, search the web for sites about "email etiquette" or go to sites such as *www.businessemailetiquette.com*, *www.iwillfollow.com/email.htm* and *www.emailreplies.com*.

Integrating Email and Incident Management Systems

Many incident management systems integrate with standard email packages (such as Microsoft Outlook and IBM Lotus Notes) to allow, for example, email messages from customers to be logged as tickets automatically. The incident management system then can automatically send a return email message to inform customers that their incidents were logged and to provide ticket numbers. Some companies' incident management systems automatically send email messages to customers whenever the status of their incident changes. Other companies send email messages with a description of the final resolution when the ticket is closed. This integration makes it possible for companies to provide customers with the convenience of using email, while still having the ability to use their incident management systems to collect and maintain incident-related data. Companies can then also combine data about incidents submitted by email with data about incidents submitted via other channels such as the telephone and the web.

Using Forms and Templates

Service desks use forms and templates to customize their email messages and to distribute and collect information electronically. A **form** is a predefined document that contains text or graphics users cannot change and areas in which users enter information. Forms can be designed to use elements such as text-entry boxes, check boxes, buttons, and pull-down menus to collect information. Forms can also be designed to require responses to any of these elements before the user can submit the form. The data entered in a form can be saved in a file or in a database. Companies that integrate their email and incident management systems typically design their forms to correspond to the entry screen of the incident management system so that incidents can be logged automatically. Customers may choose forms from a forms library, from a location within their email system, or from a web site. Figure 5-5 shows a Shutterfly Help Center web form used to submit email questions to the company's support team. Notice that the form has fields that capture customer data, such as email address and first and last name, along with fields that the customer can use to submit a question and specify the related product and category. As with most forms, in this one an asterisk (*) denotes fields that are required, and the Product and Category fields have pull-down menus that limit the data options. Limiting the data options facilitates routing the question to the correct support group within the organization and also enables effective reporting. Many organizations have extensive systems in place—such as knowledge management systems—that can use these data fields to first determine if the question can be answered automatically.

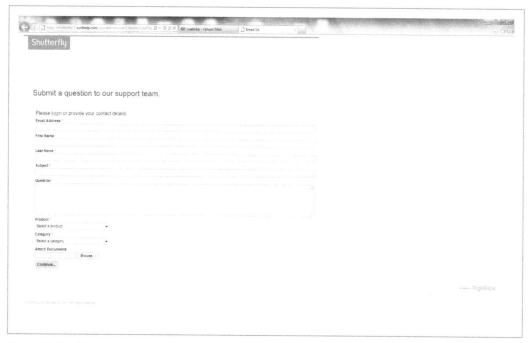

Figure 5-5 Sample web form
© 2012 Shutterfly, Inc. Reproduced by permission of Shutterfly, Inc.

Forms save time for customers, analysts, and service desk management. Customers save time because they know what information they must provide to submit an incident or service request. Analysts save time because they get all the information they need to begin working on the ticket. Service desk management saves time because the information is in a format that can be used for statistical analysis, rather than in an unstructured format.

A **template** is a predefined item that can be used to quickly create a standard document or email message. For example, service desks can prepare standard openings and closings for emails being sent to customers. Templates save analysts time because with a template, they can create documents and email messages quickly by reusing text and items such as links to web sites or pages on the service desk's web site.

Using Email Management Systems

Email management systems such as emailtopia (*www.emailtopia.com*), Kana (*www.kana.com*), and RightNow (*www.oracle.com*) enable service desks to manage high-volume chat, email, and web form messages in much the same way that ACDs enable service desks to handle telephone calls. For example, these systems enable service desks to route messages to queues; run real-time reports to determine such statistics as how many emails are received per hour, per day, and so forth; prioritize messages; and categorize messages so service desks can report on the types of messages being received. These systems also allow analysts to search and review customer messages and to view a history of a customer's activities on the support web site. In other words, service desk analysts can see the various web pages, FAQs, and so on that a customer examined prior to submitting his or her message. These systems are an excellent option for service desks that use email as their primary communication channel with customers. According to HDI, 73 percent of its members use email management systems (*2012 Support Center Practices and Salary Report*).

 Thanks to email, communicating with coworkers and customers is easier and faster. Common sense, good judgment, and good writing skills let you make the most of this powerful communication tool.

The Web

The web provides many benefits to service desks and their customers, including:

- The web provides the service desk with an invaluable source of information about the products and systems the service desk supports and about the service desk industry in general.

- The web is an excellent vehicle for communicating and collaborating with coworkers, vendors, and customers.

- The web enables the service desk, its customers, and others in the support organization to access required data, information, and knowledge at any time and via a wide variety of devices.

- The web gives the service desk an alternative and less expensive way to support customers.

- The web enables the service desk to empower customers to support themselves.

Many of today's technology-savvy customers expect services that free up their most valued commodity—time. These customers expect and feel quite comfortable using web-based self-help services, such as password resets, software and document downloads, and searchable knowledge bases and FAQs. According to HDI's *2012 Support Center Practices and Salary Report*, 82 percent of respondents offer or are currently planning to offer some form of web-based self-help services. Companies that don't have web sites appear inefficient and out of touch. Customers perceive companies that offer ineffective web sites or that don't provide customers with multiple ways to obtain support as trying to avoid direct communication.

CASE STUDY: Popular IT Portals and Blogs

A number of excellent portal sites provide the service desk industry with information about service desk-related products and services. A **portal** *is a web "supersite" that provides a variety of services, such as a site search to locate pertinent articles and white papers, a product and services buyer's guide, a discussion or message board, event calendars, and publications. Service desk portals include* www.helpdesk.com *and* www.supportindustry.com. *One of the most popular IT portals is* www.techrepublic.com. *TechRepublic serves professionals representing all segments of the IT industry (including the service desk), providing information and tools for IT decision support and professional advice by job function. The TechRepublic site also has a help desk blog at* www.techrepublic.com/topics/help+desk. *A* **blog,** *or web log, is a journal kept on the Internet. Blogs are typically updated frequently and display entries in reverse chronological order. They often contain links to other useful web sites. Blogs exist for many topics and can be located by entering the topic name, followed by the word "blog" into the search box of any browser. Blogs are a good source of industry news, commentary, and guidance. Other service desk blogs include* www.hdiconnect.com/blogs.aspx *and* blogs.forrester.com/category/service_desk.

Functionality and ease of use are the keys to a successful service desk web site. Through their web sites, some service desks provide customers:

- Answers to FAQs

- A "Call Me" button to request a phone call from an analyst to discuss an incident

- A "Chat" button to correspond in real time with analysts online

- A "Contact Us" button or tab to find other ways to contact a company or department, such as through the telephone or email

- A discussion or message board for customers to submit questions and exchange ideas with other customers

- A glossary to learn the definition of terms they may encounter

- A knowledge base of solutions to solve incidents on their own

- A place to check the status of outstanding incidents by pulling up a previously submitted ticket
- A place to maintain a personal account that houses information such as the customer's telephone number, postal address, and email address
- Customer satisfaction surveys to provide feedback
- Information about new and planned products and services
- Information about current and planned service outages
- Links to other useful web sites
- Products and product updates that authorized users can download
- The ability to use remote control systems (discussed later) to aid problem solving
- Tips, techniques, and helpful hints
- Training schedules for company-sponsored training classes
- Web forms to submit incidents and service requests

Like service desk technologies in general, the functionality that a service desk's web site provides depends on factors such as the service desk's size, company goals, the nature of the company's business, and customer expectations. Not all service desks and companies have web sites, although the number of service desks without web sites is diminishing rapidly. Figure 5-6 shows the Check Point service desk web site. This site provides news and announcements at the top of the site and access to the knowledge base. Customers can sign in to access account information and visitors to the site can initiate a chat session with a sales or support representative. Customers can also create a service request or check the status of an existing service request. Visitors to the site can select a product and access more specific information such as downloads, documentation, forums, and security alerts. Quick links allow customers to perform a variety of actions, including reporting a security issue, obtaining information about the company's policies, and joining forums to interact with the company's support staff and other customers.

Figure 5-6 Sample service desk web site
Courtesy of Check Point Technologies, Inc.

The web has changed the way customers expect support services to be delivered. Web-based services will not, however, completely eliminate the telephone and email—at least not for the foreseeable future. Some customers do not have access to the web, even if only temporarily. Some customers prefer to speak with a human being. Others may try to use the web, become frustrated, and then place a telephone call or send an email message.

Web-based services do offer a cost-effective alternate way to provide support services. Use of the web continues to grow as customers have more access to and become more comfortable with this technology. Furthermore, by integrating service desk technologies, the service desk can know that a customer accessed the web prior to using another channel and automatically route the customer to the correct line of support. For example, a customer who is unsuccessful in installing a software upgrade may use the "Call Me" button or initiate a chat session to obtain assistance from an analyst.

Web sites typically reflect one of three stages of development—passive, interactive, or real-time. Passive web sites are essentially online brochures or bulletin boards. They provide customers with access to information and they direct customers to call the service desk for additional details. Interactive web sites provide customers a more two-way experience. For example, customers can specify a symptom and obtain a solution, or customers can post messages and view the responses of other customers. Real-time web sites enable customers to have "live" contact with analysts or other customers. That contact may involve a chat, a demonstration using a whiteboard system, or the resolution of an incident using remote control software. The state of development of a service desk's web site typically corresponds to its customers' needs and expectations.

Web sites that offer the ability to interact in real time with analysts and other customers are particularly important in organizations that offer high levels of self-help and self-service. This is a growing trend for a number of reasons. One reason is that technology users have become more self-sufficient and are more comfortable attempting at least initial diagnostics on their own. Another reason is that companies have invested heavily in knowledge management systems that enable customers to attempt to resolve incidents on their own. Yet another reason is that some organizations limit, or perhaps even charge a fee for, contact with service desk analysts; but they offer a wide range of free services via their web site. This is a common practice for software publishers, hardware manufacturers, and organizations that have BYOD (bring your own device) programs. With BYOD, rather than train the service desk on every possible device that users may have, some organizations are opting to provide forums and wikis that make it possible for users to get help from other users and to access and contribute to a knowledge base of solutions. In some organizations, the service desk's role now includes monitoring those forums to ensure that users are getting answers to their questions and validating solutions submitted by customers.

INTERVIEW WITH. . .

Courtesy of CompuCom Systems, Inc.

MEG FRANTZ
VICE PRESIDENT,
eKNOWLEDGE
COMPUCOM SYSTEMS, INC.
DALLAS, TEXAS
WWW.COMPUCOM.COM

The Service Desk at CompuCom is part of the ITSM & Shared Services division and provides desktop, mobile, and software-related support for more than 75 clients nationwide.

Organization. We have 1307 people in our Service Desk who are located in Dallas and Houston, Texas; Toronto, Ontario; Santa Fe and Interlomas, Mexico; San Jose, Costa Rica; and Pune, India. We also have several hundred analysts and technicians who are located at client sites. We have a number of different job positions that offer a great deal of opportunity to our employees. Our Customer Support Specialists provide first- and second-level support for specific software and hardware products or for a suite of products. Our Field Services Specialists troubleshoot, order parts, and dispatch Field

Engineers to customer sites. We also have Client Advocates who serve as account managers for specific clients, as well as operational Team Leaders and Managers.

We have a Cross-Functional Services team that supports the integrated telephony, incident management, knowledge management, automated reporting, and workforce management systems used by our analysts and management team, as well as other tools used for e-support. Technology is important because our clients want cost-effective services but are unwilling to sacrifice value and quality. Technology enables us to satisfy our customers by offering the mix of on-site, remote, and self-assisted support they need.

Our Quality team uses the data and information from these systems to ensure we are performing processes that meet our specific quality standards. We have a number of people within the organization who have been trained to use Six Sigma techniques to continually improve our efficiency and productivity.

Our eKnowledge team uses the Knowledge-Centered Support (KCS) strategy to ensure our processes and standards for adding knowledge are consistent and that the knowledge is valuable. The KCS approach increases agent satisfaction not only because it enables our analysts to achieve a high success rate when using the knowledge management system, but also because they can contribute knowledge that is then quickly published and made available to others. Our clients benefit as this approach enables us to achieve higher first contact and overall resolution rates.

The use of technology enhances employee satisfaction in other ways as well. For example, because our clients are often able to use self-help services, our analysts have the opportunity to work on more complex and challenging issues. We are also able to offer more flexibility to our employees such as the ability to work at home. Greater flexibility benefits CompuCom as well as our employees. For example, we've been able to reduce turnover and absenteeism. We are also able to extend opportunities to a wider variety of job candidates, including retirees and disabled veterans, in addition to young people.

At the heart of our success as an organization is a commitment to continuous improvement. For example, we've adopted ITIL best practices in an effort to continually improve our service management processes. Our internal IT department has achieved ISO/IEC 20000 certification annually since 2008. This certification, achieved following an independent, third-party audit, demonstrates not only our commitment to quality, but also enables us to demonstrate compliance with relevant government regulations. We have achieved the prestigious Support Center Practices (SCP) certification every year consecutively since 1997. This program requires comprehensive on-site audits and examines the major criteria required to operate a successful service desk.

Additionally, all of our analysts are required to achieve numerous certifications within three months of being hired. These certifications include a client-specific certification, ITIL awareness, and internal certification programs that focus on our analysts' soft skills such as customer service and technical troubleshooting, as well as use of our knowledge management tools. Analysts are required to renew this training and achieve a score of 90 percent or better every six months. More than 90 percent of our analysts also hold vendor-specific certifications.

Tasks. Depending on the service level agreement we have with a client, our analysts provide first- and second-level hardware, software, and network support. Clients may use our web-based, self-help services or contact us via the telephone, email, or chat. We provide templates that make it easy for our analysts to manage chats and respond to emails in a professional, efficient way. We try to resolve incidents remotely when possible, or we can dispatch an on-site engineer. Our analysts log every customer contact, and we make every effort to ensure resolutions are thoroughly documented in our knowledge base so other analysts can use them in the future.

CompuCom is a technology company and so our employees are encouraged to make the most of our technology resources. This includes using the knowledge base before reaching out to Service Desk staff and also using technology in a professional way in support of best practices. We also have a "bring your own device" policy to enable greater flexibility and mobility.

Philosophy. Our commitment to continuous improvement and our "easy to work with and flexible" approach has led to a strong reputation for quality and an extremely loyal customer base. We know that our people are the key to that success, whether those people are interacting directly with customers or working behind the scenes developing and maintaining our processes and tools. We like to hire competent people who apply their knowledge and experience to their work and who keep the customer's perspective in mind as they do so. To keep employee retention high, we focus on a "Total Agent Package" for our employees, offering: a good work environment, a robust set of tools and technologies, a team building atmosphere, additional pay on performance, a good working relationship with others, and recognition for jobs done well.

Incident Management Systems

Incident management systems are the technology used to log and track customer contacts. By logging all customer contacts such as incidents and service requests, the service desk prevents the most common customer complaint, which is that contacts are lost or forgotten. Figure 5-7 shows a screen that an analyst might use to log a new incident. This view of the incident record provides customer data, the related SLA, the incident's priority (based on impact and urgency), and the preferred assignment group. A check box provides the ability to specify whether the incident is a major incident. The affected service (Email) and configuration item are specified; clicking on the service reveals a diagram of its configuration. Both a short and detailed description of the incident are provided, along with its category (Software -> MS Office -> Outlook). The category (Profile) field works with the Find Solutions button to search for related problems and known errors. Tabs across the top provide access to associated information and documents. Buttons across the top are used to advance the incident to the next step in the process, for example, Log & Assign or Log and Resolve/Close. Best practice is to leave the incident open until customer satisfaction with the resolution is verified. Some organizations change the status to "Resolved" once the resolution is identified, and then to "Closed" when customer satisfaction is verified.

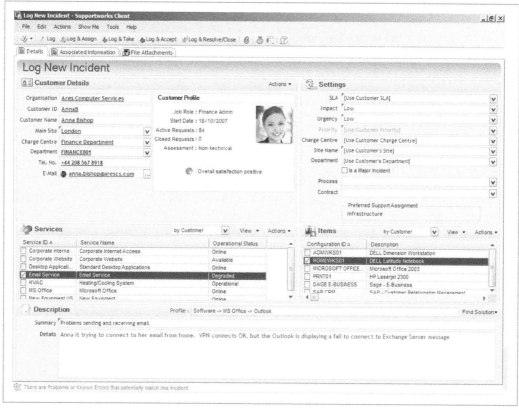

Figure 5-7 Sample incident entry screen
Courtesy of Hornbill Service Management

In some companies, customers can contact the service desk via multiple channels, such as the telephone, email, fax, and the web. In an effort to consolidate incident data, many companies integrate these systems and log incidents automatically. Or, they require analysts to log all incidents in an incident management system, regardless of how the customer reported the incident. When analysts log incidents in an incident management system, they can use the many features these tools provide to track incidents from start to finish. For example, many incident management systems generate alerts when incidents cannot be resolved immediately to remind analysts to contact customers with status updates. Many incident management systems allow analysts to access a service asset and configuration management system or knowledge management system. This allows the analysts to obtain information about the services, systems, and devices a customer is using and to access a knowledge base and obtain solutions to known errors. These systems also integrate with the information or systems used to manage SLAs such as target response and resolution times.

Logging all incidents provides the service desk with the data needed to track (and when necessary, escalate) outstanding incidents and to perform trend and root cause analysis. When incidents must be escalated, the data documented in tickets is used by level two and level three groups to further diagnose and ultimately solve the incidents. This data is also used by management to create reports and analyze trends. Analysts must work hard to ensure that the data they collect is accurate, complete, and timely. Many service desks encourage analysts to capture data in real time—for example, by logging calls while talking to a customer on the telephone.

Most analysts use telephone headsets that free their hands for typing. Incident management system features such as check boxes, buttons, and pull-down menus also help analysts quickly and accurately log incidents in real time.

Incident management systems fall into several distinct types or categories. The first category breaks down into incident management systems used by companies that provide external support and those that provide internal support. Although external and internal service desks use many of the same types of tools, they have slightly different requirements. For example, external service desks often verify that the customer is entitled to support, whereas internal service desks do not. Also, companies that provide external support often must capture information needed to create customer invoices, whereas internal service desks typically do not. The tools external and internal service desks use must enable them to automate these varying procedures.

Companies providing external support may use Customer Relationship Management (CRM) systems to track incidents and service requests, along with sales-related interactions. Using a CRM system enables anyone interacting with a customer to view the details of other interactions.

The second category of incident management systems considers the processes the system will manage, the volume of incidents and service requests that will be processed, and the number of system users expected. The number of system users includes level two and level three management and staff and, in some cases, customers, in addition to level one service desk management and staff. This second category divides incident management tools into homegrown incident tracking systems, commercially developed incident management systems, and integrated ITSM solutions.

Homegrown Incident Tracking Systems

Small service desks sometimes develop relatively simple incident tracking systems in-house. Tools developed in-house are usually referred to as "homegrown." **Homegrown incident tracking systems** tend to support only the incident management process and offer basic trouble ticketing and reporting capability. These systems are typically developed with tools such as Microsoft Access and Microsoft SQL Server and may not be able to support a high number of users or a high volume of data. Small or medium service desks that are looking for a system they can get up and running quickly often use homegrown solutions.

According to HDI's *2012 Support Center Practices and Salary Report*, 10 percent of organizations use homegrown systems. Given a good design and ongoing support, these systems can provide a small service desk with a system that meets their needs. If nothing else, these systems enable service desks to collect the data they need to justify a commercially developed system.

A downside of systems developed in-house is that they tend to be poorly documented, making it difficult to maintain and enhance the system, especially if the individual who developed the system originally has moved to another department or company. In time, most companies outgrow their homegrown system and replace it with a commercially developed system so they can rely on the vendor to support and continuously improve the product.

Commercial Incident Management Systems

Commercially developed **incident management systems** offer enhanced trouble ticketing and management reporting capability. For example, they often offer the ability to log "quick tickets" with only a click or two and to link related contacts. Like homegrown systems, these are relatively simple tools that tend to support only the incident management process; although they may also support processes such as request fulfillment, change management, service asset and configuration management, and service level management in a limited way or as an add-on module. Often, these tools are compatible with the ITIL framework. According to HDI's *2012 Support Center Practices and Salary Report*, 64 percent of the organizations surveyed indicated that ensuring tools are compatible with the ITIL framework was either necessary or very important.

These systems typically provide the automated escalation and notification capabilities that are needed in a multi-level support environment in which incidents and service requests are handed off to other analysts or specialty groups. These systems also provide more advanced diagnostic capabilities and knowledge management systems. In addition, these systems offer some customization and integration capability, such as integration with email and telephone systems. Because these tools are based on relational or structured query language (SQL) database engines, they can support a higher number of users and a higher volume of data. These tools may also be available as a cloud-based, hosted service, thus providing the flexibility to support the number of users or the volume of data required by the company.

Medium-size service desks—and smaller service desks that anticipate considerable growth— often use commercially developed incident management systems. A large service desk looking for an interim system also may use these tools.

Integrated ITSM Solutions

Integrated ITSM solutions, sometimes called enterprise solutions, are a suite of systems that companies use to manage their incident, problem, knowledge, change, and service asset and configuration management and request fulfillment processes. These tools are typically compatible with the ITIL framework. In addition, integrated ITSM solutions tightly integrate with network and systems management tools, asset management tools, and sophisticated knowledge management systems. Integrated ITSM solutions can be customized comprehensively and have many advanced features. Typically, integrated ITSM solutions are based on relational databases and on a client-server architecture, or are cloud-based, which makes these solutions able to support a high number of users and a high volume of data. For example, these solutions are often used by global companies that have IT staff in multiple locations worldwide but want to maintain a central source of information.

Medium to large service desks that require—and see the value in implementing—an integrated tool suite often use these solutions.

Locate hundreds of other vendors and products in this market by searching the web for topics such as "service desk software," "service desk tools," "service management software," and "free service desk software."

Companies tend to change their incident management systems periodically. Either they outgrow their existing systems, indicated by slow response time and inadequate functionality, or they replace their systems as new technology becomes available. Experienced service desk analysts depend on up-to-date incident management systems to provide quality support to customers. Increasingly, companies are integrating their incident management systems with knowledge management systems.

The presence of many vendors and a competitive marketplace means that technology companies are frequently acquired or simply stop doing business. For this reason, service desks must use great care when selecting technology.

Leading vendors that offer incident management systems and integrated ITSM solutions include BMC (*www.bmc.com*), Computer Associates (*www.computerassociates.com*), FrontRange Solutions (*www.frontrange.com*), HP (*www.hp.com*), Hornbill (*www.hornbill.com*), and ServiceNow (*www.servicenow.com*). Many of these vendors offer multiple products that are designed to fit an organization's size, budget, and requirements. Many of the leading incident management system vendors offer their software as a service.

CASE STUDY: Living in the Cloud

Cloud computing is affecting the service desk both in terms of the technologies the service desk uses, and in terms of the technologies that the service desk supports. Many service desks are opting to "rent" versus "buy" support solutions in much the same way that their customers are turning to cloud-based services for other business activities. **Software as a service (SaaS)** *is a software delivery model in which software and the associated data and information are centrally hosted by a vendor and made available to users via the Internet. In a SaaS model, software is paid for on a subscription basis. The cost of the subscription will vary based on factors such as the number of users that will be accessing the service and the amount of data storage that is required. Adopting a SaaS model offers many benefits such as lower initial IT costs, because the vendor retains responsibility for the infrastructure, platforms, and people needed to manage the service itself. Users access the service via any client that can access the*

Internet. With a SaaS model, companies can start small and fairly easily scale up the service as needed to meet their needs and budget. Another benefit is that the service provider manages the availability of the service to ensure that it is up and running as needed, along with upgrades to and maintenance of the service. A downside of adopting a SaaS model is that companies acquiring these services are no longer in control in terms of when upgrades and maintenance activities are performed. Other factors companies must consider include: data security and privacy, contingency planning in the event of an outage, and the fact that the company may have limited flexibility when it comes to customizing the service, or may be required to pay a premium for customized capability.

The service desk plays many different roles in a SaaS model. The SaaS providers themselves have service desks that support the external customers who are using the providers' services. Organizations and the SaaS providers will have contracts and SLAs that address areas important to the service desk such as availability, incident response and resolution times, and maintenance windows. Internal service desks must understand how the business or the service desk itself is using these third-party services and the associated contracts and SLAs that are in place. Many organizations maintain information about all services, including cloud-based services, in a service catalog. A **service catalog** *is a list of services that an organization provides to its customers. A service catalog typically provides a description of services and their deliverables, along with associated pricing and contact information, and information about supporting services, such as those provided by the service desk. Internal service desks must put in place procedures for handling incidents, problems, and access requests for these cloud-based services, just as they would any other services. These procedures must spell out when and how the internal service desk will escalate issues to the SaaS provider.*

Knowledge Management Systems

As children, we learn to work with other people and to acquire skills from them. As adults, we bring this same approach to the workplace. However, the pace of change has accelerated to the point where we can no longer depend on learning only from colleagues. As companies strive to find the optimal staff size, colleagues with the expertise an analyst needs do not always exist in the company, much less in the service desk. If colleagues with expertise do exist, they often carry a heavy workload or are busy learning new skills themselves. As a result, many companies have implemented knowledge management systems. Recall that a knowledge management system is a set of tools and databases that provide the ability to store, manage, and present information and knowledge.

These systems support what is known as the data-information-knowledge-wisdom (DIKW) hierarchy, which is illustrated in Figure 5-8. In the context of the DIKW hierarchy, **data** is a set of raw facts that is not organized in a meaningful way. For example, data about a workstation may include its manufacturer and model number. Data becomes information when it is organized in a meaningful way by, for example, analyzing relationships that exist between the data. Information is capable of answering questions such as "Who?, What?, When?, and Where?". For example, information about a workstation includes who owns it and where and when it was installed. In a service desk setting, data and information are stored in databases such as CMDBs and in databases that underpin management systems such as access management, HR, and CRM systems. These systems provide input to knowledge management systems.

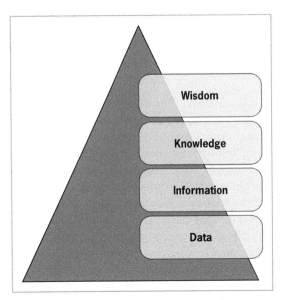

Figure 5-8 Data-information-knowledge-wisdom (DIKW) hierarchy
© Cengage Learning 2014

In the context of the DIKW hierarchy, **knowledge** is the application of information along with people's experiences, ideas, and judgments. Knowledge enables people to answer the question "How?". For example, knowledge about a workstation includes how to resolve an incident or how to upgrade that workstation. In a service desk setting, knowledge is stored in databases such as knowledge bases and known error databases that provide input to knowledge management systems.

Wisdom is the judicious application of knowledge. Wisdom enables people to answer the question "Why?". Wisdom is created when people have the knowledge and experience to make sensible decisions and judgments. Wisdom generally deals with the future and is uniquely a human characteristic. In other words, collecting and using data, information, and knowledge enables people to make wise decisions.

Knowledge management systems enable companies to capture human knowledge and make it available to others who are involved in solving problems and making decisions. Although these systems may be available to all of a company's employees and its customers, the access management process will be used to grant authorized users the right to use these systems in accordance with the company's security policies. For example, customers may only be able to view proven solutions and only those solutions that match their skills and experience. Service desk staff are typically granted greater privileges, but may still have some restrictions. For example, service desk staff may be restricted access to solutions that can only be performed by level two and level three staff. Also, service desk staff may be permitted to add, but not approve, solutions to the knowledge base. Approving solutions is typically the responsibility of a knowledge engineer.

 Customers are often able to access portions of a company's knowledge management system by clicking a Support link on the company's home page.

In the support industry, knowledge management systems and knowledge bases are widely used and provide access to information and knowledge sources such as diagnostic scripts, incident resolutions, known errors and workarounds, and documents such as user's guides, policies, and procedures. According to HDI's *2012 Support Center Practices and Salary Report*, 90 percent of companies are using or actively planning to use a knowledge management system. That percentage increases to 96 percent in larger organizations. This is primarily because most of the incident management systems and integrated ITSM solutions discussed earlier can be purchased with embedded knowledge management systems. In other words, if a company acquires a leading incident management system or integrated ITSM solution, that system either comes with a built-in knowledge base or a knowledge base can be purchased as an add-on product and integrated with the base product. Some companies do, however, purchase and implement standalone knowledge management systems. Service desks that support custom applications must use knowledge management systems that they can develop to capture knowledge in-house. Service desks that support standard industry applications from Microsoft, Lotus, Novell, and others can directly access these vendors' web sites. Service desks can also purchase commercially available knowledge bases that are pre-populated with information provided by these vendors. The pre-populated information is consolidated and formatted in a consistent manner, making it easier to use.

Knowledge management system providers include Consona Corporation (*www.consona.com*), KnowledgeBroker (*www.kbi.com*), Knowledge Powered Solutions (*www.kpsol.com*), Moxie Software (*www.moxiesoft.com*), and RightAnswers (*www.rightanswers.com*).

Whether the knowledge management capability is embedded in an incident management system or acquired as a stand-alone product, organizations can achieve the greatest return on their investment by providing access to the knowledge management system via a wide variety of channels including smartphones, email, online portals, chat, and social media. Organizations can also achieve a return on investment by taking advantage of technology advances in the areas of knowledge management and by introducing social media technologies such as forums, wikis, and social networks.

Most hardware and software vendors post answers to FAQs and solutions to known errors on their web sites. Many service desks have links to vendor web sites on the service desk web site, making them easier to access.

A reason that knowledge management technology is used widely in the support industry is because early rule-based expert systems have been replaced by more sophisticated case-based systems that are easier to use and maintain.

A **rule-based system** is made up of rules, facts, and a knowledge base or engine that combines rules and facts to reach a conclusion. Some companies tried (unsuccessfully in most cases) to implement rule-based expert systems in the mid-1980s. Rule-based systems are difficult to build and maintain because every rule added to the rule base can potentially interact with every other rule. Because of this complexity, these systems are now rarely used in the support industry.

Case-based systems have proven to be a much more viable way to manage knowledge in today's fast-paced support industry. A **case-based system** is made up of cases and a set of question and answer pairs that can be used to confirm the solution to an incident. A **case** is a unit of information, such as an online document, a database record, or the solution to a common incident, which is indexed so an analyst can easily locate it when needed. A case contains a description of the incident and a description of the solution. It also may have a frequency counter that indicates how many times the solution has been used to solve the incident or a score that indicates the relevance of the solution to the search criteria. Figure 5-9 shows the results of a Novell knowledge base search. The search form includes both a freeform short description field that the user specifies and a pull-down menu that is used to limit the list of products to valid options. The results are ranked and an indicator is provided along with a key to place results into categories such as Best Bet, Support TID (ticket ID), Articles/Tips, Documentation and so forth. Filters provide the ability to further limit the search results based on criteria such as content type, date range, and whether or not to include archived articles. Note that along with the search results, users are offered the ability to open a service request, chat with a representative, or join a support forum.

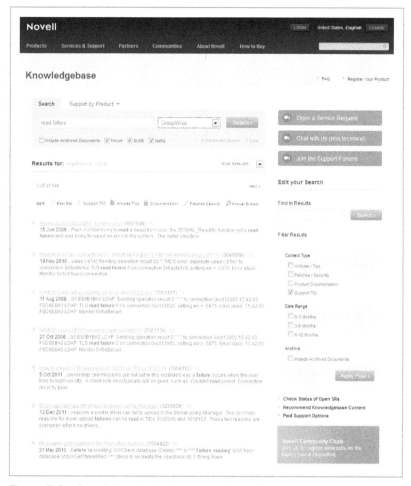

Figure 5-9 Sample knowledge base search results
Courtesy of Novell, Inc.

Case-based systems are much simpler to implement than rule-based systems and offer the service desk far more flexibility and power. They also offer the control that is needed to ensure that the information provided complies with the organization's IT governance and security policies and that intellectual property and proprietary knowledge are protected.

Knowledge management is fundamentally about ensuring that the right information is available to the right people at the right time. This can occur both formally, for example, via a well-managed case-based knowledge management system, or informally. For knowledge management to succeed, people must be willing to share their knowledge. For example, some organizations use wikis, to encourage more informal knowledge sharing. Other organizations use community portals to encourage knowledge sharing among subject matter experts. A knowledge management strategy is needed to ensure that these wikis are not used informally to capture information that should be captured more formally in the company's knowledge management system. A knowledge management strategy will also ensure that wikis do not become knowledge silos that inappropriately limit who can view or contribute to the knowledge base.

Search Retrieval Techniques

Much of the flexibility and power in a case-based system comes from the many search-retrieval technologies available. Figure 5-10 lists the most common of these technologies. These retrieval technologies allow users to specify search criteria, which is then used to retrieve similar cases. **Search criteria** are the questions or symptoms entered by a user. Some of these retrieval technologies do very simple data matching, whereas others use highly sophisticated artificial intelligence.

- Case-based reasoning
- Decision trees
- Fuzzy logic
- Keyword searching
- Query by example

Figure 5-10   Common search retrieval techniques
© Cengage Learning 2014

Case-Based Reasoning

Case-based reasoning (CBR) is a searching technique that uses everyday language to ask users questions and interpret their answers. CBR prompts the user for any additional information it needs to identify a set of possible solutions. Not only does CBR find perfect matches based on user queries, but it also retrieves cases that are similar to the perfect match. Possible solutions are ranked in order of probability from most likely to least likely to solve the incident.

Decision Trees

A **decision tree** is a branching structure of questions and possible answers designed to lead an analyst to a solution. Decision trees work well for entry-level analysts and for service desk customers because they can walk through a methodical approach to solving incidents. Senior analysts and "power users" often feel that the use of decision trees increases the time needed to identify a solution.

Fuzzy Logic

Fuzzy logic is a searching technique that presents all possible solutions that are similar to the search criteria, even when conflicting information exists or no exact match is present. For example, fuzzy logic can get results when the exact spelling of a word is not known, or it can help users obtain information that is loosely related to a topic.

Keyword Searching

Keyword searching is the technique of finding indexed information by specifying a descriptive word or phrase, called a keyword. Keywords must be indexed to be located, and an *exact* match must be found. For example, if a user specifies the keyword "computer," only records that contain the keyword "computer" are located; records that contain the keyword "PC" are not located. Some systems provide the ability to index synonyms as well as keywords to increase the number of matches found when a search is performed.

Query by Example

Query by example (QBE) is a searching technique that uses queries, or questions, to find records that match the specified search criteria. Queries can include **search operators**, which are connecting words such as AND, OR, and NOT. Search operators are also called Boolean operators. QBE also can find records that *do not* contain the search criteria or that contain a value less than, greater than, or equal to the specified search criteria.

 Search retrieval technologies have value only if the information in the knowledge base is current, complete, and accurate. If it isn't, then out-of-date, inaccurate, or incomplete information will be delivered when a search is performed.

Storage Methods

Search-retrieval techniques are complemented by interactive storage methods, such as hypermedia and hypertext retrieval. **Hypermedia** stores information in graphical forms such as images, movies, and videos. **Hypertext** is text that links to other information. **Hyperlinks** are text or graphics in a hypertext or hypermedia document that allow readers to "jump" to a related idea. Clicking a hyperlink might open a pop-up window with a definition, instructions, a diagram, a still picture, or an animated picture. Hyperlinks can also present audio or video streams, and they can jump to other web pages. Readers can easily move to more detailed information and back to a higher level by clicking hyperlinks that are embedded in the document.

Knowledge management systems allow service desk analysts access to knowledge even if the resident expert is away on vacation or in training. With knowledge management systems, the knowledge is available online whenever it is needed. Storing knowledge online also enables service desks to make that knowledge available to customers via their web sites. These systems lead an analyst or a service desk customer through troubleshooting steps that help resolve incidents, which in turn improve the analyst's and the customer's problem-solving skills.

Also, without these systems, the resident expert may spend a great deal of time answering questions and handling difficult incidents in one particular area. Sometimes, this occurs so frequently that the resident expert doesn't have the time or the energy to pursue new skills.

Being the resident expert used to be considered "job security." Today, companies want people who share their knowledge with coworkers and customers, cross-train their coworkers, and continuously develop new skills. Contributing to and using knowledge management systems enables analysts to achieve all of these goals.

 ITIL introduces the **service knowledge management system (SKMS)**, which is defined as a set of tools and databases used to manage knowledge, information, and data. The configuration management system and known error database form part of the SKMS.

Configuration Management Systems

As discussed previously, CMSs are the technologies that allow an analyst to access information about, for example, mobile devices or the components, or CIs, installed on a computer or network along with related information. Related information may include information about associated incidents, problems, service requests, known errors, changes, or releases. For example, a CMS may provide the ability to view and report on all of the incidents that have been reported about a particular hardware device or on all of the changes that have been made to that device. Related information may also include financial information such as license and warranty information.

Managed via the service asset and configuration management process, a CMS is typically one part of an integrated set of tools, rather than a single, standalone tool. For example, a CMS may be a web portal that provides the ability to view data from multiple CMDBs, KEDBs, and an incident management system. Or, a CMS may be part of an integrated ITSM solution that integrates with all the other applications in that solution.

A variety of systems may be used to collect the data and information stored in CMDBs and CMSs. For example, the incident management systems and integrated ITSM solutions discussed earlier in this chapter typically provide applications that can be used to *manually* collect and store asset and configuration data. PC and network inventory software can *automatically* collect data about networked devices and load that data into CMDBs and the CMS. Examples of vendors that offer PC and network inventory products include Absolute Software (*www.absolute.com*), Express Metrix (*www.expressmetrix.com*), Kace Systems Management Appliance by Kace (*www.kace.com*), LANDesk software (*www.landesk.com*), ZENworks by Novell (*www.novell.com*), Software Innovations UK Limited (*www.systemhound.com*), and Total Network Inventory by Softinventive Lab (*www.softinventive.com*).

Many of these vendors have products that offer the capability to manage mobile devices as well PC and network components. Other vendors offer products that focus primarily on mobile device management, such as Airwatch, LLC (*www.air-watch.com*) and Zenprise (*www.zenprise.com*).

Few organizations have the resources to manually inventory their assets and so the ability to automatically collect configuration data is critical. This is particularly true for organizations that are adopting BYOD programs and for organizations that have established PC refresh cycles in an effort to optimize support costs and invest in newer technologies. These organizations need the ability to easily inventory devices and to ensure those devices contain the required security management capabilities.

 Software that can automatically collect inventory information may also provide features such as software metering (knowing what software licenses have been purchased and where they are being used), remote control, remote monitoring, and software distribution systems.

Remote Support Technologies

Few service desks have all of their customers in one building or in one location. In companies that do, typically small companies, service desk analysts often "jump and run" to the customer's desk to diagnose and potentially solve an incident or service request. This approach is far too inefficient and costly for big companies, not to mention the fact that eventually no one is left at the service desk to answer calls. Many incidents can be solved over the telephone or via email or the web, so a better approach is to offer remote support.

The need to provide remote support is compounded by the fact that an increasing number of service desk customers are mobile or work remotely on a regular basis. For example, they work in a hotel, in an airport, at a client site, or at home. International Data Corporation forecasts that by 2015, the world's mobile worker population will reach 1.3 billion, representing more than 37 percent of the total workforce (IDC Press Release, *www.idc.com/getdoc.jsp?containerId=prUS23251912*, January 2012). Because the needs of mobile and remote workers can change daily as they move from one location to the next, supporting these workers can be quite challenging. The challenge is compounded by the fact that many organizations lack the ability to manage and secure remote devices.

Many service desks use remote support technologies to extend the service desk's reach and enhance their ability to resolve incidents, particularly remote incidents. Figure 5-11 lists the most common remote support technologies available to the service desk. Many of the PC and network inventory and mobile device management vendors discussed above have management suites that include many if not all of these technologies. The availability of these technologies depends on factors such as need and available funding.

- Remote control systems
- Remote monitoring systems
- Self-healing systems
- Software distribution systems

Figure 5-11 Common remote support technologies
© Cengage Learning 2014

Remote Control Systems

A **remote control system** is a technology that enables an analyst to view and take control of a connected device to troubleshoot incidents, transfer files, provide informal training, or collaborate on documents. Typically, a customer must first grant the analyst permission to access his or her device.

Remote control systems may be part of an operating system or application, or they may be standalone systems. For example, Microsoft Windows operating systems offer standard features such as Remote Assistance and Remote Desktop (*www.microsoft.com*). The Apple Remote Desktop product can be purchased for use with the Macintosh operating system (*www.apple.com*). Other leading systems include GoToAssist by Citrix Online (*www.gotoassist.com*), pcAnywhere by Symantec (*www.symantec.com*), and Netop Remote Control by Netop Tech (*www.netop.com*).

Although some service desks cannot use remote control systems because of security concerns, many service desks, small to large, find that that they can solve incidents more quickly when time is not lost traveling to a customer's location. Also, most customers appreciate the immediacy with which their incident can be addressed when analysts use a remote control system. Because security can be a concern, many remote control systems provide security features such as "prompt to confirm connection," which allows a computer user to permit or reject access to his or her system, and "view only mode," which allows an analyst to see but not control a computer. These systems can control remote devices over the Internet, networks, or modems.

Remote Monitoring Systems

A **remote monitoring system** is a technology that tracks and collects events generated by network, system, or application monitoring systems and passes them to a central server, where they can be automatically picked up and evaluated by the event management process. When appropriate, these events may trigger an incident. This automation—used in conjunction with the event management process—ensures that each incident that represents a risk is logged, even one that may not cause a disruption that users notice. The service desk and other support groups can then use this data to track trends and ultimately prevent incidents. This automation also ensures that incidents that may have gone undetected are addressed. Remote monitoring systems can also pass alerts to a special monitor or electronic whiteboard system that the service desk, other support groups, and even customers can view easily. As network, system, and application incidents tend to affect many users, having a monitor that can be easily viewed makes it possible to keep all analysts—even those that may be on the telephone—informed about outstanding incidents. Figure 5-12 shows a dashboard display that shows network, system, and application status information. This dashboard displays the status of services used at multiple facilities and takes advantage of color coding (not shown) to know at a glance how those services are performing. For example, services with a status of critical (CRIT) are likely shown in red, while services that are okay are shown in green. Note that analysts could click on the tabs at the top to easily view SLAs, the status of applications, and so forth.

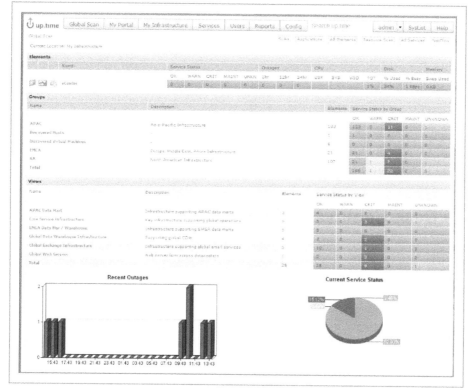

Figure 5-12   Sample service status information
Courtesy of uptime software

Self-Healing Systems

Some hardware devices and software applications can detect and correct incidents on their own, a concept known as **self-healing**. For example, VirusScanOnline by McAfee (*www.mcafee.com*) can monitor a computer for viruses, automatically attempt to clean infected files when a virus is detected, and automatically check for virus updates and software upgrades. The Microsoft Windows 8, 7, XP, and Vista operating systems (*www.microsoft.com*) can all automatically detect and resolve incidents and download software updates from the Internet.

These products and systems monitor, for example, software programs for errors. When errors are detected, these products and systems either find the source of the error and fix it, or they notify the user that an error has occurred. They can also detect whether failing hardware devices or software applications have been changed and they determine what changes could be causing an error. To correct a problem, self-healing systems may back out changes and restore the hardware or software back to its pre-change state.

Software Distribution Systems

A **software distribution system** is a technology that allows an analyst to automatically distribute software to clients and servers on the same network. Software can be distributed to lists of people. For example, all of the users in a particular department can receive software upgrades at the same time. This technology also enables software to be distributed to remote workers. Today's service desk supports a complex computing environment made up of PCs, servers, WANs, LANs, operating systems, applications, databases, mobile devices, and so on. Remote support technologies enable the service desk to centrally support this complex environment, which results in reduced cost, increased productivity for the employees of the company and its customers, and increased customer satisfaction.

Service Desk Communication Tools

Service desk communication tools are manual, electronic, and computer technologies that display or share information within a service desk or between a service desk and other support groups and customers. Service desk communication tools promote awareness with customers and within the service desk when critical incidents arise or when changes are scheduled to occur. These tools can display system status information obtained automatically from a network management system or queue activity obtained from an ACD or email management system. These tools, which include whiteboards, dashboards, instant messaging systems, and social media, enhance and complement the exchange of information that occurs with tools such as email and voice mail. These tools also integrate with smart mobile devices.

Whiteboards

Whiteboards are smooth, erasable white panels on which analysts write notes and communicate current and future events. This simple tool is a very effective way to share information and is often placed where all analysts can view it. The only downside to a whiteboard is that it is a manual device. Analysts must *neatly* write down important information in a timely fashion and remember to erase outdated information. However, that downside can be an upside, as a whiteboard can be used when other automated systems are down. **Whiteboard systems** allow two or more users on a network to view one or more user's drawings, documents, or applications being projected on an onscreen whiteboard. Some service desks use whiteboard systems to project information on a large screen that is visible to all service desk analysts. This approach is particularly useful when there is a major incident that analysts on the telephone need to be made aware of, such as a virus alert or system outage.

Dashboards

Dashboards are bright displays that send out visual and (in some cases) audible messages to service desk staff and to customer sites that have dashboards installed. Dashboards may also be called electronic reader boards. These tools can be combined with network management consoles to display real-time system and network status information. They can also be integrated with ACD management consoles, as shown in Figure 5-13, to display real-time statistics such as the number of calls in queue (CIQ), the longest call waiting (LCW), the number of analysts available to take calls (AVL), the average speed of answer (ASA), and the percentage of calls being answered within agreed service levels (SL%). Note that analysts may be on outbound calls with customers or other support providers. This is often the case when there are no calls in the queue.

Group	CIQ	LCW	AVL	ASA	SL%
CustServ	2	0:00	3	0:00	100%
Sales	5	0:02	9	0:30	92%
TechSup	7	0:30	15	1:00	88%
New CRM released this weekend. Expect high call volume.					

Figure 5-13 Dashboard showing real-time ACD statistics
© August_0802/Shutterstock.com; © 2014 Cengage Learning

Dashboards are particularly effective when used with color and sound to alert service desk staff that a situation is approaching a preset alarm threshold. For example, if the company policy is for the service desk to answer all calls within 60 seconds, a board can display a yellow message accompanied by an audible alarm when a call is nearing the targeted time. The message changes to red after the targeted time is past. Red alarms notify management that standards have been exceeded and that action is required.

Instant Messaging Systems

Instant messaging systems are text-based forms of communication that enable two or more people to communicate in real time over the Internet. Instant messaging requires that all parties be online at the same time. Companies that provide instant messaging services include AOL, Facebook, Google, Microsoft, Skype, and Yahoo!. Service desk analysts can use instant messaging to communicate with level two service providers about an ongoing incident. For example, a field service representative may use instant messaging to inform a service desk analyst that he or she has arrived at a customer site to begin work on a high-priority incident. Or, a service desk analyst may use instant messaging to communicate with a member of the network support group about a network outage. Like email, instant messaging does not provide the capabilities of an incident management system, so analysts are typically required to record any status updates obtained via instant messaging in the service desk's incident management system. Following this procedure ensures that all parties who access the incident management system have the latest information, not just the parties who are sending and receiving messages.

Communication tools such as email, whiteboard systems, and instant messaging systems are also called collaboration products, because they enable multiple users to work together on related tasks. Many companies use collaboration suites such as Google Apps, Lotus Notes, and Microsoft SharePoint to facilitate collaboration.

Social Media

The phrase **social media** is commonly used to describe any tool or service that uses the Internet to facilitate interactive communication. Unlike traditional media, which delivers content but doesn't allow viewers or readers to participate, social media allows the creation and exchange of user-generated content. According to HDI's *2012 Support Center Practices and Salary Report*, the most common applications of social media at the service desk include collaboration, wikis, forums, blogs, and social networking.

The most commonly used social networking sites are Facebook, Google+, Twitter, LinkedIn, Yammer, and Chatter. The social networking sites used will vary from one organization to the next based on factors such as target audience, demographics, and security and intellectual property considerations. Yammer, for example, is a private social network for use within organizations. Yammer is typically used by organizations that want to restrict access to their network. Facebook and Twitter are often used by schools and universities due to the ages and preferences of their customers. Twitter is often used to communicate system status information, scheduled downtime reminders, and security-related messages.

A social media policy provides guidelines regarding the use of social media at work and the types of information that can and cannot be shared with the public. Know your company's policies and remember that you are responsible for what you say and post online!

Another common application of social media is media or video sharing sites such as YouTube and Vimeo. These sites can be used to upload videos that provide, for example, information about the service desk, how to contact the service desk, how-to demonstrations, and informal training videos.

Social media is an effective way for service desks to communicate with customers. It's important to keep in mind that social media is also an effective way for customers to communicate about the quality of your company's products and services. Many organizations assign one or more people responsibility for monitoring social networking sites in an effort to identify and communicate with customers who may be dissatisfied. An effective technique is to respond in a timely, positive, and professional manner and provide the customer a telephone number or email address that can be used to communicate directly with someone who can provide assistance.

Tools Used by Service Desk Management

A number of tools are designed to help service desk supervisors and managers optimize staffing levels, prepare schedules, and monitor the performance of service desk staff. For example, larger service desks that handle a high volume of calls often use scheduling systems because these tasks (determining staffing levels, preparing schedules, and so on) can be somewhat complex and time consuming. In small service desks, managers tend to perform these tasks manually. Figure 5-14 lists some common tools used by service desk management, especially in larger service desks.

- Staffing and scheduling systems
- ACD supervisor console
- Customer surveying systems

Figure 5-14   Tools used by service desk management
© Cengage Learning 2014

Staffing and Scheduling Systems

Staffing and scheduling systems work with ACD systems to collect, report, and forecast call volumes. This information about the volume of calls received by a service desk is then used to forecast future call patterns, schedule the optimal number of staff, track analyst productivity, and prepare budgets.

ACD Supervisor Console

An **ACD supervisor console** is a system that works with ACD systems and enables supervisors to monitor call volumes and the performance of individual service desk analysts or groups of analysts. As shown in Figure 5-15, the ACD supervisor console displays statistics that are constantly updated, such as the number of analysts logged in, how many calls are in queue, and the length of time calls have been waiting. For individual analysts, supervisors are able to see information such as the skill group the analyst is logged in to, the analyst's average talk time and number of calls answered since logging in, as well as the analyst's current status.

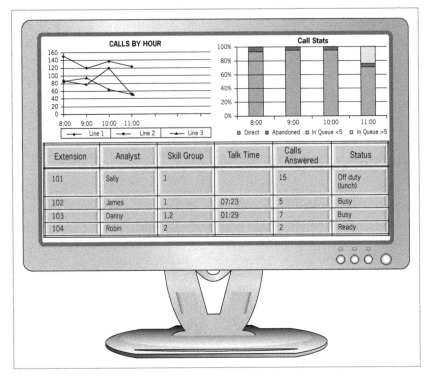

Figure 5-15   Sample ACD supervisor console
© Cengage Learning 2014

Customer Surveying Systems

Customer surveying systems are used to create and distribute questionnaires to customers and to collect and tabulate the results of their feedback. Some customer surveying systems can export the tabulated survey results to statistical-analysis packages, word processors, spreadsheets, and presentation packages.

Tools such as staffing and scheduling systems, ACD supervisor consoles, and customer surveying systems provide service desk managers with the ability to analyze service desk performance data and forecast service desk needs. As a result, service desk managers have the information they need to maximize the efficiency and effectiveness of the service desk team.

Integrating Processes and Technology

The purpose of technology is to support and enhance processes. Technology should not be added simply to automate existing processes and procedures. The reason is summed up in the adage, "If you're doing things wrong and you automate them, you'll only do them wrong faster."

Prior to selecting and implementing new technology, service desk management and staff must evaluate their existing processes and procedures to determine whether they really need new tools and technology or whether they might instead need to refine their processes. As discussed in Chapter 4, process frameworks and standards such as ITIL, MOF, and ISO/IEC 20000 offer guidance that can be used to assess and implement or improve processes. If the decision is made to implement a new technology, then service desk management and staff must select the appropriate tool, often in conjunction with other teams or groups within the IT organization. Properly implemented, technology enables an organization to keep its service desk running efficiently and effectively and, ultimately, increases customer satisfaction. On the other hand, service desk management and staff may determine through analysis that they don't need new tools. They simply need to more clearly define their processes and procedures.

Technology is not a magic pill that can cure all evils. Processes and procedures must be well defined, and *then* tools and technology can enable people to execute the processes and procedures more quickly and effectively.

Steps for Selecting Technology

With hundreds of products on the market, the process of selecting, acquiring, and implementing a support technology that will enhance the capabilities of a service desk can take six to nine months if the service desk follows all the steps required for successfully selecting a new technology. Many companies establish a committee that remains intact until a final decision is made. This committee includes representatives from all of the groups that will use the tool, such as the service desk, level two and three groups, and customers. Figure 5-16 lists the steps for selecting and implementing any technology for a support organization.

- Step 1. Define the goals.
- Step 2. Define the requirements.
- Step 3. Weight the requirements.
- Step 4. Identify candidate vendors.
- Step 5. Evaluate candidate vendors.
- Step 6. Evaluate the finalists.
- Step 7. Make a final decision.

Figure 5-16   Steps for selecting and implementing service desk technology
© Cengage Learning 2014

The next sections show how a service desk follows these steps to select an incident management system. These steps are not, however, unique to selecting an incident management system. The service desk can use this same approach, or methodology, to select and implement any new system.

Step 1. Define the Goals

The first step in selecting a new technology is to determine what the service desk and the company want to achieve by acquiring and implementing the new system. They must be as specific as possible and clearly define how people will benefit from the technology.

When implementing a change such as a new system, continuously communicate the goals of the system and how it will benefit the company, the service desk, and the people who will use it.

When defining goals, the service desk should ask for input from all of the groups and departments that will, or may, use the system to ensure that their needs are considered when making the decision. For example, possible goals for an incident management system are:

- Establish and maintain a central database of information on the status of all incidents.

- Implement a system that enables customers to report incidents easily and accurately.

- Increase the number of incidents resolved by the service desk by x percent within x months.

- Resolve incidents within the time frame defined in SLAs.

- Provide customers with timely and accurate incident status updates.

- Provide the information needed to anticipate and prevent the occurrence and recurrence of incidents.

Most of these goals are measurable, which means that the service desk will be able to statistically measure how well the implemented system attains these goals. These statistics also show management a return on investment.

Clearly defined goals enable a service desk to justify the cost of a new system and to tell vendors what the company is trying to achieve with the new system. In return, vendors can show specifically how their products help the company achieve its goals.

Step 2. Define the Requirements

A **requirement** is something that is essential. The selection committee should first define all the high-level requirements for a new system and then focus on the requirements for specific features and functions.

High-level requirements are the broad needs for a system. High-level requirements for an incident management system include operating platform, performance and growth needs, integration needs, and processes to be supported such as incident management and request fulfillment. High-level requirements provide a framework for the feature and functionality requirements.

Consider available funding when defining requirements. The cost of a system in relation to available funding can be used to include or exclude candidate vendors from the evaluation process.

Feature and functionality requirements are the specifics of how the selected tool must perform in order to support its associated processes. Service desks often break these requirements into categories. Sample categories for an incident management system include functionality requirements, configuration and customization requirements, data and reporting requirements, and security requirements. Another category may include vendor-related requirements, such as vendor stability and pre- and post-sale support.

High-level requirements, along with feature and functionality requirements, enable the selection committee to narrow the field of candidate vendors for the new system. The committee should be as specific as possible when defining requirements. Too often, companies define requirements either at such a high level that the requirements add little value to the selection process or in specific detail without considering the bigger picture. Each approach hinders their ability to identify candidate vendors.

Step 3. Weight the Requirements

The next step is to weight, or prioritize, the requirements. Although, by definition, a requirement is a necessity, some necessities are more important than others. Listing every requirement as a "must have" requirement implies that the perfect system exists, which is rarely the case. When a company weights its requirements, it is more likely to find viable vendors and products early in the search. Table 5-1 shows a sample rating system for weighing requirements.

Expect 80 percent of requirements to be satisfied "out of the box," without customizing the product.

Weight	Priority
1	Not very important
2	Somewhat important (nice to have)
3	Important
4	Very important
5	Extremely important (must have)

Table 5-1   Sample requirements rating system

© Cengage Learning 2014

Step 4. Identify Candidate Vendors

This is one of the most difficult steps in the technology selection process. Hundreds of vendors offer products, and many vendors offer multiple products or a product suite. The selection committee must research vendors and products before determining its top candidates. Resources that can be used to research vendors and products include:

- Conferences, expositions, and technology showcases such as the HDI Annual Conference (*www.thinkhdi.com*) and the itSMF Annual Conference (*www.itsmfi.org*)

 Appendix B contains a list of web sites for a number of these resources.

- Trade publications (remember that the articles are not always unbiased)
- Vendor web sites and discussion forums on the web
- Product evaluation results from research firms such as Gartner, Inc. (*www.gartner.com*) and Forrester Research, Inc. (*www.forrester.com*)

Step 5. Evaluate Candidate Vendors

Step 4 often uncovers many possible vendors to assess. There are a number of ways to approach the candidate evaluation process. Some companies simply have all of the candidates send them product literature and demo packages and then use that information to determine if the product meets the defined requirements. Problems with this approach include:

- Vendors do not always provide the needed information in their literature.
- Not all vendors provide demo packages.
- Vendors receive hundreds of requests for literature and may not respond quickly.
- This process does not use the same criteria to evaluate each of the vendors.

To overcome these problems, some companies prepare and distribute a **request for information (RFI)**, a form or letter that asks for specific product information relative to the company's requirements. Other companies prepare and distribute a **request for proposal (RFP)**, a form or letter that requests financial information as well as product information. Although sometimes perceived as a time-consuming approach, an RFI or RFP is by far the most thorough and objective way to evaluate products. It can reduce the time it takes to select a product because all of the vendors are contacted at the same time, and they have the burden of documentation. Vendors can also be given a deadline for returning their responses and informed that missing the deadline may result in their being disqualified.

Companies typically require all vendors to respond to an RFI or RFP based on the *currently available* production version and release of a product, not a future release. This protects the company in the event a vendor delays or cancels a release. Vendors are also required to clearly state when a supporting product or add-on module is needed to address a requirement. This enables a fair comparison of the vendors. Some RFIs or RFPs provide a separate section that vendors can use to describe their next release.

After vendors send in their responses to the RFI or RFP, the selection committee scores each response to determine how the products satisfy their requirements. Table 5-2 illustrates a sample rating system for scoring vendor responses.

Score	Rating
1	Poor—requirement is not satisfied
2	Fair—borderline implementation of requirement (for example, there is a workaround)
3	Good—requirement is satisfied through an add-on module or is partially satisfied
4	Very good—requirement is satisfied out-of-the-box
5	Excellent—requirement is fully satisfied out-of-the-box with added capability

Table 5-2 Sample vendor scoring system

© Cengage Learning 2014

An evaluation matrix makes it easy to collect and compare these vendor scores. Figure 5-17 shows a sample vendor evaluation matrix. The vendor's score equals its rating multiplied by the weight of the requirement.

Req #	Requirement	Weight	Vendor 1 Rate/Score	Vendor 2 Rate/Score	Vendor 3 Rate/Score	Vendor 4 Rate/Score	Vendor 5 Rate/Score
			Operating Requirements				
1	SaaS	5	4/20	5/25	4/20	4/20	3/15
2	Shared Env	5	5/25	5/25	3/15	4/20	4/20
3	Multi-channel	5	4/20	4/20	3/15	4/20	4/20
	Total Score		65	70	50	60	55

Figure 5-17 Sample vendor evaluation matrix
© Cengage Learning 2014

Step 6. Evaluate the Finalists

If the committee selected vendor candidates carefully, the final vendor evaluation scores will usually be very close. Step 6 enables the selection committee to further narrow the field of candidate vendors. To help make a final determination of the best vendor, they take the two vendors that have the highest scores and perform the following additional steps:

- Invite finalists to come to the company and demonstrate their products. Ask each person who attends a demonstration to provide feedback in writing.

- Contact vendor references and ask a pre-defined set of questions about their experiences using the vendors' products and working with the vendors. Document the references, comments, and any issues or concerns they have with the product.

- If possible, visit other sites that are using the finalists' products. Document what was learned about each product and how it is being used at the site.

- Have representative(s) of your company install and conduct hands-on testing of evaluation copies of the finalists' products. Document the results.

- Conduct tests to ensure that each vendor's product will work with other products that may be installed on the service desk's desktop. For example, run other desktop applications at the same time as the product to ensure that they will work together. Document the results.

Step 7. Make a Final Decision

When the selection committee has completed all of these steps, they then review the vendor scores compiled during Step 5 and the documented results of Step 6 activities. The committee considers the pros and cons of each product and of the vendor's performance in relation to the goals they defined for the system. All of this information and knowledge gained throughout the selection process helps the committee make a final decision. If they have taken their time, documented their efforts along the way, and worked diligently to protect the integrity of the selection process (meaning they required the same information from each and every vendor and subjected each product to the same tests), the committee's final decision should be easy.

Implementing a product goes much more smoothly when users are confident that the decision maker took care to select the best possible solution. The selection committee can encourage this confidence by preparing a report that describes the selection process and how the final decision was made. The report includes:

- **Introduction**—Describes the goals to be achieved by implementing the new system.

- **Summary of requirements**—Provides a brief overview of the requirements for the new system.

- **Evaluation methodology**—Describes the process for selecting candidates, evaluating candidates, and making a final decision.

- **Next steps**—Provides a high-level overview of the steps required to implement the selected product.

- **Appendices**—Includes all of the documentation, such as the evaluation matrix, completed questionnaires, and notes from meetings with references.

Selecting new technology is difficult and can be time consuming, but the service desk gains nothing by cutting the selection process short. It is particularly important that all potential users of the system are involved in the selection process and that every effort is made to consider their needs.

The only constant in the IT industry is change. Without support tools and technologies, this constant and pervasive change can quickly overwhelm the service desk. With the right tools and technologies, the service desk can efficiently receive customer incidents and service requests, prioritize and manage those incidents and service requests, and deliver tested and proven solutions. Support tools and technologies also enable the service desk to help customers help themselves. Properly implemented technology enables the service desk to perform its processes quickly and correctly and to be more proactive. The end result is management, employee, and, most importantly, customer satisfaction.

Chapter Summary

- A wide array of tools and technologies are available to service desks. The availability of tools within an organization depends on the number and complexity of the processes being supported and the funding on hand. Very small or new service desks may use only a telephone and a simple PC-based tracking system. Larger service desks tend to use a wide variety of tools in an effort to address incidents and service requests more efficiently and effectively.

- The telephone is a primary way that customers contact the service desk. Telephone technologies commonly used at service desks include Voice over Internet Protocol (VoIP), voice mail, fax, automatic call distributors (ACDs), voice response units (VRUs), and computer telephony integration (CTI). Telephone technologies are more effective when combined with telephone services such as automatic number identification (ANI) and caller identification (caller ID). When telephone technologies and services are implemented properly, customers are unaware that they are being used. They just know their call is being efficiently routed to the analyst who has the skills needed to provide assistance.

- Most service desks use email in some way to communicate internally, with other support groups, and with their customers. Service desks are using a number of techniques to ensure that email communications are handled efficiently and effectively, including providing service desk analysts with email etiquette training and guidance, integrating email packages and incident management systems, using forms and templates, and using email management systems. Common sense, good judgment, and good writing skills enable service desk analysts to make the most of this powerful communication tool.

- The web provides many benefits to the support industry, and companies that fail to establish web sites appear inefficient and out of touch. Conversely, companies that offer ineffective web sites and that fail to provide customers with multiple ways to obtain support are perceived as trying to avoid direct communication. Functionality and ease of use are the keys to a successful service desk web site.

- Incident management systems are the technology used to log and track customer incidents and service requests. By logging all incidents and service requests and using tools to track their status, the service desk ensures that incidents and service requests are not lost or forgotten. Small service desks tend to use simple homegrown incident tracking systems that offer basic trouble ticketing and management reporting capability. Medium to large service desks tend to use more robust incident management systems or integrated ITSM solutions that provide enhanced capability. Companies may periodically change their incident management systems because either they outgrow their existing systems or they replace their systems as new technology becomes available.

- Knowledge management systems are designed to capture human knowledge and make it readily available to people involved in solving incidents, problems, and service requests. The use of knowledge management technology has become more widespread in the support industry because these systems are often embedded in incident management systems and integrated ITSM solutions. However, they can also be implemented as standalone systems. These systems are most effective when care is taken to ensure that the information captured in the knowledge base is current, complete, and accurate.

- Tools such as configuration management systems, remote control systems, remote monitoring systems, self-healing systems, and software distribution systems extend the service desk's reach and enhance its ability to resolve incidents and service requests, particularly remote ones. The availability of these technologies depends on factors such as need and available funding.

- Service desk communication tools such as whiteboards, whiteboard systems, dashboards, and instant messaging systems promote awareness with customers and within the service desk when critical incidents arise or when changes are scheduled to occur. These tools enhance and complement the information exchange that occurs with tools such as email and voice mail. Social media technologies use the Internet to facilitate interactive communication and allow the creation and exchange of user-generated content. The most common applications of social media at the service desk include collaboration, wikis, forums, blogs, social networking, and media or video sharing.

- Tools such as staffing and scheduling systems, ACD supervisor consoles, and customer surveying systems enable service desk supervisors and managers to optimize staffing levels, prepare schedules, and monitor the performance of service desk staff. Small service desks tend to perform these tasks manually. Larger service desks that handle a high volume of calls often use these tools because tasks such as determining staffing levels and so on can be somewhat complex and time consuming.

- The purpose of technology is to support and enhance processes. However, technology is not a magic pill that can cure all evils. Processes and procedures must be well defined, and *then* tools and technology can enable people to execute the processes and procedures more quickly and effectively.

- Selecting, acquiring, and implementing technology can be challenging because there are hundreds of service desk products on the market. Goals and requirements must be defined clearly before a selection committee begins evaluating products. Evaluating products takes time and a methodical approach. The implementation of a new product goes much more smoothly, however, when users are confident that care was taken to select the best possible solution. The end result of proper selection and implementation of support tools and technology is management, employee, and, most importantly, customer satisfaction.

Key Terms

ACD supervisor console—A system that works with ACD systems and enables supervisors to monitor call volumes and the performance of individual service desk analysts or groups of analysts.

announcement system—Technology that greets callers when all service desk analysts are busy and can provide valuable information as customers wait on hold.

automated attendant—An ACD feature that routes calls based on input provided by the caller through a touch-tone telephone.

automatic call distributor (ACD)—Technology that answers a call and routes, or distributes, it to the next available analyst. If all analysts are busy, the ACD places the call in a queue and plays a recorded message, such as, "We're sorry, all of our service representatives are currently assisting other customers; your call will be answered in the order it has been received."

automatic number identification (ANI)—A service provided by a long-distance service provider that delivers the telephone number of the person calling.

available state—An ACD state that occurs when an analyst is ready to take calls.

blog—A journal kept on the Internet; short for web log.

caller identification (caller ID)—A service provided by a local telephone company that delivers the telephone number of the person calling and, where available, the name associated with the calling telephone number.

case—A unit of information, such as an online document, a database record, or the solution to a common incident, which is indexed so an analyst can easily locate it when needed.

case-based reasoning (CBR)—A searching technique that uses everyday language to ask users questions and interpret their answers.

case-based system—A system made up of cases and a set of question and answer pairs that can be used to confirm the solution to an incident.

computer telephony integration (CTI)—The linking of computing technology with telephone technology to exchange information and increase productivity.

customer surveying system—A system that is used to create and distribute questionnaires to customers and to collect and tabulate the results of their feedback.

dashboard—A bright display that sends out visual and (in some cases) audible messages to service desk staff and to customer sites that have dashboards installed; also known as electronic reader board.

data—A set of raw facts that is not organized in a meaningful way.

decision tree—A branching structure of questions and possible answers designed to lead an analyst to a solution.

dialed number identification service (DNIS)—A service that provides the number the person called when the call is made using a toll-free number or a 1-900 service.

email management system—A system that enables service desks to manage high-volume chat, email, and web form messages.

fax—An image of a document that is electronically transmitted to a telephone number connected to a printer or other output device; short for facsimile.

feature and functionality requirements—The specifics of how the selected tool must perform in order to support its associated processes.

form—A predefined document that contains text or graphics users cannot change and areas in which users enter information.

fuzzy logic—A searching technique that presents all possible solutions that are similar to the search criteria, even when conflicting information exists or no exact match is present.

high-level requirements—The broad needs for a system.

homegrown incident tracking system—Technology that tends to support only the incident management process and offers basic trouble ticketing and reporting capability.

hyperlink—Text or graphics in a hypertext or hypermedia document that allow readers to "jump" to a related idea.

hypermedia—A storage method that stores information in graphical forms such as images, movies, and videos.

hypertext—Text that links to other information.

idle state—An ACD state that occurs when an analyst is logged on to the ACD but is not accepting calls.

incident management system—Technology that offers enhanced trouble ticketing and management reporting capability.

information indicator digits (IID)—A service that identifies the origin of a call from the type or location of the telephone being used to place the call, such as a public phone, cell phone, or hotel phone.

instant messaging system—Text-based form of communication that enables two or more people to communicate in real time over the Internet.

integrated ITSM solutions—A suite of systems that companies use to manage their incident, problem, knowledge, change, service asset and configuration management, and request fulfillment processes; also called enterprise solutions.

keyword searching—The technique of finding indexed information by specifying a descriptive word or phrase, called a keyword.

knowledge—The application of information along with people's experiences, ideas, and judgments.

portal—A web "supersite" that provides a variety of services such as a site search to locate pertinent articles and white papers, a product and services buyer's guide, a discussion or message board, event calendars, and publications.

query by example (QBE)—A searching technique that uses queries, or questions, to find records that match the specified search criteria. Queries can include search operators.

queue—A line; can be used to refer to a list of calls, tickets, or email messages waiting to be processed.

recording system—Technology that records and plays back telephone calls.

remote control system—Technology that enables an analyst to view and take control of a connected device to troubleshoot incidents, transfer files, provide informal training, or collaborate on documents.

remote monitoring system—Technology that tracks and collects events generated by network, system, or application monitoring systems and passes them to a central server where they can be automatically picked up and evaluated by the event management process.

request for information (RFI)—A form or letter that asks for specific product information relative to the company's requirements.

request for proposal (RFP)—A form or letter that requests financial information as well as product information.

requirement—Something that is essential.

rule-based system—A system made up of rules, facts, and a knowledge base or engine that combines rules and facts to reach a conclusion.

screen pop—A CTI function that enables information about the caller to appear or "pop" up on the analyst's monitor and is based on caller information captured by the telephone system and passed to a computer system.

search criteria—The questions or symptoms entered by a user.

search operators—Connecting words such as AND, OR, and NOT sometimes used in queries; also called Boolean operators.

self-healing—Hardware devices and software applications that have the ability to detect and correct incidents on their own.

service catalog—A list of services that an organization provides to its customers.

service knowledge management system (SKMS)—A set of tools and databases used to manage knowledge, information, and data. (ITIL definition)

simultaneous screen transfer—A function that transfers the call as well as all the information collected in the ticket up to that point.

skills-based routing (SBR)—An ACD feature that matches the requirements of an incoming call to the skill sets of available analysts or analyst groups. The ACD then distributes the call to the next available, appropriately qualified analyst.

social media—A phrase commonly used to describe any tool or service that uses the Internet to facilitate interactive communication.

software as a service (SaaS)—A software delivery model in which software and the associated data and information are centrally hosted by a vendor and made available to users via the Internet.

software distribution system—Technology that allows an analyst to automatically distribute software to clients and servers on the same network.

staffing and scheduling systems—Systems that work with ACD systems to collect, report, and forecast call volumes.

system integration—Linking together different computer systems and applications physically or functionally.

technology—An invention, process, or method that enables the creation and enhancement of tools.

template—A predefined item that can be used to quickly create a standard document or email message.

tool—A product or device that automates or facilitates a person's work.

voice mail—An automated form of taking messages from callers.

Voice over Internet Protocol (VoIP)—A technology that translates voice communications into data and then transmits that data across an Internet connection or network.

voice response unit (VRU)—A technology that integrates with another technology, such as a database or a network management system, to obtain information or to perform a function; also called an interactive voice response unit (IVRU).

whiteboard—A smooth, erasable white panel on which analysts write notes and communicate current and future events.

whiteboard system—Technology that allows two or more users on a network to view one or more user's drawings, documents, or applications being projected on an onscreen whiteboard.

wisdom—The judicious application of knowledge.

wrap-up mode—A feature that prevents the ACD from routing a new inbound call to an analyst's extension.

Review Questions

1. Tools and technologies give the service desk the ability to more efficiently handle two primary activities. What are those activities?

2. List two reasons why companies combine or integrate tools and technologies.

3. List the two categories of costs organizations may incur when implementing technology, and provide at least three examples of each.

4. List four factors that influence the availability of tools in a service desk.

5. Describe the benefits of VoIP in a service desk setting.

6. What two things can be done to reduce customer resistance to voice mail?

7. From an analyst's perspective, what two things does ACD software do?

8. Describe four functions that an ACD console enables analysts to perform.

9. How is skills-based routing different than normal ACD routing?

10. A VRU integrates with another technology to do what? Provide one example.

11. What is a screen pop?

12. List the two most common reasons that companies implement recording systems.

13. ANI and caller ID services deliver the telephone number a customer is calling from. What does DNIS deliver?

14. Why are analysts typically required to log all incidents and service requests received via email in their company's incident management system?

15. List four benefits of integrating email and incident management systems.

16. List five of the most common services that support companies are delivering through their web sites.

17. List three reasons why web-based services will not in the foreseeable future eliminate the telephone and email as communication channels.

18. What common customer complaint is prevented when all incidents are logged?

19. Describe the pros and cons of homegrown incident tracking systems.

20. From the standpoint of managing processes, describe the difference between homegrown incident tracking systems, commercial incident management systems, and integrated ITSM solutions.

21. Integrated ITSM solutions often offer tight integration with what other tools?

22. What symptoms might companies experience when they have outgrown their incident management systems?

23. Explain the DIKW hierarchy.

24. Describe three ways that service desks can establish or gain access to knowledge bases.

25. What process is used to manage a configuration management system?

26. What are two reasons that companies implement remote support technologies?

27. Describe two of the remote support technologies available to the service desk.

28. List one very simple tool and one more sophisticated tool that service desks can use to communicate within the service desk.

29. Describe three ways that social media can be used by service desks to communicate with customers.

30. Describe two systems that service desk supervisors and managers can use to optimize staffing levels and monitor the performance of service desk staff.

31. What is technology's purpose?

32. List the seven steps involved in a technology selection project.

33. What are the benefits of preparing and distributing an RFI or RFP?

34. Describe three ways to evaluate vendors after they have been selected as finalists.

Hands-On Projects

1. **Discuss experiences using technology to obtain help.** Talk to at least three friends, family members, or fellow students about their experiences with any of the technologies described in this chapter. For example, they might have been prompted to make a selection from a list of options ("Press 1 for . . . , Press 2 for . . . ," and so on) on a telephone call, waited in a telephone queue to speak with the next available analyst, used a web form to submit an email inquiry, or used a company's web site to obtain support. Find out about their experiences, for example:

   - How did they feel about interacting with support technology?

   - What (if anything) was positive about their experience?

   - What (if anything) was negative about their experience?

   Prepare a brief summary of each of their experiences. Given what you have learned in this chapter, explain what could have been done to make their experiences more positive.

2. **Describe the benefits of self-service.** Think about the different ways you use self-service technologies as you go about your day. For example, perhaps you use a credit card to pay for gas at the pump or you use an app on your smartphone to check your bank account balance. Write a report that lists the self-service technologies you use and explain why you use them. What are the benefits? Also, describe ways you feel the self-service technologies you use could be made easier or more useful.

3. **Visit a service desk industry portal site.** Visit one or more of the service desk industry portal sites described in this chapter, such as *www.helpdesk.com* or *www.supportindustry.com*. Join the site, if necessary (membership is typically free). Prepare a brief report that answers the following questions:

- What functionality did the site provide?

- How was information on the site organized?

- Was the site easy to use? Explain.

- What was one thing you learned, or learned more about, by visiting this web site?

4. **Learn about web-based support.** Visit the web site of an organization you do business with (such as the company that manufactured the computer you use or the publisher of a software package you use). Find out such information as:

- Does the company provide a way for you to submit an incident or service request? If so, how—an email, a web form, or both?

- Can you check the status of an outstanding incident or service request?

- Does the company provide answers to FAQs?

- What self-services does the company offer?

- What social media technologies does the company use to communicate with its customers?

Prepare a brief report that describes your findings.

5. **Make it easy for customers to wait in a call queue.** Recall that a queue is a line, in this instance, of calls waiting to be processed. Assemble a team of at least three classmates or use your school's online message or discussion board, and discuss ways that technology can be used to enhance the experience of customers waiting in a queue. For example, one way might be to offer customers the option of leaving a voice mail message. Prepare a list of at least five more ways to enhance customers' experiences.

6. **Learn about using support technology.** Select a class representative who can arrange a site visit to a large service desk or call center in your area. Before the site visit, prepare a list of the technologies discussed in this chapter that you want to see in use. As a courtesy, have the class representative send this list to your tour guide in advance of your visit so that he or she knows that the goal of your visit is to see these technologies. While onsite, ask your tour guide to describe how the service desk or call center uses technology to support its customers. After the tour, prepare a short paper that answers the following questions:

- What technologies were being used?

- What technologies were not being used, and why?

- Were you in any way surprised by what you saw? If yes, explain why.

7. **Learn about incident management systems.** Go to the web sites of the incident management systems or integrated ITSM solution vendors mentioned in this chapter. Download demonstration or trial versions of two of the systems. Complete the demonstration or explore the trial software. For example, log an incident and perform a search. Using what you can learn from the companies' web sites and their demonstration software, prepare a table or spreadsheet that compares the features and benefits of the two products you've selected.

8. **Learn about remote control software.** Go to the web sites of at least three companies that publish remote control software. Use the companies mentioned in this chapter or search the web for "remote control software." Prepare a table or spreadsheet that compares the features of the remote control products manufactured by the vendors you've selected. Also, briefly describe how each of these products addresses any security concerns that may arise from their use.

9. **Make effective use of a whiteboard.** Recall that a whiteboard is a simple tool found in most service desks. Work alone or with a classmate and brainstorm ways to effectively use this simple tool to enhance communication within a service desk. Prepare a drawing of a whiteboard that illustrates the type of information you would record and that shows how the most important information can be displayed prominently.

10. **Investigate the use of social media at a service desk.** Visit your school's service desk web site and determine the various ways that it uses social media to communicate with its customers. If your school does not have a web site, or if it does not use social media, login to social media sites such as Facebook or Twitter (free registration may be required) and search "university service desk." Explore the different ways that universities use these social media sites to communicate with customers. What are these organizations doing well? How could they improve the quality of their communications with customers? Discuss your findings with your classmates.

11. **Prepare to check vendor references.** Checking vendor references is an important part of any technology selection effort. Assemble a team of at least three classmates and develop a questionnaire that can be used to question vendor references. What questions would you ask about:

- The company's environment?
- How the company is using the vendor's product?
- How satisfied the company is with the vendor's product?
- How satisfied the company is with the support the vendor provides?
- How difficult or easy the product was to implement?
- How difficult or easy the product is to maintain?

Compare your questionnaire to the questionnaires developed by other teams in your class.

Case Projects

1. **University Service Desk.** A university is preparing to install a wireless network on its campus and the service desk is expecting an increase in its contact volume as a result. Search the web for information using searches such as "university service desk" and "university service desk wireless." Prepare a brief report describing the most common tools, technologies, and techniques universities use to help students and faculty gain access to and get help using their wireless networks. Include examples of universities that currently offer wireless services, along with service desk support for those services.

2. **Creating a social media policy.** You manage the service desk and want to use social media to communicate with your customers. Search the web for information about how to create a social media policy. Prepare a presentation for the service desk team that includes the following:

   - Typical responsibilities, policies, and procedures included in a social media policy

   - Key considerations for using social media at work

   - What to do when you are unsure a post, comment, or video is acceptable

The Information Component: Service Desk Performance Measures

In this chapter you will learn:

- ◎ How information is a resource
- ◎ The most common data categories captured by the service desk
- ◎ The most common team performance metrics
- ◎ The most common individual performance metrics
- ◎ How individuals contribute to team goals

As customer expectations about service rise, businesses make every effort to meet those expectations. In addition, companies must optimize costs and their staffing levels and at the same time increase overall productivity. As a result, today's savvy customers have high expectations for the service desk, and managers have high expectations for their employees. Every department, including the service desk, is expected to contribute to the goals of the business, and every employee is expected to contribute to the goals of his or her department. Information is used to determine how departments and employees are contributing to these goals. The most important goal for the entire company is customer satisfaction.

Customer satisfaction is essential for keeping current customers and attracting new ones. Companies focus on customer satisfaction by understanding their customers' needs and expectations in all areas of the business. They do this by analyzing data and creating information. Customers who contact the service desk need and expect prompt, courteous service. Their expectations—whether reasonable or not—set the standard for service desk performance. Companies use metrics to evaluate the performance of their service desks and of their employees against these expectations. Information is used to create these metrics. The more clearly a company defines how performance is measured, the more successfully the company, departments, and service desk analysts can meet their goals and their customers' expectations.

When working in a service desk, you must understand its goals, the goals of your department, and the goals of your company—as well as the metrics that your manager uses to measure your contribution to those goals. Also, you must know that customers, managers, and coworkers use the data you collect on a daily basis to create information. The accuracy and completeness of your work directly influence how customers and managers perceive your contribution to all these goals. When others perceive your work positively, you create and receive greater opportunity to advance your career.

Information as a Resource

Service desks can improve customer service and meet their goals by using many of the technologies discussed in Chapter 5. These technologies extend the service desk's ability to gather, organize, and use information. It takes time and effort to capture, or collect, the data needed to create accurate and meaningful information. Data and information are resources, in the same way that well-trained employees, well-defined processes, and well-implemented technology are resources.

Service desks that recognize information as a resource are more proactive than reactive. A **reactive service desk** simply responds to events that occur each day, while a **proactive service desk** uses information to anticipate and prevent incidents and prepare for the future. Some service desks are so understaffed and so overwhelmed with their responsibilities that they capture little or no data. Without data to analyze, these service desks cannot determine the underlying cause of incidents or make strategic decisions, and so they remain reactive.

Reactive service desks tend to:

- Capture little, if any, data.

- Perform little trend analysis. As a result, analysts identify incidents when they happen but do not have the information to predict or prevent incidents.

- Avoid activities such as logging, tracking, and providing status updates because analysts and perhaps supervisors see these activities as too time consuming.

- Rediscover incidents, which means that several analysts independently find solutions to the same incident rather than one of them being able to look up the solution found earlier by another and logged in a knowledge management system.

- Fail to formally define processes and, as a result, have unclear roles and responsibilities.

- Fail to clearly communicate who owns incidents (for example, level one, level two, and so on). As a result, no one takes ownership of incidents, or many people take ownership of incidents, which can result in confusion and wasted effort.

- Handle incidents and service requests randomly rather than based on priority.

- Work without clear individual, team, and department goals and performance measures.

- Use what little data is available to criticize or blame rather than to identify opportunities to improve.

- Experience high costs due to inefficiencies and lack the ability to forecast costs.

- Ignore customer needs, resulting in low customer satisfaction.

Because reactive service desks capture little data, they have trouble creating the information necessary to understand customer needs and expectations and to measure customer satisfaction. As a result, they waste precious time focusing on activities that are unimportant to customers. Without information, reactive service desks must rely primarily on their hardworking, sometimes overworked people because they cannot justify or implement other resources, such as processes and technology, which would enable their people to be more efficient and effective. Companies must begin to capture data—even if only basic data in an incident management system—if they want to break the cycle of having insufficient resources to produce the information needed to justify additional resources.

Successful companies realize that they can derive many positive benefits by viewing all pertinent information as a resource. Service desks in these companies tend to be more proactive in nature. Proactive service desks tend to:

- Capture all pertinent data.

- Perform trend and root cause analysis in an effort to predict and prevent incidents.

- Automate activities such as logging, tracking, and providing status updates where possible.

- Minimize incident rediscovery by ensuring that all known solutions are stored in a knowledge management system.

- Clearly define processes, which leads to clear roles and responsibilities.

- Clearly define ownership. Owners manage by exception, which means owners are required to take action only when incidents and service requests are not being handled in a timely fashion.

- Handle incidents and service requests within predefined target resolution times that reflect their priority.

- Meet clearly defined individual, team, and department goals.

- Use data to identify opportunities; continuous improvement is a way of life.

- Control costs; the entire support organization can accurately forecast costs.

- Meet customer needs and enhance customer self-sufficiency by providing the tools and information customers need to resolve incidents and answer questions on their own, resulting in high customer satisfaction.

Proactive service desks rigorously analyze data and use the resulting information to justify other resources such as people, processes, and technology. They use this information to analyze the impact that incidents have on IT services and on the business, and they try to identify ways to minimize that impact. They also use this information to increase customer satisfaction, enhance productivity, improve the quality of products and services, deliver services more efficiently and effectively, and create new products and services.

HOW THE PROS DO IT: Demonstrating Productivity

One of the most difficult things for service desks to demonstrate is that they are increasing customer productivity by proactively preventing incidents or by providing self-services, such as a web site that enables customers to support themselves. A common technique is to capture a starting point, or **baseline**, metric. For example, prior to adding wireless networking-related FAQs to the service desk's web site, the incident management system can be used to create a baseline metric that shows the number of wireless networking-related "how to" questions the service desk receives on a monthly basis. Six months after the FAQs are implemented, the service desk can create a current metric. If the current metric indicates that the number of wireless networking-related "how to" questions has gone down, it can be surmised that the FAQs are a success. The service desk could also show the number of **page hits**—web page visits—the FAQs are receiving, or it could use exit polls to show that the FAQs are being used and that customers consider them helpful. On the Internet, **exit polls** combine questions such as "Was this information helpful to you?" with Yes and No buttons that customers can use to provide feedback. If a greater percentage of poll responses indicates that the information was helpful, it can be further surmised that the FAQs are a success.

Service desks are not, however, *all* reactive or *all* proactive. Many service desks are highly reactive but demonstrate proactive tendencies. For example, they may do a good job of communicating information verbally within the service desk team and with other support groups. As a result, they can stay on top of things in the present, although in the long run they suffer because the data and information is not being captured for future reuse. On the other hand, proactive service desks can demonstrate reactive tendencies. For example, they may experience an exceptionally busy time during which they are unable to focus on improving and instead focus on dealing only with daily demands.

One reason is that collecting useful data is difficult and can be costly. Even if the service desk's tools and technologies facilitate the collection of data, it takes effort to ensure that data is always accurate, current, and complete. It also takes effort and skill to analyze the data and produce meaningful and useful information—and ultimately—knowledge.

Service desks cannot move from a reactive state to a proactive state overnight. They must follow a systematic plan to become more proactive over time. That plan involves recognizing that information is valuable, determining what categories of information to collect, setting up efficient processes to collect data, and gaining analysts' acceptance and enthusiasm for collecting and sharing information. These last two points are key. If the data is simple to capture, analysts will capture it completely and accurately, making the resulting information invaluable. If analysts understand the value of information, they will collect and share it willingly and openly. This enables the service desk to provide world-class customer service and meet its goals.

The amount of data a service desk captures is determined by how much access to information management wants and what tools the service desk has. If senior management cares about and trusts the information produced by the service desk, they will encourage and direct the service desk to capture data. Service desk management may also encourage analysts to capture data to gain senior management's trust and to increase their commitment to back the service desk's goals and provide needed resources. When the service desk has appropriate tools and technology, capturing data takes little time. Analysts accustomed to logging contacts and who understand the value of the captured information consider logging contacts to be part of their job. In fact, service desk managers often include capturing data in the analyst's job description, use it as a criterion to measure job performance, and reward analysts who collect quality data.

Data Categories Captured by Service Desks

Service desks that capture information divide that information into various data categories. Because most service desks perform similar processes, these data categories tend to be similar from service desk to service desk. Each service desk captures additional data categories specific to its business or industry. Figure 6-1 lists the most common data categories captured by service desks.

- Customer data
- Incident data
- Status data
- Resolution data

Figure 6-1 Common data categories
© Cengage Learning 2014

This data, typically captured through fields in the organization's incident management system or integrated ITSM solution, enables service desks to track incidents; measure team, individual, and process performance; and perform trend analysis. Be aware that the actual field names used in the data categories vary from one service desk to the next.

Some service desks handle service requests via their incident management process. Others have a separate request fulfillment process in which similar data categories are defined and captured for all service requests.

Customer Data

Customer data is identifying details about a customer. Customer data includes the customer's name, telephone number, email address, department or company name, physical address or location, customer number, and employee number or user ID. This data is stored in fields. All of the fields that describe a single customer are stored in a **customer record** in one or more CMDBs. Customer records are linked to incident records, which are stored in the incident management system, by a unique *key* field such as customer number, employee number, or user ID.

A **field** is a location in a database that stores a particular piece of data. A **record** is a collection of related fields.

Customer records may be housed in a CMDB that is maintained by another department and then used by the service desk and other departments via the CMS. For example, in internal service desks, the company's human resources department may maintain the customer records, because it is responsible for maintaining all employee-related data. In external service desks, the company's sales department may maintain the customer records, because it is responsible for maintaining all customer-related data. In the absence of a CMS, the service desk's incident management system may be linked directly to another department's database—for example, the human resources database. In other cases, such as in companies where security is a concern, only the data needed to log incidents is exported from the human resources database and imported into the service desk's incident management system. This data may be imported once and then maintained by the service desk going forward. Or, a program may run periodically to keep the two databases in sync, in which case the human resources department continues to maintain the data. Optimally, a definitive, single source of data is identified and maintained.

Incident Data

Incident data is the details of an incident or service request. Incident data includes incident type (such as an incident or service request), channel used to submit (such as telephone, email, or web request), category (such as hardware or software), affected service, system or device (such as a printer or monitor), the symptom, the date and time the incident occurred, the date and time the incident was logged, the analyst who logged the incident, the incident owner, a description, and a priority. This data is stored in fields, and all of the fields that describe a single incident are stored in an **incident record** in the incident management system. Each incident record is assigned a unique identifier, such as a ticket number, that can be used to retrieve the record or link it to other records. For example, incident records may be linked to CI records in a CMDB, to problem records, or to knowledge base articles. Incident data fields are used to describe an incident and can also be used to research and track trends or to search the knowledge management system for solutions. Figure 6-2 shows a sample trend report that uses the incident category field.

Some incidents, such as major incidents, are reported by multiple customers. Many organizations create a master, or "parent," incident record and then link to it "child" records for each customer that reports that incident. Analysts update the status of the single parent incident record, but also have the ability to communicate with, and report on, the many impacted customers.

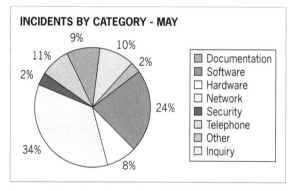

Figure 6-2 Sample trend report
© Cengage Learning 2014

Status Data

Status data is details about an incident that are used to track the incident throughout its lifecycle. Status data includes incident status (such as assigned, awaiting parts, resolved, and closed), the person or group assigned, the date and time assigned, and a priority. This data is stored in fields in the incident record in the incident management system. After an incident record is created, that record is continuously updated as new data— such as status data and resolution data—becomes available. These fields can be used to report on the status of outstanding incidents and to monitor SLA attainment. Figure 6-3 shows a sample incident aging report, which can be used to monitor whether outstanding incidents are being resolved within their target resolution time.

Assigned To	<1 Day	2–3 Days	4–5 Days	6–10 Days	>10 Days	% Within Target
Field Services	24	6	3	1	2	98
Network Support	54	23	15	9	13	94
Development	76	54	8	2	1	87
Vendor	93	27	3	4	12	75

Figure 6-3   Sample incident aging report
© Cengage Learning 2014

Resolution Data

Resolution data describes how an incident was resolved. Resolution data includes the fields required to track service level compliance and perform trend analysis, such as the person or group who resolved the incident, resolution or workaround description, the date and time the incident was resolved, an indicator of customer satisfaction, the date and time the incident was closed, and a possible cause. This data is stored in fields in the incident record and the data is added as it becomes available. Reusable resolutions are incorporated into FAQs or recorded as solutions in the knowledge management system.

In most companies, the status of an incident is set to *resolved* when a level one or two analyst delivers a solution and is set to *closed* only after the incident owner verifies that the customer is satisfied with the resolution.

Service desk analysts and managers use these customer, incident, status, and resolution data fields to create detailed tracking and summary reports and to perform trend analysis. In addition, managers use these data fields to calculate many team and individual performance measures.

Team Performance Measures

Service desk managers are under constant pressure to demonstrate the value of the service desk and to justify the funds and resources the team needs. Managers use performance measures to prove the importance of the service desk team to the company and to demonstrate the service desk's contribution to critical success factors and key performance indicators. A **critical success factor (CSF)** is a measurable characteristic that must exist for something—such as a process, project, or team—to be viewed as successful. For example, maintaining high levels of customer satisfaction is a CSF for the service desk. A **key performance indicator (KPI)** is a key metric used to manage a process. For example, resolving all incidents within the time frame specified in SLAs is a KPI for the incident management process. KPIs underpin, or support, CSFs. For example, an organization that considers minimizing business impact by resolving incidents as quickly as possible a CSF may define the percentage of incidents resolved at first contact by the service desk as a KPI. This is because resolving the incident at the service desk reduces any delays that might occur when incidents are escalated to second or third level support.

Team performance measures assess characteristics such as:

- **Efficiency**—A measure of the time and effort required to deliver services in relation to their cost

- **Effectiveness**—A measure of how completely and accurately services are delivered

- **Quality**—A measure of how well services meet customer requirements

Individual performance measures also measure the characteristics of efficiency, effectiveness, and quality.

The goal is to achieve a balance among efficiency, effectiveness, and quality without overemphasizing any one of these characteristics. This balance is needed because any one of these characteristics can, on its own, result in negative consequences. For example, in an effort to drive down costs, some organizations strive for high levels of efficiency. They may achieve these efficiencies by eliminating checkpoints designed to ensure quality. For example, in an effort to close incidents more quickly, a service desk may eliminate the step that involves verifying customer satisfaction with the solution. While eliminating such a step may, in fact, increase efficiency, it may also decrease effectiveness or quality as the service desk may fail to quickly recognize that incidents are being chronically resolved incorrectly. To achieve a balance, many service desks track the percentage of incidents that are reopened within a predefined period of time. Another example is that a service desk may strive to deliver such high-quality services that the cost to deliver those services is greater than customers are willing to pay. To achieve a balance, many service desks use SLAs to define the level of service expected and the agreed upon cost. Achieving a balance among efficiency, effectiveness, and quality ensures the right services are delivered the right way at the right cost.

A balanced set of knowledge management-related metrics includes: number of solutions in the KMS, number of times customers access the KMS, and incidents resolved using the KMS.

Team performance metrics measure the combined efforts of the service desk team and show that not only is the service desk working hard but also that it is meeting its business goals and its customers' expectations. Furthermore, clearly defined performance measures enable the service desk management and team to objectively evaluate their performance, celebrate their achievements, and develop strategies for improvement. Figure 6-4 lists the most common ways that service desks define and measure team performance.

- Service desk goals
- Service Level Agreements (SLAs)
- Customer satisfaction surveys
- Benchmarking

Figure 6-4 Common team performance measures
© Cengage Learning 2014

Service desk goals provide the information that service desks need in order to know whether they are continually improving. SLAs provide the information to understand customer expectations. Customer satisfaction surveys and benchmarking provide the information to identify areas for improvement. These measures enable the service desk management and team to satisfy customers at an appropriate cost to the organization. The best companies also consider job satisfaction of their employees in the team setting an important component of their overall performance.

Service Desk Goals

Service desk goals are measurable objectives that support the service desk's mission. Most organizations establish specific goals each year in an effort to clarify what analysts are supposed to focus on, to eliminate conflicting goals, and to encourage analysts to produce the desired results. Sample service desk goals include:

- Achieve an average four out of five rating on the annual customer satisfaction survey.

- Provide each analyst with eight hours of training each month.

- Resolve 70 percent of reported incidents at level one.

- Reduce support costs by 5 percent by year's end or by implementing a new technology.

- Maintain a cost per contact at or below the industry average.

Cost per contact, historically called cost per call, is the total cost of operating a service desk for a given period (including salaries, benefits, facilities, and equipment) divided by the total number of contacts (calls, emails, faxes, web requests, and so on) received during that period. According to HDI's *2012 Support Center Practices and Salary Report*, the industry average cost per contact ranges from $10 (chat) to $17 (phone).

Cost per contact increases dramatically when contacts are escalated to more highly specialized resources. Moving incidents from level three to level one or self-service and eventually to elimination results in real cost savings to the organization. Some companies also calculate **cost per unit**, which is the total cost of operating a service desk for a given period divided by the total number of units (such as services, systems, and devices) supported during that period.

Many companies distinguish between goals and operational performance metrics, such as those reflected in SLAs. Goals represent what the service desk is *striving* to achieve. Operational metrics represent what the service desk is *expected* to achieve as determined by its SLAs.

 The most effective goals are SMART: specific, measurable, achievable, relevant, and time-bound.

Service Level Agreements

An SLA is a written document that spells out the services the service desk will provide to the customer, the customer's responsibilities, and how service performance is measured. Senior management representatives from the service desk and from the customer community typically negotiate the terms of SLAs, which are designed to:

- Ensure that the service desk's services match their customers' needs.

- Ensure that the service desk and customers have the same expectations about the services the service desk will provide.

- Ensure that the service desk and customers clearly understand their respective responsibilities.

- Provide measurable performance metrics for the service desk.

- Provide a point of reference that can be used to discuss service desk and customer performance and to communicate the need to modify or enhance that performance.

- Ensure that all parties understand and are willing to follow the processes managed by or through the service desk.

SLAs ensure that both the service desk and its customers understand their responsibilities. For example, an SLA may state that customers must report incidents to the service desk versus another group or person within the IT organization. The SLA will also state the time frame within which the service desk must respond to and resolve incidents based on their priority.

Eighty-one percent of HDI's members have SLAs with some or all of their customers (*2012 Support Center Practices and Salary Report*, HDI). Most service desks have SLAs because they realize that they can't keep pace with customers' rising expectations. While negotiating SLAs, the service desk and the customer discuss the company's cost to meet the customer's expectations. This ensures that the expectations do not exceed the benefit that customers will obtain from a service. Consequently, service desks use SLAs as a tool for managing customer expectations, and when possible and appropriate, enhancing customer self-sufficiency.

SLAs are an excellent way to measure team performance because they show how well the team is meeting customer expectations. The service desk does not have to *guess* at what customers want and how they can satisfy their needs—they *know* what customers want and need because it is all clearly defined in the SLAs.

SLAs can be quite complex or they can be simple one-page documents, such as the sample shown in Figure 6-5. For example, because it is a legally binding contract, an SLA between a company and a supplier that provides service desk outsourcing will tend to be quite complex. On the other hand, an SLA between a service desk and a department in a company may be fairly simple and used primarily to clarify expectations and responsibilities.

SLAs are used to measure the performance of the entire IT department as well as the service desk. They measure IT service characteristics such as availability, security, IT service continuity, and capacity-related characteristics such as response time and performance.

ABC SERVICE DESK
SERVICE LEVEL AGREEMENT

This document is an agreement between the ABC service desk and its customers. This service level agreement (SLA) has been designed to promote a common understanding about the services the service desk provides, and customer responsibilities relative to those services. This document also describes how service level performance is measured.

Parties: The *service desk* provides a single point of contact for the ABC IT Department. *Customers* are ABC employees who seek technical support services from the ABC IT Department.

Responsibilities: The *service desk* provides first level support to customers using the processes and technology implemented by the ABC IT Department. The service desk also facilitates second and third level support by engaging resources as needed to resolve incidents beyond the scope and authority of the service desk. *Customers* obtain service using the processes and technology implemented by the ABC IT Department and described in this document. Specifically, ABC employees must contact the service desk when support services are needed.

Hours of operation: The service desk is available to ABC employees 24 hours a day, 7 days a week.
- During *normal business hours*—Monday through Friday 7 a.m. to 8 p.m.—customers can contact the service desk and speak directly with an analyst.
- *After-hours*—8 p.m. to 7 a.m. weekdays, weekends, and holidays—customers can access the service desk's web site. For *priority* 1 incidents only, customers can contact the service desk and obtain support from on-call analysts.

Contact methods: Customers can use the following methods to obtain support:
- Telephone—Customers can contact the service desk by calling **(555) 451-4357**. The target response time for calls is thirty (30) seconds. Following a brief introduction, customers may hear a system outage message. This message is broadcast only when a priority 1 incident exists.

- Voice mail—Voice mail is offered to customers who call the service desk during normal business hours after a two (2) minute delay. Customers can use this option in lieu of waiting in the queue. Voice mail messages will be answered within thirty (30) minutes during normal business hours. Customers calling with a priority 1 incident are encouraged to wait in the queue. Voice mail messages left after-hours will be answered the next business day.

- Email—Email messages sent to **servicedesk@abc.com** will be answered within one (1) hour during normal business hours. Emails sent after-hours will be answered the next business day.

- Internet—The service desk's web site at **servicedesk.com** provides forms that can be used to submit incidents and service requests. Submitted incidents and service requests are automatically logged in the service desk's incident management system and are handled according to their priority. The Web site also provides self-services such as FAQs, a solution knowledge base, a password reset utility, and access to remote diagnostic and control utilities.

Incident priorities: Incident priority reflects the impact of an incident on the ABC business and when the incident must be solved. Service desk analysts and customers will work together to determine the priority, using the following guidelines:

Priority	Business Impact	Target Resolution Time
1	Service, system, or device down, business halted	2 hours
2	Service, system, or device down or level of service degraded, business impacted	8 hours
3	Not critical, customer can wait without business impact	48 hours

This agreement is effective through December 31st of the current year and will be evaluated and republished yearly or as needed.

Figure 6-5 Sample service desk SLA

A number of different service desk tools are used to create SLA metrics, including ACDs and incident management systems. Sample SLA metrics captured with ACDs include:

- **Abandon rate percent**—The percentage of abandoned calls compared to the total number of calls received. An **abandoned call** is a call in which the caller hangs up before an analyst answers. For example, a caller who tires of waiting in a queue or becomes confused using a VRU may choose to hang up before an analyst answers. Organizations often exclude from this calculation calls that have a queue message prompting the caller to hang up. For example, a message may encourage the caller to use the service desk's self-help web site; a different message may indicate that queue wait times are exceptionally long and will encourage calling back at a less busy time.

- **Average speed of answer (ASA)**—The average time it takes an analyst to pick up an incoming call.

- **Average wait time**—Also known as average queue time—the average number of seconds or minutes a caller waits for an analyst after being placed in the queue by an ACD.

Service desks also use their incident management systems to capture SLA metrics. Sample SLA metrics captured with these systems include:

- **Response time**—The length of time a customer waits for a reply to a fax, email, or web request. Response time is comparable to the ASA metric used for telephone calls.

- **First contact resolution rate percent**—The percentage of contacts resolved during a customer's initial contact compared to the total number of contacts received at the service desk for a given period of time.

- **Level one resolution rate percent**—The percentage of incidents resolved at level one (not necessarily during the customer's initial contact).

- **Incidents resolved within target time percent**—The percentage of incidents resolved within a target resolution time. Service desks base the target resolution times on the priority of the incident.

- **Reopened percent**—The percentage of closed incidents that had to be opened back up within a given period of time. This usually occurs because the incident symptom recurs, which implies that the service desk or a level two or level three service provider initially delivered an incorrect or incomplete solution.

Service desks that don't have formal SLAs can still use performance metrics. They can set internal goals for the service levels they strive to achieve and measure their performance against those goals.

When negotiating SLAs or establishing internal goals, companies often look for "industry standard" metrics to use as a starting point. Such metrics are difficult to find because no one organization represents the support industry as a whole. Organizations such as HDI (*www.thinkhdi.com*), the Technology Services Industry Association (*www.tsia.com*), and supportindustry.com (*www.supportindustry.com*) all provide their version of these metrics. Some of these organizations charge a fee. Typically, these organizations determine metrics by surveying their members or clients and by conducting surveys via the Internet.

Customer satisfaction is another common SLA metric that is usually captured by conducting customer satisfaction surveys and totaling the results. For example, an SLA may state that the service desk is expected to achieve an average four out of five rating on the annual overall customer satisfaction survey. Customer satisfaction is an excellent quality metric that serves to balance out the efficiency and effectiveness metrics.

Customer Satisfaction Surveys

Customer satisfaction surveys are a series of questions that ask customers to provide their perception of the support services being offered. Whether conducted annually or on an ongoing basis, customer satisfaction surveys are an excellent way to measure the strengths and weaknesses of existing support services. Surveys provide insight as to whether customers *perceive* their needs are being met and so are a subjective metric, unlike more quantifiable or objective metrics, such as the number of calls answered per hour or the average time to resolve an incident. Surveys can be conducted during telephone calls, by sending out surveys via email, or by asking the customer to provide feedback via the web.

Most unhappy customers never tell companies about their dissatisfaction, so it is extremely important to *ask* customers for feedback.

The two most common customer satisfaction surveys are event-driven surveys and overall satisfaction surveys. **Event-driven surveys** are a series of questions that ask customers for feedback on a single, recent service event. The results of these surveys give management the ability to measure the performance of the service desk team. These surveys can also be used to measure individual performance because they give feedback on the performance of the analyst who handled the event. Typically, the service desk conducts event-driven surveys immediately following the service event or within 24 to 48 hours of the service event. Figure 6-6 shows a script for a sample event-driven survey conducted via the telephone.

Event-Driven Survey

Hello (customer's name), this is (analyst's name) from the Service Desk. On (date from incident ticket), you placed a call to us for assistance about (incident description from ticket). Would you mind answering a few brief questions regarding that call?

Thank you.

Rating Scale

1   Very dissatisfied
2   Dissatisfied
3   Neither satisfied nor dissatisfied
4   Satisfied
5   Very satisfied

How satisfied are you with:

The speed with which your question was answered?

The courteous manner of the analyst who handled your call?

The knowledge of the analyst who handled your call?

The overall service you received?

Do you have any comments or suggestions regarding this call?

_____

_____

Thank you very much for your feedback. Please give us a call whenever you need assistance.

Figure 6-6   Sample event-driven survey
© Cengage Learning 2014

Overall satisfaction surveys are a series of questions that ask customers for feedback about all contacts with the service desk during a certain time period. Service desks use these responses to identify areas for improvement and to identify areas where the service desk is performing well. Some service desks also send these surveys to customers who *did not* contact the service desk in the previous 6 or 12 months to determine what, if any, additional services are required to meet their needs. Usually, the service desk conducts overall satisfaction surveys annually or semiannually. Figure 6-7 shows a sample overall satisfaction survey.

OVERALL SATISFACTION SURVEY

This survey has been designed to identify areas in which the service desk can improve the quality of service it provides to you, our customer. In addition, we would like to begin trending the performance of frequently-used applications. Please take a moment to complete this brief survey and return it to the service desk by _____.

Most used applications: 1) _____ 2) _____ 3) _____

1. How often do you call the service desk?

   ☐ Daily   ☐ Once a week   ☐ Never

   ☐ More than once a week   ☐ Once a month

2. When you call with an incident, is the incident resolution explained to you?

   ☐ Always   ☐ Usually   ☐ Sometimes   ☐ Never

3. Does the service desk notify you of system outages shortly after or prior to when they occur?

   ☐ Always   ☐ Usually   ☐ Sometimes   ☐ Never

4. Why do you usually call the service desk?

   ☐ System incidents ➤ workstation, printer, etc. not working

   ☐ Output incidents ➤ missing, late, misdelivered, etc.

   ☐ Other   ➤ Please Explain: _____

_____

5. Have you received adequate training on how to effectively use your computer and/or printer?

   ☐ Yes   ☐ No

6. Are you kept informed about the status of incidents that cannot be solved immediately?

   ☐ Yes   ☐ No

7. Do you currently receive the Service Desk Newsletter?   ☐ Yes   ☐ No

8. Please rate the competence and courtesy of the service desk staff:

   Most Competent   4   3   2   1   Least Competent

   Most Courteous   4   3   2   1   Least Courteous

OPTIONAL

NAME: _____

TITLE: _____

LOCATION: _____

Figure 6-7   Sample overall satisfaction survey
© Cengage Learning 2014

Overall satisfaction surveys may be used to measure customers' satisfaction with the entire IT organization during a certain period of time. In such cases, care must be taken to ensure the questions asked enable the ability to distinguish actions taken by the service desk, versus other support groups within IT. For example, the survey may ask, "Did the service desk provide you with an incident tracking number?" Or, the survey may ask, "Did the Desktop Support Technician arrive at your office at the agreed time?" This ensures a fair evaluation of the service desk's performance and also ensures the service desk can identify improvement opportunities within its control.

Overall satisfaction surveys are an excellent way to measure the quality of service desk services because customers provide direct feedback. Management uses the feedback obtained from these surveys when defining the service desk's goals.

Benchmarking

Benchmarking is the process of comparing the service desk's performance metrics and practices to those of another service desk in an effort to identify improvement opportunities. Companies that provide benchmarking services require participants to complete comprehensive surveys that explore all aspects of their service desk, and they store the results in a database. This data can then be used to compare one company to others—usually companies that are similar in size or industry. Benchmarking services can be quite costly. Because they know that they are comparing their metrics and practices to a true group of their peers, companies striving to be world class are often willing to pay for these services. These services often are also accompanied by consulting services that result in a clear roadmap that leads to specific improvement goals.

Companies that provide service desk benchmarking services include HDI (*www.thinkhdi.com*), Gartner, Inc. (*www.gartner.com*), and MetricNet (*www.metricnet.com*).

Companies benefit most from benchmarking when they identify opportunities for improvement rather than simply compare metrics. In other words, a service desk must not only determine whether its metrics are better than or worse than another company's; it must also thoroughly analyze benchmarking results to uncover practices in place at the other company that it can implement to improve. However, the service desk must also ensure that any changes it makes fit the needs of its customers. There is no guarantee that one company's practices will satisfy another company's customers or improve its performance.

Customers and management can use all of these techniques—service desk goals, SLAs, customer satisfaction surveys, and benchmarking—to measure service desk performance. Although not all companies use all of these techniques, successful ones understand that they can't manage or improve what they aren't measuring; therefore, they use as many of these techniques as possible. No single technique can be used to measure service desk performance fully. They all work together to enable the service desk to meet its commitments to customers and to identify areas for improvement. Also, many performance metrics influence each other. Placing too great an emphasis on any one metric can produce unintended results. For example, emphasizing efficiency can reduce the average queue time but could cause customer dissatisfaction because customers feel they are being rushed off the phone. On the other hand, emphasizing effectiveness by devoting an extensive number of analysts to research may produce high-quality solutions, but it might also cause customer dissatisfaction because customers have a long average queue time.

The best companies strive to achieve a balance among efficiency, effectiveness, and quality when establishing performance measures. These companies rigorously collect the data required to measure performance and promote their performance achievements to customers and management.

Individual Performance Measures

Team performance is only as good as the performance of the analysts on the team. Every analyst influences the team's ability to achieve its goals and expected service levels. If every analyst in the service desk achieves his or her individual performance goals, then the team will achieve its goals. Like team performance measures, individual performance measures gauge and try to balance characteristics such as efficiency, effectiveness, and quality. The goals of measuring individual performance are to:

- Set performance expectations.

- Reward positive performance.

- Set up a plan to improve weak performance.

- Measure changes in performance throughout the year.

- Document when an improvement plan is successful and when it is unsuccessful.

Figure 6-8 lists the most common ways that service desks measure individual performance.

- Individual performance goals
- Employee performance plans
- Monitoring
- Skills inventory matrix

Figure 6-8   Common individual performance measures
© Cengage Learning 2014

These techniques provide service desk management and staff with a framework for setting performance expectations and identifying the data they will use to measure and manage individual performance. Service desk analysts often create the data that will measure their performance. Analysts who log all incidents as close to real time as possible, for example, are able to show their contribution to the service desk and its goals. Analysts who do not log all incidents or who fail to use care when logging incidents create inaccurate or incomplete data, and so are often unable to statistically demonstrate their contribution.

Some analysts dislike performance measures and mistakenly believe that management cannot measure their performance if the data is not available. The flaw in this line of thinking is that management still measures performance; they simply do it without facts. In other words, management measures performance based on what they *perceive* an analyst has accomplished. By capturing data and learning to use data to create information, analysts can maximize their contribution to service desk goals and communicate that contribution to management.

Stating the number of incidents logged and resolved is far more meaningful to management than hearing that an analyst handled "a lot" of incidents in a given week.

Individual Performance Goals

Individual performance goals are measurable objectives for analysts that support the service desk mission. These goals are communicated to analysts at the time they are hired and during performance reviews. How and when performance reviews are conducted varies from one company to the next. Some companies informally review metrics with analysts on a weekly basis and conduct more formal reviews quarterly, semiannually, or annually. Other companies conduct, for example, a semiannual review to discuss performance. Most companies then conduct an annual review that determines any changes to the employee's compensation package (that is, salary, benefits, training or certification allotment, and so on). Frequent performance reviews are best because they enable analysts to know how they are doing and they provide a forum for discussing ways that analysts can improve.

As with team performance goals, a number of different service desk tools are used to create individual performance metrics, such as an ACD and the incident management system. Sample individual performance metrics captured with an ACD include:

- **Availability**—The length of time an analyst was signed on to the ACD compared to the length of time the analyst was scheduled to be signed on.

- **Average call duration**—The average length of time required to handle a call.

- **Time idle**—The average length of time an analyst was idle during a given period of time.

- **Wrap-up time**—The average length of time an analyst was in wrap-up mode during a given period of time.

An excessive amount of idle or wrap-up time is undesirable because it delays service to the customer. However, most service desk managers recognize that some idle or wrap-up does not mean an analyst is being unproductive. For example, an analyst may be in the middle of providing critical information to a coworker or a supervisor who is at his or her desk when a call arrives. On the other hand, some analysts forget to log off the ACD when they step away from their desk, and others fail to make themselves unavailable when extra time is needed to escalate a call. In such cases, the service desk manager or supervisor will counsel the analyst on the importance of avoiding unnecessary or excessive idle or wrap-up time.

Some companies avoid excessive amounts of idle or wrap-up time by having senior analysts or specialists work offline for a predefined period of time. During this time, the senior analysts or specialists can analyze problems, assist with difficult incidents, and provide training to handle similar incidents in the future. These senior analysts or specialists do not log on to the ACD, so they are not eligible to receive calls.

ACD metrics are combined with metrics produced using the service desk's incident management system. Sample individual performance metrics captured with incident management systems include:

- **Reopened percent**—The percentage of closed incidents that an analyst opens back up within a given period of time.

- **Resolution percent**—The percentage of incidents an analyst resolves compared to the total number of incidents that analyst handled during a given period of time.

- **Application of training investments**—A comparison of an analyst's resolution percent before and after attending training.

Customer satisfaction is a common individual performance metric. It is captured through the results of event-driven customer satisfaction surveys, which capture information about an analyst's performance handling individual events, as opposed to the overall team performance. Monitoring is another way service desks measure the quality of an individual's performance and determine whether an analyst is meeting his or her individual goals. Service desk management, in conjunction with customer management, establish these individual goals, such as maintaining an average customer satisfaction rating of four out of five.

Certification also can be used to measure individual performance. **Certification** is a document awarded to a person who has demonstrated that he or she has certain skills and knowledge about a particular topic or area. Often, the person must pass a test after receiving instruction or doing self-study. Because certification requires analysts to demonstrate their mastery of a subject by taking a test, companies consider it an excellent way to measure an analyst's knowledge. Companies may also baseline an analyst's performance before training and compare that to the analyst's performance after a certification is achieved. For example, a company may evaluate the percentage of incidents an analyst is able to resolve before and after achieving an industry-standard certification. One such certification is the **CompTIA A+** certification, which measures a technician's knowledge of hardware and operating system technologies and concepts, along with topics such as security, safety and environmental issues, and communication and professionalism.

Certification is discussed in detail in Chapter 8.

As with team performance measures, no single metric can measure individual performance accurately. They work together and can influence each other. By monitoring all of these metrics, individuals can identify areas where they can improve. Service desks often incorporate individual performance goals into employee performance plans. Service desks that do not use employee performance plans or that do not provide job descriptions with measurable objectives will typically still set individual performance goals.

Employee Performance Plan

An **employee performance plan** is a document that clearly describes an analyst's performance requirements and individual improvement objectives. Unlike job descriptions, which can be generic and static, employee performance plans change as the employee's performance improves or deteriorates. Figure 6-9 shows a sample employee performance plan.

EMPLOYEE PERFORMANCE PLAN

My personal mission is to provide the highest-quality technical support in a courteous and professional manner. I am also committed to communicating customer needs to the appropriate teams within the IT organization. In order for the service desk to be successful, I will strive to meet the following goals:

Technical Knowledge

- Maintain a high level of knowledge in the services, systems, and devices for which I am recognized as an expert
- Increase my level of knowledge in the following services, systems, and devices over the next three months:
    - A
    - B
- Continuously seek out ways to improve my technical support skills

Customer Service Quality

- Provide courteous, quality, responsive, and responsible support
- Show genuine interest in every customer concern
- Maintain a high level of support policy knowledge
- Utilize all available tools and procedures to resolve customer issues
- Continuously seek out ways to improve my customer service skills

Contact Resolution and Work Quality

- Log all contacts received
- Reduce the number of contacts I escalate by x% within the next three months
- Improve my average call duration from _____ to _____ minutes per call within the next three months

Teamwork

- Work well with others, participate constructively in team meetings, and assist other team members when needed
- Adhere to assigned shift schedules

Figure 6-9 Sample employee performance plan

© Cengage Learning 2014

Employee performance plans are most effective when analysts are given the tools—in this case, reports—they need to monitor their daily performance. Analysts then can meet weekly or monthly with their supervisor or team leader to review and discuss the results. At that time, they can refine the employee performance plan as needed.

266

Monitoring

Monitoring occurs when a supervisor or team leader monitors an analyst's interactions with customers in order to measure the quality of an analyst's performance. Monitoring may include listening to a live or recorded call or reviewing emails and chats. Used properly, monitoring is an excellent quality metric. It encourages analysts to put themselves in the customer's shoes and objectively assess the quality of their service from the customer's perspective. In addition, it promotes the consistent handling of contacts and provides employees and supervisors with information on which they can base performance improvement plans.

Monitoring is also an excellent training technique because supervisors and team leaders can give analysts specific feedback on how they could have handled a contact better and how they can handle similar contacts in the future. Just under 62 percent of HDI's members use monitoring as a method for training new hires on the service desk (*2012 Support Center Practices and Salary Report*, HDI). Some supervisors and team leaders occasionally watch analysts handle contacts so they can also provide guidance in areas such as the ergonomics of the analyst's workspace, the analyst's use of tools, and the analyst's ability to stay organized and calm while working.

 Chapter 7 explores how to set up an ergonomic workspace.

A monitoring program must be implemented carefully in order to be effective, or it can become demoralizing and invasive. Most companies involve the service desk staff when designing their monitoring programs. Management and staff jointly define guidelines for how and when employees will be monitored. For example, they may agree to monitor contacts two to ten times each month. Other guidelines include agreeing not to monitor partial contacts or personal contacts.

One of the keys to a successful monitoring program is a checklist given to analysts that describes the specific criteria supervisors or team leaders are using to measure the quality of a call. Figure 6-10 shows a sample monitoring checklist. Without this checklist, analysts are unsure what supervisors and team leaders are looking for when they monitor the calls, and therefore, may perceive the results as subjective.

MONITORING CHECKLIST

☐ Use standard greeting:
  - Service desk.
  - This is Lizette.
  - How may I help you?

☐ Listen actively:
  - Respond to the customer (uh-huh, I see, I understand).
  - Ask questions.
  - Verify understanding (state back, paraphrase).
  - Listen to *what* is being said and *how* it is being said.

☐ Demonstrate a *can do* attitude:
  - Positive, caring.
  - Avoid negatives (such as I can't, We don't, etc.).

☐ Build rapport:
  - Use the customer's name (including titles when appropriate, such as Dr., Professor, etc.).

☐ Ask skill assessing questions (when appropriate).

☐ Collect the required information to log the call in the same order every time.

☐ If the incident must be escalated:
  - Determine the incident priority.
  - Recap next steps.
  - Provide an incident number.
  - Provide a workaround (if possible).

☐ If a solution can be provided:
  - Deliver the solution at the customer's skill level.
  - Direct the customer to self-help resources (when applicable).

☐ Verify customer satisfaction.

☐ Use standard closing:
  - Ask if there is anything else I can do.
  - Thank the customer for calling.
  - Let the customer hang up first.

Figure 6-10   Sample monitoring checklist
© Cengage Learning 2014

Skills Inventory Matrix

A **skills inventory matrix** is a grid that rates each analyst's level of skill on every service, system, and product supported by the service desk. A skills inventory matrix is an excellent tool that management can use to determine hiring needs, develop training and cross-training plans for both individual analysts and the service desk team, and establish and measure how well analysts are attaining their improvement goals. Also, companies that use skills-based routing typically require analysts to create and maintain a skills inventory. Some companies have analysts complete the skills inventory matrix during their job interview in an effort to compare the knowledge and expertise of job candidates. Analysts can also use the skills inventory matrix to assess and document their skill levels and identify areas that need improvement. Furthermore, analysts can use the skills inventory matrix to determine the best person to consult when they need assistance in a particular area. Figure 6-11 shows a sample skills inventory matrix. Note that a skills inventory matrix can reflect soft skills, business skills, and self-management skills in addition to technical skills.

Team Members	Customer Service	Windows 8	Microsoft Word	Add New Required Skills As They Are Identified
Isabella	3	1	4	
Rama	1	3	2	
Bill	1	3	1	

Sample rating scale:

1   Expert; certified expert

2   Expert; able to train; write documentation; install

3   Confident; able to assist; not able to train

4   Somewhat able to assist; not totally confident

NA   Not Applicable; no skill required

Figure 6-11   Sample skills inventory matrix

© Cengage Learning 2014

Employee performance plans, individual performance goals, monitoring, and the skills inventory matrix are all ways service desk management can measure the performance of individual analysts. Organizations can use one, all, a combination, or none of these techniques. Although these techniques are interrelated, they can also be used independently of each other. Each of these techniques requires and uses information and, when rigorously supervised, will result in customer and employee satisfaction.

Individual Contributions to Team Goals

Although management directs most of the performance metrics analysts must meet, energetic analysts can suggest additional metrics and supply other information that further demonstrates their contribution to the team's goals. For example, if a company seems focused on efficiency, analysts may propose an effectiveness or quality metric that can balance the service desk's services. Many managers in a team setting try to involve their staff when establishing performance measures, and they encourage their staff to suggest how team and individual performance can be measured and improved. Even simple things such as suggesting possible solutions to an incident rather than finding fault or complaining will raise an analyst's standing in management's eyes.

Embracing and suggesting performance metrics shows management that you are a team player. If you suggest a way to increase efficiency, effectiveness, or quality, capture a baseline metric that can be used to prove your suggestion was a success.

Management appreciates summarized information and can make decisions more quickly and in a less arbitrary manner when they have facts. A powerful technique is to statistically communicate information about a cause and effect to management. This information can indicate both positive and negative trends. For example, service desk management might report to senior management that "We've taken on support for a new product without increasing our staffing levels and as a result we're experiencing a longer average speed of answer (ASA)." Or, service desk management might report, "We implemented a new knowledge management system and can now resolve 15 percent more incidents than before." Capturing data and using information also moves the service desk from a reactive state to a proactive state—which is a much less stressful state for service desk analysts and their customers.

In business, everyone's performance is measured, from the most junior associate to the most senior executive. Employees cannot just work hard and *hope* that management recognizes their efforts. To be successful, you must *show* management your commitment and competency. The best way to do that is to ensure that you understand the goals of your department and company and become skilled at using information to demonstrate how you contribute to those goals.

Chapter Summary

- Today's savvy customers have high expectations for the service desk, and business managers have high expectations for their employees. Every department, including the service desk, is expected to contribute to the goals of the business, and every employee is expected to contribute to the goals of his or her department. The most important goal for the entire company is customer satisfaction. Companies focus on customer satisfaction by understanding their customers' needs and expectations in all areas of the business. They do this by analyzing data and creating information.

- Data and information are resources in the same way that well-trained employees, well-defined processes, and well-implemented technology are resources. Service desks that recognize information as a resource are more proactive than reactive. A reactive service desk simply reacts to events that occur each day, whereas a proactive service desk uses information to anticipate and prevent incidents and prepare for the future.

- Service desks that capture data divide that data into categories such as customer, incident, status, and resolution data. Service desk analysts and managers use this data, typically captured through fields in the service desk's incident management system, to create detailed tracking and summary reports and to perform trend analysis. In addition, managers use this data to calculate many team and individual performance measures.

- Service desk performance measures typically reflect the efficiency, effectiveness, and quality of the services being delivered by the service desk team and by individuals within the team. Common team performance measures include service desk goals, SLAs, customer satisfaction surveys, and benchmarking. Common individual performance measures include individual performance goals, employee performance plans, monitoring, and a skills inventory matrix.

- In business, everyone's performance is measured, from the most junior associate to the most senior executive. Employees cannot just work hard and *hope* that management recognizes their efforts. To be successful, you must understand the goals of your department and company and become skilled at using data and information to demonstrate how you are personally contributing to those goals.

Key Terms

abandon rate percent—The percentage of abandoned calls compared to the total number of calls received.

abandoned call—A call in which the caller hangs up before an analyst answers.

application of training investments—A comparison of an analyst's resolution percent before and after attending training.

availability—The length of time an analyst was signed on to the ACD compared to the length of time the analyst was scheduled to be signed on.

average call duration—The average length of time required to handle a call.

average speed of answer (ASA)—The average time it takes an analyst to pick up an incoming call.

average wait time—The average number of seconds or minutes a caller waits for an analyst after being placed in the queue by an ACD; also known as average queue time.

baseline—A metric used to show a starting point.

certification—A document awarded to a person who has demonstrated that he or she has certain skills and knowledge about a particular topic or area.

CompTIA A+—A certification that measures a technician's knowledge of hardware and operating system technologies and concepts, along with topics such as security, safety and environmental issues, and communication and professionalism.

cost per contact—Historically called cost per call; the total cost of operating a service desk for a given period (including salaries, benefits, facilities, and equipment) divided by the total number of contacts (calls, emails, faxes, web requests, and so on) received during that period.

cost per unit—The total cost of operating a service desk for a given period (including salaries, benefits, facilities, and equipment) divided by the total number of units (such as services, systems, and devices) supported during that period.

critical success factor (CSF)—A measurable characteristic that must exist for something—such as a process, project, or team—to be viewed as successful.

customer data—Identifying details about a customer, including the customer's name, telephone number, email address, department or company name, physical address or location, customer number, and employee number or user ID.

customer record—All of the fields that describe a single customer.

customer satisfaction survey—A series of questions that ask customers to provide their perception of the support services being offered.

effectiveness—A measure of how completely and accurately services are delivered.

efficiency—A measure of the time and effort required to deliver services in relation to their cost.

employee performance plan—A document that clearly describes an analyst's performance requirements and individual improvement objectives.

event-driven survey—A customer satisfaction survey that asks customers for feedback on a single, recent service event.

exit poll—A measurement technique that, on the Internet, combines questions such as "Was this information helpful to you?" with Yes and No buttons that customers can use to provide feedback.

field—A location in a database that stores a particular piece of data.

first contact resolution rate percent—The percentage of contacts resolved during a customer's initial contact compared to the total number of contacts received at the service desk for a given period of time.

incident data—The details of an incident or service request, including incident type (such as an incident or service request), channel used to submit (such as telephone, email, or web request), category (such as hardware or software), affected service, system, or device (such as a printer or monitor), the symptom, the date and time the incident occurred, the date and time the incident was logged, the analyst who logged the incident, the incident owner, a description, and a priority.

incident record—All of the fields that describe a single incident.

incidents resolved within target time percent—The percentage of incidents resolved within a target resolution time.

individual performance goals—Measurable objectives for analysts that support the service desk mission.

key performance indicator (KPI)—A key metric used to manage a process.

level one resolution rate percent—The percentage of incidents resolved at level one (not necessarily during the customer's initial telephone contact).

monitoring—When a supervisor or team leader monitors an analyst's interactions with customers in order to measure the quality of an analyst's performance.

overall satisfaction survey—A customer satisfaction survey that asks customers for feedback about all contacts with the service desk during a certain time period.

page hit—A web page visit.

proactive service desk—A service desk that uses information to anticipate and prevent incidents and prepare for the future.

reactive service desk—A service desk that simply responds to events that occur each day.

record—A collection of related fields.

reopened percent—The percentage of closed incidents that had to be opened back up within a given period of time.

resolution data—Details that describe how an incident was resolved, including all the fields required to track service level compliance and perform trend analysis, such as the person or group who resolved the incident, resolution description, date and time resolved, customer satisfaction indicator, date and time closed, and possible cause.

resolution percent—The percentage of incidents an analyst resolves compared to the total number of incidents that analyst handled during a given period of time.

response time—The length of time a customer waits for a reply to a fax, email, or web request.

service desk goals—Measurable objectives that support the service desk's mission.

skills inventory matrix—A grid that rates each analyst's level of skill on every product, system, and service supported by the service desk.

status data—Details about an incident that are used to track the incident throughout its lifecycle, including incident status (such as assigned, awaiting parts, resolved, closed), the person or group assigned, the date and time assigned, and a priority.

time idle—The average length of time an analyst was idle during a given period of time.

wrap-up time—The average length of time an analyst was in wrap-up mode during a given period of time.

Review Questions

1. How are metrics used in a service desk setting, and how are they created?

2. What causes an organization to stay in a reactive state?

3. List at least five ways that proactive service desks use information.

4. How can a service desk move to a proactive state?

5. What factors influence the amount of data captured by a service desk?

6. List the four main data categories captured by most service desks.

7. How is resolving an incident different from closing an incident?

8. List and describe the three characteristics that service desk team and individual performance measures assess.

9. List the four most common ways that service desks measure team performance.

10. How is cost per contact calculated?

11. What is the distinction between service desk goals and operational performance metrics?

12. How are SLAs used to control costs?

13. List three service level metrics that measure the efficiency of the service desk team.

14. List three service level metrics that measure the effectiveness of the service desk team.

15. What is the difference between first contact resolution rate and level one resolution rate?

16. What is target resolution time based on?

17. What performance characteristic does a customer satisfaction survey measure?

18. How are event-driven surveys used differently than overall satisfaction surveys?

19. What is the benefit of benchmarking?

20. Why is it important that companies thoroughly analyze benchmarking results?

21. What are the goals of individual performance management?

22. What are the four most common ways that service desks measure individual performance?

23. List two ways to measure an individual's efficiency.

24. List two ways to measure an individual's effectiveness.

25. List two ways to measure the quality of an individual's performance.

26. Used properly, what perspective does monitoring encourage analysts to adopt relative to the services they are delivering?

27. List two ways that managers use a skills inventory matrix.

28. List two ways that analysts use a skills inventory matrix.

29. How do service desk analysts benefit when service desks use information to move from a reactive state to a proactive state?

30. How can you ensure that management recognizes your efforts?

Hands-On Projects

1. **Learn how a service desk measures performance.** Select a class representative who can arrange to have a manager or analyst from a local service desk come and speak to your class. Prior to the presentation, prepare a list of the team and individual performance measurements discussed in this chapter. As a courtesy, have your class representative send this list to your speaker ahead of time so that he or she knows the goal of your class is to learn how these techniques are used. Prepare a report that answers the following questions:

   - Do employees have performance plans?

   - If yes, how and when are they updated?

   - Do employees have job descriptions?

   - If both, how are the performance plans related to the job descriptions?

   - What metrics do they use to measure team performance?

   - What metrics do they use to measure individual performance?

   - What tools do they use to capture their metrics?

   - What is the team's philosophy with regard to capturing data and creating information?

   - What is the team's philosophy with regard to performance measurements?

2. **Evaluate performance measurements.** Assemble a team of at least three of your classmates or use your school's online message or discussion board. Discuss the metrics being captured by the company you interviewed in Project 6-1 and examine its philosophy toward performance measurements. Discuss the following questions and then document your team's conclusions:

   - Is this company collecting a balanced set of metrics? In other words, is it measuring efficiency, effectiveness, and quality?

   - If not, what metrics does your team recommend the company begin capturing in an effort to be more balanced? Explain.

   - What, if any, observations can you make concerning the company's philosophy with regard to performance measurements?

   Present and compare your conclusions with the rest of the class.

3. **Learn about creating meaningful goals and metrics.** Setting goals and creating metrics can be difficult. Focusing on the wrong goals and metrics can drive negative behavior. Search the web for tips that can be used to set goals and produce meaningful metrics. Example searches may include: "creating meaningful metrics," "creating balanced performance metrics," and "how to create SMART goals."

   Prepare a brief report that describes the top five tips you learned from reading this chapter and from visiting these sites about setting goals and creating metrics. Include conclusions you can draw about the importance of using care when setting goals and producing metrics.

4. **Learn how companies measure customer satisfaction.** Visit the web site of an organization you do business with (such as the company that manufactured your computer or that published a software package you use).

   - Does the site contain a customer satisfaction survey? If not, does it provide some other way for customers to provide feedback?

   - What kind of feedback does it request (for example, feedback on its efficiency, effectiveness, or quality)?

   - Does the organization give any indication of how it will use customer feedback?

   - Did you feel compelled to give feedback? In other words, did the company make you feel that your feedback was important, and did the site make it easy for you to provide feedback?

   - If the site did not contain a survey, or if you did not feel compelled to give feedback, what techniques could the company use to obtain your feedback?

5. **Identify ways to reduce abandoned calls.** An abandoned call means the caller hangs up before an analyst answers the call. Prepare a list of reasons that customers abandon calls. Eliminate positive reasons that callers hang up (such as a message encouraging use of the service desk's web site). Then, using everything you have learned, prepare a second list that proposes ways to reduce the number of abandoned calls. Assemble a team of at least three of your classmates or use your school's online message or discussion board. Compare and discuss your lists. Can you add any additional items to your lists?

6. **Learn how team and individual performance is measured.** Interview a friend, family member, or classmate who works in a team setting. (It does not have to be a service desk.) Ask this person the following questions:

   - How is the team's performance measured?

   - How is your individual performance measured?

   - Do you feel that your manager has communicated clearly what you must do to receive a positive performance evaluation?

   - What techniques do you use to communicate your achievements to management?

   - How do you feel about the amount of information management requires you to provide about your personal performance? Why?

   Prepare a brief report that presents conclusions you can draw from this discussion.

7. **Evaluate a single performance characteristic.** Choose among the characteristics of efficiency, effectiveness, and quality. List the pros and cons of focusing on this single performance characteristic. For example, list the pros and cons of focusing only on how efficiently the service desk is performing while ignoring its effectiveness or the quality of its services.

   You can work with two of your classmates to complete this project by holding a debate. Each classmate could present the merits of a single performance characteristic and state why he or she believes that characteristic is more important than the others.

You could then end the debate by summarizing the pros and cons of focusing on a single performance characteristic. Present your conclusions to the class.

8. **Learn how service desk outsourcing companies measure performance.** Search the web to locate two companies that provide service desk outsourcing. For each company, summarize in a few paragraphs what you were able to learn about its performance management program from the web site. In your summary, include the answers to such questions as:

   - Does the company appear to use any of the techniques discussed in this chapter to measure overall team performance?

   - Does it give any indication of how it measures the performance of individual staff members?

   - How does it measure customer satisfaction?

   - Can you determine from the company's web site if the company addresses all of the performance characteristics (efficiency, effectiveness, and quality)?

9. **Interview a manager.** Talk to someone you know who is in a management position. The person doesn't have to be the manager of a service desk. Document his or her answers to the following questions:

   - How do you measure the performance of your team?
     - Overall?
     - Individually?

   - Do you feel you have all the information needed to, for example, justify resources, enhance productivity, and evaluate performance? If not, why?

   - How do you communicate to upper management the contribution of your team to the organization's goals?

   - How do you communicate to upper management your individual contribution to the organization's goals?

   Summarize any conclusions you can draw from this discussion about the importance of using information as a resource.

Case Projects

1. **ABC Electronics.** You've recently been promoted to service desk supervisor at ABC Electronics. The service desk does not currently capture any team or individual performance measures. Everyone is extremely busy, but you're not having any luck convincing management that additional resources are needed. The service desk does not have a sophisticated telephone system such as an ACD, but it does have a simple incident management system. Currently, only high-priority incidents that must be assigned to other groups are logged, and very little information is captured.

The service desk manager asks you to recommend ways the service desk can justify additional resources and communicate its value to management. Prepare a brief report outlining your recommendations.

2. **Technology Support Unlimited.** You have been hired as a consultant to help Technology Support Unlimited (TSU) measure customer satisfaction with its support services. TSU provides service desk outsourcing services. It has SLAs with all of its customers that describe measurable performance goals regarding the efficiency and effectiveness of its services. It wants to use customer satisfaction surveys to measure the quality of its services and identify opportunities to offer additional services. It has asked you to develop a survey.

Begin by interviewing several of TSU's customers. (You can use classmates, friends, family members, or coworkers who have contacted a service desk in the past.) Determine what they think are the characteristics of quality service desk service. Narrow their suggested list of characteristics down to no more than five key measurable characteristics. Create a one-page survey that asks customers to rate TSU's performance in those areas. Remember also to ask customers if they have any suggestions about how TSU can improve its services. You may want to look on the web or collect sample surveys from restaurants and so forth to get ideas for the format of your survey.

The Service Desk Setting

In this chapter you will learn:

◎ Factors that influence the service desk's location and layout

◎ How analysts can improve the ergonomics of their personal workspaces

◎ Work habits to get and stay organized and achieve personal success

Having the right processes, technologies, and information—and knowing how to use them properly—is only part of supporting customers effectively. In order to provide top-quality customer service and support, an analyst needs a good work environment, good work habits, and a great attitude. Some days, walking into a service desk is like walking into an amusement arcade. Lights are flashing, alarms are ringing, and everyone is talking at once. The larger the service desk, the more active and exciting—or intimidating—it can be. Focused, organized people who thrive on challenge will find this dynamic environment invigorating.

Service desks, whether large or small, are high-energy and high-activity places. The constant stream of contacts from customers in need requires friendly and patient analysts. Companies that create a pleasant, comfortable working environment make it easier for their analysts to be understanding and effective.

Whether or not a company provides the optimal working environment, analysts can set up their personal workspaces for optimal comfort and functionality. They can also establish routines to organize their time. To be a successful service desk analyst, you must understand how the physical layout of your workspace can benefit (and sometimes detract from) your performance. Also, it is important to understand that you can arrange your physical workspace and adopt behaviors to increase your comfort and productivity.

Service Desk Setup

Service desks come in all shapes and sizes, and the setup of service desks varies from one company to the next. The service desk setup includes both its location and its layout. Several factors influence the service desk's location, such as accessibility, the need for security, and the company's commitment to the well-being of its staff. Factors such as size, technical sophistication, and the nature of problem solving analysts do influence the service desk's physical layout. All of these factors together affect analysts' comfort in the workplace and how efficiently they work.

Location of the Service Desk

Location refers to the physical site of the service desk in the building. When choosing a location, companies may place the service desk near other support groups (such as level two and level three support groups). This physical proximity allows the service desk to interact more easily with the people in those groups and vice versa. The service desk may be placed near groups that report to a different department but that interact regularly with the service desk. For example, the service desk may be located near the training department in recognition of the service desk's need for ongoing education and training, or the service desk may be located near or with the data center operations control team so that both teams can share service and network monitoring systems. An external service desk may be located near the sales group. Companies may also place the service desk near their customers. This allows the service desk to build rapport with its customers and develop an understanding of the environment in which its customers work. Location may also be influenced by the need to provide for continuous operations in the event of an emergency. For example, some companies have multiple service desks that are linked by technology. This enables the company to transfer service desk operations to an alternate site in the event that one site is affected by a natural disaster or other extreme condition. Figure 7-1 lists factors that influence the location of the service desk.

- Accessibility
- Security
- Wellness

Figure 7-1 Factors that influence service desk location
© Cengage Learning 2014

A company's commitment to creating a safe and attractive workplace for its employees and its willingness to make the financial investment required to do so also have considerable bearing on the service desk location.

Accessibility

Accessibility determines how easily the service desk can be reached by service desk staff, other employees of the company, and customers. Historically, many service desks were located behind closed doors in the computer room. Today, service desks are situated more centrally. Accessible service desks enable analysts to interact more freely with level two and level three support groups and, when appropriate, with internal or external customers. For example, some service desks offer walk-in service. Because it can be distracting if customers begin speaking to an analyst who is on the phone—with headsets, it's sometimes hard to tell if an analyst is on the phone—many service desks set up a desk or counter that customers report to when they arrive at the service desk for walk-in service. The customers then receive service on a first-come, first-served basis. This type of highly personalized service is costly ($16 per contact), but is common in the education industry and in smaller organizations (*2012 Support Center Practices and Salary Report*, HDI).

In a decentralized service desk setting, the factors that influence the location of the service desk vary from one site to the next.

Some service desks offer tours of their facilities to customers, visitors from other companies, remote employees who have come to corporate headquarters for a meeting or training, and so on. When efforts are made to ensure that visitors do not disrupt analysts who are on the phone, having customers and other support groups visit the service desk is an excellent way to let them see the service desk in action and help them understand the service desk's role.

Security

Data and equipment protection, along with the personal safety of employees, affect where a service desk is located and the measures taken to secure the area. Some service desks are in remote parts of the building or can be accessed only by using a key or a card key or by signing in with a guard. Some organizations use biometrics to grant or restrict access. **Biometrics** involves measuring a person's physical characteristics, such as finger or palm prints, facial features, or parts of a person's eye such as the retina or iris. The permissions or authority the service desk has to make system changes also influence the need for security. For example, service desks with access to master computer consoles need greater security to prevent unauthorized system changes. The safety of the service desk staff is also a consideration. Service desks that operate 24 hours per day, 7 days per week need more security than those that function only during regular business hours. Service desks that are open around the clock often secure the service desk area so after-hours workers are safe.

Wellness

Wellness is the condition of good physical and mental health, especially when maintained by proper diet, exercise, and habits. Exposure to natural light, access to clean air, and the ability to exercise are just a few things that influence workers' physical and emotional well-being both at and away from the workplace. A well-lit environment encourages the positive attitude service desk analysts need. Many people prefer to work in an area that has good ventilation or windows they can open for fresh air and that is located far from a designated smoking area. People are also more comfortable when they work in an open workplace that allows them to move about or in a building that has an indoor gym or other room where they can exercise when it is too hot or cold outside. Companies that promote wellness design their workplaces to provide these types of positive influences. A well-designed workplace that takes into consideration the comfort and safety of employees prevents workplace injuries, reduces fatigue and stress, and increases productivity.

Wellness resources and programs—such as fitness memberships or facilities on site, flu shots, smoking-cessation classes, nutritional counseling, and child care—also help organizations reduce absenteeism, retain employees, and contain rising health-care costs.

Physical Layout of the Service Desk

Physical layout refers to how the service desk is arranged into workspaces. A **workspace** is an area outfitted with equipment and furnishings for one worker. The physical layout might be a result of how the service desk was formed. Recall that some large service desks grew from small service desks, whereas others evolved from the consolidation of several small service desks or from a corporate merger or acquisition. A company's desire to create an attractive workplace also has considerable bearing on its physical layout. Figure 7-2 lists other factors that influence the physical layout of the service desk.

- Size
- Tools and technology
- Interaction

Figure 7-2 Factors that influence the service desk's physical layout
© Cengage Learning 2014

Size

The number of analysts who work at a service desk greatly influences its physical layout or how the workspaces are arranged. For example, small service desks place analysts close together to enhance their ability to work together as a team. Larger service desks want analysts to be able to work together as a team, but they must also accommodate the needs of service desk management and other supporting groups, such as knowledge engineer, technical support, and perhaps a training group.

In a very small service desk—consisting of one or two people—analysts typically sit in cubicles. The analysts in a small service desk with more than two people may sit side by side in large cubicles that face each other across an aisle so they can communicate easily. These service desks also may devote some space to equipment such as a multi-function printer, whiteboard, and network monitors. Figure 7-3 illustrates a small service desk setting.

 The supervisor or manager of a very small service desk (if there is one) may reside in the service desk and handle customer contacts, but will typically move to a nearby cubicle or office as the service desk grows.

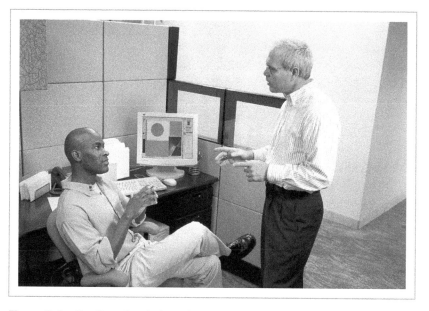

Figure 7-3 Small service desk setting
© Comstock / Photos.com

284

Medium service desks use a different layout than small service desks do. Medium service desks have between 10 and 25 people on staff and can take on the characteristics of both small and large service desks. As the service desk grows to 25 people or so, some companies arrange cubicles around an enclosed common area—sometimes called a "bullpen"—to minimize the noise entering and leaving the service desk, as well as to enable analysts to share resources such as equipment and books or manuals. Communication tools such as a whiteboard, an electronic reader board, or network monitors are positioned so they can be viewed easily by all analysts. Figure 7-4 shows a medium service desk setting.

Figure 7-4 Medium service desk setting
Courtesy of Mesh.net
Photo by Nu-Design.com

Medium and large service desk settings sometimes contain common areas, such as a lab or meeting area. They may also set aside an cubicle or two for use by level two or level three staff who periodically visit the service desk for informal training or who are on site when a new system is launched. The cubicles may also be used for certification testing or testing of job applicants.

Large service desks that grew from small or medium service desks sometimes did so without the benefit of an expansion plan. For example, some service desks may take up two or more floors of a building due to office space constraints. In other service desks, analysts may reside in long rows of standard cubicles and must leave their cubicles to communicate with coworkers and service desk management. Worse yet, they may shout through cubicle walls or stand on their chairs in an effort to communicate.

In contrast to these unplanned settings, some large service desks are created with employee comfort, safety, and productivity in mind. These service desk settings consider in their layout factors such as noise, lighting, and the analyst's personal workspace. Workspaces are often arranged in clusters or "pods" designed to reduce noise, facilitate communication, and increase teamwork. These clusters may represent teams of analysts within the service desk who have similar skills, such as hardware skills, software skills, or mobile computing skills. In an external service desk or service agency, these teams may consist of analysts who support a single customer, or they may consist of analysts who support several customers, such as several small companies that require a limited amount of support.

In a well-designed setting, the cubicle walls between the workspaces typically are low—three to four feet—enabling analysts to interact easily and view electronic reader boards, network monitors, and even pictures mounted around the perimeter of the service desk. Figure 7-5 illustrates a large service desk setting.

Figure 7-5 Large service desk setting
Courtesy of CompuCom Systems, Inc.

Regardless of a service desk's size, the physical layout of the service desk must facilitate efficient communication among analysts in an effort to avoid situations such as having more than one analyst working on the same incident. It is also important to have a mechanism such as a whiteboard or a reader board that can be used to quickly notify all analysts when there is a major incident.

Tools and Technology

The size of the service desk often reflects its use of tools and technology, which, in turn, influences its physical layout. Furthermore, the size of the service desk and its technical sophistication often go hand in hand. For example, small service desks may need only a multi-function printer and a whiteboard, whereas larger service desks may use electronic reader boards and network monitors. Some service desks, regardless of size, have lab areas with the same hardware and software configurations as their customers. Analysts can use these lab areas to obtain hands-on training, simulate customers' incidents, and develop and test potential solutions. All service desks can benefit from technology, and the service desk's physical layout must accommodate whatever tools and technology the service desk uses or plans to use in the future.

Interaction

Both the level of interaction and the nature of problem solving performed by the service desk staff influence its physical layout. For example, service desks in which analysts interact constantly and work together to solve incidents use low-walled, open cubicles that are arranged to face a common area. Service desks where analysts work independently researching complex incidents or debugging programs use higher cubicle walls or even private offices.

Growing service desks often add on to their existing location without considering or being able to consider these factors—size, tools and technology, and interaction. This ad hoc design hinders productivity. Companies that are designing new service desks, or redesigning existing ones, are in the best position to consider all of these factors in their physical layout plans.

More and more, companies recognize that a well-designed work environment enhances the service desk's productivity and improves analysts' ability to communicate and share information. Also, many organizations conduct research on work environments and provide recommendations. For example, the **National Institute for Occupational Safety and Health (NIOSH)** is a part of the U.S. Centers for Disease Control and Prevention (CDC) that is responsible for conducting research and making recommendations for the prevention of work-related illnesses and injuries (*www.cdc.gov/niosh/homepage.html*). The **Occupational Safety and Health Administration (OSHA)** is an agency of the U.S. Department of Labor that is dedicated to reducing hazards in the workplace and enforcing job safety standards (*www.osha.gov*). OSHA also implements and improves health programs for workers. These organizations provide companies and individuals with the information needed to create safe and comfortable workspaces.

Analysts' Personal Workspace

Analysts often have no control over the location and the layout of the service desk, but they can improve the ergonomics of their personal workspaces. **Ergonomics** is the science of people-machine relationships that is intended to maximize productivity by reducing operator fatigue and discomfort. Some symptoms of a poorly designed workspace include headaches, wrist and shoulder pain, backaches, and swollen ankles. Unfortunately, people often do not know until it is too late that these symptoms of poor ergonomics can be prevented.

Good ergonomics practices (discussed below) help reduce these symptoms and prevent repetitive stress injuries. **Repetitive stress injuries (RSIs)** are physical symptoms caused by excessive and repeated use of the hands, wrists, arms, and thumbs; they occur when people repeatedly perform tasks using force, strenuous actions, awkward postures, or poorly designed equipment. For example, too much typing on handheld devices such as smartphones could cause repetitive strain injuries to users' thumbs. RSIs include carpal tunnel syndrome, tendonitis, bursitis, and rotator cuff injuries. **Carpal tunnel syndrome (CTS)** is a common repetitive stress injury that affects the hands and wrists and is linked to repetitious hand movements, such as typing on a computer keyboard and working with a mouse. CTS is caused by constant compression of the main nerve to the hand as it passes through the carpal tunnel of the wrist. The service desk team is susceptible to RSIs such as CTS because analysts do a considerable amount of keyboarding and mousing.

Also, analysts are susceptible to computer vision syndrome. **Computer vision syndrome** encompasses a variety of ailments such as headaches and eyestrain that occur as a result of staring at a computer monitor for a prolonged period of time.

 To learn more about ergonomics and how to prevent and treat conditions such as CTS and computer vision syndrome, go to *www.healthycomputing.com*.

A majority of ergonomic problems can be eliminated by making simple, no-cost adjustments to the analyst's personal workspace. Analysts can easily adjust their chairs, monitors, keyboards, mouse devices, telephones, headsets, and lighting to create a workspace that fits their needs. Making these adjustments goes a long way to helping analysts stay healthy on the job.

Chair

In each workspace, the placement and use of the chair, monitor, keyboard, and mouse are related, and all must be aligned properly with each other and with the analyst. How analysts adjust and sit in their chairs is equally important. Analysts should adjust the chair until the back is erect, slightly back, and firm against the backrest. Figure 7-6 illustrates a typical office chair that can be adjusted to promote good posture and back support. Adjustment features may include the ability to adjust arm height, arm width, seat height, seat tilt, and support for the lumbar region (also known as the small of the back).

Figure 7-6   Ergonomic office chair and footrest
Courtesy of Relax the Back

If necessary, analysts can further support their backs with a lumbar pillow or a rolled-up towel. Legs should be relaxed, and feet should be flat on the floor. Analysts can also place a footrest or a box under the desk to keep their feet from dangling.

 To learn more about how to adjust your chair, go to *www.osha.gov/SLTC/etools/computerworkstations*. This site also offers information about how to adjust the keyboard and mouse and how to improve workspace lighting.

Monitor

The chair height can both affect and be affected by the monitor placement. The best position for a monitor is directly in front of the analyst at or just below eye level. When analysts are sitting straight with their heads erect, the monitor should be at least 20 inches away from their eyes. If necessary, analysts can place a book under the monitor to raise it up to the right level. If the monitor is too high, they can remove anything under it to lower it, adjust their chair, or, as a last resort, replace the desk or table with a lower one.

Factors such as monitor size and resolution also affect productivity. For example, widescreen displays make it possible for analysts to view multiple windows and can reduce scrolling. Higher resolution displays reduce eyestrain and make it easier for analysts to read text and view detailed diagrams. Figure 7-7 shows a typical monitor.

Figure 7-7 Typical monitor
© Semisatch/Shutterstock.com

If you're encountering monitor glare, treat the glass surface with an antiglare coating or install a filter over the screen.

Keyboard and Mouse

Correct placement and use of the keyboard and mouse combined with good work habits can help analysts avoid repetitive stress injuries. The proper form for typing and using the mouse is to keep wrists straight and to avoid resting them on hard surfaces. Elbows should be kept close to the body and should be bent between 90 and 120 degrees. Keys should be pressed gently rather than pounded to prevent injury to both the hands and the keyboard. Also, the mouse should be held loosely. Analysts can also consider using ergonomic keyboards and sloping keyboard trays to reduce the symptoms of carpal tunnel syndrome. A wrist rest—a firm cushion that lays parallel to the keyboard—can also help. Wrist rests that are too soft allow the wrists to sink in, putting unnecessary pressure on the wrists. Figure 7-8 illustrates how a wrist rest can be used in front of a keyboard and a mouse.

Figure 7-8   Keyboard and mouse wrist rest

 Periodically shake out your hands and perform shrugging exercises to relax your shoulders. Squeeze a stress ball to keep blood flowing through your fingers and arms, strengthen your grip, and relieve stress. Keep it loose!

All these components—chair, monitor, keyboard, and mouse—work together. The chair should be aligned with the monitor and keyboard so that, when an analyst sits up straight in the chair, the monitor is at or below eye level and the wrists are straight on the keyboard. Whenever analysts adjust their chairs, they will most likely need to readjust their monitor and their keyboard and mouse as well. Figure 7-9 illustrates the relationship between the chair, monitor, and keyboard.

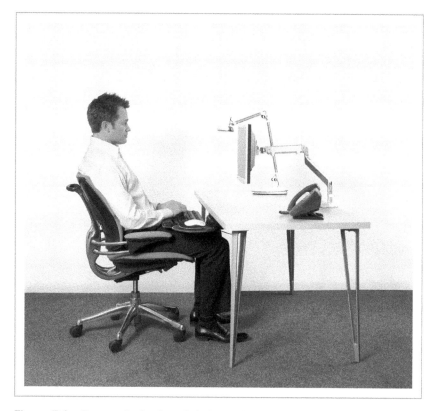

Figure 7-9 Ergonomically aligned chair, monitor, and keyboard
Courtesy of Humanscale

The person in this figure is sitting up straight with his feet resting comfortably on the floor and with the chair supporting his lower back. Also, the monitor is at eye level, the person's wrists are straight, and his fingers are resting lightly on the keyboard. This is the optimal placement of the technology for this person. Another person would likely need to make adjustments to achieve optimal placement of the technology.

Telephone and Headset

A telephone is one of the most basic pieces of equipment at service desks. The type or style of telephone is less important than its correct position in relation to the computer. Analysts who have to stretch or turn around to answer the telephone are at risk for a repetitive stress injury. A good rule of thumb for analysts is to place the telephone either directly in front of them or at less than a 25 degree angle and no more than 10 inches away.

Telephone headsets rid analysts of the traditional handheld receiver. Headsets relieve stress and tension by freeing analysts' hands for typing, and they prevent neck pain by eliminating the need to balance the receiver between the head and shoulder. Wireless headsets provide the added ability to stand up and move about the service desk. As shown in Figure 7-10, headsets are available in numerous styles, including over-the-ear models and headbands that fit over one ear or both ears.

Your head is your heaviest body part. Although headsets are fairly light, avoid ones that make you tilt or hang your head. These can quickly cause tension in your neck, shoulders, and back.

For a series of videos demonstrating neck stretches for the workplace, go to *www.mayoclinic.com/health/neck-stretches/MM00708*. Scroll down for additional videos such as forearm, upper body, standing, and seated stretches for the workplace.

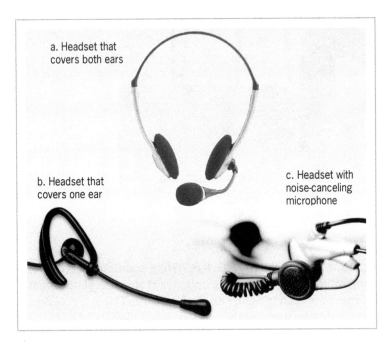

Figure 7-10   Available headset styles
Source: a. © badahos / Shutterstock.com b. © Christopher Tan Teck Hean / Shutterstock.com c. © Alexander Gordeyev / Shutterstock.com

Anyone who wears a telephone headset for long periods, as most analysts do, is at risk for hearing loss or acoustic shock. Hearing loss can occur when the headset volume is turned up excessively high for a prolonged period of time. NIOSH says that exposure to sound averaging 85 decibels for more than eight hours a day presents a risk of hearing loss (*Noise and Hearing Loss Prevention*, The National Institute for Occupational Safety and Health, 2011). Note that a conversation between two people typically measures 60 decibels. **Acoustic shock** is the term used to describe the symptoms, such as discomfort and pain, that a person may experience after hearing a loud, unexpected sound via a telephone or headset. Analysts should see a doctor if they experience ringing in the ears or a problem with hearing.

Minimize your risk by taking occasional breaks and maintaining your headset at a comfortable volume level. Also, select a headset that offers protection against loud, unexpected noises.

If possible, analysts should try on several headset models before making a final selection. Although the style of headset a person selects is a matter of personal choice, each style changes how much the wearer can hear. For example:

- Some headsets cover only one ear so people can remain aware of what is going on around them.
- Some headsets cover both ears so people can block out noise.
- Some headsets offer a noise-canceling microphone to help filter out noise that the customer may hear from the service desk, such as phones ringing, announcements, and people talking nearby.

Regardless of the style, a headset should keep the user's head and neck in a neutral position and should free the hands for activities such as typing.

Lighting

The brightness of a workspace can greatly affect an analyst's well-being. Too much overhead lighting or ambient light from a window can produce a glare on the monitor, which can cause eyestrain, headaches, and fatigue. Glare can also prompt analysts to shift their posture to a more awkward position, increasing the chance of neck or back strain. Analysts can reduce this glare by spraying an antiglare coating on the glass surface or by installing an antiglare filter. Too little lighting can cause analysts to squint and strain in order to see paperwork or the monitor.

As a preventative step, analysts should have routine hearing and eye exams.

Adjustable task lighting on the desk provides directed lighting to supplement the overhead lighting and can be shifted to prevent glare. Task lighting can be used to spotlight desk tasks, such as writing and reading, and can also be used to reduce the high contrast of light and dark areas that occur in a workspace. Figure 7-11 shows the use of task lighting.

Figure 7-11 Effective task lighting
Courtesy of Dazor Manufacturing Corp.

When using a task light:

- Position the light away from your computer screen to prevent glare.

- If you are working with a document holder next to the computer screen, shine the light directly on the document holder and not on your computer screen.

- Position the light 15 to 20 inches (depending on your height) directly over paper documents that are placed on your desk.

- Position the light slightly below eye level.

- Always keep the light head facing down so that it does not shine in your eyes.

- Place the task light where it can be easily adjusted by hand or moved to the area of the desk where you are working.

In addition to overhead and task lighting, analysts need regular or periodic exposure to natural light. This is because natural light, or the lack of it, can influence analysts' moods. A study conducted by the National Institute of Mental Health found that the shorter days and fewer sunlight hours during winter trigger a change in many people's brain chemistry. The change may set off a cycle of depression, which is now recognized in medical literature as Seasonal Affective Disorder (SAD).

Also, regular light bulbs emit light in only a narrow scope of the visual spectrum, whereas natural light has a balanced spectrum that renders colors perfectly. Because of this, natural light is much more pleasing than artificial light. Analysts can experience a positive psychological lift by making a conscious effort to look out a window periodically throughout the day or by going outside, even if only for a brief period of time. People with more severe cases of SAD respond well to exposure to bright, artificial light. **Light therapy** involves sitting beside a special fluorescent light box for several minutes day. A health care professional should be consulted before beginning light therapy.

Your work habits contribute to the amount of stress and tension you experience on the job. Take regular breaks, periodically look out a window, stretch, and be aware of your posture and wrist positions.

At any new office or workspace, analysts should take the time to arrange the equipment to meet their requirements. If they need additional equipment, such as a task light or footrest, they should request it from their managers. In addition to these physical equipment adjustments, analysts can adapt their work habits as well.

Good Work Habits for Analysts

Customer support is a tough job. In fact, it's one of the most stressful professions you can have. This is because analysts cannot predict what crisis will occur on any given day. Difficult customer situations and a lack of time to update one's skills or insufficient resources such as tools, procedures, and knowledge sources also contribute to the stress that can occur in a service desk setting. To reduce stress and the possibility of getting injured on the job, analysts can ensure that they are ready to *respond*, not react, to whatever comes their way. Figure 7-12 lists good work habits analysts can use on a daily basis to get and stay organized and to achieve personal success.

Skills and techniques analysts can use to achieve longer-term success and advance their career are discussed in Chapter 8.

- Create a beginning of day (BOD) procedure.
- Manage priorities.
- Create a "What I Need to Know" list.
- Create a "What Coworkers Need to Know" list.
- Utilize peak productivity times.
- Eliminate or minimize time robbers.
- Place a mirror on your desk.
- Take breaks.
- Recognize learning as the labor of the information age.

Figure 7-12   Good work habits for service desk analysts
© Cengage Learning 2014

Each of these items helps reduce the stress that can occur in a service desk setting and contributes to the personal success of service desk analysts and, ultimately, to the success of the service desk and the company.

Create a Beginning of Day (BOD) Procedure

Successful analysts develop routines that enable them to stay organized and remember things. A **beginning of day (BOD)** procedure is a list of tasks an analyst performs at the start of each workday. For example, an effective BOD includes:

- Greet coworkers.
- Straighten desk (if time did not allow you to do so at the end of the previous day).
- Check and respond to your work-related voice mail, email, and text messages.
- Check the status of incidents and service requests.
- Follow up on any critical issues from the previous day.
- Create or update a "To Do" list for the day.
- Note any current "hot" (or major) incidents.
- Take a deep breath and get ready for anything!

 Arrive a few minutes early so that you can complete your BOD before signing on to take calls. A BOD is a habit that sets the tone for the rest of the day. Start the day off right.

In addition to a BOD procedure for each analyst, some service desks create a BOD for the entire service desk. An EOD (end of day) procedure is also a good idea. Service desks that work in shifts also may have a beginning and end of shift procedure, also known as a shift turnover procedure. The policies of the service desk determine what tasks are included in these procedures.

Manage Priorities

Once analysts are organized for the day, they need to determine in what order to complete the tasks on their "To Do" list. A "To Do" list must be prioritized daily. Analysts assign a priority to each task to indicate the order they will work on tasks that day. A simple priority scale rates each task on a scale from A to D, as shown in Table 7-1.

Rating	Priority
A	Urgent, must do today
B	Important, should do this week
C	Do when time permits
D	Delegate

Table 7-1 Simple priority scale

© Cengage Learning 2014

After each task has a priority rating, analysts check for a balance of priorities. When faced with more "A" priority tasks than can be completed in one day, analysts can consider the following questions about each task:

1. **Who asked me to complete this task?**
   A task assigned by a customer or a manager may have a higher priority than a task assigned by a coworker.

2. **Am I the proper person to complete this task?**
   You don't have to accept a task just because someone asks. The person asking you to complete a task may not know that another person on the team is responsible for the work being requested. If your manager is asking you to complete a task that you do not feel qualified to complete, discuss the matter with your manager and ask for any help you need prior to proceeding.

3. **What is the risk if I don't complete this task? What is the value if I do complete this task?**
   Failing to complete a task may cause the analyst (or someone waiting on the analyst's input) to miss a critical deadline. Consistently completing tasks on time helps make an analyst eligible for a raise or a promotion.

4. **When am I expected to have this task done? That is, what is my deadline for this task?**
   If the task is due that day, it is a high priority for the day. If it is not due for several weeks, the analyst can assign a lower priority and strive to simply start the task even though it may not get completed that day.

 To avoid overcommitting yourself, ask the person assigning a task when it needs to be completed, rather than offering to complete it immediately. Also, ask how important the task is so that you can assign an appropriate priority.

Based on their answers to these questions, analysts can refine the priorities of the tasks on their "To Do" lists.

Some people find the task of assigning priorities to all of the tasks on their "To Do" lists overwhelming. Some people also lack the time or inclination required to rewrite "To Do" lists at the end of each day or week and so may end up with multiple, out-of-date "To Do" lists, which tends to only make them feel more disorganized. Simpler, electronic organizers can be just as effective, such as Evernote (*www.evernote.com*), LeanKit Kanban (*www.leankitkanban.com*), and OneNote (*www.office.microsoft.com/en-us/onenote*). These systems enable you to set up electronic folders or whiteboards that can be moved around using the "click and drag" technique as priorities change. Pages or cards associated with each of your assigned projects or tasks can also be easily maintained.

Regardless of what system you use, a key to success is collecting all of your "To Do's," ideas, and project-related data in one place or system, and then developing the habit of regularly maintaining that system. Having an easy-to-use system will not only allow you to be more organized, it will also help to control the stress that is inevitable when you have an abundance of commitments.

Create a "What I Need to Know" List

Lists of commonly used information are a great way for analysts to get and stay organized. Analysts should create a list of important telephone numbers, filenames, dates, and so on that they need on a fairly regular basis and place it in clear view. These items are not necessarily ones they use daily, which analysts tend to memorize, but are pieces of information they may use often during a short period of time, such as the rollout date of a new system.

Lists help you work more efficiently and effectively. However, don't make your lists so complex and difficult to maintain that they become counterproductive.

Create a "What Coworkers Need to Know" List

Similar to the "What I Need to Know" list, the "What Coworkers Need to Know" list contains important information coworkers may need to know if an analyst is out of the office for a few days or weeks. For example, the analyst could be at a training class, on vacation, and so on. This list should include the status of any current and ongoing projects, the location of documents the analyst is responsible for maintaining, the dates during which the analyst will be gone, and the names of people who provide backup in their absence. During work-related travel, such as attending a training class or offsite meeting, analysts may include a way for coworkers to reach them in the event of an emergency.

Set up an Out of Office message for voice mail and email boxes when leaving the office for an extended period of time. Use a script or template to ensure the message is professional and provides essential information such as the dates you will be gone and who to contact if immediate assistance is needed in your absence.

Utilize Peak Productivity Times

Are you an early bird or a night owl? Most people have about four hours each day during which they are most productive and alert. Successful, results-oriented people develop the habit of tackling their biggest, hardest, and most important tasks during their peak productivity time. Because this time varies from person to person, each analyst should determine his or her personal peak productivity time. If possible, the analyst should schedule work to take advantage of the time during which he or she functions best.

Don't waste your peak productivity time on frivolous tasks or on tasks that don't support your goals. Discipline yourself to stay focused on your highest priority tasks until those tasks are complete.

Eliminate or Minimize Time Robbers

Time robbers are activities that take up time and do not add value to the work that analysts perform. In fact, time robbers usually decrease productivity and increase stress levels. Analysts can use the following techniques to avoid time robbers:

- **Log contacts as they come in.** This avoids the need to handle the contact twice, eliminates the possibility that analysts forget critical information, and ensures that the time stamps that indicate when the incident record was entered correspond to when the incident was actually reported by the customer. Real-time logging also ensures that other analysts and customers who may be checking ticket status online can get the information they need, when they need it, preventing a waste of their time.

- **Avoid distractions.** Overall, analysts should stay focused on their work and resist the temptation to get involved in every conversation going on around them. It is, however, appropriate for analysts to get involved when it appears there is a major incident and they need a status update or to participate in joint problem solving with a coworker.

- **Avoid procrastination.** Putting off a task until the last minute can cause analysts to miss a critical deadline or produce a low-quality product. The best way for analysts to avoid this is to break large tasks into smaller ones and try to complete the task a little bit at a time. Also, they can set a time limit and work on a task for at least that period of time. Even if it's only 10 minutes, at least they will have started. Who knows—they may find that the project captures their interest and they will want to keep going.

- **Ask for help when you need it.** It is human nature to want to figure things out on our own, but sometimes we need help. Analysts need to try to distinguish between just "taking a little more time to figure things out" and needing help and guidance to avoid aggravation and wasted time.

- **Keep desk and files organized.** Clutter is distracting and a waste of space and time. Disorganization in the form of loose power cables and overburdened electrical outlets can be hazardous. Physical clutter—such as disorganized stacks of files and loose papers—and digital clutter—such as an out-of-control email box or poorly labeled files and folders—all add up to lost time, and potentially add up to rework. Organization is a key to success. Analysts should devise a system that they can use to get and stay organized. This may involve acquiring or downloading functional and easy-to-use desk accessories or filing systems. It may also include getting in the habit of always putting away or digitizing files after they use them and handling papers and folders only one time. A good rule of thumb is: do it, file it, or dump it (that is, recycle junk mail or other unneeded paperwork). A similar technique that can be applied to email is: answer it, mark it for follow-up, file it, or delete it.

- **Suggest constructive ways to make improvements.** Complaining wastes time, is typically perceived as whining, and can give an analyst a bad reputation. The analyst may be viewed as negative and uncooperative or unwilling to be a team player. If analysts see opportunities to make improvements, they should—in a constructive manner—tell their team leader or send an email or memo that outlines the steps they think could help eliminate or minimize a problem.

- **Reap the benefits of technology.** Every job contains tasks that must be done repeatedly. Furthermore, everyone can use help now and then remembering appointments and assignments. Analysts should identify these tasks and then use technology to automate these tasks. Desktop shortcuts and Internet browser features such as favorites and bookmarks can be used to access frequently used software programs and web sites. Tools such as Microsoft Outlook and IBM Lotus Notes provide the ability to create folders for filing emails and flag emails for follow-up. These tools, along with services such as Google Calendar (*www.google.com/calendar*) and Zoho Calendar (*www.zoho.com/calendar*), provide the ability to set up a calendar and schedule appointments. Smartphones offer many of these same capabilities. At a minimum, many cell phones provide the ability to maintain contact information or have an alarm clock feature to help you remember appointments. File storage services such as Dropbox (*www.dropbox.com*) and Google Drive (*drive.google.com*) make it easy to manage and share digital files and folders.

Numerous books and articles on time and stress management are available online and at your local library. These books and articles contain excellent tips about how to manage time wisely and how to avoid and alleviate stress.

To learn more about time management, go to *www.time-management-guide.com*. For time management tips for students, go to *www.d.umn.edu/student/loon/acad/strat/time_man_princ.html*. To learn more about stress management, go to *stress.about.com* or *www.webmd.com/balance/stress-management/default.htm*.

Developing excellent time management skills will serve you well throughout your life.

Place a Mirror on Your Desk

Facial expression mirrors mood, and mood mirrors facial expression. Also, good posture improves the quality of the voice and makes it easier for customers to understand what analysts are saying. To monitor their facial expressions and posture, analysts can place a mirror at eye level when they are sitting straight. By taking a quick look in the mirror before they answer the phone, analysts can ensure that they have a relaxed and pleasant facial expression. They can put a smile on their face, give the customer (whom they pretend to see in the mirror) their full attention, take a deep breath to get focused, and then answer the telephone. This mirror technique helps analysts ensure that they demonstrate concern when a customer is dissatisfied and when they sense anger building (their own or the customer's). Again, they should relax their faces and assume a caring expression, take a deep breath to stay calm, and make sure they are listening actively to the customer. A mirror also enables analysts to see a person who walks up from behind, preventing them from being startled while on the telephone or while focused on a task.

Take Breaks

Working nonstop often leads to fatigue and burnout. Analysts should take time throughout the day to rejuvenate: stretch, spend a moment looking out the window, or simply close their eyes and take a few deep breaths to regain a sense of calm. They can take a short walk, even if it's only to the restroom or to get a drink of water. Fatigue is one of the first signs of dehydration, so analysts should make sure they are drinking plenty of water. Drinking plenty of water increases your energy level and mental capacities. A side benefit is that, when you drink plenty of water, your body lets you know when it's time to take a break.

Taking a break can also involve performing a low-stress task such as opening mail, filling out a time sheet, putting away reference books or magazines, or tidying your desk. Completing such small, seemingly trivial tasks provides a rejuvenating sense of accomplishment, and eliminating clutter from your workspace lets you refocus your energies.

Recognize Learning as the Labor of the Information Age

Friends, family, and coworkers often refer to analysts as "computer experts," and at any given point they *are* experts. However, technology changes quickly. The skills and experience that served an analyst well in the past may, at any time, outlive their usefulness or relevance. Then it is time to replace them with new skills. True experts take the time and energy to continually update and improve their knowledge and skills. Working at a service desk provides constant opportunity for change, which an analyst can resist or embrace. Choose to embrace it!

Good work habits represent the discipline analysts need to feel in control during exceptionally busy times at the service desk and to stay motivated during slow times. Getting and staying organized, knowing how to manage stress, and continuously rejuvenating oneself are habits that enable people to view work as a challenge to be enjoyed. These habits, combined with a properly set up workspace, enable analysts to maintain physical and mental fitness on the job and to achieve personal success.

Chapter Summary

- To provide top-quality customer service and support, analysts need a good working environment, good work habits, and a great attitude. Companies that create a pleasant, comfortable working environment make it easier for their analysts to be friendly and patient when interacting with customers. Whether or not a company provides the optimal working environment, analysts can set up their personal workspaces for optimal comfort and functionality. They can also establish routines to organize their days.

- Factors such as accessibility, the need for security, and the company's commitment to the wellness of its staff influence the service desk's location. Factors such as size, the tools and technology the service desk uses, the level of interaction required, and the nature of problem solving that analysts perform influence the service desk's physical layout. All of these factors affect how safe and comfortable analysts are in the workplace.

- Analysts often have no control over the location and the physical layout of the service desk, but they can improve the ergonomics of their personal workspace. A well-arranged workspace can reduce the chances that analysts will suffer repetitive stress injuries such as carpal tunnel syndrome. Analysts can easily adjust their chair, monitor, keyboard, mouse, telephone, headset, and lighting to create a workspace that fits their personal needs.

- Customer support is a tough job. In fact, it's one of the most stressful professions you can have. Good work habits help to reduce stress and the possibility of getting injured on the job. They also enable analysts to get and stay organized and to achieve personal success. Analysts working in a service desk setting must strive to *respond*, not react, to daily events. Good work habits can help.

Key Terms

accessibility—How easily the service desk can be reached by service desk staff, other employees of the company, and customers.

acoustic shock—The term used to describe the symptoms such as discomfort and pain that a person may experience after hearing a loud, unexpected sound via a telephone or headset.

beginning of day (BOD)—A list of tasks an analyst performs at the start of each workday.

biometrics—Measurements of a person's physical characteristics, such as finger or palm prints, facial features, or parts of a person's eye such as the retina or iris.

carpal tunnel syndrome (CTS)—A common repetitive stress injury that affects the hands and wrists and is linked to repetitive hand movements, such as typing on a computer keyboard and working with a mouse.

computer vision syndrome—A variety of ailments such as headaches and eyestrain that occur as a result of staring at a computer monitor for a prolonged period of time.

ergonomics—The science of people-machine relationships that is intended to maximize productivity by reducing operator fatigue and discomfort.

light therapy—A treatment for Seasonal Affective Disorder (SAD) that involves sitting beside a special fluorescent light box for several minutes day.

location—The physical site of the service desk in the building.

National Institute for Occupational Safety and Health (NIOSH)—A part of the U.S. Centers for Disease Control and Prevention (CDC) that is responsible for conducting research and making recommendations for the prevention of work-related illnesses and injuries; located on the web at *www.cdc.gov/niash/homepage.html.*

Occupational Safety and Health Administration (OSHA)—An agency of the U.S. Department of Labor that is dedicated to reducing hazards in the workplace and enforcing mandatory job safety standards; also implements and improves health programs for workers; located on the web at *www.osha.gov.*

303

physical layout—How the service desk is arranged into workspaces.

repetitive stress injuries (RSIs)—Physical symptoms caused by excessive and repeated use of the hands, wrists, arms, and thumbs; they occur when people repeatedly perform tasks using force, strenuous actions, awkward postures, or poorly designed equipment.

time robbers—Activities that take up time and do not add value to the work that analysts perform, and in fact usually decrease productivity and increase stress levels.

wellness—The condition of good physical and mental health, especially when maintained by proper diet, exercise, and habits.

workspace—An area outfitted with equipment and furnishings for one worker.

Review Questions

1. Briefly describe the three factors that influence where a service desk is located.
2. Why is the service desk often situated in a centralized location?
3. Describe three ways that companies promote wellness when designing a workplace.
4. What is a workspace?
5. Briefly describe the three factors that influence a service desk's physical layout.
6. Describe a typical layout for a small service desk.
7. What are the benefits of arranging workstations in clusters or "pods"?
8. Why do companies install low cubicle walls in a service desk setting?
9. What are the benefits of a well-designed workspace?
10. Define the term *ergonomics.*
11. List four symptoms analysts may experience if their workspace is not arranged ergonomically.
12. What service desk activities put analysts at risk for carpal tunnel syndrome?
13. How should analysts adjust and sit in a chair?
14. How should a monitor be situated on the analyst's desk?

15. When typing and using the mouse, what four work habits can analysts adopt to avoid carpal tunnel syndrome?

16. Describe two benefits and two potential disadvantages of using a headset.

17. What are two factors you might consider when selecting a headset?

18. Briefly explain the impact of having too much light in a workspace, and suggest two ways to alleviate that problem.

19. Briefly explain the impact of having too little light in a workspace, and suggest a way to alleviate that problem.

20. Why is natural light important, and what are two ways that analysts can reap its benefits?

21. What should you do anytime you move into a new office or workspace?

22. What is a BOD, and why is it an important habit?

23. Briefly explain what you should do if faced with more "A" priority tasks than you can complete in one day.

24. What are time robbers, and why should they be eliminated?

25. What can happen if you procrastinate the completion of a task?

26. Why is it important to take breaks?

27. What are the benefits of drinking plenty of water?

28. Why must analysts recognize learning as the labor of the information age?

29. Describe two work habits that enable people to view work as a challenge to be enjoyed.

Hands-On Projects

1. **Learn about ensuring employee comfort and safety**. If the company where you work or the school you attend has a health and safety representative, interview that person. Or, interview a manager in any business setting (it doesn't have to be a service desk manager). Determine what that person has done to ensure the comfort and safety of the employees of his or her company. Document the answers to the following questions:

   - What have you (or what has your company) done to:
     - Provide for the comfort and safety of employees?
     - Facilitate communication and the sharing of health- and safety-related resources?
   - Do you teach employees about ergonomics? If so, what components of their work environment can employees adjust?

- If you do teach employees about ergonomics, do you feel these efforts are beneficial? If so, in what ways?

- If you do not teach employees about ergonomics, do you feel it would be beneficial to do so? If so, in what ways?

2. **Learn about repetitive stress injuries**. Use the web to research repetitive stress injuries. Select a device you use on a daily basis and determine what RSIs you are susceptible to as a result of using that device. For example, what injuries can occur from using a laptop, a gaming device, or a smartphone? Prepare a paper that answers the following questions:

- What are the symptoms of repetitive stress injuries?

- How are they caused?

- How are they treated, or how can their symptoms be controlled?

- How long does it take to relieve the symptoms?

- How can they be prevented?

3. **Evaluate your workspace**. A properly arranged workspace increases productivity and reduces stress and fatigue. Look closely at the workspace where you complete most of your writing, computer work, reading, and studying. This workspace could be at home, work, or school. Then, briefly outline your answers to the following questions:

- Have you ever experienced any of the negative symptoms of a poorly designed workspace, such as headaches, wrist and shoulder pain, back pain, or swollen ankles?

    o If so, given what you have learned in this chapter, were your symptoms the result of poor workspace design or poor work habits?

- In what ways can you improve the ergonomics of your workspace?

- In what ways can you improve your work habits?

Unless you share your workspace, arrange your workspace so that it meets your ergonomic requirements.

4. **Correct your workspace lighting**. Assess the lighting in the area where you do most of your reading, writing, and computer work. Do you have adequate lighting to read, write, and use your computer (if you have one) without experiencing negative side effects? If not, use the information presented in this chapter to determine what you can do to correct the lighting. Prepare a paper that describes the steps you can take to improve the lighting situation and the negative side effects the steps will alleviate. If the lighting situation is acceptable, explain why.

5. **Reduce noise in the service desk**. Assemble a team of at least three of your classmates or use your school's online message or discussion board. Brainstorm and prepare a list of ways that service desk staff can work as a team and as individuals to reduce the noise that can occur in a service desk setting. For example, the service desk might avoid the use of speakerphones.

6. **Create checklists**. Envision that you are starting a new job as a service desk analyst and complete the following tasks:

- Create a BOD checklist. Include a list of tasks you must complete before leaving the house to ensure that you arrive at work on time and prepared. While creating your BOD, consider the last couple of weeks. Were there days when you felt disorganized or when you forgot items you needed? Include tasks on your BOD that can prevent the frustration of this type of situation.

- Create a "What I Need to Know" checklist. Given what you have learned in this and previous chapters, create a list of the types of information you will likely use on a regular basis.

Share your lists with your classmates so that you can benefit from their ideas as well.

7. **Practice using a mirror**. Place a mirror near where you often sit while talking on the phone, and then look in it before you answer the phone and while you are talking on the phone to a friend or family member. Regardless of how you feel, practice putting a smile on your face and using a pleasant upbeat tone every time you answer the phone. Experiment with different facial expressions while you are on the phone. For example, if you are laughing, try to look sad. Or, if you are frustrated, try smiling. Pretend that what you are seeing in the mirror is what the person on the phone would see if you were speaking with them in person. Write a paragraph describing how the mirror affected your conversations. For example, how did using different facial expressions affect the tone of your voice? How did the person you were speaking with respond to your tone of voice? Did imagining that the person could see your facial expressions affect your interactions with him or her?

8. **Experiment with organizational systems**. Depending on your organizational needs, conduct one of the following experiments:

- Access the websites of the free organizational systems referenced in this chapter such as Evernote (*www.evernote.com*), LeanKit Kanban (*www.leankitkanban.com*), or OneNote (*www.office.microsoft.com/en-us/onenote*).

- Or, search the web or online app stores for free "To Do" list Apps if you are a smartphone user.

- Or, access the web sites of the file storage services referenced in this chapter such as Dropbox (*www.dropbox.com*) and Google Drive (*drive.google.com*).

- Use your school's online message or discussion board to learn what organizational systems your classmates are using, or to share what system you are using.

- Debate the pros and cons of the various systems.

- If you are not currently using an organizational system, select a system and commit to using that system for 21 days—the time it typically takes to form a habit.

- Experiment with new systems until you find one that you can sustain on a day-to-day basis.

9. **Identify time robbers**. Review the list of time robbers discussed in this chapter. Make a list of any time-robbing activities that regularly cause you to waste time. For example, you may regularly procrastinate or allow your desk and files to become unorganized. Go to the library or search the web for information about time management. Identify three specific things you can do to eliminate or minimize the source of your time robbers. Prepare a brief paper describing (1) your time robbers, (2) your course of action, and (3) any goals you may choose to set. For example, you may set a goal to clean off your desk within three days.

10. **Learn about the benefits of water**. This chapter briefly discussed the benefits of drinking plenty of water. Search the web for the keywords "health benefits of drinking water." Prepare a report that provides additional detail about the benefits of water. Include the following:

   - The amount of water you should drink each day

   - The symptoms of not drinking enough water

   - The symptoms of drinking a sufficient amount of water

   - Tips for consuming an adequate amount of water each day

Case Projects

1. **Design New Service Desk Facilities**. You are the supervisor of a small service desk that has seven analysts, and your manager just informed you that the service will be moving to a new building at the end of the year. Your manager asks you to suggest the best way to design the new facilities. Goals include enabling collaboration while at the same time dealing with the noise and distractions that are inherent in a service desk setting. She also wants you to recommend ways to make your new facilities "analyst-friendly." Prepare a sketch of your suggested layout, and provide notes that outline the rationale for your design. You can search the web or do library research to get ideas for the layout.

2. **Ergonomics 101**. You've been hired as a consultant to help a large service desk implement an ergonomics program. The analysts in this service desk use a wide array of mobile devices on a daily basis. Do research to determine the steps involved in setting up an ergonomics program. Identify up to five specific tips each related to laptop-, tablet-, and smartphone-related ergonomics. Prepare a brief report for management outlining the steps to be taken and the benefits to be derived. Include in your report the specific tips that you identified and steps that management should take to ensure the ongoing success of this program.

CHAPTER 8

Customer Support as a Profession

In this chapter you will learn:

◎ Service desk industry trends and directions

◎ The role of certification in the service desk

◎ How to maintain technical skills while learning service desk management skills

◎ How to prepare for a future as a service desk professional

Tremendous opportunities exist for people interested in a service desk career. Companies worldwide realize that they must provide high-quality customer service and support or risk losing their customers to a company that does. Departments that deliver internal customer support realize that they too must provide high-quality service and support and that they must understand and align their services with their company's business goals. In the future, the most successful companies will be those that keep a close eye on both business and service desk industry trends and embrace the ones that enable them to achieve their goals. These companies need and reward people who are innovative, flexible, and professional, and who thrive on satisfying customers.

Companies and departments worldwide are working hard to attract and keep people who have the energy, enthusiasm, and skills needed to deliver the quality support services their customers demand. These organizations are seeking people who have the desire and ability not only to support increasingly complex and tightly integrated technologies being used by customers, but also to use and promote the equally complex and tightly integrated technologies that service desks use to deliver support. These companies also need people who can assume the important supporting roles in a service desk, such as knowledge engineer, service management and improvement, and technical support for the service desk's tools and technologies.

The support industry is growing and changing rapidly and constantly. To seize the opportunities offered by this dynamic industry, you must be aware of service desk industry trends and objectively evaluate how your skills match those trends. You must determine your strengths and interests and seek out jobs and experiences in which you can excel. A successful service desk career occurs when you continuously leverage your experiences, refine your skills, and keep an eye on the future.

Service Desk Industry Trends and Directions

An almost irreversible dependence on technology has prompted customers to demand ever-cheaper, faster, and better technical customer support services. This demand has prompted companies to considerably expand the role of the service desk. Although in the past companies considered service desk jobs to be entry-level positions, today the service desk has a more strategic position because the service desk can and does contribute to the company's bottom line. This is because the service desk helps companies to make the most of their technology investments and also helps to minimize the impact when that technology fails.

The service desk offers—and will for the foreseeable future continue to offer—considerable opportunities to people who want to be a part of this dynamic and growing industry. For example, pursuing a career in the service desk provides the opportunity to:

- Learn about and support a wide range of computing technologies, such as hardware, software, databases, applications, and networks.

- Work with people and with technology.

- Use relevant skills acquired in other industries, such as customer service skills, to gain entry into the computer industry.

- Gain entry into a company at which you want to work.

- Learn about all the various departments within a company and gain a full appreciation of the opportunities available within that company.

- Advance your career along either a technical career path or a managerial career path.

As service desks continue to evolve, they face many challenging business trends. These trends influence the direction in which the service desk industry is heading and the opportunities available to people pursuing a service desk career. These trends, many of which were touched on in previous chapters, include those listed in Figure 8-1. Each of these trends affects how service desks are run and the opportunities they present to service desk analysts.

- Multigenerational support

- Multichannel support

- Anytime, anywhere, any device support

- Collapsing support levels

- 24/7 support

- Fee-based support

- Global support

- Increased use of best practice frameworks and standards

- Outsourcing

- Service desk as a profession

Figure 8-1   Service desk industry trends
© Cengage Learning 2014

Multigenerational Support

The workforce is more diverse today than ever before in history. The demographics span four different generations of workers, including the mature, World War II generation, the Baby Boomers, Generation X, and the Millennials (also known as Generation Y). These different generations of technology users tend to have varying needs and expectations with regard to the service desk and support.

By 2020, Millennials will make up nearly half (47 percent) of the workforce (*The 2020 Workplace*. J. Meister. K. Willyerd. HarperCollins Publishers, 2010).

Most customers in Generation X and the Millennials have grown up interacting heavily with technologies such as social networking sites, wikis, blogs, and podcasts, and tend to be quite comfortable using these technologies for self-help. Service desks must respond by providing these self-help resources and ensuring that these resources provide customers the answers they need in an efficient and effective way.

Younger customers also tend to bypass formalized support channels such as the telephone or email and turn first to crowdsourcing as a means of problem solving. **Crowdsourcing** involves outsourcing a task traditionally performed by a single individual to a large group of people or community (i.e., a crowd). In the context of technical support, crowdsourcing may involve posing a question or problem to a large group of people via Facebook, Twitter, or an online forum in an effort to quickly get an answer. While this approach could be viewed as desirable as it reduces contact volumes at the service desk, crowdsourcing can be ineffective. For example, the "crowd" may not have a solution and so the customer wastes time waiting on a solution. Also, the solutions provided might not be the best solutions, or they might violate existing policies, such as security policies. Service desks must respond by offering facilitated social media channels and forums that are monitored to ensure that customers get the right answers at the right time or are directed to more formalized channels.

Generally speaking, older workers do not fit any one profile; their level of comfort using technology varies. Some older workers feel quite comfortable using self-help and crowdsourcing as their first option, while others require help adapting to these technologies. Still other older workers have "grown up" contacting a help desk or service desk and so may be more comfortable obtaining human assistance and receiving step-by-step instructions. Service desks must respond by ensuring that self-help isn't viewed as a one-size-fits-all solution that becomes a barrier to customer service.

 Older generations are increasingly expected to work longer, many beyond the normal age of retirement, and some retired workers will return to the workforce for a variety of reasons. These reasons may include a desire to be a productive member of society, for personal satisfaction, or perhaps in response to financial pressures.

Regardless of age, today's customers demand better and faster service and are increasingly willing to use any and all options provided. These demanding customers want the freedom to choose when, where, and how they obtain support, and they want whatever option they choose to be easy to use and effective.

Multichannel Support

Customer experience is a critical component of customer satisfaction, and multichannel support is one way that service desks can positively influence customer experience. The telephone will continue to be a heavily used contact channel for some time. One reason is that self-help isn't always an option, whether because of poor connectivity or because the customer is experiencing a unique or complex issue that is beyond the scope of self-help. Another reason is that some workers are unwilling to take the time required to use self-help options and view calling the service desk as the fastest way to obtain support. Examples include highly compensated workers, such as lawyers and doctors, and workers who handle financial transactions such as stock brokers or workers taking orders in a call center. Furthermore, some people simply prefer to speak with a human being, particularly when they need help.

Customers are also willing to use alternative support channels such as email and web-based services, such as self-help, online chat, and video demonstrations. A "trend within a trend" is that many interactions involve multiple technologies. For example, customers may begin interacting with the service desk via the telephone or a chat session and be directed to download a fix from a web site. Customers may begin interacting with the service desk via a web site and be directed by an avatar to download a video demonstration. In the context of computing, an **avatar** is a computer user's representation of himself or herself. Avatars may be three-dimensional, such as those found in video games, or two-dimensional, such as those used in many Internet-based instant messaging forums such as Skype. Or, customers may begin interacting with an avatar embedded in an application or service, and the avatar directs the customer to the service desk only if automated diagnostic techniques fail to produce a solution.

Service desks should provide input to service design activities that result in support being a natural extension of people's work. In other words, meet customers where they are, and where they need support, rather than requiring that customers conform to the processes that are convenient or cost-effective for the service desk.

Historically, companies have tended to handle these alternative support channels informally—for example, incidents might not be logged—and few, if any, metrics were captured. However, to meet the needs of today's technically savvy and demanding customers, service desks must look at multichannel support differently.

Smart service desks know that customers will embrace self-help and web-based services only if the content is current, well organized, and easy to use. As with telephone calls, chat services must enable customers to interact with a knowledgeable professional who can quickly deliver a resolution. These same service desks also know that, as discussed previously, some customers are still going to use channels such as the telephone and email to obtain support.

And herein lies the trend. Multichannel support changes the skills that service desk analysts must have and the types of incidents and service requests they resolve. Because customers can handle their simpler incidents through the web, they contact the service desk with more complex incidents or with incidents that require an immediate resolution, such as connectivity-related incidents. As a result, good problem-solving skills are important for analysts. Writing skills are important because analysts must interact with customers through email and chat and because they are expected to contribute to the content that customers access on the web. Internet skills, such as the ability to use browsers, find content online, and use Internet-based diagnostic tools such as remote control systems, also are imperative.

Multichannel support also creates a need for people to develop, maintain, and support the service desk's systems. Roles such as technical support and knowledge engineer have greater importance, as service desks rely more heavily on their support systems and use these systems to collect and maintain content for their web sites.

314

Service desks also face the challenge of ensuring that they are capturing the data needed to efficiently and effectively manage the various support channels they offer to customers. This means they must determine how best to integrate the various tools needed to capture this data, such as ACDs, email response management systems, integrated service management tools, and web-based systems, to name just a few. Service desks must also begin to produce meaningful metrics, such as response time and cost per contact, relative to each channel they offer. They must track usage trends, understand their customers' preferences, and invest in options that reflect those preferences. They must understand that, when sites are well designed, web-based contacts cost *less* than contacts that involve analysts—but still they are not free. Companies must bear the cost of maintaining their web sites, and they must work hard to keep them useful and current, or customers will turn to another channel. Companies must also understand that telephone contacts will cost more, because they represent complex and unique incidents that typically cannot be resolved using self-services.

Social media has made it easier for service desks to understand their customers' preferences. For example, smart service desks monitor Facebook and Twitter postings and respond quickly to customer complaints and suggestions.

Anytime, Anywhere, Any Device Support

A number of IT industry trends are prompting changes to how the service desk is structured, along with its policies and processes. These IT industry trends include BYOD, desktop virtualization, and cloud computing, just to name a few. As discussed in earlier chapters, each of these trends is impacting the service desk in its own right as they result in a more complex computing environment.

Collectively, these trends are enabling the even swifter adoption of what was already a strong trend, worker mobility. The variety of mobile and wireless devices and applications, combined with the speed at which individuals are adopting these devices, make supporting mobile workers particularly challenging for service desks.

Mobile devices such as tablets and smartphones are also being used by level two and level three support groups and service desk managers, prompting many service desks to revise their escalation and notification procedures.

This constant barrage of new technologies, and in some cases an absence of standards with regard to these technologies, are causing service desks to realize that they must look strategically at how to serve their customers going forward. The complexities of supporting a multivendor environment, compounded by the emergence of technologies such as cloud computing, reinforce this need to take a strategic view. Such a strategic assessment includes assessing the skills of their staff, redesigning their processes, evaluating their tools, and rethinking their data and information needs. In other words, service desks must holistically address all aspects of their service to meet the requirements of their customers whenever they need assistance (anytime), wherever they are (anywhere), regardless of the device they are using (any device).

 The challenges facing today's service desks can be overcome by effectively using people, processes, technology, and information.

In response to these trends, service desks are getting engaged earlier in the service lifecycle and working with other parts of the IT organization to define standards in terms of what devices and applications best serve the needs of technology users and ensure the security of corporate data assets. Service desks are also participating in efforts to modify SLAs to include policies and procedures relating to process areas such as information security management, change management, service asset and configuration management, and access management.

In light of these trends, service desks recognize that today's workers are increasingly technically savvy and self-sufficient. When they do need support, however, their need is often immediate and so the service desk must be prepared. Practices such as improved knowledge management, self-help, and the introduction of social or communal forms of support can help but are still relatively reactive in nature.

To make the transition to a more strategic, proactive service desk, a more formalized approach to problem management is needed—one that not only feeds knowledge management (e.g., workarounds and known errors), but also seeks to eliminate recurring incidents, thus freeing service desk resources to work on new and more complex incidents. Therein lies an important point: self-help can be used effectively to handle known issues and can also be used to automate recurring requests (such as password resets). However, the technological changes facing the IT industry are resulting in new incidents, many of which are complex in nature because people want to be able to access data, information, and knowledge across a wide array of platforms and technologies. Furthermore, as organizations adopt practices such as virtualization and cloud computing, connectivity becomes critical, and incidents that stand in the way of that connectivity are now viewed as major.

This transition to a more strategic, proactive service desk and the focus on continual process improvement is supported by the expanded role service desks are taking as organizations adopt ITIL best practices. This expanded role has broadened the service desk's scope of responsibility and has created jobs that require more advanced skills, pay better, and offer a greater diversity of advancement opportunities for service desk analysts.

The constant barrage of new technologies creates job opportunities as well and requires people in support positions to continuously update their skills. Many companies offer a considerable amount of training in an effort to attract and retain analysts who have, and want to maintain, state-of-the-art skills and who are comfortable using and supporting state-of-the-art technologies.

Collapsing Support Levels

Historically, service desks have used a multi-level support model. Although three levels was the standard, many organizations have collapsed that model to only two levels of support. Level one triages contacts, resolves those that can be resolved at the service desk, and escalates those that cannot to other support groups. Incidents that are escalated are handled by specialists, such as the network group or an applications support group. A "trend within a trend" is for major incidents to be handled by virtual teams of experts that come together to resolve incidents and then disband; this practice is also known as swarming. Gartner defines **swarming** as a work style characterized by a flurry of collective activity by anyone and everyone conceivably available and able to add value (*www.gartner.com/it/page.jsp? id=1416513*). Although such an approach would prove too costly for all incidents or for noncritical incidents, it represents a more efficient way to handle complex or critical incidents than the historical approach of escalating incidents from one level of support to the next.

This trend to collapse support levels is prompted by the need to resolve incidents quickly and minimize the impact of those incidents on business operations. It also reflects the fact that many customers are unwilling to be placed on hold, transferred from one group to the next, or told they will receive a call back. Instead, they want an immediate resolution.

Because of this trend, companies are striving to ensure that their service desks are able to assist customers at the first point of contact whenever possible. To do so, techniques companies are using include hiring and promoting more highly skilled and certified analysts as well as using technologies, such as knowledge management systems and remote control systems, to expand analysts' capabilities. Companies also are using ACD features, such as skills-based routing, VRUs, and web-based features such as chat because these technologies make it possible to route contacts directly to the analyst who has the skill needed to handle the incident or service request. All of these techniques enable organizations to reduce handoffs. As a result, the level one service desk is able to handle contacts previously handled by both level one and level two. These techniques also make it possible for companies to reduce the number of escalated incidents (and therefore more effectively use IT resources), reduce wait times, and provide the immediate response today's demanding customers require.

24/7 Support

Customers are challenging companies to provide **24/7 support**, which means that support services are provided 24 hours a day, 7 days a week. The need to support an increasingly self-sufficient customer base, a global customer community, a mobile workforce, or a business that operates around the clock leads to this demand for continuous support.

24/7 support does not mean that service desk analysts must be on site at all times. Many service desks use their phone system to direct customers to their web site after hours where they can use self-help services, submit an incident or service request, or obtain the status of an outstanding incident or service request. Some service desks forward calls to a data center or supplier after hours where the calls are then logged and handled. Some service desks use their phone system to transfer callers to analysts who are working at home or to instruct callers about how to obtain emergency support if needed—typically by contacting an on-call analyst. Some service desks enable customers to chat via the service desk's web site with analysts who may be working at home.

Emergency support is often provided by on-call analysts who carry smart mobile devices. The compensation that on-call analysts receive varies by company. For example, some companies pay an hourly overtime rate, which is typically 1.5 times the analyst's base rate. Some companies offer analysts compensatory time ("comp time"), which means employees earn time off when they work extra hours. Some companies convert on-call availability time to comp time. For example, two to four hours of on-call time equals one hour of comp time. Other companies are more generous. A night of on-call time equals a day off. Conversely, some companies simply expect analysts to be on call as a regular part of their job. They may, however, pay a flat rate per incident, which means analysts are compensated only when they actually handle customer contacts. Or, they may pay a bonus when an analyst spends a lot of time working on a particularly severe or complex incident.

This 24/7 support trend creates many opportunities for service desk professionals. It creates positions for service desk analysts as well as positions for team leaders and supervisors. Companies that provide 24/7 support often have three work shifts: a day shift, a midday (or "mid") shift, and a night shift. The hours that these shifts work vary from company to company. Companies often pay a shift premium, or shift differential, to employees who work an undesirable shift such as the night shift. The shift periods that qualify for a premium and the amount paid vary from one company to the next. Most shift premiums range from 5 to 8 percent of an employee's salary.

Companies that provide 24/7 support often offer very flexible schedules for their employees. For example, people may work 10 hours per day for four days and then have three days off. Or they may work part-time, such as 20 hours per week. These scheduling alternatives help accommodate the needs of people such as students and retirees who want to continue their education, have family demands, and so on.

 Flexibility is an important characteristic for both individuals and companies. To meet dynamic business challenges, companies will increasingly adopt on-demand staffing models that give the flexibility to scale staffing levels up or down based on current needs.

This trend also creates opportunities for people who assume supporting roles in the service desk. For example, the service desk's technical support staff maintains the service desk's web site, which allows customers to gain access to web-based self-services after hours. Knowledge engineers also make it possible for customers to get answers to FAQs and search knowledge bases for solutions after hours.

For some companies, demand for support may be light after hours. As a result, support may be provided by a supplier, by an on-call employee, or via the web. Customers may not receive the same depth of service after hours that they receive during normal business hours. Most customers are satisfied, however, if they are at least able to find answers on their own, submit a request to obtain service during normal service desk business hours, or obtain support in the event of an emergency.

Fee-Based Support

With **fee-based support**, customers pay for support services on a per-use basis. In other words, each time a customer contacts the service desk or accesses a designated area of the company's web site for billable services, a fee is charged. Service desks that charge for support then have funds available to acquire resources and continuously improve their services. This creates job opportunities. Also, charging for support is an effective way to manage customer expectations. For example, the service desk can charge a higher rate for premium or value-added services. As a result, higher-level, more challenging, and higher-paying job positions are created.

Chapter 2 discussed some advantages and disadvantages of fee-based support in the "Service Desks as Cost Centers or Profit Centers" section.

The trend is that some web-based support services will most likely continue to be free, such as FAQs, online knowledge bases, downloadable software fixes, and so on. However, more service desks will likely charge for at least some of their services, such as premium services. As the BYOD policies put in place by some companies are requiring that a service contract is in place for the device itself, it is also likely that there will be an increase in the number of companies providing fee-based consumer support services.

People entering the service desk industry need to be aware of this trend and determine whether and how their employer, or prospective employer, charges for support. A company's policy on this practice greatly influences how analysts account for their time and effort as well as how they interact with customers. For example, analysts who work at service desks that charge for their services are typically required to log all incidents and to verify that a customer is entitled to support before they begin working on an incident. Service desk managers value people who understand that the service desk is a "business within a business" that must justify its existence and that can be run profitably.

Global Support

Some companies are being challenged to provide **global support**, which means they support customers anywhere in the world. This demand for global support may be caused by the need to support a large company that has foreign divisions and subsidiaries or by the need to support customers who are doing business with the company through the web. Companies providing global support must address the culture, language, time zone, and legal issues that come with working in an international market. They also must consider matters affecting the regions of the world in which they do business such as economic conditions, natural disasters, crime, and terrorism. They can do that several ways, including:

- **Regional, in-country service desks**—Traditionally, large companies establish multiple, in-country service desks that each provide localized support. These in-country service desks are able to provide highly personalized service because they understand issues such as language, culture, and local expectations. Some companies prefer this highly personalized form of support even though it can be expensive. To mitigate their costs, these companies may require that all service desks use the same processes and technologies, such as cloud-based technologies. Each service desk may also produce a standard set of metrics that are forwarded to the corporate headquarters for review. Conversely, some companies allow each service desk to establish its own processes and technologies and focus only on its own needs and the needs of its customers.

- **Follow the sun support**—Follow the sun support means that companies establish two or more service desks, each on a different continent, and as one service desk closes, another opens. For example, if a company has service desks in Australia, the United Kingdom, and the United States, when Australia completes its business day, support transfers to the service desk in the United Kingdom. When its business day is complete, the United Kingdom service desk transfers support to the service desk in the United States, which transfers support back to Australia when its day is done. These service desks use common tools and common processes and are able to share common data and information sources such as knowledge and configuration management systems. The advantage of this approach is that the company is able to leverage technology and maximize its ROI, while analysts within each service desk are able to deliver personalized service to their customers—that is, service that addresses issues such as language and culture. This approach also eliminates the costs associated with shift work as each service desk works only a single shift. Large, multinational companies often take a follow the sun approach.

- **One centralized, global service desk**—One centralized, global service desk means that one physical service desk provides 24/7 support. This approach tends to be less costly than follow the sun support because companies are not required to set up and staff multiple facilities, nor are they required to replicate their processes and technologies across multiple sites. These companies must, however, address issues such as language and culture, and they must also determine how to deliver localized support when necessary. For example, a service desk may need to determine how to ship a replacement laptop to a mobile worker in another country. Companies that need to provide global support but lack a large support staff, such as a small web-based company, often opt to have a single global service desk.

Regardless of how companies provide global support, this trend presents a number of opportunities for people pursuing a service desk career. First, companies that provide global support often operate 24 hours a day, 7 days a week, which means more job opportunities. Second, people with the right skills may be given the opportunity to travel and gain experience working abroad. Third, global support often requires people who speak multiple languages and understand the cultural issues that are unique to a particular part of the world. For example, in Germany, people consider it rude to address someone by their first name prior to being given permission. In the United States, however, people often use first names. Also, while some companies provide information and deliver support through the web in English only, others offer a choice of languages. These companies often depend on their analysts to translate solutions and publish them in a variety of languages. Companies that provide global support value and are willing to reward people who understand cultural differences and can read and write as well as speak multiple languages. Rewards may include higher salaries and perks such as the opportunity to telecommute or travel abroad.

Use of Best Practice Frameworks and Standards

The trends discussed above require service desks to determine how best to utilize each of the components discussed throughout this book: people, processes, technology, and information. Many companies are taking the first step toward meeting this challenge by using a best practice framework such as ITIL to redesign their processes. ITIL views the service desk as a critical role within IT, and so adopting it often results in increased responsibility and opportunity for service desk professionals.

Some companies are using the ITIL framework along with ISO/IEC 20000 specifications to redesign their processes. ISO/IEC 20000 requires evidence in the form of records and documents that the specifications are being met. This evidence is often created by the service desk or uses data and information collected by the service desk.

By redesigning their processes, service desks are able to determine how best to utilize their existing people and technology, before hiring new people or acquiring new technology. Service desks can use information to determine which processes need to be designed (or redesigned), and they can also use information to measure the efficiency and effectiveness of their new processes.

Most process-related initiatives are handled as projects to ensure all stakeholders are engaged and to ensure the new processes and associated tools achieve the desired outcome. These initiatives present tremendous opportunities for individuals who understand these frameworks and standards and who also have some project management skills, whether as a project manager or as an effective project team member. These initiatives also demand many of the soft and self-management skills discussed in this book, such as being a good listener, being an effective communicator, and being able to manage stress. Individuals with these skills who understand the benefits of a best practice approach are in the best position to survive and even thrive in today's rapidly changing workplace.

 The more you can contribute to improvement initiatives and bottom-line benefits, the more valuable you become to an organization. At a minimum, you gain marketable experience that enhances your resume.

Outsourcing

Many of the service desk industry trends discussed above, combined with the need to reduce costs, prompt companies to outsource some or all service desk services. While the outsourcing of services is cyclical, sometimes up and sometimes down, outsourcing will always be a part of the service desk industry for a number of reasons. Companies that outsource may want to take advantage of an outsourcer's experience or flexibility, such as an outsourcer's ability to accommodate peak periods, seasonal call volumes, or after-hours call volumes. Companies that outsource may also want to leverage an outsourcer's investment in and use of new technologies. Frequently, companies are partnering with these external service agencies to deliver high-quality support services at a reduced cost. Some companies outsource all of their support services. Others outsource a portion of their services, such as after-hours support, hardware support and repair, or off-the-shelf PC software support. Some companies outsource support for these industry-standard hardware and software products so they can dedicate their resources to supporting systems developed in house. This desire to outsource all or some support services has spawned a tremendous increase in the number of companies that offer service desk outsourcing services and, consequently, an increase in the number of job opportunities.

 Outsourcing requires that the two companies involved—the supplier and the company that hires them—work closely together to define the services to be delivered and the expected level of performance.

This outsourcing trend represents a great opportunity for people who want to pursue a service desk career because it has created many jobs that offer a lot of flexibility. Each outsourcer needs the right number of people with the right skills to support its clients. Outsourcers are constantly looking for people who have great customer service skills along with the necessary mix of business and technical skills to satisfy their customers' needs, which naturally vary considerably from one customer to the next. As a result, people have the opportunity to work with a diversity of customers while being employed by one company. Outsourcers often base raises and bonuses on people's performance and ability to satisfy customers. The best and the brightest people are regularly rewarded and promoted. Service agencies also tend to offer flexible work hours and even the opportunity to work on a contract basis. This means that people who want to work for a time and then take time off (for example, to go to school or to care for a child or family member) have the opportunity to do so as long as they give the supplier adequate notice.

People working in service desks tend to be frightened by the prospect of outsourcing because it can result in the loss of jobs. However, successful outsourcing *creates* job opportunities for the external supplier, which they may then offer to service desk employees. It is not uncommon for companies to allow a supplier to hire qualified members of their service desk staff when it takes over support because knowledge about the customer community is very important. This is particularly true when the supplier employees who deliver support services are physically located at the company's facilities. Companies may enter into this type of arrangement for security reasons or because they want to leverage an existing investment in technology. Regardless of where the analysts are physically located, people with the right skills are valued.

Service Desk as a Profession

Historically, the service desk was considered a stepping stone to other professions. Today, a number of trends indicate that the service desk has been elevated to a profession in and of itself. For example:

- In many organizations, service desks report directly to a Chief Information Officer (CIO) or senior executive. This shows the importance of service desks within companies.

- Many companies have rewritten their service desk job descriptions to create higher-level job positions. This reflects the expanded responsibility of the service desk. Because the expanded responsibility includes the service desk being asked to solve more incidents at level one, many companies are increasing the amount of training and authority given to analysts. In addition, some companies have been raising the starting salaries for service desk positions.

- Organizations often offer bonuses based on a person's performance and ability to satisfy customers.

- Some companies are creating new team leader and supervisor positions within the service desk in recognition of the need to provide feedback, coaching, and counseling to front-line staff. As a result, more management positions are available.

- Some companies rotate personnel through different positions in the department or company in an effort to reduce burnout and increase the experience and skill of service desk analysts. This practice enables front-line staff to acquire a broad base of experience and to better understand the needs of the business. This practice also enables service desks to reduce turnover and retain the knowledge and experience of seasoned analysts.

- Individual and site certification programs are being used by service desk managers and service desk analysts to demonstrate their business, technical, soft, and self-management skills.

The service desk is no longer an entry-level position that people enter and leave as if through a revolving door. The number of opportunities the service desk offers continues to expand, as shown in Figure 8-2.

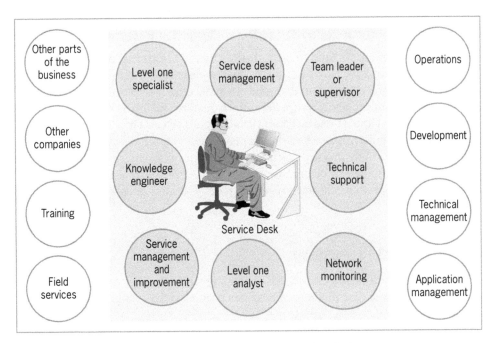

Figure 8-2   Career opportunities within and beyond the service desk
© Cengage Learning 2014

INTERVIEW WITH...

Courtesy of Forrester Research, Ltd.

JOHN RAKOWSKI
ANALYST & ADVISOR
FORRESTER RESEARCH, LTD.
SOUTHHALL, UNITED KINGDOM
www.forrester.com

John Rakowski, interviewed by Donna Knapp, August 2012

Question: I've heard you refer to this as the 'age of the customer.' What do you mean by that?

Answer: The world is changing. For companies that provide IT-related services, it used to be about having great salespeople who could communicate the company's value to its customers. Today, customers can rate your company's products and services via the web. People are relying on the recommendation of other customers, and people believe what other customers are saying. For internal IT organizations, it used to be that the enterprise IT department dictated heavy laptops and big, complex applications. Today, consumerization trends such as bring your own device (BYOD), bring your own application (BYOA), and cloud-based computing are changing the way employees acquire technology. Employees want to use whatever device or application helps with their own personal productivity, including tools that enable them to maintain a work-life balance.

All this adds up to the fact that companies must make customer experience a priority. If companies get it wrong, it has become easier for customers to change providers. If companies get it right, customers will sing their praises. It is no different for enterprise IT departments. IT departments that don't have a service orientation run the risk of customers switching services and service providers, making the IT department less relevant.

A natural reaction is fear and for companies and IT departments to think they are losing control. There is only, however, so much that can be controlled. Shadow IT—building and using IT services inside an organization without organizational approval—is happening because people are looking for quicker ways to do their jobs in increasingly complex environments.

An outside-in approach is needed that ensures customer experience is at the forefront of every business decision; a feat that is easier said than done, as customers' expectations are constantly changing.

Question: How do you see changing business and customer expectations influencing the role of the service desk in the years to come?

Answer: The service desk's importance will increase over the next decade. The service desk provides a window into the information about how services are being used and how important they are to the business. Many service desks still operate in a traditional fashion in that they view their role as supporting the needs of business, versus that of a business partner.

Service desks must shift from this traditionally reactive approach to a more proactive approach aimed at detecting what service experience customers require. Service desks must be innovative. They must understand that the service desk is in a unique position in terms of understanding whether the organization's customer experience efforts are meeting the needs and wants of customers, as well as the industry requirements of the business. Having the business know-how to understand the challenges the industry is facing will be a key skill for service desk professionals in the coming years.

Question: In addition to business know-how, what skills do people working in IT and in service desks need to meet customers' rising expectations?

Answer: Soft skills, particularly communication skills, remain critical. IT professionals must be able to take technical concepts and make them understandable and they must do so simply, concisely, and without the technical jargon. They must be helpful. They must make an effort to understand the customer they are speaking to so that they are appropriately acknowledging that customer's role in the organization.

As the role of IT shifts to more of an advisory role, it will be important to present concepts in a more business-oriented way. Rather than simply talking about a technology's features and functionality, the focus must be on how the technology increases productivity, saves costs, enables the company to be more competitive, and so forth. IT professionals should not neglect simple business skills—balance sheets, profit and loss statements, and the core concepts and functions within business.

IT professionals must understand the advertising and marketing hype around trends and must learn how to respond in a way that best reflects business and customer requirements. Why and how can the technology be used? Is the company ready for the technology? Is the technology appropriate given the company's risk profile?

IT professionals shouldn't be afraid to make recommendations. They must, however, present those recommendations in the form of a business case that gives a clear understanding of how the business will benefit based on an understanding of the challenges customers are facing. To do this, IT professionals should read about the industry that they are working in or are interested in. They should have an eye out for breaking news about companies who are the innovators in that industry or about ways in which technology can improve that industry. They can build good relationships with other business units in an effort to better understand their industry.

It's not enough, however, to just have ideas. Solutions are only of value if you can market and execute on those ideas. IT professionals should understand the project lifecycle. Understanding what's involved in a good project and how to work with stakeholders are all good core skills.

Question: What business and IT trends do you think will have the greatest impact on the service desk in the years to come?

Answer: One of the great challenges that service desks face is determining how best to use collaboration technologies to implement social support. Social support makes it easier for customers to support other customers, but there needs to be some governance to ensure that customer needs are, in fact, being met. With social support, the service desk's metrics indicate that incidents are going down, but that's not the case. The incidents just aren't being reported to the service desk. Service desks need to embrace the informal forms of support that are happening now and determine how best to use these channels to ultimately provide better support to customers.

Technology innovation is also allowing service desks to adopt a more decentralized model while at the same time having centralized processes. Such an approach enables service desks to be embedded in the organization with their customers and to understand what they are doing and their requirements.

The challenge is to embrace the right technologies and models. There has to be the right mix of self-service, automation, and personalized support. Service desks need to do more with less but not to the point where they are alienating customers or impacting the business.

The service desk has been an expensive area for the business. To be viewed as vital, service desks must make sure they proactively understand and are working to meet customer requirements. This is something that sometimes gets lost when companies outsource their service desks in an effort to reduce costs.

Customers are more technically-savvy and technology is becoming easier to use; however, more service offerings and a more complex back-end infrastructure mean there is still a great need for support.

Enterprise IT and the service desk will still be important in 10 to 20 years. However, we have to move away from being IT engineers to being customer-focused, service-centric professionals. There is a lot of hype surrounding trends such as BYOD and it is being suggested that employees will go around IT. A large majority of companies aren't there yet and many employees still want services provided by IT. That doesn't mean that IT and the service desk can continue to do things the way they've always been done. We must respond to customer experience and customer preferences.

The service desk of the future won't be staffed and measured the way it is today. The role will change from supporting technology to advising customers on technology choices in a controlled way.

Question: What advice would you give to a young person who is currently working in a service desk or pursuing a career in the technical customer support industry?

Answer: IT isn't always perceived as an exciting or sustainable career. IT is exciting. If you want to help companies become more innovative and competitive, IT is a great profession to be in. If you want to interact with a variety of employees at all levels of the business, IT is a great profession to be in.

Help desks and service desks have gotten some bad press through the years, but that is changing. The key is to be customer-centric. Understand your customers. Not all employees want to bring their own device. This is hype that is being driven by the marketing perspective. Put the needs of your business and your customers in the context of trends. Technical customer support is a people business and you are first and foremost operating from a service perspective. If you adopt a service-centric approach, your customers will understand that you are helping.

Understand too that we're living in a social world. That doesn't necessarily have to do with the technology. A core skill in business is the ability to communicate.

Role of Certification in the Service Desk

The idea of certifying professionals has existed for years. Examples include certified public accountants (CPAs), certified electricians, certified mechanics, and certified teachers. The practice of certifying IT professionals began in the late 1980s and was prompted by the growing complexity of technology coupled with a shortage of people with IT skills. Early IT certification programs focused primarily on people's technical skills. In the 1990s, organizations began to also value nontechnical certifications for IT professionals. For example, the support industry offers certification programs that focus on the soft and self-management skills needed by service desk professionals. Certifications related to topics such as IT service management and project management are also valued because they represent the skills IT professionals need to contribute to improved processes, increased productivity, and the achievement of business goals.

Certifications are necessary for organizations that provide service desk outsourcing services. When evaluating potential suppliers, potential clients often consider both site and individual certifications held by service desk management and staff.

To become certified, people must pass an exam after receiving instruction or doing self-study. Most certifications have recommended or mandatory prerequisites that people must meet to be eligible for the exam. These prerequisites may include hours of instruction, years of experience, or another certification. For example, many advanced certifications require people to hold a basic or foundation certificate or a given degree. Some certification programs require people to complete a project or in some way apply the skills that they have learned, in addition to taking an exam. Because becoming certified is hard work, companies find that certification is an excellent indicator of a person's skills and knowledge about a given subject as well as his or her willingness to learn new skills. To ensure that people maintain their knowledge, many certification programs require people to periodically renew their certificates.

Certification, coupled with experience, is what is most valued in today's competitive job market, along with a willingness to learn new skills and stay current.

Many companies use certifications to distinguish among job candidates. Some companies even require certification as a condition of employment. Although these companies might hire people who are not certified, uncertified employees may receive a lower salary and may be required to obtain their certification within a predefined time. Or, they may be required to obtain a certification before being considered for a promotion.

Because the IT industry is constantly changing, training and certification provides people the ability to distinguish themselves from other job candidates, secure higher salaries or promotions, and pursue new opportunities. The most sought-after certifications vary over time and from one company to the next. This is one of the downsides of certification: a hard-earned certification may become irrelevant or obsolete over time.

For this reason, the most successful job candidates and valued employees hold both technical and nontechnical certifications and combine those certifications with real-world experience. The most successful IT professionals also recognize the importance of continually learning new skills—whether tied to a certification or not—and using those skills to solve business problems and meet business goals.

The number of available IT certifications, both technical and nontechnical, is considerable. However, certifications such as those listed in Figure 8-3 are particularly relevant for people pursuing a service desk career. Some certifications, such as those offered by HDI and the Technology Service Industry Association (TSIA), are specific to the service desk. These certification programs enable individuals to focus on and demonstrate that they possess the industry knowledge and skills needed to deliver excellent customer support. Certifications related to topics such as ITIL and project management help individuals acquire a broader understanding of IT industry best practices and provide a bigger picture perspective than technical certification programs tend to offer. Technical certifications range from generic certifications, such as those offered by the Computing Technology Industry Association (CompTIA), to those that are vendor specific, such as those offered by Cisco and Microsoft.

- HDI certification
- TSIA certification
- ITIL certification
- Project management certification
- CompTIA certification
- Vendor certification

Figure 8-3   Certification programs relevant to a service desk career
© Cengage Learning 2014

HDI Certification

HDI certification is an open, standards-based, internationally recognized certification program for service desk professionals (*www.thinkhdi.com/certification*). Certification levels include Customer Service Representative, Support Center Analyst, Desktop Support Technician, Support Center Team Lead, Support Center Manager, Desktop Support Manager, and Support Center Director. HDI also offers the HDI Support Center Certification program. This site certification recognizes a support center's commitment to excellence, efficiency, and service quality and is based on the internationally recognized HDI Support Center Standard. The standard specifies criteria relative to successful leadership, strategic planning, people management, resource and technology optimization, and service delivery; it is designed to produce performance and satisfaction results.

Site certifications are conducted by an independent auditor who requires evidence that the organization is complying with the criteria specified in the standard. Individuals working in the organization may be interviewed, observed working, or have their work examined.

TSIA Certification

The TSIA individual certification training program is designed to prepare support professionals at all levels to perform within industry standards and to earn international certification (*www.tsia.com/awards_and_certifications/support_staff_excellence/individual_certification*). The four levels of TSIA individual certification available include: Customer Service Qualified, Certified Support Professional, and Certified Support Professional Supervisor. TSIA membership is required to participate in the TSIA Certification program. TSIA's programs are geared to companies that provide external customer support.

ITIL Certification

ITIL certifications are individual certifications that are based on the ITIL Qualification Scheme (*www.itil-officialsite.com/Qualifications/ITILQualificationScheme.aspx*). This scheme enables an individual to gain credits for each ITIL-related exam they take. There are four levels within the scheme: Foundation, Intermediate (Lifecycle and Capability), ITIL Expert, and ITIL Master. The Foundation certification focuses on the key concepts, terminology, and processes of ITIL and is a prerequisite for all other ITIL certifications. The Intermediate and ITIL Expert certifications cover more advanced concepts and are oriented to specific roles within an organization. For example, an Intermediate certification called "Operational Support and Analysis" covers subjects such as the service desk function and processes such as event management, incident management, request fulfillment, problem management, and others.

Many organizations that are adopting the ITIL framework or improving their ITIL processes provide their employees with ITIL-related training so they can understand basic concepts and how ITIL best practices benefit both IT and the business. With this knowledge, individuals can contribute to efforts to improve the quality of IT services and IT service management processes. It is common for individuals to also acquire the ITIL Foundation and other certifications on their own in an effort to enhance their resume. The exams are offered by accredited examination institutes that provide individuals the ability to download exam requirements, locate accredited training providers, and register for exams (*www.itil-officialsite.com/ExaminationInstitutes/ExamInstitutes.aspx*).

Another IT service management certification is ISO/IEC 20000 Foundation, which is offered by the Examination Institute for Information Science (EXIN), a global, independent, not-for-profit IT examination provider (*www.exin.org*).

The ITIL Foundation certification was ranked tenth on TechRepublic's list of "Top Certifications by Salary," which shows the positive association between training and salary

(*www.techrepublic.com/whitepapers/2012-it-skills-and-salary-report/4227993*).
ITCareerFinder.com also included ITIL Foundation on its 2012 list of "IT Certifications in
Demand for 2012/Best Certifications to Get a Job" (*www.slideshare.net/ITCareerFinder/
top-it-certifications-in-demand-for-2012-best-certs-to-get-a-job*).

Project Management Certification

Project management is the process of planning and managing a project. Project management
certifications frequently appear on lists of top IT certifications. These certifications validate
that an individual has learned project management fundamentals such as how to initiate, plan,
and execute projects. Holders of these certifications must also demonstrate the ability to
estimate required resources, identify and mitigate project risks, prepare and maintain a
project budget, and gain customer acceptance and sign-off. These certifications are valued
because they enable holders to understand the discipline needed to effectively plan and
manage projects—regardless of the size or nature of the project—and emphasize the
communication and collaboration skills needed to build and manage a project team. Service
desks continuously have projects underway, whether to improve the service desk's processes,
procedures, and tools or to introduce new technologies the service desk is expected to
support. Project management skills enable service desk professionals to participate in these
projects and ensure the service desk's needs are being fully addressed. These skills also enable
service desk managers, team leaders, and senior analysts, for example, to plan and manage
projects aimed at improving service desk operations.

The Project Management Institute (PMI) (*www.pmi.org*) is a membership organization that
offers globally-recognized standards and credentials. All PMI certifications are based on
A Guide to the Project Management Body of Knowledge (PMBOK® Guide), a comprehensive
guide that describes project management best practices. The most widely recognized PMI
certifications are Project Management Professional (PMP), designed for project managers,
and Certified Associate in Project Management (CAPM), designed for project team members.
All PMI certifications require experience and education.

CompTIA offers the CompTIA Project+ certification, which gives project managers the skills
necessary to complete projects on time and within budget (*http://certification.comptia.org/
getCertified/certifications/project.aspx*). This certification also creates a common project
management language among project team members.

The highest salaries are paid to individuals who combine experience with a certification. Salaries may also
reflect how difficult a certification is to obtain and whether individuals are required to maintain their
certification through continuing education.

CompTIA Certification

CompTIA is a membership organization dedicated to advancing IT industry growth through
its educational programs, market research, networking events, professional certifications, and
public policy advocacy. The CompTIA A+ certification (*http://certification.comptia.org/
getCertified/certifications/a.aspx*) is the most widely recognized and required certification for

entry-level service technicians (such as service desk analysts and field service technicians). Some organizations will hire individuals and require that they achieve the A+ certification within a predetermined period of time—typically three to six months following employment.

The certification consists of two exams. The CompTIA A+ Essentials exam is mandatory and validates a candidate's technical understanding of computer technology, networking, and security, as well as the communication skills and professionalism now required of all entry-level IT professionals. The second exam, CompTIA A+ Practical Application, is an extension of the knowledge and skills identified in CompTIA A+ Essentials, with a more hands-on orientation focused on scenarios in which troubleshooting and tools must be applied to resolve problems.

Other CompTIA certifications include areas such as cloud essentials, networking, servers, convergence, Linux, security, document imaging, and Green IT.

 A complete list of CompTIA certifications is available at *http://certification.comptia.org/getCertified/certifications.aspx.*

Vendor Certifications

Many vendors that manufacture hardware and publish software products, such as those listed in Figure 8-4, offer technical certifications. Information about the certifications offered can typically be found on the company's web site. Many of the certifications these vendors offer are advanced certifications that require years of professional experience and may require a candidate to pass multiple exams.

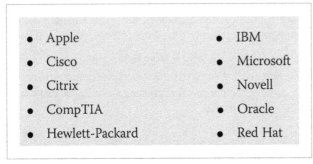

- Apple
- Cisco
- Citrix
- CompTIA
- Hewlett-Packard
- IBM
- Microsoft
- Novell
- Oracle
- Red Hat

Figure 8-4 Vendors that offer technical certification programs
© Cengage Learning 2014

Certification programs can be costly and time consuming to complete successfully. Many individuals and organizations believe that the cost and effort is justified, as certification represents industry recognition and the ability to demonstrate a level of competency based on industry best practices. Although becoming certified does not automatically guarantee individuals will be hired or promoted, being certified does enable individuals to distinguish themselves from other job candidates and may make them eligible for raises or bonuses. For example, some companies have a formal policy about raises for certification, whereas others leave it to the discretion of the employee's manager.

One of the most common incentives for becoming certified is when companies pay for the training and for the cost of the exam that leads to certification. Many companies pay for certification to reward their employees, and they view it as a way to retain people who have the skills needed to support today's sophisticated technology environments. As this cost can be substantial, some companies require individuals to sign a contract that requires them to stay at the company for a specified period of time once they become certified. Employees who choose to leave the company before the specified time may be required to reimburse the company all or a portion of the cost of certification.

Some companies also reward individuals who demonstrate that they are applying the lessons learned through certification and sharing those lessons with others. In an effort to validate, quantify, and ultimately reward an increase in a person's level of competence, some companies compare metrics before certification (such as first contact resolution and customer satisfaction) to metrics after certification.

Certifications are becoming a necessary credential for service desk professionals. Managers value people who dedicate the time and effort necessary to get certified. As a result, certified individuals often get better jobs, receive higher salaries, and advance more quickly.

The fact that certification programs exist for the service desk serves as true validation that customer support is now a recognized profession. These programs emphasize the importance of interpersonal and technical skills, and they ultimately ensure that people who choose customer support as a career are rewarded for those skills.

Preparing for a Career in the Service Desk

Every day, the world changes dramatically. People and businesses are being called upon to continuously reinvent themselves in order to compete. Unlike the past, when people worked for the same company most of their lives, today's college graduates will have 10 to 12 jobs during three to five careers. If you choose to pursue a service desk career as one of those, the skills you develop will serve you well throughout your life because they are very transferable and relevant to any number of endeavors.

A successful service desk career begins with the decision that you want such a career. This is easily determined by asking yourself a few simple questions:

- Do you have a positive attitude?
- Do you enjoy helping others?
- Do you enjoy solving problems?
- Do you like change?
- Do you enjoy learning new skills and acquiring new knowledge?
- Do you have the ability to see the good in people and to be objective in difficult situations?

If you answer yes to these questions, you possess the fundamental characteristics needed to be successful.

A second set of questions deals with your ascent through the service desk:

- Are you interested in pursuing a technical career?

- Are you interested in pursuing a management career?

- Are you interested in pursuing a customer service career?

Your answers to these questions will determine the work experience you seek, the focus of your education and training, and the nature of your self-study.

Work Experience

Although prior service desk experience is optimal when looking for a job in the service desk industry, companies that are hiring people for service desk positions will also consider relevant work experience that represents some form of customer service. For example, working at a store in the mall or at a restaurant is valuable experience because these jobs require a lot of customer interaction. Other relevant fields include teaching and social work because they require someone who enjoys working with people and who can communicate effectively. Having relevant work experience can help in that search for your first service desk job.

Education and Training

Not all companies require candidates to have an MIS or computer science degree when applying for service desk positions. Because communication skills are so important, companies also consider candidates with English or communications degrees. Companies undertaking knowledge management and process improvement initiatives often hire degreed technical writers. In addition, companies look at applicants' certifications because they can differentiate one candidate from another. Good computer literacy and software skills also are important. Regardless of the type of technology they support, most companies require that their employees *use* technology to do their jobs. A high level of comfort using technology will give you a competitive edge over other candidates.

Self-Study

No one can predict what the future holds. Today's trends, however, provide some insight. Take it upon yourself to do reading and studying over and above that which is required at work or at school. To be successful in the service desk, continuously follow trends both in the service desk and in business; gain an understanding of their impact on your skills and on the support industry; and determine how you can seize the opportunities they present. Ongoing study will keep you competitive and prepared for changes.

Appendix B lists books, self-study programs, and organizations you can use to obtain additional information about the technical customer support industry.

To have a successful service desk career:

(1) Decide to make it your career. In other words, rather than view working in a service desk as just a job or as just a stepping stone to some other profession, decide you're going to pursue technical customer support as a career. Paramount to this decision is understanding that, to be successful, you must thrive on dealing with customers, not just technology. In fact, you've got to love complaining and demanding customers. You must understand that complaints are opportunities for you to make or recommend improvements. You must also be confident that, in difficult situations, you can really shine.

(2) Become a life-long learner. Determine all of the areas where you lack experience, and begin to fill in the blanks. Be curious. Learn more about business. Learn more about your company's business and its goals. Identify ways you can contribute to the attainment of those goals and explore ways to make those contributions. Learn about emerging technologies. Learn which of those technologies your company views as strategic and expand your knowledge in those areas. The only thing constant in any career today is change. The more confident you are in your ability to continually learn new skills, and the more willing you are to continually learn new skills, the easier it will be for you to adapt when things change.

(3) Market your skills and gain exposure outside of your department and company. While we all hope that our bosses and perspective employers will just know what great people we are and what great jobs we do, the reality is you've got to market yourself. In other words, you've got to create your own opportunities. Ways to market your skills include:

- **Create a personal brand**—In the context of business, a **brand** is a name, term, design, symbol, or any other feature that differentiates a company's goods or services from those of its competitors. Similarly, a personal brand portrays you in a professional way and differentiates you from others. Once you've established your brand, you can then promote that brand online by, for example, adding it to your Twitter profile. You can also set up a professional profile on a social networking site such as LinkedIn (*www.linkedin.com*). Because your employer, potential employers, your peers, and perhaps even your customers may be viewing your profile, keep it up-to-date and ensure that your profile accurately reflects your qualifications, experience, and skills.

- **Get published**—There are literally thousands of web sites, magazines, and ezines to which you can submit articles, white papers, or solutions to technical problems. If you need to, take a technical writing class or use books about writing to improve your skills.

- **Hone your speaking skills**—You can hone your presentation skills and gain exposure by speaking at conferences, user group meetings, and within your company. If you don't feel comfortable speaking or want to improve your interpersonal skills, use training programs such as Toastmasters (*www.toastmasters.org*), Dale Carnegie (*www.dalecarnegie.com*), or speech classes to gain the confidence you need.

- **Build relationships**—Work at building relationships with employees in other parts of your company. For example, get to know the people in your company's training department or quality department. Let them know what's happening in the support department, and learn about what they do and how they can help you and your team. You can also join professional associations that enable you to build relationships with people who work at other service desks in your community. Associations that may have local chapters in your area include HDI (*www.thinkhdi.com/membership/local-chapters.aspx*) and itSMF (*www.itsmfusa.org/?page=localinterestgroups*).

Creating a personal brand, publishing articles, speaking in public, and building relationships will get people to recognize your name and abilities, and it will help you build a portfolio over time that you can share with prospective employers or clients.

Once perceived as a profession that simply required people to be nice, technical customer support is increasingly complex and challenging. The technologies that service desks support are complex, the tools they use to deliver support are complex, their customers are demanding, and the businesses they serve are demanding. That represents a lot of opportunity for people who want to use the best of all their skills—business, technical, soft, and self-management—to have a rewarding career.

Transitioning to a Management Position

Whether you plan to pursue a career in management or are promoted into a management position as a reward for excellent technical performance, the transition to a management position can be trying. This is especially true for people who pride themselves on their technical abilities. Technicians often have a hard time "giving up" the technical skills they have worked so hard to develop in order to acquire the business skills they need to be a manager. This is because technicians often believe the amount of respect they receive from other technicians is based solely upon their technical ability. Also, technicians often find it difficult to manage people who were previously their peers. The tips listed in Figure 8-5 are designed to ease this transition.

- Focus on the big picture.
- Learn about managing and working on projects.
- Serve as a consultant to your staff.
- Learn to delegate.
- Lead and coach your staff.
- Learn to use information.
- Broaden your skills base.

Figure 8-5 Tips for transitioning to management
© Cengage Learning 2014

Following these tips will give people with strong technical skills who choose to pursue a management career the confidence to focus on management issues. For individuals who aren't interested in pursuing management positions, these tips can also be used to enhance their flexibility, keep themselves motivated, and create value for their customers and company—all critical skills in a competitive business environment.

Focus on the Big Picture

Successful managers strive continuously to understand how their team or department fits into the company as a whole and how it contributes to the company's goals. This perspective enables them to understand how the actions of their team impact the company's performance. Understanding the big picture also enables managers to continuously identify ways their team can improve and more fully contribute to the company's bottom line. The best managers can communicate this bigger-picture perspective to their staff. Having this understanding improves staff morale and increases people's perception of their job value.

Learn About Managing and Working on Projects

In today's business world, change is constant, so people working in a service desk are continuously exposed to projects. It is critical that technical professionals, particularly those interested in transitioning to a management position, understand how projects are run and the keys to project success. This can be accomplished by taking advantage of any training that is offered, seeking out self-study, or by asking a seasoned project manager to serve as a mentor. This understanding can also be achieved simply by being observant and being an active participant when working on a project team.

At a minimum, individuals in management positions must understand how to contribute to, produce, and understand key project deliverables. These include a **project scope**, which describes the work to be done, and a **project plan**, which is a summary document that describes the project, its objectives, and how the objectives are to be achieved. For smaller projects, the project plan may consist of submitting a service request or request for change and documenting the tasks to be completed in the record. For larger projects, a more formal approach is taken, and the project plan typically contains a **work breakdown structure (WBS)**, which is a task-oriented breakdown of the work to be done. The WBS is used to logically arrange the tasks to be completed and to define milestones. A **milestone** is a key or important event in the life of a project. The WBS is also used to assign resources to tasks, estimate costs, and create schedules. As illustrated in Figure 8-6, a **Gantt chart** is a type of bar chart that is often used to illustrate a project schedule.

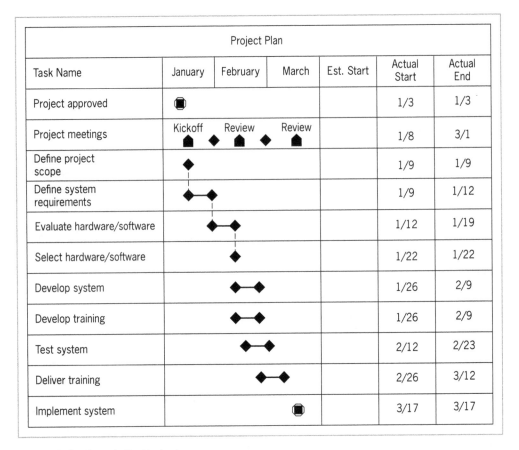

Project Plan						
Task Name	January	February	March	Est. Start	Actual Start	Actual End
Project approved	▣				1/3	1/3
Project meetings	Kickoff ⬆ ◆	Review ⬆ ◆	Review ⬆		1/8	3/1
Define project scope	◆				1/9	1/9
Define system requirements	◆—◆				1/9	1/12
Evaluate hardware/software	◆—◆				1/12	1/19
Select hardware/software		◆			1/22	1/22
Develop system		◆—◆			1/26	2/9
Develop training		◆—◆			1/26	2/9
Test system		◆—◆			2/12	2/23
Deliver training			◆—◆		2/26	3/12
Implement system			▣		3/17	3/17

Figure 8-6 Sample Gantt chart
© Cengage Learning 2014

Widely used software products that support project scheduling, management, and collaboration activities include: Basecamp (*www.basecamp.com*), Mavenlink (*www.mavenlink.com*), Microsoft Project (*www.microsoft.com/project/en-us/project-management.aspx*), and Zoho Projects (*www.zoho.com/projects*). Free, open source project management tools are also available that can be downloaded from the Internet or used via a web browser.

Being an effective manager involves being a team player and supporting projects, even when you disagree with the project objectives. Missing deadlines or being viewed as someone who stands in the way of progress will do little to advance your career or gain acceptance for your point of view. Learning how projects are run will enable you to begin initiating projects aimed at implementing your own ideas.

 Individuals between jobs often are able to work as independent contractors or take advantage of freelance opportunities to stay active in the workplace. Project management skills serve them well in these situations.

Serve as a Consultant to Your Staff

A consultant is a professional who analyzes clients' needs and helps them develop systems to improve employee performance, company productivity, customer satisfaction, and so on. Good consultants do not always have all the answers right away. They do, however, know where to get information when they need it. Also, consultants typically have a broad base of experience and can offer alternative ways of getting things done. Serving as a consultant to his or her staff allows a manager to stay focused on the bigger picture, while providing staff members with what they need to focus on the details.

Learn to Delegate

Delegating is a tough skill for every new manager to learn, but it is particularly difficult for people with strong technical skills. This is because technicians often fear that, if they do not use their technical skills, they will lose them. Also, many technicians learn new skills by doing a task. They roll up their sleeves and figure out how to do what they need to do by trial and error. Although delegating tasks may make new managers feel like they are depriving themselves of the opportunity to practice and learn new technical skills, it will free up the time they need to acquire management skills.

Delegating is not simply "dumping" work on another person. Effective delegators share the responsibility and authority to successfully complete the task with others, and they also hold people accountable for their performance of the task. Effective delegation includes coaching people on the expected results of the work to be done and on where that work fits relative to other priorities. The most effective managers clearly communicate *what* needs to be done, and then empower people to determine *how* best to complete the assigned task. Managers must also work with employees to ensure they have the time, skills, and resources—such as financial and technical resources—needed to successfully complete the assigned task.

Lead and Coach Your Staff

A good manager understands that he or she can't motivate other people. Motivation comes from within. What managers can do, however, is provide leadership and a motivating, well-managed environment. A leader guides people by communicating a vision and inspiring people to achieve that vision. A leader also coaches people and teaches them how to be self-motivated and empowered.

Successful service desk managers lead their staff by helping them to understand the role of the service desk in its company or its department, the service desk's importance to the company or the department, and the scope of the service desk's responsibilities. Managers must also create a clear vision of where the service desk is heading in the future and must passionately move the service desk toward that future state by setting clear, attainable goals. Furthermore, managers must help people understand the bigger issues that are involved in their management decisions and activities. In other words, *why* the service desk is doing things the way it is doing them and *why* the service desk is heading in the direction it is heading. Educating their staff about these higher-level activities enables managers to engage their staff in the decision-making process when appropriate, thus instilling a sense of responsibility and a feeling of ownership relative to the results.

According to Frederick Herzberg, a behavioral scientist who in the 1950s developed a theory about motivation that continues to be relevant today (*The Motivation to Work*, Wiley & Sons, New York, 1959), responsibility is one of the factors that leads to job satisfaction. Herzberg studied motivational influences and concluded that the things that satisfy workers, such as responsibility, are entirely different from the things that dissatisfy workers. Furthermore, Herzberg concluded that the things that dissatisfy workers are not just the opposites of things that satisfy workers. Figure 8-7 lists some of the work "dissatisfiers" that Herzberg found in his studies.

- Company policy administration
- Lack of job security
- Poor working conditions
- Insufficient or unfair salary and compensation
- Too much or too little supervision

Figure 8-7 Herzberg's work dissatisfiers
© Cengage Learning 2014

Table 8-1 lists some of the work satisfiers that Herzberg found in his studies, along with examples of these work satisfiers in a service desk setting.

Herzberg's Work Satisfiers	Examples of Satisfiers in a Service Desk Setting
Achievement	Clearly defined goals
	Special projects
	Team-building activities
Interesting work	Job shadowing
	Complex incident and problem solving
	Using a variety of skills
Opportunity	Technical and managerial career paths
	Project management
	Training and certification
Recognition	Incentive programs
	Peer recognition programs
	Thanks, praise, and feedback
Responsibility	Flexible work hours
	Mentoring
	Representing the team at meetings and on projects

Table 8-1 Herzberg's work satisfiers and examples in a service desk setting
© Cengage Learning 2014

Herzberg theorized that managers should not assume that by eliminating dissatisfiers, they have created satisfaction. Herzberg also concluded that job satisfiers are the source of motivation, as they have a positive, intrinsic impact on workers.

Herzberg's theory makes perfect sense when you assume the perspective of a worker. For example, have you ever had a bad boss, or have you ever felt you weren't being paid fairly? Such scenarios cause dissatisfaction. Eliminating these dissatisfiers may not, however, cause job satisfaction. If you are doing a job that is boring (and from your perspective, meaningless), you will be dissatisfied, regardless of a great boss or a good salary. In other words, it is possible to love your boss or to be making a lot of money and still hate your job.

Remember, motivation comes from within. As a manager, all you can do is create a motivating environment. You can do that through:

- **Teamwork**—Creating a shared vision and positive relationships.

- **Education**—Continuously promoting the benefits of your vision and providing people with the education and training they need to be successful.

- **Empowerment**—Communicating values (that is, right and wrong ways of doing things) and requiring each and every person on your team to take responsibility for their actions and for their role in attaining the desired future state.

- **Setting goals**—Breaking the vision into smaller attainable goals, thus enabling a sense of achievement.

- **Recognizing accomplishments**—Celebrating the attainment of both team and individual goals. Effective managers understand that they never lose credit when they give credit and recognition to their individual employees and to their team.

Taking credit for others' ideas and accomplishments is dishonest, demoralizing, and counter-productive. It will cause people to mistrust you and will lessen their willingness to work with you. Give credit where credit is due and you will get credit for creating a strong and productive team.

Remember, too, that not all workers are highly motivated. Managers must sometimes deal with poor performers or risk damaging the morale of the whole team. Successful managers continuously coach their employees by providing constructive feedback and guidance. The best managers regularly tell people *specifically* what they are doing right and, when necessary, *specifically* what they are doing wrong and how they can improve.

Numerous books and articles on leadership, motivation, and coaching are available online and at your local library. Refer to Appendix B for examples.

Successful managers also regularly recognize the efforts of their workers in meaningful ways. One of the best ways to do this is by learning about employees as individuals: What is important to them? What are their personal goals? How do they take in information?

People take in information differently. Some people are auditory, which means they take in information by listening. Auditory workers like to be told they are doing a good job. Saying "thank you" or "great job" to an auditory worker, in person when possible, is an excellent way to acknowledge his or her efforts. Some people are visual, which means they take in information by seeing. You can usually tell visual people, as they have "stuff" all over their desks. Visual people really appreciate being given something they can look at, such as a thank you note, a letter of recognition, or a certificate. Some people are kinesthetic, which means they take in information by touching; they like a "hands-on" approach. You can acknowledge a kinesthetic person's efforts by shaking her hand or by giving him a pat on the back.

Learning about people as individuals is a life skill that will serve you well, whether or not you are a manager and regardless of your chosen profession.

Learn to Use Information

It is imperative that service desk managers understand that information is a resource, just as people, processes, and technology are resources. Managers must ensure that the data their staff collects is meaningful, and they must add context and value to that data and create information that can be shared with others throughout the company. For example, managers must be able to use data and information to understand, influence, and communicate the performance of processes and their staff. Service desk managers must also be able to present information in financial terms by, for example, understanding and communicating the costs associated with service outages, with each contact channel, and with escalating incidents and service requests to higher levels of support.

Managers must be able to use information to justify investments and put together a business case for proposed initiatives. A **business case** is a report that describes the business reasons that a change is being considered, along with its associated costs, benefits, and risks. Managers who request resources without being able to justify the cost versus the benefit of those resources rarely receive what they need. Similarly, managers who cannot give other managers in their department or company the information they need to make informed decisions or contribute to business cases for improving the quality of products and services rarely earn the respect and cooperation they want.

Broaden Your Skills Base

Managers need to add to all the skills (business, technical, soft, and self-management) that they depended upon as analysts. They must quickly acquire or fine-tune skills such as team building, project management, presentation, and meeting skills. These skills involve building relationships and working with others to obtain their confidence and commitment. Classes and online resources are available, and libraries and bookstores are filled with books, DVDs, and CDs that can help managers expand their knowledge in these areas.

It is important to understand that promotion to a management position means that you will be expected to acquire and demonstrate management skills. Analysts don't always realize the impact this will have on their ability to maintain their technical skills. Furthermore, not all technicians enjoy doing the work that managers are required to do. Because not everyone on the service desk team is interested in pursuing a management career, many companies are developing technical and managerial career paths that enable people to focus on their personal strengths and interests. Continuous self-assessment and the exploration of available opportunities will help you to determine and choose what path to take on your way to a long and rewarding career.

The future is bright for people who can find and fill the gaps that may exist in their company's service desk organization or in the service desk of a prospective employer. To locate and fill these gaps, you need to be aware of service desk industry trends and be able to objectively evaluate how those trends affect your skills. You must develop a balanced set of skills—business, technical, soft, and self-management—and be able to communicate the value of those skills. Most importantly, you must learn to leverage and effectively integrate service desk people, processes, technology, and information and use them as stepping stones to the future.

Chapter Summary

- Tremendous opportunities exist for people interested in pursuing a service desk career. This is because companies and departments worldwide are working hard to attract and keep people who have the energy, enthusiasm, and skills needed to deliver the high-quality services their customers demand. These companies also need people who can assume the increasingly important supporting roles in a service desk, such as knowledge engineer, service management and improvement, and technical support for the service desk's tools and technologies. To seize the opportunities offered by this dynamic industry, you must be aware of service desk industry trends and objectively evaluate how your skills match those trends. You must determine your strengths and interests and seek out jobs and experiences in which you can excel and that enhance your resume.

- An almost irreversible dependence on technology has prompted customers to demand ever cheaper, faster, and better support services. This demand has prompted companies to considerably expand the role of the service desk. Trends such as the need to provide multigenerational and multichannel support; anytime, anywhere, any device support; support with fewer escalation levels; 24/7 support; fee-based support; and global support are further influencing the direction in which the service desk industry is heading. Many companies are responding to this challenge by using best practice frameworks and standards and by outsourcing some or all of their support services. Each of these trends affects how service desks are run and the opportunities they present to service desk professionals.

- The idea of certifying professionals, such as accountants and electricians, has existed for years. Organizations also recognize the importance of certifying both the technical and nontechnical skills of IT professionals. Certifications particularly relevant for people who are pursuing a service desk career include those offered by HDI and TSIA that are specific to the service desk. Certifications related to topics such as ITIL and project management are also relevant, as are technical certifications, which range from generic certifications to those that are vendor specific. Certification programs can be costly and time consuming to complete successfully. Many individuals and organizations believe that the cost and effort is justified, as certification represents industry recognition and the ability to demonstrate a level of competency based on industry best practice.

- A successful service desk career begins with the decision that you want to have a service desk career. You must then decide which type of career you want to pursue. Are you interested in pursuing a technical career? Are you interested in pursuing a management career? Are you interested in pursuing a customer service career? Your answers to these questions will determine the work experience you seek, the focus of your education and training, and the nature of your self-study. To have a successful career, view working in a service desk as more than just a job or just a stepping stone to some other profession. Become a life-long learner and take the steps needed to fill any knowledge or experience gaps. Market your skills and gain exposure outside of your department and company.

- Technicians who choose or are promoted into a management position must work hard to acquire the business skills needed to be a manager. Tips for making this transition include focusing on the big picture, learning how to manage and work on projects, and serving as a consultant to your staff. Managers must also learn to delegate, provide leadership, and create a motivating environment. They must understand that information is a resource, just as people, processes, and technology are resources. They must add to the business, technical, soft, and self-management skills that they depended upon as analysts. Not everyone is interested in pursuing a management career, and so many companies are developing technical and managerial career paths that enable people to focus on their personal strengths and interests. Continuous self-assessment and the exploration of available opportunities will help you to determine and choose what path to take on your way to a long and rewarding career.

- The future is bright for people who develop and maintain a balanced set of skills— business, technical, soft, and self-management—and who are able to communicate the value of those skills. Most importantly, learn to leverage and effectively integrate service desk people, processes, technology, and information and use them as stepping stones to the future.

Key Terms

24/7 support—Support services that are provided 24 hours a day, 7 days a week.

avatar—A computer user's representation of him- or herself.

brand—A name, term, design, symbol, or any other feature that differentiates a company's goods or services from those of its competitors.

business case—A report that describes the business reasons that a change is being considered, along with its associated costs, benefits, and risks.

crowdsourcing—Outsourcing tasks traditionally performed by single individuals to a large group of people or community (i.e., a crowd).

fee-based support—Support services that customers pay for on a per-use basis.

Gantt chart—A type of bar chart that is often used to illustrate a project schedule.

global support—Support for customers anywhere in the world.

milestone—A key or important event in the life of a project.

project management—The process of planning and managing a project.

project plan—A summary document that describes a project, its objectives, and how the objectives are to be achieved.

project scope—A description of the work to be done in a project.

swarming—According to Gartner, Inc., a work style characterized by a flurry of collective activity by anyone and everyone conceivably available and able to add value.

work breakdown structure (WBS)—A task-oriented breakdown of the work to be done in a project.

Review Questions

1. What must companies do to avoid losing customers?
2. Why have companies elevated the service desk to a more strategic position?
3. Will a one-size-fits-all approach to customer service meet the needs of today's multigenerational workforce? Explain your answer.
4. Provide four examples of steps that service desks are taking to adopt a more strategic, proactive approach to technical customer support.
5. Provide two examples of how multichannel support changes the skills that service desk analysts must have.
6. Describe why and how companies are using technology to collapse support levels.
7. What are four ways that companies provide 24/7 support?
8. Why do people need to determine whether or how their employer, or prospective employer, charges a fee for support?
9. What issues must companies providing global support address?
10. Briefly describe three ways that companies can provide global support.
11. What knowledge and skills enable people to contribute to process-related improvement initiatives?

12. List four reasons why companies outsource some or all of their support services.

13. What can service desk analysts do to capitalize on the outsourcing trend?

14. List four indications that the service desk has been elevated to a profession.

15. What two trends initially prompted corporate managers to recognize the importance of certifying IT professionals?

16. Certifications specific to the service desk focus on what skills?

17. Why are certifications related to IT service management and project management valued?

18. True or False. People with certifications are always paid higher salaries. Explain your answer.

19. What are three ways that managers show they value the time and effort that individuals put into becoming certified?

20. List at least five of the fundamental characteristics you must possess to have a successful service desk career.

21. What type of work experience will companies consider when hiring people for service desk positions?

22. Why is it important to continuously follow service desk and general business trends?

23. Describe three ways that people with strong technical skills can ease the transition to a management position.

24. Describe two traits of an effective leader.

25. Describe five ways a manager can create a motivating environment for employees.

26. How can managers use information when requesting resources?

27. What skills must you develop to have a balanced set of skills?

28. What components of a service desk must you learn to leverage and use as a stepping stone to the future?

Hands-On Projects

1. **Discuss the current and future state of technical and customer support.** The support industry has changed dramatically and is expected to continue to change for the foreseeable future. Companies have taken great strides to improve the quality of their support services, and yet the media continues to report that service is poor. Assemble a team of at least three classmates or use your school's online message or discussion board and briefly discuss, in general, the current state of technical and customer support. Discuss the following:

- **Current state:** Is service getting better? Why is there such a gap between the efforts companies are making to improve their services and customer perceptions about those services?

- **Future state:** Predict the impact that the trends discussed in this chapter will have on the support industry. How can the support industry respond to these trends and satisfy the needs of their increasingly demanding customers while at the same time maintaining costs?

Present your conclusions and predictions to the class.

2. **Evaluate a local service desk.** Visit the service desk where you work, at your school, or at a company in your community. Determine the following:

   - What services does the service desk provide?

   - What skills does it require of its employees?

   - Does it encourage or require its employees to become certified? If so, what types of certifications are required (such as technical certifications, service desk certifications, or both)?

   - How does it interview job candidates? What qualities does it look for in job candidates?

   - How does it measure the performance of its analysts?

   - What processes does it have in place?

   - What technologies does it use?

   - What data does it capture? How does it use that data to create information?

   - Does it provide 24/7 support? If so, how? If not, does it provide after-hours support? If so, how?

   - How does the manager envision meeting his or her customers' needs in the next five years?

   - What strategies are in place to address trends influencing the service desk? Include trends such as social support, self-help, BYOA, BYOD, desktop virtualization, and cloud computing.

   Given everything you have learned in this book, what conclusions can you draw from visiting this service desk? Write a report that summarizes your findings and conclusions.

3. **Interview a service desk employee.** Arrange to interview a manager or analyst who works in a service desk either at your school or in the community. Before the interview, prepare a list of questions you would like answered and send it to the person so that he or she can prepare. For example, you may ask the person to describe:

   - How is the service desk organized? (If possible, obtain a copy of the company's organization chart.)

   - What job categories are included in the organization chart?

- What skills are required for each job category?

- What, if any, certifications are encouraged or required?

- What career path opportunities exist within the service desk?

- What career path opportunities exist beyond the service desk?

- What processes determine the work that person performs on a daily basis?

- What technologies are used by the service desk?

- What data is that person required to collect? How is the data used?

- What terminology is used? Obtain an understanding of any new terms that person introduces or terms that are used differently than those described in this book.

Write a report that summarizes what you learned from this person.

4. **Learn about service desk certification.** Visit the web site of one of the companies or organizations discussed in this chapter that certifies service desk professionals. Determine the following:

- What levels of certification are available?

- What skills are certified?

- What prerequisites must you meet before you can get certified?

- What are the benefits of being certified?

Write a report that summarizes what you have learned about certification from visiting this web site.

5. **Analyze the impact of technology dependence.** Assemble a team of at least three classmates or use your school's online message or discussion board. Explore and analyze the ways that corporations, government agencies, and academic institutions are dependent on information technology.

- Prepare a list of both the positive and negative effects of this dependence on these organizations.

- Search the web for articles about "IT outages," "computer outages," and "technology outages."

- Document at least three recent examples of significant computer outages. How did these outages impact the affected organizations and their customers? What caused the outages (where provided)?

- Prepare a list of steps organizations must take to minimize the negative effects of technology dependence and to minimize the impact of computer outages.

Compare your ideas with those developed by other teams or individuals in your class.

6. **Evaluate and learn to market your skills.** Search the web for service desk-related jobs. Review the ads and select one to evaluate in depth. Compare your education,

training, and work experience to the ad and prepare for a job interview with the selected company. Present to your class a three- to five-minute description of the skills needed for the job compared to the skills you have that you believe qualify you for consideration for this position.

7. **Learn about managerial skills.** Interview a friend or family member who is in a management position. Ask this manager how he or she developed business and financial management skills, team-building skills, project management skills, presentation skills, and meeting skills. How important does this person feel it is for a manager to have these skills? What other skills does this person feel are needed to be a manager? Summarize what you learned from this interview.

8. **Learn what motivates workers.** Assemble a team of three to five classmates, optimally classmates of varying ages. Discuss what motivates workers who are part of the different generations discussed in this chapter. How are these workers different? How are these workers the same? For each generation, prepare a list of the following:

- Three work dissatisfiers

- Three work satisfiers

- Three specific examples of each work satisfier

Present and discuss your conclusions with the class.

9. **State your career goals.** The section "Preparing for a Career in the Service Desk" presented a series of questions that describe the fundamental characteristics needed to have a successful service desk career. Ask yourself these questions, and assess your desire to pursue a service desk career. The section also presented a second set of questions that relate to your ascent through the service desk. Ask yourself these questions, and again assess your desire to pursue a service desk career. Write down a description of your service desk career goals based on your answers to these questions. Explain why you want to pursue this direction.

10. **Evaluate your online presence.** Search the web for your name and examine all the ways people can obtain information about you online (e.g., via Facebook, Twitter, LinkedIn). What impression do your usernames, profiles, photographs and so forth give to your employer or perspective employers? In light of the career goals identified in Hands-on Project 9, are you clearly communicating your personal brand and making the desired first impression online? Consider asking your classmates or a trusted mentor to critique your online presence. Prepare a list of ways that you can improve your online presence. Present and discuss your conclusions with the class.

Case Projects

1. **University Service Desk.** A university service desk recently installed a wireless network on its campus. Most of the faculty and students are quite comfortable using the web and mobile devices. You work as a service desk analyst and think the service desk can enhance its services by using Web 2.0 technologies and social media. Use the

web to research the use of Web 2.0 technologies and social media at the service desk and analyze ways these technologies can be used to serve the university's faculty and students. After you finish your research and analysis, prepare a brief report of your findings. The report could outline, for example, what the introduction of Web 2.0 technologies and social media will mean to your customers and how Web 2.0 technologies and social media will enable the university to provide cost-effective support services. Provide any information you can about how other universities and companies are using these technologies to support their customers. Finally, prepare a list of changes you recommend making to the service desk so that the team will be prepared to use and promote the use of these technologies. Consider all aspects of the service desk—people, processes, technology and information.

2. **Bayside Consulting Services, Inc.** You are the supervisor for a service desk that supports the internal customers of Bayside Consulting Services, Inc., a small consulting company that has recently moved to a new and much smaller corporate headquarters. Only the company's executives and managers will work at the headquarters. All of the company's consultants will work from their home offices. Most of the consultants will use company-supplied laptops, tablets, and smartphones. Some consultants will participate in an experimental "bring your own device" program. As a result, you are expanding your service desk. You are very committed to satisfying customers and resolving a high percentage of incidents, and you know that many of the traditional techniques used to support workers, such as going to the worker's office to diagnose an incident or upgrade a system, aren't going to be possible or practical now that the consultants are working remotely, and now that consultants will be using a wider array of technologies. Search the web for articles about topics such as "supporting remote workers" and "supporting telecommuters." Use the articles to prepare a brief presentation outlining the people, process, technology, and information issues you must address at the service desk in preparation for this change. Outline how the responsibilities of your customers must change as well.

3. **Bulldog Boards Manufacturing.** You work as a service desk analyst for Bulldog Boards Manufacturing Company, a producer of high-quality wakeboards, bindings, and boots. The company recently established a service desk for the company's employees who use a newly introduced sales ordering and product manufacturing system. The company's employees are quite comfortable using the web, and numerous employees have suggested that the service desk begin offering a live chat service. The company has also received this suggestion from external customers. As a result, the service desk manager has asked you to research live chat best practices. Search the web for articles about topics such as "live chat best practices" and "live chat etiquette." Use the articles to prepare a brief presentation outlining the top five tips for using live chat to communicate with customers as well as the benefits of using live chat for customer service. Also include a recommendation about the skills and training analysts need to use this technology.

Job Descriptions for the Service Desk

This appendix provides sample service desk job descriptions. These job descriptions provide you with a basic overview of the job responsibilities and activities as well as the professional experience and education required for each position. Be aware that these job titles and descriptions will vary from company to company. The following sample job descriptions are provided:

- Level One Analyst
- Level One Specialist
- Service Desk Team Leader
- Service Desk Manager
- Knowledge Engineer

Level One Analyst

REPORTS TO

Service Desk Team Leader

POSITION CONCEPT

As directed by the Service Desk Team Leader, delivers quality customer service to service desk customers by providing them with a single point of contact to report incidents and service requests or to make inquiries. Handles incidents and service requests throughout their lifecycle and works on special projects as assigned.

DUTIES AND RESPONSIBILITIES

1. Ensures customer satisfaction by responding to service desk contacts. Logs all incidents and service requests and tracks the same through to resolution.

2. Ensures customer incidents and service requests are handled in a timely manner by documenting the impact to the customer and by assigning an appropriate priority and target resolution time.

3. Conducts initial diagnosis using documented procedures and available tools. Records incident symptoms and status information in a timely fashion in an effort to communicate with and properly use senior IT staff.

4. Ensures incident resolution by maintaining an action plan for incident resolution; by initiating and tracking incident escalations to technical resources, vendors, and so on; and by keeping the customer updated on the status of incident resolution.

5. Ensures management awareness of major incidents or incidents that are nearing or exceeding documented targets.

6. Receives, records, and handles service requests.

7. Confirms customer satisfaction and closes incidents and service requests.

8. Builds team spirit by assisting and coaching other staff members.

REQUIRED SKILLS AND ABILITIES

1. Strong dedication to quality customer service and a working knowledge of enterprise-wide service delivery procedures.

2. Strong interpersonal skills and strong verbal and written communication skills. Superior telephone and email etiquette and an ability to interact effectively with customers, vendors, peers, and management via multiple contact channels.

3. Strong problem-solving skills and decision-making ability.

4. Good initiative and assertiveness. Good project management skills, the ability to organize work efficiently, and the capacity to work well under stress and time pressures.

5. Good working knowledge of the day-to-day operating environment, available tools, operating techniques, and customer applications.

Education: Associate's degree or equivalent technical training. CompTIA A+ certification and ITIL® Awareness education within six months of employment.

Experience: One to three years of computer-related support experience.

Level One Specialist

REPORTS TO

Service Desk Team Leader

POSITION CONCEPT

Possesses a broad understanding of the company's information technology along with a depth of expertise in a specific subject area. Resides in the service desk for his or her assigned shift, handling complex incidents and service requests and mentoring Level One Analysts. Helps maintain the organization's hardware and software inventory and knowledge management system.

DUTIES AND RESPONSIBILITIES

1. Resides in the service desk for assigned shift.

2. Diagnoses and resolves incidents and service requests referred by Level One Analysts.

3. Researches complex incidents and service requests and develops solutions.

4. Participates on project teams related to his or her area of expertise and determines the service desk's needs with regard to new products and systems.

5. Demonstrates excellent verbal and written communication skills.

6. Demonstrates commitment in areas of strategic importance to the organization.

REQUIRED SKILLS AND ABILITIES

Level One Specialists are fully qualified to resolve most customer incidents and those service requests designated as the responsibility of the service desk. Additional or more specific educational or professional background may be required for a candidate to be selected for a support position associated with a particular client organization. The following criteria are considered minimal for the position:

Education: Bachelor's degree or equivalent technical training. CompTIA A+, ITIL® Foundation, and relevant technical certifications related to areas of expertise.

Experience: Three to five years of computer-related support experience; considerable work experience in area of specialty.

Service Desk Team Leader

REPORTS TO

Service Desk Manager

POSITION CONCEPT

Oversees the day-to-day operation of the service desk. Works closely with front-line service providers to ensure that they have the resources needed to perform their duties efficiently. Ensures that all incidents and service requests reported by both IT customers and staff are recorded and monitored. Ensures that the service desk is meeting its Service Level Agreement (SLA) commitments.

DUTIES AND RESPONSIBILITIES

1. Ensures that all incidents and service requests are logged.

2. Ensures prompt, accurate status and feedback of all incidents and service requests to customers and management.

3. Monitors SLA compliance.

4. Performs trend analysis to alleviate recurring incidents experienced by customers.

5. Ensures that front-line service providers have the resources needed to resolve as many incidents and service requests as possible.

6. Develops and maintains service desk procedures based on ITIL® best practices and ensures that procedures are followed.

7. Works with the Service Desk Manager to monitor and evaluate the performance of service desk staff.

8. Develops training plans and ensures that service desk analysts are properly trained.

9. Performs other duties when required.

REQUIRED SKILLS AND ABILITIES

Strong supervisory, communication, and teamwork skills are essential, as well as a demonstrated ability to provide excellent customer service.

Education: Bachelor's degree or equivalent work experience. ITIL® Foundation and relevant advanced certifications.

Experience: Five years of customer service and support experience.

Service Desk Manager

REPORTS TO

Senior Service Desk Manager

POSITION CONCEPT

Provides the primary interface between IT management and customer management on matters involving the service desk. Works with service level management on activities such as reviewing reports and analyzing statistics, establishing SLAs, and ensuring that the service desk's processes and technologies are meeting the needs of the company. Works closely with the Senior Service Desk Manager to prepare the service desk's budget and to plan its activities for the coming year.

DUTIES AND RESPONSIBILITIES

1. Plans and directs training activities for the development of personnel.

2. Supervises all service desk personnel and maintains proper staffing to ensure that objectives are met.

3. Coordinates the implementation of support-related technology changes that impact service desk customers.

4. Interfaces with service level management on behalf of the service desk.

5. Interfaces with multiple vendors regarding service, maintenance, and performance.

6. Makes recommendations to management for the purchase of service desk tools and technologies.

7. Performs other duties as assigned.

REQUIRED SKILLS AND ABILITIES

Extensive management experience is required. Necessary skills include the ability to prepare budgets and reports along with the ability to analyze statistics. Must demonstrate the ability to establish goals and plan improvement initiatives.

Education: Bachelor's degree or equivalent business training. ITIL® Foundation and relevant advanced certifications.

Experience: Five to 10 years of customer service and support experience.

Knowledge Engineer

REPORTS TO

Service Desk Manager

POSITION CONCEPT

Responsible for the content, maintenance, and administration of knowledge resources such as the knowledge management system, the service desk web site's FAQ list and solution database, and commercially available knowledge bases that are applicable to the technology environment supported by the service desk. Identifies and promotes web-based knowledge resources that are applicable to the technology environment supported by the service desk.

DUTIES AND RESPONSIBILITIES

1. Promotes and facilitates knowledge sharing throughout the organization.

2. Maintains the knowledge management system.

   a. Develops and distributes resolution documentation standards such as the format and writing style to be used when preparing resolutions.

b. Reviews resolutions submitted by service desk analysts, technical resources, subject matter experts, vendors, and so forth.

c. Ensures that resolutions (1) are technically valid, (2) are reusable, (3) are presented in a clear, consistent, logical manner, (4) conform to knowledge management standards, and (5) do not duplicate an existing resolution.

d. When necessary, confers with technical staff to clarify resolution procedures, verbiage, or placement within the resolution database.

e. Approves or rejects resolutions as appropriate.

f. Ensures that analysts can quickly and easily retrieve resolutions added to the knowledge management system.

g. Provides education and counseling as needed to improve the quality of submitted resolutions.

3. Reviews knowledge management system trend data, technical bulletins, and vendor forums. Proactively includes in the knowledge management system resolution information relative to the supported technology environment.

4. Identifies and recommends improvements to the design and functionality of the company's technical knowledge resources.

5. Leads or participates in project teams dedicated to improving the efficiency, effectiveness, and quality of technical knowledge resources.

6. Acts as a consultant to the Service Desk Manager with regard to how technical knowledge resources are being used.

REQUIRED SKILLS AND ABILITIES

1. Excellent problem-solving and incident analysis skills.

2. Strong verbal and technical writing skills.

3. Extensive experience with the company's technical environment (including operating systems, local and wide area networks, telecommunications, hardware, and system and application software).

4. The ability to identify and verify valid resolutions and workarounds to technical incidents.

5. The ability to provide technical resolution data in a form that analysts can easily retrieve and apply to reported incidents and service requests.

6. An in-depth understanding of service desk operations.

7. An interest in keeping abreast of the most recent technical bulletins and vendor forums related to relevant product defects, resolutions, and available workarounds.

Education: Bachelor's degree or equivalent work experience.

Experience: Three to five years' experience providing technical customer support.

Service Desk Resources

This appendix lists resources for additional information about the service desk industry that you can use to learn more about this dynamic industry and advance your career. Many of these resources can be obtained through your local library or via the web. Many of the magazines can be obtained free of charge by subscribing through the magazine's web site. The magazines and the membership organizations are excellent sources of the most up-to-date information about the industry. The following resources are provided:

- Books
- Certification bodies
- Self-study programs
- Magazines
- Membership organizations

Books

The Complete Idiot's Guide to MBA Basics. T. Gorman. Alpha Books, 2011.

Dictionary of Business Terms, Fifth Edition. J. Friedman. Barron's Educational Series, 2012.

The Essential Drucker. P. Drucker. HarperBusiness, 2001.

A Guide to Computer User Support for Help Desk & Support Specialists, Fourth Edition. F. Beisse. Course Technology, 2010.

A Guide to Customer Service Skills for the Service Desk Professional, Third Edition. D. Knapp. Course Technology, 2010.

The Handbook of Technical Writing, Tenth Edition. G. Alred. St. Martin's Press, 2011.

Introduction to the ITIL® Service Lifecycle (ITIL® 2011 Edition). A. Orr. The Stationery Office, 2011.

ISO / IEC 20000-1: 2011 A Pocket Guide. M. Rovers. Van Haren Publishing, 2012.

ITIL® Continual Service Improvement. The Stationery Office, 2011.

ITIL for Dummies (ITIL® 2011 Edition). P. Farenden. John Wiley & Sons, Ltd., 2012.

ITIL® Service Design. The Stationery Office, 2011.

ITIL® Service Strategy. The Stationery Office, 2011.

ITIL® Service Operation. The Stationery Office, 2011.

ITIL® Service Transition. The Stationery Office, 2011.

ITIL® V3 Small-scale Implementation. S. Taylor, I. Macfarlane. The Stationery Office, 2009.

The ITSM Process Design Guide. D. Knapp. J. Ross Publishing, Inc., 2010.

Metrics for IT Service Management. P. Brooks (Lead Author), Jan van Bon (Chief Editor). Van Haren Publishing, 2006.

Microsoft Operations Framework 4.0: A Pocket Guide. D. Pultorak (Lead Author), C. Henry, P. Leonard. Van Haren Publishing, 2008.

The Portable MBA, Fifth Edition. Authors (Various). John Wiley & Sons, Inc., 2010.

Process Mapping, Process Improvement, and Process Management. D. Madison. Paton Press LLC, 2005.

Six Sigma for IT Management. Authors (Various), Jan van Bon (Chief Editor). Van Haren Publishing, 2006.

Certification Bodies

The Computing Technology Industry Association (CompTIA)
www.comptia.org

CompTIA works with experts and industry leaders from the public and private sectors, including training, academia, and government to develop broad-based, foundational exams that validate an individual's IT skill set.

HDI
www.thinkhdi.com

HDI certification is an open, standards-based, internationally recognized certification program for service desk professionals.

ITIL® Exam Institutions
www.itil-officialsite.com/ExaminationInstitutes/ExamInstitutes.asp

ITIL-related examinations are offered by a number of accredited examination institutes (EIs). EIs work with a network of accredited training organizations (ATOs) and accredited trainers with accredited materials.

Project Management Institute (PMI)

www.pmi.org

PMI's family of credentials supports the project management profession and its practitioners and promotes ongoing professional development.

Technology Services Industry Association (TSIA)

www.tsia.com

TSIA offers a family of awards, recognition and certification programs that are designed to recognize the accomplishments of and prepare support professionals at all levels.

Self-Study Programs (DVDs, CDs, and Seminars)

American Management Association (AMA)

www.amanet.org

The AMA offers seminars in topics such as communication, customer service, finance and accounting, leadership, management, project management, and time management.

CareerTrack, Inc.

www.careertrack.com

CareerTrack, in partnership with Fred Pryor Seminars, offers seminars on topics such as conflict and stress management, computer skills, customer service, grammar and writing, team building, and time management.

HDI

www.thinkhdi.com

HDI publications include *SupportWorld* magazine and its Focus Book Series. These publications provide timely articles on topics affecting the service desk.

ITSM Bookstore

www.itsmbookstore.com

ITSM Bookstore offers ITSM-related book titles including OGC's Official ITIL books and Key Element Guides and Official *it*SMF Pocket Guides.

JWA Video

www.jwavideo.com

JWA Video offers seminars in topics such as customer service, communication skills, management and supervision, writing and presenting, and time management.

The Telephone Doctor
www.telephonedoctor.com

The Telephone Doctor offers soft skills training for customer service professionals. Other topics include leadership and management and meeting openers for staff meetings and training sessions.

Magazines

The following publications provide information resources for service and support professionals and are available by subscription or online:

Contact Professional
www.contactprofessional.com

SupportWorld
www.thinkhdi.com/resources/publications

Membership Organizations

Association of Support Professionals (ASP)
www.asponline.com

ASP is an international membership organization for customer support managers and professionals. ASP publishes research reports on a wide range of support topics and provides its members with career development services.

HDI
www.thinkhdi.com

HDI provides targeted information about the technologies, tools, and trends of the service desk and customer support industry. HDI offers a variety of services to meet the evolving needs of the customer support professional.

IT Service Management Forum (itSMF)
www.itsmfi.org

itSMF is an independent and internationally recognized membership organization for IT Service Management professionals. itSMF has 53 officially approved chapters worldwide that offer membership, events, and publications to its members.

Technology Services Industry Association (TSIA)
www.tsia.com

TSIA is an industry trade group for service and support professionals. TSIA provides market research, programs, certifications, and information resources.

Glossary[1]

24/7 support — Support services that are provided 24 hours a day, 7 days a week.

A

abandon rate percent — The percentage of abandoned calls compared to the total number of calls received.

abandoned call — A call in which the caller hangs up before an analyst answers.

access management — The process responsible for granting authorized users the right to use a service in accordance with the company's security policies while preventing access to nonauthorized users.

accessibility — How easily the service desk can be reached by service desk staff, other employees of the company, and customers.

ACD supervisor console — A system that works with ACD systems and enables supervisors to monitor call volumes and the performance of individual service desk analysts or groups of analysts.

acoustic shock — The term used to describe the symptoms such as discomfort and pain that a person may experience after hearing a loud, unexpected sound via a telephone or headset.

active listening — Listening in which the listener participates in a conversation and gives the speaker a sense of confidence that he or she is being understood.

announcement system — Technology that greets callers when all service desk analysts are busy and can provide valuable information as customers wait on hold.

application of training investments — A comparison of an analyst's resolution percent before and after attending training.

automated attendant — An ACD feature that routes calls based on input provided by the caller through a touch-tone telephone.

automatic call distributor (ACD) — Technology that answers a call and routes, or distributes, it to the next available analyst. If all analysts are busy, the ACD places the call in a queue and plays a recorded message, such as, "We're sorry, all of our service representatives are currently assisting other customers; your call will be answered in the order it has been received."

automatic number identification (ANI) — A service provided by a long-distance service provider that delivers the telephone number of the person calling.

availability — The length of time an analyst was signed on to the ACD compared to the length of time the analyst was scheduled to be signed on.

available state — An ACD state that occurs when an analyst is ready to take calls.

avatar — A computer user's representation of him- or herself.

average call duration — The average length of time required to handle a call.

average speed of answer (ASA) — The average time it takes an analyst to pick up an incoming call.

average wait time — The average number of seconds or minutes a caller waits for an analyst after being placed in the queue by an ACD; also known as average queue time.

B

baseline — A metric used to show a starting point.

beginning of day (BOD) — A list of tasks an analyst performs at the start of each workday.

benchmarking — The process of comparing the service desk's performance metrics and practices to those of another service desk in an effort to identify improvement opportunities.

best practice — A proven way of completing a task to produce a near optimum result.

best-in-class — Refers to a company that is the finest in its industry peer group. For example, a best-in-class manufacturing company is considered excellent by its customers when compared to other manufacturing companies.

biometrics — Measurements of a person's physical characteristics, such as finger or palm prints, facial features, or parts of a person's eye such as the retina or iris.

blended call center — A call center that receives incoming calls and makes outgoing calls.

blog — A journal kept on the Internet; short for web log.

brainstorming — A technique performed by a group of people and designed to generate a large number of ideas for solving a problem.

brand — A name, term, design, symbol, or any other feature that differentiates a company's goods or services from those of its competitors.

bring your own device (BYOD) — A practice that involves using personally-owned mobile devices to access business applications.

business case — A report that describes the business reasons that a change is being considered, along with its associated costs, benefits, and risks.

business process management (BPM) — A systematic approach to improving an organization's business processes.

business relationship management — The process responsible for maintaining a positive relationship between a service provider and its customers. (ITIL definition)

business relationship manager — An employee who has in-depth knowledge of a specific customer community and is responsible for maintaining the relationship with that customer.

business skills — The skills people need to work successfully in the business world, such as the ability to understand and speak the language of business; the skills that are unique to the industry or profession the service desk supports, such as accounting skills or banking skills (industry knowledge); and the skills that are specific to the customer service and support industry, such as understanding the importance of meeting customers' needs and knowing how to manage their expectations (service industry knowledge).

C

call center — A place where telephone calls are made or received in high volume.

caller identification (caller ID) — A service provided by a local telephone company that delivers the telephone number of the person calling and, where available, the name associated with the calling telephone number.

carpal tunnel syndrome (CTS) — A common repetitive stress injury that affects the hands and wrists and is linked to repetitious hand movements, such as typing on a computer keyboard and working with a mouse.

case — A unit of information, such as an online document, a database record, or the solution to a common incident, which is indexed so an analyst can easily locate it when needed.

case-based reasoning (CBR) — A searching technique that uses everyday language to ask users questions and interpret their answers.

case-based system — A system made up of cases and a set of question and answer pairs that can be used to confirm the solution to an incident.

categorization — Recording the type of incident being reported. Categorization also involves recording the type of problem, service request, or change being reported.

cause and effect analysis — A technique used to generate the possible problem causes and their effect.

centralized service desk — A single service desk that supports all of the technologies used by its customers.

certification — A document awarded to a person who has demonstrated that he or she has certain skills and knowledge about a particular topic or area.

change advisory board (CAB) — A group or a committee that supports the assessment, prioritization, authorization, and scheduling of changes. (ITIL definition)

change management — The process responsible for controlling the lifecycle of changes, enabling beneficial changes to be made with minimal disruption to IT services. (ITIL definition)

change manager — The person who coordinates all change management activities and ensures approved changes represent an acceptable level of possible and probable risk and impact.

channel — A route of communication to and from the service desk, such as the telephone, voice mail, email, and the web.

community of practice (CoP) — A group of people who are bound together by similar interests and expertise.

CompTIA A+ — A certification that measures a technician's knowledge of hardware and operating system technologies and concepts, along with topics such as security, safety and environmental issues, and communication and professionalism.

computer-based training (CBT) — Computer software packages used to train and test people on a wide range of subjects.

computer telephony integration (CTI) — The linking of computing technology with telephone technology to exchange information and increase productivity.

computer vision syndrome — A variety of ailments such as headaches and eyestrain that occur as a result of staring at a computer monitor for a prolonged period of time.

configuration item (CI) — Any component or other service asset that needs to be managed in order to deliver an IT service. (ITIL definition)

configuration management database (CMDB) — A database that is used to store configuration records throughout their lifecycle. (ITIL definition)

configuration management system (CMS) — A set of tools and databases for managing IT asset information and linking that information to related incidents, problems, known errors, changes, and releases.

configuration record — A record containing details of a configuration item. (ITIL definition)

contact — A generic term used to describe different types of customer transactions such as questions, incidents, and service requests.

contact center — A call center that uses technologies such as email and the web in addition to the telephone.

cost-benefit analysis — A business calculation that compares the costs and benefits of two or more potential solutions in order to determine an optimum solution.

cost center — A service desk in which the budget items required to run the service desk are considered a cost (expense) to the company.

cost per contact — Historically called cost per call; the total cost of operating a service desk for a given period (including salaries, benefits, facilities, and equipment) divided by the total number of contacts (calls, emails, faxes, web requests, and so on) received during that period.

cost per unit — The total cost of operating a service desk for a given period (including salaries, benefits, facilities, and equipment) divided by the total number of units (such as services, systems, and devices) supported during that period.

362

costs — The amounts paid to produce a product, such as workers' wages, salaries and benefits; the facilities and equipment workers use; and any materials and supplies they consume.

critical success factor (CSF) — A measurable characteristic that must exist for something—such as a process, project, or team—to be viewed as successful.

crowdsourcing — Outsourcing tasks traditionally performed by single individuals to a large group of people or community (i.e., a crowd).

customer — A person who buys products or services.

customer data — Identifying details about a customer, including the customer's name, telephone number, email address, department or company name, physical address or location, customer number, and employee number or user ID.

customer entitlement — The determination of whether the customer is authorized to receive support, and if so, the level of support the customer should receive.

customer relationship management (CRM) — A program that involves using customer contact and relationship information to generate additional sales and to increase levels of customer service and retention.

customer record — All of the fields that describe a single customer.

customer satisfaction — The difference between how a customer expects to be treated and how the customer perceives he or she was treated.

customer satisfaction survey — A series of questions that ask customers to provide their perception of the support services being offered.

customer service — Services that ensure customers receive maximum value for the products or services they purchase.

customer support — Services that help a customer understand and benefit from a product's capabilities by answering questions, solving problems, and providing training.

customer surveying system — A system that is used to create and distribute questionnaires to

customers and to collect and tabulate the results of their feedback.

D

dashboard — A bright display that sends out visual and (in some cases) audible messages to service desk staff and to customer sites that have dashboards installed; also known as electronic reader board.

data — A set of raw facts that is not organized in a meaningful way.

decentralized service desks — Multiple service desks, each of which supports specific products or customer communities.

decision tree — A branching structure of questions and possible answers designed to lead an analyst to a solution.

development — The construction of new systems.

dialed number identification service (DNIS) — A service that provides the number the person called when the call is made using a toll-free number or a 1-900 service.

dispatcher — The person who initially handles customer contacts; also called a service desk agent, customer care agent, customer service representative, or call screener.

dispatch — To send.

E

effectiveness — A measure of how completely and accurately services are delivered.

efficiency — A measure of the time and effort required to deliver services in relation to their cost.

electronic learning (eLearning) — Technology-supported learning and teaching.

email management system — A system that enables service desks to manage high-volume chat, email, and web form messages.

emergency change — A change that must be introduced as soon as possible to repair an error in an IT service that has a high impact on the business.

employee performance plan — A document that clearly describes an analyst's performance requirements and individual improvement objectives.

ergonomics — The science of people-machine relationships that is intended to maximize productivity by reducing operator fatigue and discomfort.

escalation (or escalate) — To raise an incident from one level to another, such as from level one to level two, to dedicate new or additional resources to the incident.

ethical behavior — Conduct that conforms to generally accepted or stated principles of right and wrong.

ethics — The rules and standards that govern the conduct of a person or group of people.

event — A change of state that has significance for the management of an IT service or other configuration item. (ITIL definition)

event-driven survey — A customer satisfaction survey that asks customers for feedback on a single, recent service event.

event management — A process that captures and logs events, analyzes them, and determines an appropriate action.

exit poll — A measurement technique that, on the Internet, combines questions such as "Was this information helpful to you?" with Yes and No buttons that customers can use to provide feedback.

external customer — A person or company that buys another company's products and services.

external service desk — A service desk that supports customers who buy its company's products and services.

F

fax — An image of a document that is electronically transmitted to a telephone number connected to a printer or other output device; short for facsimile.

feature and functionality requirements — The specifics of how the selected tool must perform in order to support its associated processes.

fee-based support — Support services that customers pay for on a per-use basis.

field — A location in a database that stores a particular piece of data.

first contact resolution rate percent — The percentage of contacts resolved during a customer's initial contact compared to the total number of contacts received at the service desk for a given period of time.

Five Whys — A technique that involves repeatedly asking the question "Why?" until the root cause of a problem is determined.

flowchart — A diagram that shows the sequence of tasks that occur in a process.

follow the sun — A service desk approach that enables an organization to provide 24-hour coverage by scheduling regional service desks to work only during the usual business hours for their location.

form — A predefined document that contains text or graphics users cannot change and areas in which users enter information.

framework — A structure designed to enclose something.

front-line service provider — Service desk staff who interacts directly with customers.

functional escalation — Escalation that transfers an incident from one line of support to the next; occurs when greater knowledge or authority is required to resolve an incident or a target time frame is approaching or has been exceeded.

fuzzy logic — A searching technique that presents all possible solutions that are similar to the search criteria, even when conflicting information exists or no exact match is present.

G

Gantt chart — A type of bar chart that is often used to illustrate a project schedule.

global support — Support for customers anywhere in the world.

governance — How an organization controls its actions.

H

help desk — A single point of contact within a company for technology-related questions and incidents.

hierarchic escalation — Escalation that occurs when management is involved in the incident management process, even if only for information purposes; occurs when steps are taking too long, there is contention about assignments, or additional resources are needed to resolve a incident.

high-level requirements — The broad needs for a system.

homegrown incident tracking system — Technology that tends to support only the incident management process and offers basic trouble ticketing and reporting capability.

hyperlink — Text or graphics in a hypertext or hypermedia document that allow readers to "jump" to a related idea.

hypermedia — A storage method that stores information in graphical forms such as images, movies, and videos.

hypertext — Text that links to other information.

I

idle state — An ACD state that occurs when an analyst is logged on to the ACD but is not accepting calls.

impact — A measure of the effect an incident, problem, or change is having on business processes. (ITIL definition)

inbound call center — A call center that receives telephone calls from customers and may answer questions, take orders, respond to billing inquiries, and provide customer support.

incident — An unplanned interruption to an IT service or a reduction in the quality of an IT service. (ITIL definition)

incident data — The details of an incident or service request, including incident type (such as an incident or service request), channel used to submit (such as telephone, email, or web request), category (such as hardware or software), affected

service, system, or device (such as a printer or monitor), the symptom, the date and time the incident occurred, the date and time the incident was logged, the analyst who logged the incident, the incident owner, a description, and a priority.

incident management — The process responsible for managing the lifecycle of incidents. (ITIL definition)

incident management system — Technology that offers enhanced trouble ticketing and management reporting capability.

incident owner — An employee of the support organization who acts as a customer advocate and proactively ensures that an incident is resolved to the customer's satisfaction.

incident ownership — A practice that ensures that, when the service desk analyst cannot resolve an incident during the first contact or escalates the incident to a person or group outside of the service desk, an incident owner is designated.

incident record — All of the fields that describe a single incident.

incident tracking — The practice of following *one* incident from identification to closure.

incidents resolved within target time percent — The percentage of incidents resolved within a target resolution time.

individual performance goals — Measurable objectives for analysts that support the service desk mission.

information — Data that is organized in a meaningful way.

information indicator digits (IID) — A service that identifies the origin of a call from the type or location of the telephone being used to place the call, such as a public phone, cell phone, or hotel phone.

Information Technology Infrastructure Library (ITIL) — A set of best practices for IT service management.

inquiry — A customer request for information, such as "When will the new release of software arrive?"

installations, moves, adds, and changes (IMACs) — Activities that include moving equipment, installing and configuring new systems, and upgrading existing systems; also known as *moves, adds, and changes (MACs)*.

instant messaging system — Text-based form of communication that enables two or more people to communicate in real time over the Internet.

integrated ITSM solutions — A suite of systems that companies use to manage their incident, problem, knowledge, change, service asset and configuration management, and request fulfillment processes; also called enterprise solutions.

internal customer — A person who works at a company and at times relies on other employees at that company to perform his or her job.

internal service desk — A service desk that responds to questions, distributes information, and handles incidents and service requests for its company's employees.

internal service provider — A department or a person within a company that supplies information, products, or services to another department or person within the same company.

International Organization for Standardization — A network of the national standards institutes of 164 countries; also known as ISO.

Internet — A global collection of computer networks that are linked to provide worldwide access to information.

Internet-based training (IBT) — A training system that people can access from any device that has an Internet connection and a browser.

intranet — A secured, privately maintained web site that serves employees and that can be accessed only by authorized personnel.

inventory management — A process that focuses only on collecting and maintaining information about IT assets, not the relationships that exist among those assets. See also *service asset and configuration management*.

ISO 9000 — A set of international standards for quality management.

ISO/IEC 20000 — An international standard for IT service management.

IT governance — The processes that ensure the effective and efficient use of IT in enabling an organization to achieve its goals. (Gartner, Inc. definition)

IT Operations Control — The function within IT that monitors the entire IT infrastructure from a central console or set of consoles.

IT service — A service that is based on the use of information technology and supports business processes.

IT service management (ITSM) — A discipline for managing IT services that focuses on the quality of those services and the relationship that the IT organization has with its customers.

K

Kaizen — A Japanese term that, when applied to the workplace, means continuing improvement involving everyone—managers and workers alike.

Kepner-Tregoe problem analysis — A proprietary problem analysis technique developed by Charles Kepner and Ben Tregoe that involves defining and describing the problem, establishing possible causes, testing the most probable cause, and verifying the true cause.

key performance indicator (KPI) — A key metric used to manage a process.

keyword searching — The technique of finding indexed information by specifying a descriptive word or phrase, called a keyword.

knowledge — The application of information along with people's experiences, ideas, and judgments.

knowledge base — A logical database that contains data used by a knowledge management system. See also *knowledge management system (KMS)*.

knowledge base administrator (KBA) — Another name for a *knowledge engineer*.

knowledge engineer — The person who develops and oversees the knowledge management process and ensures that the information contained in the knowledge management system is accurate, complete, and current; also called a *knowledge base administrator (KBA)*.

knowledge management — The process responsible for gathering, storing, and sharing information and knowledge within an organization.

knowledge management system (KMS) — A set of tools and databases that are used to store, manage, and present information sources such as customer information, documents, policies and procedures, incident resolutions, and known errors.

known error — A problem that has a documented root cause and a workaround.

known error database (KEDB) — A database that contains known error records. See also *knowledge management system (KMS)*.

L

large service desk — An internal service desk that has more than 25 people on staff or an external service desk that has as many as several hundred people on staff.

Lean Six Sigma — A process improvement approach that combines the concepts of Lean Manufacturing (removing waste) and Six Sigma (reducing defects).

level one — The first point of contact for customers.

level one analyst — A person who receives and logs contacts, answers questions, and resolves incidents and service requests when possible; also called service desk analyst, customer support analyst, or service desk technician.

level one resolution rate percent — The percentage of incidents resolved at level one (not necessarily during the customer's initial telephone contact).

level one specialist — A person who researches complex incidents and handles service requests that require more skill or authority—or, in some cases, more time—than a level one analyst can devote to a single contact; also called service desk specialist, technical support specialist, or customer support specialist.

level three — The person or group that resolves complex incidents that are beyond the scope of level two.

level two — The person or group that resolves incidents that are beyond the scope or authority (such as system access rights or permissions) of level one.

level zero — Customers solving incidents on their own; see also *self-help*.

light therapy — A treatment for Seasonal Affective Disorder (SAD) that involves sitting beside a special fluorescent light box for several minutes day.

local service desk — A service desk that is located close to its customers.

location — The physical site of the service desk in the building.

M

major incident — An incident that is causing significant business impact.

malicious software (malware) — Harmful software such as viruses, worms, Trojan horses, spyware, and adware that is designed to damage or disrupt a computer, computer system, or computer network.

medium service desk — A service desk that has between 10 and 25 people on staff; can take on the characteristics of both small and large service desks.

mentoring program — A program that enables a less experienced or less knowledgeable person to receive guidance or advice from a more experienced or knowledgeable person.

metrics — Performance measures.

Microsoft Operations Framework (MOF) — A collection of best practices, principles, and models that offers guidance to IT organizations for managing their IT services.

milestone — A key or important event in the life of a project.

mission — A description of the customers the service desk serves, the types of services the service desk provides, and how the service desk delivers those services.

monitoring — When a supervisor or team leader monitors an analyst's interactions with customers in order to measure the quality of an analyst's performance.

moves, adds, and changes (MACs) — Service desk activities that include moving equipment, installing and configuring new systems, and upgrading existing systems; also known as *installations, moves, adds, and changes (IMACs)*.

multi-level support model — A common structure of service desks, where the service desk refers incidents it cannot resolve to the appropriate internal group, external vendor, or subject matter expert.

N

National Institute for Occupational Safety and Health (NIOSH) — A part of the U.S. Centers for Disease Control and Prevention (CDC) that is responsible for conducting research and making recommendations for the prevention of work-related illnesses and injuries; located on the web at *www.cdc.gov/niash/homepage.html*.

near-shore outsourcing — Obtaining services from another company in a neighboring country.

network monitoring — Activities that use tools to observe network performance in an effort to minimize the impact of incidents.

notification — The activities that inform all of the stakeholders in the incident management process (including management, the customer, and service desk analysts) about the status of outstanding incidents.

O

Occupational Safety and Health Administration (OSHA) — An agency of the U.S. Department of Labor that is dedicated to reducing hazards in the workplace and enforcing mandatory job safety standards; also implements and improves health programs for workers; located on the web at *www.osha.gov*.

off-the-shelf — Personal computer software products that are developed and distributed commercially.

offshore outsourcing — The exporting of work from one country to another part of the world.

one-stop shop — A service desk that is fully responsible for resolving all incidents and service requests, even if the solution requires extensive research or even programming changes.

onshore outsourcing — Obtaining services from another company in the same country.

367

out-of-scope service request — A request that is beyond the capabilities of the service desk.

outbound call center — A call center that makes telephone calls to customers, primarily for telemarketing.

outsource — To have services provided by an outside supplier instead of providing them in-house.

overall satisfaction survey — A customer satisfaction survey that asks customers for feedback about all contacts with the service desk during a certain time period.

ownership — Tracking an incident to ensure that the customer is kept informed about the status of the incident, that the incident is resolved within the expected time frame, and that the customer is satisfied with the final resolution.

P

page hit — A web page visit.

Pareto analysis — A technique for determining the most significant causes from a list of many possible causes of a problem.

peer-to-peer support — A practice in which users bypass the formal support structure and seek assistance from their coworkers or someone in another department.

people — The service desk component that consists of the staff and structure put in place within a company or department to support its customers by performing processes.

physical layout — How the service desk is arranged into workspaces.

podcast — A method of distributing digital media files over the Internet to personal computers and portable media players.

policy — A formal document that describes the intentions and expectations of management.

portal — A web "supersite" that provides a variety of services such as a site search to locate pertinent articles and white papers, a product and services buyer's guide, a discussion or message board, event calendars, and publications.

post-sales support — Helping people who have purchased a company's product or service.

pre-sales support — Answering questions for people who have not yet purchased a company's products or services.

priority — A category that defines the relative importance of an incident, problem, or change and is based on impact and urgency. (ITIL definition)

proactive service desk — A service desk that uses information to anticipate and prevent incidents and prepare for the future.

problem — The cause of one or more incidents. (ITIL definition)

problem management — The process responsible for managing the lifecycle of problems. (ITIL definition)

problem manager — An employee of the support organization who coordinates all problem management activities and ensures problems are resolved within SLA targets.

procedure — A step-by-step, detailed set of instructions that describes how to perform the tasks in a process.

process — A collection of interrelated work activities that take a set of specific inputs and produce a set of specific outputs that are of value to a customer.

productivity — An efficiency measure that relates output (goods and services produced) to input (the number of hours worked).

profit center — A service desk that must cover its expenses and perhaps make a profit by charging a fee for support services.

program — An approach used to manage one or more interdependent projects.

project — A temporary endeavor undertaken to complete a unique product, service, or result.

project management — The process of planning and managing a project.

project plan — A summary document that describes a project, its objectives, and how the objectives are to be achieved.

project scope — A description of the work to be done in a project.

Q

quality — A characteristic that measures how well products or services meet customer requirements.

query by example (QBE) — A searching technique that uses queries, or questions, to find records that match the specified search criteria. Queries can include search operators.

question — A customer request for instruction on how to use a product, such as "How do I . . . ?"

queue — A line; can be used to refer to a list of calls, tickets, or email messages waiting to be processed.

R

reactive service desk — A service desk that simply responds to events that occur each day.

record — A collection of related fields.

recording system — Technology that records and plays back telephone calls.

remote control and diagnostic systems — Systems that allow the service desk to take remote control of the keyboard, screen, or mouse of connected devices and then troubleshoot problems, transfer files, and even provide informal training by viewing or operating the customer's screen.

remote control system — Technology that enables an analyst to view and take control of a connected device to troubleshoot incidents, transfer files, provide informal training, or collaborate on documents.

remote monitoring system — Technology that tracks and collects events generated by network, system, or application monitoring systems and passes them to a central server where they can be automatically picked up and evaluated by the event management process.

reopened percent — The percentage of closed incidents that had to be opened back up within a given period of time.

repetitive stress injuries (RSIs) — Physical symptoms caused by excessive and repeated use of the hands, wrists, arms, and thumbs; they occur when people repeatedly perform tasks using force, strenuous actions, awkward postures, or poorly designed equipment.

request for change (RFC) — A request to change the production environment.

request for information (RFI) — A form or letter that asks for specific product information relative to the company's requirements.

request for proposal (RFP) — A form or letter that requests financial information as well as product information.

request fulfillment — The process responsible for managing the lifecycle of service requests. (ITIL definition)

requirement — Something that is necessary or essential.

resolution data — Details that describe how an incident was resolved, including all the fields required to track service level compliance and perform trend analysis, such as the person or group who resolved the incident, resolution description, date and time resolved, customer satisfaction indicator, date and time closed, and possible cause.

resolution percent — The percentage of incidents an analyst resolves compared to the total number of incidents that analyst handled during a given period of time.

response time — The length of time a customer waits for a reply to a fax, email, or web request.

return on investment (ROI) — A business calculation that measures the total financial benefit derived from an investment—such as a new technology project—and then compares it with the total cost of the project.

root cause — The most basic reason for an undesirable condition or problem, which if eliminated or corrected, would prevent the undesirable condition or problem from existing or occurring.

root cause analysis — A methodical way of determining why problems occur and identifying ways to prevent them.

rule-based system — A system made up of rules, facts, and a knowledge base or engine that combines rules and facts to reach a conclusion.

S

screen pop — A CTI function that enables information about the caller to appear or "pop" up on the analyst's monitor and is based on caller information captured by the telephone system and passed to a computer system.

search criteria — The questions or symptoms entered by a user.

search operators — Connecting words such as AND, OR, and NOT sometimes used in queries; also called Boolean operators.

self-healing — Hardware devices and software applications that have the ability to detect and correct incidents on their own.

self-help — Customers solving incidents on their own. See also *level zero*.

self-management skills — The skills, such as stress and time management, that people need to complete their work effectively, feel job satisfaction, and avoid frustration or burnout.

senior service desk manager — The person who typically establishes the service desk mission and focuses on the service desk's strategic or long-term goals; also called a *service desk director*.

service — A means of delivering value to customers by facilitating outcomes customers want to achieve without the ownership of specific costs and risks. (ITIL definition)

service asset and configuration management (SACM) — The process responsible for ensuring that the assets required to deliver services are properly controlled, and that accurate and reliable information about those assets is available when and where it is needed.
(ITIL definition)

service catalog — A list of services that an organization provides to its customers.

service desk — A single point of contact within a company for managing customer incidents and service requests.

service desk director — Another name for the *senior service desk manager.*

service desk goals — Measurable objectives that support the service desk's mission.

service desk manager — The person who works closely with the senior service desk manager to prepare the service desk's budget and plan its activities for the coming year.

service desk supervisor — The person who oversees the day-to-day operation of the service desk, which includes making sure the service desk is meeting its SLA commitments, monitoring and evaluating the performance of service desk staff, and ensuring that the staff is properly trained; also called *team leader.*

service knowledge management system (SKMS) — A set of tools and databases used to manage knowledge, information, and data. (ITIL definition)

Service Level Agreement (SLA) — A written document that spells out the services the service desk will provide to the customer, the customer's responsibilities, and how service performance is measured.

service level management — The process of negotiating and managing customer expectations by establishing SLAs, which spell out the services the IT organization—including the service desk—provides to the customer, the customer's responsibilities, and how service performance is measured.

service management and improvement — Activities such as monitoring service desk performance and identifying and overseeing improvements to the service desk.

service request — A request from a user for information, advice, or a standard change.

severity — The impact an incident is having on the business.

simultaneous screen transfer — A function that transfers the call as well as all the information collected in the ticket up to that point.

Six Sigma — A disciplined, data-driven approach for eliminating defects in any process.

skills-based routing (SBR) — An ACD feature that matches the requirements of an incoming call to the skill sets of available analysts or analyst groups. The ACD then distributes the call to the next available, appropriately qualified analyst.

skills inventory matrix — A grid that rates each analyst's level of skill on every product, system, and service supported by the service desk.

small service desk — A service desk that has one to 10 people on staff.

social learning — Learning by interacting with other people.

social media — A phrase commonly used to describe any tool or service that uses the Internet to facilitate interactive communication.

soft skills — The qualities that people need to deliver great service, such as active listening skills, verbal skills, customer service skills, problem-solving skills, temperament, teamwork skills, and writing skills.

software as a service (SaaS) — A software delivery model in which software and the associated data and information are centrally hosted by a vendor and made available to users via the Internet.

software distribution system — Technology that allows an analyst to automatically distribute software to clients and servers on the same network.

software piracy — The unauthorized use or reproduction of copyrighted or patented software.

staffing and scheduling systems — Systems that work with ACD systems to collect, report, and forecast call volumes.

standard — A document that contains an agreed-upon, repeatable way of doing something.

standard change — A preapproved change that is low risk and follows a procedure.

status data — Details about an incident that are used to track the incident throughout its lifecycle, including incident status (such as assigned, awaiting parts, resolved, closed), the person or group assigned, the date and time assigned, and a priority.

subject matter expert (SME) — A person who has a high level of experience or knowledge about a particular subject.

support — Services that enable the effective use of a system.

swarming — A work style characterized by a flurry of collective activity by anyone and everyone conceivably available and able to add value. (Gartner, Inc. definition)

system integration — Linking together different computer systems and applications physically or functionally.

T

target escalation time — A time constraint placed on each level that ensures that incident resolution activities are proceeding at an appropriate pace.

target resolution time — The time frame within which the support organization is expected to resolve an incident.

target response time — The time frame within which the service desk or level two acknowledges the incident, diagnoses the incident, and provides the customer with an estimated target resolution time.

team leader — Another name for the *service desk supervisor.*

technical skills — The skills people need to use and support the specific products and technologies the service desk supports.

technical support — A wide range of services that enable people and companies to effectively use the information technology they have acquired or developed.

technology — An invention, process, or method that enables the creation and enhancement of tools.

telemarketing — The selling of products and services over the telephone.

template — A predefined item that can be used to quickly create a standard document or email message.

time idle — The average length of time an analyst was idle during a given period of time.

time robbers — Activities that take up time and do not add value to the work that analysts perform, and in fact usually decrease productivity and increase stress levels.

tool — A product or device that automates or facilitates a person's work.

total cost of ownership (TCO) — The total amount that a company or person spends on information technology over its lifetime. A considerable portion of the TCO is technical support.

Total Quality Control (TQC) — The system that Japan developed to implement *Kaizen*, or continuing improvement.

Total Quality Management (TQM) — A management approach to long-term success through customer satisfaction.

trend analysis — A methodical way of determining and, when possible, forecasting service trends.

triage — The process of determining a customer's need and routing him or her to the appropriate support group.

U

ubiquitous computing — An environment where people have access to their information from multiple computing devices and systems and even from public shared access points.

urgency — A measure of how long it will be until an incident, problem, or change has a significant impact on the business. (ITIL definition)

user — A person who consumes products or services.

V

value — The perceived worth, usefulness, or importance of a product or service to the customer.

virtual service desk — A service desk that gives the impression of a centralized service desk by using sophisticated telephone systems and the Internet. In reality, the service desk analysts may be located in any number of locations, including their homes.

voice mail — An automated form of taking messages from callers.

Voice over Internet Protocol (VoIP) — A technology that translates voice communications into data and then transmits that data across an Internet connection or network.

voice response unit (VRU) — A technology that integrates with another technology, such as a database or a network management system, to obtain information or to perform a function; also called an interactive voice response unit (IVRU).

W

Web 2.0 — A concept that emphasizes enabling web users to interact, collaborate, and generate content via, for example, blogs, wikis, and social networking sites, rather than passively view content created by others.

webinar — A method used to deliver presentations, lectures, workshops or seminars over the web; short for web-based seminar.

wellness — The condition of good physical and mental health, especially when maintained by proper diet, exercise, and habits.

whiteboard — A smooth, erasable white panel on which analysts write notes and communicate current and future events.

whiteboard system — Technology that allows two or more users on a network to view one or more

user's drawings, documents, or applications being projected on an onscreen whiteboard.

wiki — A web site whose users add, modify, or delete its content using a web browser.

wisdom — The judicious application of knowledge.

work breakdown structure (WBS) — A task-oriented breakdown of the work to be done in a project.

workaround — A temporary way to circumvent or minimize the impact of an incident.

workspace — An area outfitted with equipment and furnishings for one worker.

world class — Refers to a company that has achieved and sustains high levels of customer satisfaction. For example, a world class manufacturing company is considered excellent by its customers when compared to other service companies, regardless of what industry they are in.

World Wide Web (WWW or web) — A collection of documents on the Internet with point-and-click access to information that is posted by government agencies, businesses, educational institutions, nonprofit organizations, and individuals around the world.

wrap-up time — The average length of time an analyst was in wrap-up mode during a given period of time.

wrap-up mode — A feature that prevents the ACD from routing a new inbound call to an analyst's extension.

Index

A

abandoned calls, **257,** 270
abandon rate percent, **257,** 270
Absolute Software, 218
access management, **22,** 154, 173
access-related incidents, 154
account managers, 170
ACD. *See* automatic call distributor (ACD)
ACD supervisor console, **225,** 235
acoustic shock, **292,** 302
active listening, **88,** 104
ad-hoc training, 42, 43
Airwatch LLC, 218
AlliedSignal, 122
all things to all people syndrome, 39
amanet.org Web site, 86
analysts, 14, 78, 217, 263–264
  email etiquette training and
    guidance, 197
  good work habits, 295–301
  logging incidents, 262
  personal workspace, 286–295
  skills, 313
ANI. *See* automatic number
    identification (ANI)
announcement systems, **190,** 235
antiglare filter, 293
antivirus software, 83
anytime, anywhere, any device
    support, 314–315
AOL, 224
Apple Computer, Inc., 36, 187
Apple Remote Desktop, 220
approvals, 154
ASA. *See* average speed of answer
    (ASA)
ASP. *See* The Association of
    Support Professionals (ASP)
assessment, 161
assets, identifying and managing,
    164–169
The Association of Support
    Professionals (ASP), 23, 25
authorized users, 154

B

automated attendants, **192,** 235
automatic call distributor (ACD),
    190–192, 235
automatic number identification
    (ANI), **195,** 235
availability, **263,** 270
available state, **191,** 235
avatars, **313,** 342
average call duration, **263,** 270
average speed of answer (ASA),
    257, 270
average wait time, **257,** 270

Baby Boomers, 311
Bank of America, 124
Barclay's, 124
Basecamp, 336
baseline, metric, **248,** 270
beginning of day (BOD) procedure,
    296, 302
benchmarking, **100,** 104, 261
best-in-class, **13,** 27
best practice, **6**–7, 27, 320
biometrics, 302
bizhotline.com Web site, 86
Blackbaud Web site, 23
blended call centers, **36,** 67
blogs, **42,** 67, **160, 201,** 235
BMC, 210
BOD procedure. *See* beginning of
    day (BOD) procedure
Boeing, 124
books, 355–356
Boolean operators, 217
BPM. *See* business process
    management (BPM)
brainstorming, **150,** 151, 173
brands, **333,** 342
breaks, 301
bring your own application
    (BYOA), 323
bring your own device (BYOD), **10,**
    27, 204, 323
British Airways, 124
business, 343

C

business cases, **340**
businessemailetiquette.com web
    site, 197
business process management
    (BPM), 117, 174
business relationship management,
    170–171, 174
business relationship managers,
    170–171, 174
business rules triggering alerts, 143
business skills, **21, 83**–87, 104
BYOA. *See* bring your own
    application (BYOA)

CAB. *See* change advisory board
    (CAB)
call centers, 27, 36
caller identification (caller ID), **195,**
    235
candidate vendors, 230–232
can-do attitude, 93
careertrack.com Web site, 86
carpal tunnel syndrome (CTS),
    287, 289, 302
case-based reasoning (CBR), **216,**
    235
case-based systems, **214**–217, 235
cases, **214**
CaseTracker, 55–56
categories, priority, 136–139
categorization, **134**–139, 174
categorizing incidents, 135–136
cause and effect analysis, 151, **151,**
    174
CBR. *See* case-based reasoning
    (CBR)
CBT. *See* computer-based training
    (CBT)
CDC. *See* U.S. Centers for Disease
    Control and Prevention
    (CDC)
Central Computer and
    Telecommunications
    Agency (CCTA), 6
centralized global service desks, **319**

CENGAGE**brain**.com

Buy. Rent. Access.

Access student data files and other study
tools on **cengagebrain.com**.

For detailed instructions visit
www.cengage.com/ct/studentdownload.

Store your Data Files on a USB drive for maximum efficiency in
organizing and working with the files.

Macintosh users should use a program to expand WinZip or PKZip archives.
Ask your instructor or lab coordinator for assistance.